Bierman, J.

D0493075

FIRE IN THE NIGHT

FIRE IN THE NIGHT

Wingate of Burma, Ethiopia, and Zion

JOHN BIERMAN
and
COLIN SMITH

Macmillan

First published 1999 by Random House

This edition published 2000 by Macmillan
an imprint of Macmillan Publishers Ltd
25 Eccleston Place, London SW1W 9NF
Basingstoke and Oxford
Associated companies throughout the world
www.macmillan.co.uk

ISBN 0333 72576 X

A CIP catalogue record for this book is available from
the British Library.

Printed and bound in Great Britain by
Mackays of Chatham plc, Chatham, Kent

In salute to,
and in memory of,
all the brave men
who pass through these pages

Contents

FIRE IN THE NIGHT

Prologue

The General took off at nightfall, his plane rising from the airstrip at Imphal to bank across the line of the distant Naga Hills before setting course for the jungle airfield at Hailakandi, one hundred miles to the west, near the Indian-Burmese border.

Below his aircraft the slopes were blanketed by forests of teak and pine, interspersed with great stands of bamboo and pierced here and there by pinpoints of light. Each pinpoint denoted a village more concerned by the possibility of a marauding tiger or an obliterating herd of elephants than by the war on its doorstep.

The General had a long-standing fear of flying, not helped by a recent incident in which his chief staff officer's plane had collided with a kite hawk on takeoff. But constant aerial inspection trips from unit to unit under his command, lately deep inside enemy-held territory, were an inescapable part of the General's duties, and he had long since learned to feign unconcern by burying his aquiline nose into a book—Tolstoy, Voltaire, Jane Austen, the Old Testament: his tastes and interests were wide-ranging and cultivated.

To put on a show of nonchalance was the General's way. He knew fear; he also knew that he must never show it.

For this particular flight the weather forecast was mainly fair, although there were reports of isolated storms in the region. An encounter with an enemy fighter plane at night and so far inside friendly territory was unlikely. So, despite the urgings of his chief of staff to put off the trip, and despite his own vague unease—not quite a premonition, perhaps, but an impulse that made him turn back before boarding to lavish unexpected praise on a subordinate—the General saw no reason to change his travel plans.

Although born into his country's military caste and raised in its institutions, the General viewed war as an evil, albeit in this case a very necessary one, analagous to a surgical operation in which violence must be done to the body in order to save it. And although born into a fundamentalist Christian family and raised according to its precepts, the focus of the General's unswerving faith was not the gentle Redeemer dying on the cross for the sins of mankind but the stern Jehovah of the Israelites, demanding trust and exacting obedience. The books of ancient Israel's kings and prophets were the General's unvarying guide in life, and often in battle, and he had assumed as his own the struggle of the modern Israelites to recover their ancestral homeland.

Knowing nothing of this, the young American pilot sitting beside the General at the controls of the B-25 bomber thought nonetheless that, with his profuse black beard and piercing gaze, he looked more like an Old Testament prophet than a Limey officer. Even the Victorian-era solar topee the General habitually wore, an affectation that had assumed the status of a trademark, did not manage to make him look any less biblical.

The Americans, officers and enlisted men alike, who were serving alongside the General and his British and colonial troops, called him The Beard or, more simply, The Man. And those were terms of respect. They knew him as a wildly unconventional commander and a hard-driving son of a bitch who was breaking new ground in jungle warfare—so new and so exciting that the Pentagon had raised a private air force just so that he would have all the air support he wanted when he wanted it, no questions asked and no objections raised.

Not surprisingly, the young pilot was somewhat in awe of the General, and it may have been for that reason that he failed to tell him he was not entirely happy about this last leg of his daylong tour of inspection. Earlier in the day, there had been something about the pitch of one of his aircraft's twin engines that the pilot did not quite like. But he was not about to interrupt the General's schedule on account of it; this was a guy you did not hold back without a very good reason.

So the B-25 roared on into the dark, bearing the General and all on board toward a common fate . . .

O my brother, the fire in the night.

Book One

EARLY
LIFE

We were reared on a diet of porridge, bread and dripping, and the "sincere milk of the Word."
—SYBIL WINGATE

I do not profess to try to follow the teachings of Christ in many respects, as they are wholly incompatible with the conditions of my life.
—ORDE WINGATE

Chapter 1

Unity state that aircraft has definitely never landed and are making every effort to locate. Hailakandi operations are also trying to trace aircraft. Shall I sign sitrep?
—MESSAGE FROM SPECIAL FORCE TTQ, IMPHAL, DATED 0200 HOURS, 24 MARCH 1944

Boy born today and Ethel has haemorrhage and desire prayer for her.
—TELEGRAM FROM COL. GEORGE WINGATE, NAINI TAL, DATED 1800 HOURS, 26 FEBRUARY 1903

ORDE CHARLES WINGATE entered the world as he left it, amid a flurry of urgent telegrams.

His mother's confinement and labor were fast and easy, as routine and unremarkable a business in its way as the flight from Imphal to Hailakandi should have been. But just as the doctor was leaving the house where he had delivered "an unusually fine large baby weighing nine pounds," a cry of alarm from the nurse brought him back.

Ethel Wingate was hemorrhaging, and for the next several hours she hung between life and death, so weak that Nurse Carroll had to hold a hand in front of her mouth to make sure she was still breathing. The attendant physician, a Dr. Fayrer, was at a loss, but Colonel George Wingate had no doubt about what to do. In the space of an hour he sent off eight telegrams to relatives and friends around the globe, begging them to pray for his wife's survival. "I never lost hope," he said in a subsequent letter to his mother-in-law, "because I was relying on prayer."

This was no mere figure of speech. George and Ethel Wingate were Protestant fundamentalists of the purest stamp, to whom the efficacy of prayer was a self-evident fact. Like Ethel's parents, Mr. and Mrs.

Charles Orde-Browne, they were members of the Plymouth Brethren, an austere evangelical sect that, dispensing with any form of priesthood, believed in the imminence of the Second Coming and the most direct kind of commerce between Man and his Maker.

So throughout the long night George Wingate and the Orde-Brownes, and the other coreligionists to whom the colonel had cabled, prayed ceaselessly, until "at 4 o'clock on Friday morning I thought I saw a change and I knew then prayer had been heard. By 8 o'clock A.M. it was beyond doubt that she was reviving—Dr. Fayrer was very surprised."

Once it was clear that his wife was out of danger, Wingate sat beside her bed and read the Thirtieth Psalm out loud—"Thou hast turned for me my mourning into dancing: thou hast put off my sackcloth and girded me with gladness, . . . O Lord my God, I will give thanks unto thee forever."

The Wingates' drama of faith and deliverance took place in a rented guesthouse at Naini Tal in the United Provinces of India. Naini Tal was one of those hill resorts to which the British raj customarily fled to escape the heat of the plains, although in this out-of-season instance the colonel and his lady were in flight not from the heat but from the mumps. Their daughters Rachel and Sybil were suffering from this dangerously contagious ailment, with consequent risk to the baby their mother was carrying, and had been left at home with their ayah.

Nonconformist religiosity ran deep on both sides of the Wingate family.* George's father, the Reverend William Wingate, having been born to wealth and being something of a playboy in his early years, turned to religion and good works in his late twenties following the death of his first wife in premature childbirth. After two years as an evangelical lay missionary in his native Glasgow, he decided that his true purpose in life was to convert the Jews to Christianity. So, abandoning the family shipping firm and defying the wishes of his father, who subsequently disinherited him, he went to Berlin, where he learned German and Hebrew before being ordained as a minister in 1843 in the Church of Scotland's mission to the Jews of Hungary.

---

*It's a fine irony, though, that one of the most celebrated of all English Dissenters, John Bunyan, should have been victimized by a Wingate ancestor, Judge Euston Wingate, who sent him to jail in 1660 for preaching without a license.

During his time in Budapest, the Scottish church split in two, and William joined the more fundamentalist of the two factions. This eventually became the Free Church of Scotland, colloquially known as the "Wee Frees." In the mid-1850s, after the Protestant missions in Hungary were forced to leave as a result of Catholic pressure, William returned to Britain, where he continued his evangelical work among the Jews of London until his death at ninety-one.

George, his second son by his second wife, went into the army with a purchased commission and was serving in India when he underwent a religious experience similar to his father's. Evidently the Wee Frees were not strict enough for his taste, and in a blinding moment of revelation he resolved to join the Plymouth Brethren. As an act of piety, and while still a serving officer, he set up and financed a missionary center to propagate the Christian faith among the fiercely Islamic Pathans of the Northwest Frontier. During a campaign on the other side of India, against the Naga headhunters who inhabit the hills that mark the frontier between Assam and Burma, he refused to march his men on the Sabbath and escaped without so much as a reprimand.

It was while he was on home leave in England in 1878 that George Wingate was introduced to the Orde-Brownes, a pious but well-to-do couple who ran a mission to slum dwellers in Woolwich and lived nearby in middle-class Plumstead. Charles Orde-Browne was an ex–army officer who, while serving in the Crimean War, had undergone the spiritual experience, similar to that of William and George Wingate, which led him to join the Plymouth Brethren.

George was twenty-six at the time he met the Orde-Brownes. Their eldest daughter, Ethel, was twelve. But despite the difference in ages it was understood on both sides that one day they would marry. And so they did—although not until twenty years later.

A century on, this all seems very strange: a serving army officer in a particularly turbulent part of the empire diverting time and attention from soldiering to evangelism, without apparent damage to his career; a man of twenty-six falling for a girl of twelve, with the approval of her family, and then waiting twenty years for her hand. But manners and perceptions change, and what seems distinctly odd in the sexually savvy and irreligious close of the twentieth century was unexceptional during the Victorian high season, when empire was clearly God-ordained and—*honi soit qui mal y pense*—a gentleman's feelings for a prepubescent girl could seem entirely wholesome.

Orde Wingate was five months old when his parents took him and his sisters to England for a spell of home leave. Seven months after that the colonel and his lady returned to India, leaving their children behind in the care of the Orde-Brownes. During that period of separation the austere Colonel Wingate revealed an unexpectedly sentimental side of his nature, writing to his two small daughters—"my own sweet little Rae [Rachel] and Tibaloo [Sybil]"—in unabashed baby talk: "Mummy is always thinking of Ray and Sybil and she wants to send them a picky, so Papa is taking Mummy to be photographed today." And so forth.

By the middle of 1905, Colonel Wingate and his wife were back in England, this time for good. George, now aged fifty-two, had been put on the Supernumerary List—in effect, retired—with a pension almost equal to his full pay. And after a number of moves within the Home Counties, near London, the family came to roost in 1914 at Summerhill, a large house in the Surrey market town of Godalming. By this time there were seven children—four daughters and three sons—and Orde was eleven years old.

George's pension and Ethel's inherited private income meant that the family was comfortably off. But the time and money they devoted to evangelical good causes meant that their lifestyle fell some distance short of affluence. George contributed substantially to a number of missionary societies, and he and Ethel together wholly supported a mission that sought to bring Christianity to the Muslims of central Asia.

Beyond the financial sacrifices such pieties incurred, the Wingate household lived under conditions of considerable austerity as dictated by George and Ethel's puritanical beliefs. "We were reared on a diet of porridge, bread and dripping, and 'the sincere milk of the Word,' " Sybil Wingate would recall.

> Winter was one long purgatory of bitter cold. . . . No room was ever warmed. . . . We sat in our overcoats in ice-cold rooms with our

hands clasped round our necks for warmth. . . . The perpetual fear of damnation [was] the fundamental cause of our daily unhappiness.

On Sundays the entire family dressed in black, attended the Brethren's prayer meetings (which George frequently addressed) in the morning, and devoted the rest of the day to Bible studies and other "improving" pastimes. George was austere, remote, harsh, and dictatorial, frequently chastising his children simply "for the good of their souls," doubtless in the spirit of Proverbs 13:24—"He that spareth his rod hateth his son; but he that loveth him chasteneth him betimes." In her bitter memoir of childhood, composed in late middle age and apparently not intended for publication, Sybil wrote:

[My father] was, I think, the most unhappy, the most lonely creature I have ever known. This was the inevitable consequence of his own nature, which was gloomy pessimistic and deeply tinged with suspicion and hostility. . . . [My mother] was by temperament as different from him as one human being can be from another. She loved him; she sacrificed her life to him: for nearly 40 years she suffered unhappiness and isolation which . . . were simply the product of his morose and misanthropic temperament. But she never understood him.

And between George Wingate and his children, as Sybil recalled it, there was "an impenetrable wall of reserve and estrangement, which no amount of pity or even affection could remove." He beat them "at fairly frequent intervals," she and Orde being "easily the most frequent victims." Orde was also the usual target of his father's "incessant scolding and grumbling, especially at mealtimes," enduring "years of dumb humiliation which left their mark on him."

Orde's younger brother Nigel had similarly bitter recollections of life at Summerhill, describing it as "a temple of gloom" whose occupants lived in "the most poisonous and repressive religious atmosphere that it is possible to conceive." Orde himself has left no written evidence of his feelings toward his father, but it should be said that he always wrote respectfully to him and claimed at the age of twenty-nine that "we realise more as we grow older all you have done for us and thank God that we have had such a father all these years." Since it was certainly not in his nature to butter up anyone, we must assume that the mature Orde had come to appreciate his father's moral qualities and to forget the beatings and the verbal bullying.

However that might be, existence was not entirely joyless and cramped for the Wingate children. There were annual seaside holidays when they sailed dinghies and roamed happily amid rock pools at low tide, and, as Sybil would also recall—this time in a less embittered (and published) reminiscence—their mother was, for all her fundamentalist beliefs, "a woman of very considerable mental gifts, full of a lively intellectual curiosity, extremely well read, her conversation larded with quotations from the English classics, and with two years at a Paris finishing school and an almost professional musical training behind her."

> Throughout our childhood Mother was a bright light in the darkest moments, as well as a source of entertainment and fun. Her naturally happy temperament was a reassurance in itself and did a good deal to counteract the severer side of the evangelicalism in which she, like my father, had been brought up. . . . She gave us that most essential element in children's upbringing, the knowledge that they are loved.

George Wingate's Christianity was inevitably of the muscular kind, and he believed in cultivating stamina in his children by taking them on demanding cross-country hikes. Orde, as the oldest son, was expected to lead the way in manly pursuits, and he became obsessed with the idea of constantly testing his courage and endurance. Nevertheless, the Wingate parents' strict beliefs and fears of "contamination" kept the children from mixing with outsiders, beyond unavoidable contacts at school. Consequently, the intellectual atmosphere in which they grew up was, as Sybil put it, "somewhat apocalyptic."

Apart from intensive study of the Bible—with heavy emphasis on the Old Testament and the Psalms, chunks of which they had to learn by heart—the children were taught to believe that Christ would return to earth in their own lifetime, ushering in a reign of peace, truth, justice, and mercy. The reverse side of this benign notion was that the wicked would be punished in hellfire while the good basked in the sunshine of the Savior, and Orde, as he later told his wife, came to believe that he was inherently sinful.

Possibly this had something to do with the approach of puberty and "impure" thoughts, but for whatever reason the boy began to have nightmares in which his soul was carried off by the Devil. At the same time, he was afraid that his siblings, being so much better than he, might be carried off to heaven by angels. He was particularly concerned that he might lose his baby brother Granville in this fashion and used to tuck him tightly into his bed at night so that the angel would find it difficult to snatch him.

Orde's education, like that of his siblings, was initially in the hands of his mother, who taught her children the three R's. As the Wingate children grew older their parents found the money to hire a procession of tutors and governesses—seven at their most numerous—to instruct them in such subjects as mathematics, piano, French, and history. Orde was slow at learning to read and consequently slow to catch up with his older sisters in Bible studies, Sybil ascribing this as "partly due to the mental paralysis produced by sheer misery." His choices of secular reading matter were restricted, but Orde would recall in later years becoming engrossed in such children's standards as *Grimm's Fairy-Tales, Jock of the Bushveldt, Swiss Family Robinson,* and (obviously in a heavily bowdlerized version) *Tales from the Arabian Nights.*

As an escape from the austerities of their existence the Wingate children enjoyed a rich fantasy life in a make-believe country they called Lodolf. As Sybil described it, "Lodolf was a serial romance, or rather a play to which new acts were perpetually being added. . . . The dramatis personae . . . included characters from every historical romance or poem we had ever read, especially Charlotte Young's [sic] *Little Duke,* Fouqué's *Sintram,* tales of the Round Table and of the Peers of Charlemagne, Scott's *Lord of the Isles* and *Lady of the Lake.*"

Rachel, the oldest, was the dramatist and producer of this serial and, recalled Sybil, "we moved with perfect sureness of foot from the one world to the other, keeping them inviolably separate and confiding in no adult the existence of our refuge."

At the age of eleven Orde began his formal education as a day pupil at Hill Side, a private junior school in the locality where boys were prepared for later entry into Charterhouse, the archetypal English public school, which was also located on the outskirts of Godalming. As a day boy, both at Hill Side and Charterhouse, he would be to a large extent sheltered, as his parents intended, from the "corrupting" influences of high Anglicanism and social conformity—the prevailing ethos of the public school system, which existed primarily to turn out soldiers to police and guard the empire and civil servants to administer it.

Orde left little impression behind in either school, except that a contemporary at Hill Side remembered him in later years as one whose unbiddable and unsociable character automatically provoked the ire of conventional schoolmasters. Among his peers, this contemporary recalled, he was "the sort of boy who used to be kicked from one end of the school to the other for the good of his soul. Nobody, however, kicked Wingate. He feared no one."

Cut off as he and his siblings had been from contact with other children, Orde had of course had no chance to acquire any social skills, and when he was admitted to Charterhouse at the age of thirteen his status as a day boy and his surly demeanor again set him apart from the majority of his fellows.

Colonel Wingate's insistence that he be excused attendance at Anglican services in the school chapel, Orde's dislike of team sports, and his overall indifference to the "school spirit" on which his teachers and contemporaries kept harping, made him even more the outsider. His excessive piety set him apart, too, one teacher remembering that he would go off by himself to pray while the other boys kicked around a football. Nor did his appearance help: his clothes were of markedly cheaper cut and quality than those of his fellows, and he felt especially humiliated by having to wear heavy boots while the other boys wore shoes.

School photographs show an undersized boy with a large head and piercing gaze. He was nicknamed "Stinker," and one of his contemporaries later recalled him as "a little rat-like fellow." This uncharitable character witness added, however, that "you could see even then that he had a will."

Another, a fellow day boy, recalled the time he mentioned to Wingate that his parents were taking him to a concert on the following Sunday. Orde was appalled at the thought of such desecration of the Sabbath. "If you go you'll bring your soul into danger of hellfire!" he warned. Another classmate admitted, well after Wingate had achieved fame in World War II, that he had "no memory of him at all nor any idea now what he looked like."

If he was a flop socially, Orde was no great achiever academically. His marks were indifferent and he consistently ranked near the bottom of his class. Even in the school's Officers' Training Corps he was an undistinguished cadet, never rising above the rank of lance corporal and scoring little success in such soldierly pursuits as boxing and marksmanship.

In short, and to put it kindly, Orde was not considered an adornment to the school. Nevertheless, Charterhouse is now proud to carry in the entrance to the school chapel a plaque, unveiled in 1946 by Lord Mountbatten of Burma, commemorating the nonconforming nonachiever who became one of its most celebrated and admired Old Boys.

Despite his indifferent performance as an Officers' Training Corps cadet, Wingate embarked on a military career on leaving Charterhouse at age seventeen. As the oldest son, it was natural that he should follow in his father's footsteps, and for all the horrors of World War I, just ended, the family remained army-minded. The theme of Sword and Bible ran strong in the traditions of British Nonconformism, and "Onward, Christian Soldiers" was considerably more than a mere figure of speech.

In any case, Orde's poor academic record hardly qualified him for university and one of the civilian professions. Nor, of course, could there be any question of his seeking a career in the parentally despised Church of England, another traditional occupation for the sons of the British upper middle class of the time. And he had no interest in or aptitude for commerce; his mother, being something of a snob, would not have welcomed the idea of his "going into trade." Another factor in his choice of a military career, as he claimed in later years, was his belief that without an armed force to back it up the newly formed League of Nations would be unable to keep the peace, making another major war inevitable.

So the army it was, but not into a fashionable or glamorous regiment. Young officers in the Household Cavalry, the Brigade of Guards, or one of the smarter county regiments were expected to be well off enough to support an appropriate lifestyle, but Orde's parents, drained by their missionary efforts, were not able to subsidize his meager army pay. Consequently he applied for admission to the Royal Military Academy at Woolwich, where entrants were trained for the bread-and-butter work of the army in the Corps of Engineers or the Royal Artillery.

To gain entry Orde had to pass an examination in eight obligatory subjects—English, English history, geography, arithmetic, intermediate mathematics, French or German, physics, and chemistry—and one further optional subject. All that was needed to scrape through was a score of 33 percent in all except for arithmetic, where 75 percent was required. And scrape through he did, coming in sixty-third out of sixty-nine successful candidates.

For most of the ensuing three years at Woolwich, Orde cut no better a figure as a gentleman cadet than he had as a pupil at Charterhouse. At 129 pounds and five feet six inches he was fully grown physically, but in terms of his mental discipline and intellectual development he still had a long way to go.

Most of Wingate's intake took easily enough to the Woolwich environment. The academy, known to generations of its alumni as "The Shop," was not all that different from the boarding schools they had attended, although the bullying of juniors—known as "snookers"—by the senior cadets was even more prevalent than under the public school fagging system, and the drill sergeants and lecturers were even more determined than the schoolmasters to break down individuality in order to create fully conforming officers and gentlemen.

As a day boy at school, Orde had never been exposed to the full blast of such a regime, and attempts to force him into the Woolwich mold served only to make him even more surly and rebellious. Sartorially, his appearance tended toward the untidy, a considerable offense in any military establishment. Academically, he was inclined to work only as hard as he needed to avoid expulsion. As for rules and regulations, a contemporary would recall, "He and I had one basic common belief: regulations are made by sods for fools and they are to be circumvented and not obeyed where inconvenient."

But Wingate's mode of rebelliousness was not entirely grim and humorless. Irritated by the manner of a sergeant major who insisted that gentlemen cadets should slap their rifles harder while executing the second movement of the "present arms," he and a fellow cadet named

Lance Perowne* studiously took a Lee-Enfield rifle apart by removing the screws that held it together and replacing them with matchsticks, so that, as an eyewitness would recall: "On the following day when the Sergeant-Major gave his favourite exhortation, there was a loud crash and a rifle disintegrated."

In his spare time Wingate read voraciously, but nothing more demanding than thrillers and pulp romances. The only soldierly activity in which he appeared to take a serious interest was horsemanship, and in this—although he had no previous experience—he excelled.

Among the many bizarre customs of the academy that were intended to whip gentleman cadets into shape was a weekly event known as the Snooker Dance. Its purpose was to familiarize cadets with the social art of ballroom dancing—a necessary pre-mating ritual for the officer class—and to impress on the junior cadets their lowly place in the military hierarchy. Attendance was compulsory and so was the dress code: senior cadets in full mess dress and snookers, acting out the role of female dancing partners, in white vests and flannel trousers.

For the juniors there was further humiliation to follow. After each dance, according to a contemporary account, they were "herded into a crowd and organised to perform various antics. . . . These varied from ludicrous to rough and usually a certain number of cadets sustained minor injuries. At the end of the session the snookers had to run the gauntlet of the other terms on the way back to their houses."

An even more demeaning ritual was the practice of "running" a cadet who had broken some pettifogging rule or other. This unofficial but time-hallowed and authority-sanctioned punishment consisted of making the offender strip naked and run a gauntlet of knotted towels before being tossed into a tank of water. Wingate's general demeanor and unpopularity made him an obvious candidate for this shaming (if not particularly brutal) treatment, and by the time he had reached his third term it only took one insignificant offense to bring it about.

He went against the rules of the academy's riding school by keeping a horse out longer than allowed, thereby depriving another cadet of a recreational ride. This antisocial misdemeanor was enough for a senior underofficer with a particular dislike of Wingate to call for retri-

*Many years later Perowne was to become one of Wingate's brigade commanders in Burma.

bution and, in accordance with custom, a baying pack of senior cadets went to his room after dark, pronounced sentence, and led him out to the rugby field.

Resistance would have been futile, and when the mob came for Wingate he walked with quiet dignity to the place of "execution." Most victims got their punishment over quickly by cupping a hand over their genitals and running, head down, as fast as possible through the gauntlet. But not Wingate. He faced his persecutors down by standing as tall as his five feet six inches would allow and looking them in the eye. Then, as senior cadet Derek Tulloch would recall:

> Orde walked, very slowly, the whole way down the line, with a dangerous look in his eye, which I have frequently had cause to recognise since. Few of us could bring ourselves even to apply the knotted handkerchiefs and many of us came away feeling ashamed of the part we had played in it.

Having contemptuously walked the line, Wingate vaulted to the edge of one of the nearby water tanks, calmly took his stance, and dived in, completing his moral victory over those who had presumed to humiliate and punish him for being different.

Trivial though the affair may seem, it may have been one of the transforming events of Wingate's life. It scarred him deeply, making him chronically hostile to mindless custom and blimpish higher authority—not a mind-set conducive to a successful military career. But on the credit side, the experience seemed to fire his dormant ambition and trigger the awakening of his sleeping intellect. If, as Francis Bacon had said, "knowledge itself is power," then he would acquire knowledge so that the rabble should never again have power over him.

So when, a few days later, the Woolwich academy commandant, Sir Webb Gillman, sent for Wingate and warned him that he must study harder and smarten up all around or risk expulsion, he was pushing at an open door. Contemptuous though he was of those in higher authority who, like Gillman, sanctioned such practices as "running," Wingate had already resolved to pay due and proper attention to his classroom studies and waste no more of his spare time on pulp fiction. He made a bonfire of his books and plunged voraciously into a wide range of weightier subjects—history, philosophy, political science, economics, and world literature: Tacitus and Tolstoy, Machiavelli and

Marx, Aristotle and Adam Smith. As Sybil would observe, "His mind had suddenly awakened and was crying out for food."

As an odd by-product, the experience of being "run" also taught Wingate to overcome the inhibitions about nudity that his puritan upbringing must surely have implanted. In later life he would frequently greet visitors to his rooms or his field headquarters in a state of seemingly unself-conscious nakedness—a habit that contributed greatly to his reputation for eccentricity.

It was as though he was reenacting his moment of triumph over the mob and demonstrating his continuing contempt for the norms of a hypocritical society.

Chapter 2

WINGATE'S SUDDEN APPLICATION to his studies, coming as it did toward the end of his time at Woolwich, was too late to enhance his passing out performance to any great extent. In July 1923, he graduated fifty-ninth out of seventy cadets, was commissioned into the Royal Artillery, and posted as a subaltern to a medium battery at Larkhill, on Salisbury Plain.

His duties there were none too arduous. Five years after the end of the Great War the British army was in a semicomatose condition, traumatized by its recent experiences in the meat grinder of industrialized warfare, disoriented by the return to peacetime routine, and both impoverished and demoralized by government penny-pinching, with most infantry regiments reduced to two battalions—one for home service and the other for abroad. The down-at-the-heels appearance of the artillery depot at Larkhill reflected the army's plight. Except during the brief summer training season, life at Larkhill revolved mainly around "square bashing" and "bull," otherwise foot drill and hours spent polishing leather and brass for interminable kit inspections. Tulloch, who was also serving at Larkhill and had become a firm friend of Wingate's, recalled that

> on morning parades . . . the number of men who were left after the fatigues and duty men were marched off could be counted on one hand. These were usually dismissed for weeding the garden, whitewashing the ropes around the huts, or some such innocent pastime. Senior officers were still suffering from the aftermath of the war, and young subalterns were left very much to their own devices.

This state of affairs gave Wingate plenty of time for his reading and for a newfound outdoor passion—fox hunting. This pastime, calling for dash and daring as well as a high level of horsemanship, was con-

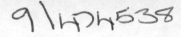

sidered by the army brass to be excellent training for young officers, who were given the services of a charger and groom and encouraged to turn out for the local hunt. For officers at Larkhill, the local hunt was the South and West Wiltshire at Motcombe, and Wingate and Tulloch regularly rode with it, and with the Portman Hunt in neighboring Dorset, during the three years they were at Larkhill together. Wingate, forever testing the limits of his courage and physical endurance, rapidly acquired a reputation for reckless daring in the chase. Where more prudent riders would seek a less direct route in pursuit of the hounds, Wingate would frequently break away from the field to take a risky straight-line course, over wide ditches and streams, high hedges and gates.

He sometimes went purposely out of his way to jump a challenging gate and often fell, though without ever sustaining serious injury or losing his nerve. He also developed a remarkable knack for divining the best place to cross a river that might seem unfordable to others, displaying an innate talent for reading difficult terrain. "As the seasons went on he rapidly became a legendary character," Tulloch recalled, although, being strapped for cash, "his hunting kit became steadily more deplorable."

> Neither of us were fashion plates, but his hat was definitely unbeatable and usually resembled a furry concertina; he seldom failed to land on it less than twice a day.

While Wingate was admired for his skill and verve, he was criticized by many of his fellow huntsmen for the merciless way he drove his mounts. In later years he would drive the men under his command just as relentlessly but, as his men well knew, never harder than he drove himself. For Wingate, the hunt was far more than a mere weekend pastime, however stimulating. In a revealing, if overheated, letter to Dr. Claude Fothergill, a fashionable doctor who fancied himself as a part-time evangelist, he laid bare his feelings on contemplation of "a day of pure happiness" in the saddle:

> It was seven when I woke, and the sun had only just risen. The skies were damp and gloomy but their appearance could bring nothing but satisfaction to me. That very dampness and gloom that meant disheartenment to the rest of the world meant the anticipation of a

good scent to me, and filled me with joyous anticipation. And there was no lying abed, no lazy folding of the hands to sleep, as would descend on me before a day of parades, but a glad leap from the warmth, a good wash before dressing—not in the King's uniform but in that much more glorious hunting uniform—and a good English breakfast of eggs and bacon washed down with tea. And what a joy to feel around my neck that emblem of sport—a stock—and on my legs a pair of fine topboots in place of the melancholy attire of war.

"Today," I said to my soul, "you will forget this tawdry life of reality, this vulgar present, this banal undistinguished existence . . . such trivialities as 'the great heart of the people,' 'liberty, fraternity and equality,' 'humanity,' 'evangelicanism,' 'the dictatorship of the proletariat,' and other dreary coarsenesses! Today, in the only world I will admit to be real, the real world of dreams, of fancies, of departed glories brought nigh, in this world . . . you are about to move. Black is the past, black may be the future, but the present, oh my courageous soul, is glorious. Today I shall be like a god."

Wingate ran this panegyric past his sister Sybil before posting it to Fothergill. She advised him not to bother, saying Fothergill was as incapable of understanding his feelings "as an amoeba is of appreciating the Ninth Symphony."

At about this time, Wingate came into a legacy of about two thousand pounds from an uncle and, Tulloch would recall, "his immediate reaction was to help his impecunious friends and I think at least one hundred went in this way. I know I received a tenner to help out towards my hay bill, which was not repaid for some time after, and many of his loans were not repaid at all; he did not expect it."

Wingate was similarly generous in making loans, which were seldom repaid, to a handful of old soldiers who had fallen on hard times. He also helped out his siblings whenever they were in need, which was frequently—so much so that his sister Rachel felt bound to entreat him: "Don't run through all your legacy money now. You'll want it badly for the Staff College or something else later on."

But he could not resist the temptation posed by a secondhand sports car, which Tulloch taught him to drive and which he would steer as fast and as recklessly as he rode to hounds, though with considerably less skill. "[The car] had only two speeds—flat out and full stop," Tulloch would recall. "The drives were far more exciting than the hunts."

Not surprisingly, Wingate's legacy dwindled rapidly and, disregarding the precepts of his puritan upbringing, he was not averse to an occasional flutter on the horses to top up his bank balance. He opened an account with White, Fisher and Co., "the world's premier sporting accountants, of Geneva and Glasgow," under the nom de plume of "Wetterhorn." There is no surviving record of how well, or how badly, he fared. His parents would have been horrified. His officers' mess bills reveal that he also liked to play billiards, another pastime frowned on by the pious, and, like any other young officer, he liked his liquor and occasionally fell behind in paying for it.

A dunning letter from John Smith and Sons, "dealers in wines and spirits" of Weedon, Northhants., demanded payment of seventeen shillings and fivepence, "which is now much overdue and requesting its immediate settlement to avoid unpleasantness," while another vendor of alcohol, C. Marshall of High Street, Tisbury, Wilts., became so impatient that he wrote to Wingate's commanding officer demanding payment of three pounds, ten shillings, and fivepence. The proprietor of the Queen's Head at Weedon also had recourse to Wingate's CO, writing, "I cannot get any money from him. I have sent several times, kindly see into this matter and oblige."

And, of course, there were girls, although the written record fails to disclose how far he went with them. He must have been discreet, for Tulloch thought that "he had no use for girls whatsoever and concentrated on physical fitness and his horses." But surviving invitations and letters make it clear that at least the opposite sex were interested in him, if not obviously vice versa. A Wiltshire girl named Cecily Bullock, one of the fox-hunting crowd, wrote, "Do come and dine here the night of the 25th and bring anyone you like, too, that's to say if you are coming to the dance. Do bring lots of men friends as we all want partners." Another Wiltshire gel named Ruth, whose P. G. Wodehouse vernacular would fit any Bertie Wooster and Jeeves plot, enthused, "How sporting of you to come along. It will be topping to see you."

A young woman named Elizabeth, writing from an address in fashionable Knightsbridge, sounds rather more flirtatious: "I know nothing about your morals. I should think you have some pretty stiff ones if anyone bothers to look far enough." She added, teasingly: "How weak of you to go to a cinema once a week. It is the last thing I can imagine you doing. I suppose you sit there and turn up your nose with disgust, having no sense of romance."

Otherwise, Wingate seems to have remained a world away from the bright young things of the Jazz generation. As the twenties roared on and the music of the American speakeasies reached Britain, Wingate's main pleasures remained resolutely rural and would have been instantly recognizable by an ensign from the Duke of Wellington's army. From fox hunting, he and Tulloch graduated to an even more testing equine pursuit: steeplechasing. His first time out, Wingate—a 15 to 1 outsider—won the West Wilts Cup by two lengths, while Tulloch came in third, a perfect paradigm of their future relationship in wartime Burma, where Wingate would command a division with Tulloch as his chief staff officer.

Wingate went on to win several more trophies, which he kept at home in Godalming. Inevitably, his involvement in the raffish world of steeplechasing, with its punters, bookmakers, and tic-tac men, did not please his parents. But Ethel could not entirely overcome a feeling of maternal pride in her firstborn son's derring-do:

> I am proud of your pluck and horsemanship [she wrote after his first win] but I know that this point-to-point, however good for you professionally, must throw you into a wildly unconverted set and make it harder every day to follow Christ. . . . That is a danger that fills me with dread whenever I think of it and I pray God to keep you from the two special sins that are as a rule associated with success in horsemanship.

And his father, having seen a newspaper photograph of his son in a spectacular steeplechase fall, enquired, "Is it a warning from God?"

> You have been brought up in "the fear and nurture of the Lord." . . . Can you cut with horse-racing fever? As a Christian it is the only safe thing to do. This time, in answer to our prayers, you have escaped—next time it may be a broken leg or concussion of the brain, or something else that will disable you for life.

Wingate, of course, ignored these parental warnings, but it is clear from his diary entries that he was not immune to fear: "Before the first race my bowels turned to water and I gasped with fear. . . . At the fifth fence I was knocked out of the saddle by another horse. The air seemed full of oaths and no wonder; there were 20 starters and only seven finished, I think! I got up again and went on over the blind ditch and so up the slope towards the haystack, fumbling vainly for my stirrups and praying desperately."

Another diary entry at about this time gives some account of a winter weekend when for once Wingate was not riding to hounds or steeplechasing: "Sunday. Went to church. Ball aching sermon as usual. The Church of England is no church. . . . Music before lunch. Beethoven's Ninth, which I like better and better—especially parts 3 and 4 of presto finale movement. . . . Lunch. Ate too much Stilton—why has no one paid for a little port to moisten it?"

In January 1926, the army sent Wingate on a six-month course to its principal riding school at Weedon, in Northamptonshire. It was a privilege usually offered only to officers in fashionable cavalry regiments, but Wingate, the not-so-humble gunner, refused to be overawed by his admittance into the holy of holies of classical horsemanship. True to form, he infuriated his instructors by disregarding their textbook notions of correct style while consistently making winning performances over the jumps. And in July 1926, despite his contrary attitude and unorthodox style, he graduated as a qualified instructor of equitation.

On completing the course, Wingate—by now a full lieutenant and studying for promotion to captain—took a brief leave before being sent to rejoin his battery, which was now based at Fort Brockhurst, in Hampshire. There he met the girl who was to be the first serious love of his life: Enid Margaret Jelley, known to her friends as Peggy. She was the younger daughter of a retired colonel who was in the habit of offering hospitality to the young officers based nearby. He did not think much of Wingate, whose unconventional behavior and unorthodox ideas clearly irritated him. According to the Jelleys' older daughter Mary, her parents only put up with him because they realized how much Peggy loved him. If Mary is to be believed, Wingate had the habit of dropping his cigarette ends wherever he pleased and, as a frequent houseguest, would preempt Colonel Jelley's copy of *The Times* at breakfast and, having read it, discard it in a crumpled condition. Not surprisingly the colonel and his lady thought of Wingate as "that rude young man."

But Peggy was undeterred by his social shortcomings. For her, these were offset by lean good looks, sparkling conversation, and infectious enthusiasm. A serious-minded girl, she found herself entranced by the intensity of his monologues on politics, philosophy, religion, music, and literature and moved by his occasional lapses into silent introspection. She was able to read his moods and was flattered to find herself becoming the repository for his hopes and fears. He was quite unlike the other young men of her acquaintance and soon they had an "understanding"—not yet a formal engagement—that some day they would marry. As an army brat she realized that day might be far off: a young officer without private means was in no position to marry until he had won promotion, and Wingate had often told her of his ambition to serve overseas and make his mark before settling down.

During his six months at Weedon, Wingate had infuriated his snobbish cavalry-regiment messmates no less than he had irked his instructors by haranguing them at mealtimes on contentious subjects, such as the principles of Marxism, with which he claimed to agree. He was almost certainly doing this for effect—"he only does it to annoy, because he knows it teases"—for, as he assured his concerned sister Sybil, he was too firm a believer in God ever to become a Communist.

But if not a Communist, he was clearly inclining toward the left. He ran an account with a Charing Cross Road bookshop billing its wares as "Literature of the Left" and known colloquially as "The Bomb Shop." An invoice dated 13 June 1925 listed his purchase of *War and Peace* in three volumes, six shillings; George Bernard Shaw's *Getting Married, You Never Can Tell,* and *Arms and the Man,* two shillings each; *The Communist Party Manifesto,* threepence; and *Sexual Health and Birth Control* by Ettie Rout, one shilling.

Some idea of Wingate's musical tastes at the same period may be gleaned from a Gramophone Exchange invoice detailing his purchase of an HMV table gramophone for £20—more than a month's salary—and recordings of Beethoven's Violin Concerto no. 5, Symphony no. 3, and *Apassionata* Piano Sonata, plus the larghetto from Mozart's Clarinet Quintet—"the most beautiful melody I know," noted Wingate. And he was beginning to pay a little more attention to his appearance, going to a Saville Row tailor to be fitted for a civilian suit and to Sulka on Bond Street for shirts and ties, although he rarely managed to look really well turned out, either in uniform or mufti.

As the clothes, the books, the booze, and the billiards suggest, Wingate had by now broken free of the austere and restrictive religious ideology drilled into him by his parents. By his own account, he could no longer be termed a Christian in any formal sense. In a 1925 letter to an evangelist with whom his sister Monica—by that time a student at Newnham College, Cambridge—had been corresponding he wrote:

> Personally, I do not profess to try to follow the teachings of Christ in many respects, as they are wholly incompatible with the conditions of my life: and permit me to say without any idea of being offensive, with the life of every officer, ipso facto. If the so-called disciples of Christ would only read his TEACHINGS with honesty and not refuse to accept as allegorical everything that does not to some extent fit in with his preconceived idea of life, not one in a million of so-called Christians would continue to be so called. . . .
>
> Do let us be sincere and not always trying to replace the powerful revolutionary teachings of Christ with the emotional dogmas of the churches which call themselves by his name. . . . Indeed, religion in the past has always been responsible for the greatest crimes—the Crucifixion, the burning of Joan of Arc, the massacre of St. Bartholomew—and a thousand other villainies. This is that very emotional dogmatic religion that you value so highly and consider a sine qua non of salvation.

Some might interpret this as agnosticism, or even atheism, but such was not the case. Despite his rejection of Christian dogma—the divinity of Jesus, the Virgin Birth, the Resurrection, the Trinity, et al.—Wingate remained, and would remain throughout his life, absolutely certain of the existence of the Judeo-Christian God, not just as some remote prime mover but as a personal deity, and one moreover who intended him for some great purpose, as yet unrevealed. "I have the strongest belief in the existence and goodness of God," he said in a letter to Sybil, "and I rejoice in the conviction that there is a plan in life for those that will believe it." This was the God whose will and presence were indelibly imprinted on his mind in childhood by parental precept and study of the Old Testament, the Jehovah whose will and presence remained for him tangible in everyday affairs, just as were the will and presence of Evil.

Reconciling that bedrock belief in the existence of God with the product of his late-flowering intellectual curiosity, his eager rummaging in the storehouse of Western secular thought would surely cause profound inner conflict. Here was a skeptical twentieth-century humanist harnessed to a God-intoxicated seventeenth-century mystic—a Shaw inside a Bunyan if you will. Wingate would prove able to work his way through the paradox, but it would take a decade or so for him to encounter and embrace a cause able to resolve it completely and in so doing to direct his life toward a goal from which it would never deviate.

Chapter 3

WINGATE HAD long considered service in the Middle East, where Britain still held imperial sway and kept substantial armed forces, as the route to promotion. His family name had considerable resonance throughout the region, for his father's first cousin, Sir Reginald Wingate, had been successively governor-general of the Sudan, commander of the Egyptian army, and, during World War I, Britain's high commissioner in Cairo—effectively the ruler of Egypt.

Now retired at the age of sixty-six, but still wielding great influence in Whitehall and Westminster, "Cousin Rex," as he was known to his Wingate relatives, was living in Scotland but maintained a pied-à-terre in London, where Orde met him for the first time in 1925. In the course of conversation, the older Wingate told Orde of a less overt connection with the Arab world—that T. E. Lawrence, celebrated as "Lawrence of Arabia" for his part in fomenting the Arabs' wartime revolt against the Ottoman Empire, was a distant cousin through Orde's mother's side of the family.*

Sir Reginald advised Orde that if he wanted a posting to the Middle East he would do well to apply for an intensive course in Arabic at London University's prestigious School of Oriental Studies. Orde took his advice and in September 1926 his application was approved. He sold his horses, said good-bye to Tulloch, who was off on a posting to India, and moved to digs in London to start the course. It was hard, concentrated work, but by now Wingate had completely overcome his former sloth in the classroom, and in March 1927 he graduated with an 85 percent examination mark.

---

*As the imperial proconsul in Cairo during World War I, Sir Reginald had provided the large sums of gold with which Lawrence had bribed the tribes of the Arabian peninsula to take up arms against the Turks.

His next step was to apply for six months' leave so that he could travel in the Middle East and perfect his Arabic by daily use. But his application was turned down on the grounds that he had not yet completed the five years' service required to qualify for a long leave. Six months later he applied again, and this time he was successful: Cousin Rex had made a discreet intervention on his behalf, and Orde, the inveterate outsider, had learned a lesson that would serve him well in the future—that the "system," however much he might despise it, could be made to work for him if he were to cultivate the influential insider.

Before taking his leave Orde went to visit his cousin at his Scottish home in Dunbar, East Lothian.* There Sir Reginald advised him to go to Khartoum, enlist in the advanced Arabic classes held for members of the Sudan administration, and try to get himself seconded to the elite Sudan Defence Force. He gave his young cousin a letter of introduction to the SDF commander, or *ka'id al amm,* to use his Arabic title, Major General H. J. Huddleston, better known in the Middle East as "Huddleston Pasha."

The SDF was a somewhat strange organization, reflecting the peculiar status of the Sudan as a quasi-colony under the joint rule of Britain and Egypt, which was itself little more than a protectorate. The force—only forty-five hundred officers and men to keep the peace in a territory of almost one million square miles—had been created in January 1925, after the murder of the governor-general, Sir Lee Stack, by Egyptian nationalists led the British to expel the Egyptian military from the Sudan. The new force's officers were almost entirely British, and despite the hard and lonely conditions, the SDF was considered a glamorous posting. Competition for a five-year secondment from their regiments was intense among young and single British subalterns, bored by garrison life in postwar Britain and eager to do some "real soldiering." In many ways it was the equivalent of what special forces such as the SAS or Green Berets have become to young British and American officers in the years since World War II.

The idea of the Sudan was irresistibly romantic to a generation of public schoolboys brought up on Kipling, Newbolt, and the *Boys' Own Paper*—the Sudan of the Fuzzy-Wuzzy ("You're a pore benighted 'ea-

*Although he was of Scots descent on his father's side and his future wife was Scottish, this was to be Orde's first and only visit to Scotland.

then, but a first-class fightin' man") and "the square that broke," of the Mad Mahdi and a dashing young war correspondent named Winston Churchill. Wingate, as we have seen, had little respect for the public-school ethos, but he was anxious for the career boost to be derived from service on the outposts of empire and command of a company of native troops.

With a recommendation from his influential Cousin Rex in his back pocket—and despite the fact that he had not completed the required five years' army service before he could, strictly speaking, be considered for the SDF—Wingate knew that he stood a good chance of being accepted.

Before leaving for the Middle East he went to Godalming to say good-bye to his parents and siblings. His mother's health was none too good, her doctor having found her heart "very tired." Sir Thomas (later Lord) Horder, the specialist to whom she had been referred ("at the top of the tree, alas! a four-guinea wallah") told her that he would have heart trouble, too, if he gave his heart the amount of work to do that she was giving hers, and she had spent several weeks in bed.

In those days, before air travel became common, the usual route to the Middle East was by boat-train from London and Dover to Calais and Paris, south by rail to Marseilles, and thence by sea to Alexandria. Wingate, ever the nonconformer, decided to go by sea from Harwich to the Hook of Holland and then bicycle across Europe, through the Netherlands, Germany, Czechoslovakia, Austria, and Yugoslavia, to Italy, where he would embark from Genoa for Alexandria.

For one who had never left Britain before, the journey was full of incident. He averaged a punishing seventy miles a day on his bicycle, was robbed of one hundred Austrian schillings by an apparently friendly tinker in Prague, and was arrested for vagrancy in Vienna. On the Yugoslav-Italian border he sold his bicycle for five pounds and walked across the frontier to Trieste. There he found the Italian carabinieri to be "the best-behaved officials, if you can call them so, in Italy," always ready to "help you defeat the avarice of [their] fellow countrymen."

From Trieste he caught the train to Venice, which he found entrancing. He loved the absence of traffic noise (thanks to the canals), the beauty of the Piazza San Marco, and the locals' "delightful habit" of strolling up and down the square in twos and threes from six to ten o'clock each evening. "I cannot believe that Beatrice was more beautiful or Dante more romantic than some of these superb creatures," he wrote. But he found the English abroad less appealing—they were "so much more English" than they were at home, with "the appearance, views and habits of the Victorian era." "I avoid them," he added.

In a vaporetto going down the Grand Canal, he found himself under the gaze of an Englishman who "looked like a retired official or officer in some smart regiment" and his wife, a woman with "a faded, querulous face." Impelled by his seemingly insatiable need to provoke and irritate, Wingate got into animated conversation with an Austrian "about the sort of subjects that Englishmen simply don't talk about with Huns":

> I pointed out to the Austrian what a mess Lloyd George and Clemenceau* had made of Central Europe. I drew his attention to the fact that a reckoning was inevitable, and that no right-minded man could wish to prevent it. I deplored the French nation. I admired the Germans. And I was gratified by the look of incredulous horror and loathing that crept over the faces of my fellow-countrymen.

From Venice he caught the night train to Genoa—"a revolting town . . . hot, dusty, dirty, garish, ugly and expensive"—and took his berth in a third-class cabin on the *Italia,* a passenger ship bound for Alexandria, four days' sailing away. He shared the cabin with "a Gypo doctor, an Austrian hairdresser (dames), a German secretary, a Levantine, and lastly Blunt"—a fellow British officer. "I was very relieved to see him. I knew him hunting in England, and he is now running the intelligence in Cairo. He's a clever fellow and interesting." With the unconscious arrogance of the same kind of Englishman abroad that he had been deploring a few paragraphs before, Wingate continued:

> We took charge of the cabin between us, and did pretty much as we pleased, with due consideration for our fellow passengers' feelings. Filthy habits, such as turning off the fan at night, shutting the porthole except in a rough sea, smoking in the cabin, etc., we could not permit. We further discouraged others from getting up at the same time as ourselves, which would make movement difficult.

---

*The British and French World War I leaders who had been the principal architects of the Versailles Treaty, whose humiliating terms were loathed by most Germans, especially veterans such as the Austrian-born former corporal Adolf Hitler.

It is revealing that this chatty, uninhibited letter was addressed to the father Wingate had for so long considered forbidding and unapproachable. With manhood and independence from the stifling home atmosphere, he had evidently overcome his fear of the parent who used to beat him for no other reason than to strengthen his character and succeeded in putting their relationship on a soldier-to-soldier basis of mutual respect. It's no less interesting that he seemed to expect his stuffy, Victorian parent to share his "enlightened" contempt for the stuffy, Victorian British abroad. Or was he trying to provoke him, too?

After the *Italia* docked at Alexandria, Wingate took the train to Cairo, where he stayed ten days in the flat of a former fellow student from the School of Oriental Studies, visited the usual tourist sites, and called on the bigwigs to whom Cousin Rex had given him letters of introduction. These included the Sudan agent and Sir Reginald's former secretary, the venerable Ibrahim Bey Dimitri, who readily put himself out for "a cousin of our beloved Master and Chief" and in turn introduced him to a number of influential Egyptian and Syrian effendis, who were equally fulsome in their remembrances to the ex–high commissioner.

From Cairo Wingate took the train south to Wadi Halfa and thence by Nile steamer to Khartoum. Plagued by toothache while the side-wheeler clattered upstream, Wingate fell into conversation with an officer of the Sudan Political Service named A. L. W. Vicars-Miles, who was returning from home leave to his post in Rashad, in the mountainous Kordofan Province. Despite Wingate's customarily unkempt appearance and unorthodox views, Vicars-Miles took a liking to him— though the magic of the family name must have helped—and offered him some painkiller for his toothache. He also offered the hospitality of his remote outpost, should Wingate not find Khartoum to his liking.

In Khartoum, Wingate called on Huddleston Pasha, who promised to find a place for him in the Sudan Defence Force, subject to War Office approval. But there would not be a vacancy until the following April, and Wingate soon found himself beggared by the cost of living in Khartoum. "Expenses here are terrible unless you are on the rate of pay in the country," he complained. "I'm not drinking a drop, literally, I smoke moderately, I'm even economising in fans, and I have no amusements of any sort."

So with six months to kill Wingate decided to take Vicars-Miles up on his invitation and traveled by riverboat and camel to join him at

Rashad, his administrative outpost in the Nuba Mountains, where he anticipated—correctly—that he would be able to live within his slender means.

As a guest, Wingate was a decidedly mixed blessing. At close quarters, Vicars-Miles found his eccentricities and outlandish opinions increasingly hard to take. As at the Jelleys', Wingate tended to litter the floor with his cigarette ends. Some days he would stretch out on the sofa, sucking sugarcane for hours on end to test the dietary usefulness of unrefined sucrose in tropical conditions. On one occasion Vicars-Miles was startled to find Wingate sitting bareheaded and stripped to the waist in the blinding heat of the midday sun. Asked what he thought he was doing, Wingate replied that he was conducting an experiment to find out how long it would take him to get sunstroke. Appalled by such recklessness in the pursuit of knowledge, Vicars-Miles ordered Wingate indoors. His exposure left him badly sunburned, but Wingate, who was chronically unable to accept received wisdom—on sunstroke or any other subject—felt the experiment had been worthwhile.

At table and over after-dinner whiskies, Wingate would punctuate brooding silences with the lengthy expression of anti-establishment opinions of the kind that had occasionally caused consternation in the officers' mess at Larkhill and Weedon. However much he might feel provoked, Vicars-Miles schooled himself to accept such monologues as the outpourings of a lively and well-stocked mind that enjoyed controversy for its own sake. But Vicars-Miles's young subordinate officers were not so forgiving. What they wanted in a companion was "a jolly decent chap" of their own kind; what they had instead was a show-off, constantly parading his knowledge on every subject under the sun, not to mention his objectionable opinions.

In the idiom of the period, and of their public school background, Wingate seemed an "absolute bounder," totally lacking in respect for the value system in which they—and presumably he—had been brought up. In the claustrophobic atmosphere of a remote and isolated tropical station, his presence was an irritant they could well do without.

So they were considerably relieved when, receiving word that his application for a secondment to the SDF had been approved by the War Office in London, Wingate left for Khartoum, sporting a moustache that he had grown partly because it was less trouble than shaving and "partly because the Arabs pay more attention to one wearing that appendage."

From Khartoum, he was sent to the headquarters of the SDF's East Arab Corps,* in Kassala Province, for familiarization with the customs and methods of this unique miniature army, and within two months took up his first command, taking charge of a company, or *idara*, of 275 native troops, with the local and temporary rank of *bimbashi*, the rough equivalent of major.

He was based at Gedaref, a remote outstation where he was the only European. His three junior officers and the Other Ranks were nearly all Muslims, mostly from the tribes of central and eastern Sudan, with a sprinkling of Somalis and Nubians. Many of the men were accompanied by their wives, concubines, and children, living in family groups in mud huts scattered around the outstation headquarters. As the rules and customs of the SDF required, Wingate was not just a commanding officer to these men and their families, but also a father, philosopher, and guide. "I lived and moved among these people," he would recall. "They were delightful. . . . All the squabbles of the married quarters were brought to me."

Wingate soon became acutely conscious that he exercised powers not only of severe physical punishment—up to a maximum of twenty-five lashes with a rhinoceros-hide whip—but literally of life and death. On one occasion he exercised that power to save one of his men from being either hanged for murder or serving a long jail sentence for manslaughter. In the course of a dispute over a woman, this man had hit his rival with a steel-shod stick and unintentionally killed him. Wingate could have referred the case to corps headquarters for court-martial, but he decided otherwise:

> I said to myself "Here is an ignorant peasant. His mind is quite un-
> complicated . . . he is capable of showing great virtues, as I know,
> and he is also capable of suffering mental distress. . . . To inflict on
> such a man the hardship of prison for a term of years, to shut him
> away from his natural surroundings, would be in my opinion a

*The SDF's other principal components were the West Arab Corps, the Equatorial Corps, and the Camel Corps.

crime greater than this particular manslaughter." When I arrived at these conclusions I talked to the prisoner and told him I was not going to send up his case.

If Wingate was deeply reluctant to punish his subordinates by imprisonment, he was more ready to impose the lash and even, on occasion, to punch or kick a man who provoked his unruly temper by some display of incompetence or insubordination. For an officer to strike a British Other Rank was forbidden. But although by the standards of his day Wingate was no racist, his men were natives, after all, and the finer points of disciplinary procedure were rarely observed in the remote outstations of the Sudan.

Because it was the rainy season when he took up his command at Gedaref, military activity was restricted, allowing Wingate time to concentrate on his Arabic studies, with a view to obtaining a first-class interpreter's certificate. He also studied for his promotion examinations and read up in the hope of qualifying for entry into the Staff College, looking ahead with considerable self-confidence to his longer-term future:

> I doubt very much whether the Sudan will be useful to me for longer than five years at the outside [he wrote to his father]. There's no future for a soldier in the Sudan, but the responsibility (not to mention the pay) is most valuable to a young soldier like myself. . . . I daresay if I made a dead set at it, and fortune favoured me, I might become Ka'id el Amm here one day, but I feel disposed to attempt something bigger.

Such moments of exuberant self-confidence, however, were interspersed with what he called "nervous attacks." With the benefit of current psychiatric knowledge it seems clear that these were symptoms of a temporarily debilitating form of clinical depression, a condition that was to haunt him throughout his life, but that he would reveal only to a handful of intimates. Peggy Jelley was one of these. "I have been in such a state of nerves during the last week or two that I have read an omen of death into everything," he told her, describing the onset of one attack:

> The tree that blew down outside my house; a worm-eaten tree; the owl that visited my garden each night and hooted at me; the skele-

ton I've just seen in a landslide; the crows that have been cawing over my head just now—all are omens of approaching death.

These incidents became familiar. When depression struck for the first time he had "nothing to hang on to, not even the knowledge of when it would end." Eventually, he hit on "a sort of formula which I said to myself as the waters closed over my head and went on repeating":

> "God is good," I used to say over and over again. It had to be some-thing simple because my anguish prevented any thought process, and it had to be something comprehensive that I really believed or it would have been no good to me. These words summed up my whole belief and when I hung in the abyss they were all that I had the strength to utter.

When Peggy was herself feeling depressed over the death of a friend, Wingate wrote back: "I know how you feel . . . I have felt the same. There's no way out of it—no escape from the cruelty of life. . . ." But he added this stoic advice:

> He that is down need fear no fall, he that is destitute no mischief. Little Peggy, we must have the courage to live. Don't be frightened by death. We know nothing about it except that it is the end of mor-tal life—life as we know it. If you don't know how to die you don't know how to live. . . . When punishment comes you set your teeth—one grows soft too easily.

It is surely no coincidence that the onset of his "particular curse," as Wingate was to call it, should occur while he was serving in the Sudan. It is a harsh and forbidding terrain whose savage extremes of tempera-ture, immense horizons and massive cloud formations, limitless night skies and primal solitudes, merciless predators and arid expanses all combine to induce a sense not so much of the wonder of Nature as of its indifference, even malevolence.

Confronted by the howling emptiness of this universe, Wingate had only his belief in a personal God to hold on to as a lifeline to sanity. He believed because he had to believe; it was what enabled him to endure the recurring nightmare of clinical depression and drive off the demons that pursued him so that—usually, he reported, in two or three days—he could return to the world of challenge and achievement.

In learning to live with his affliction—which also to a lesser degree affected some of his siblings—Wingate came to believe that "it has two sides—mental (or spiritual) and physical," the latter being amenable to "rest, recreation, society, a mild indulgence in narcotics, a fatherly attitude towards oneself, etc." The spiritual trouble should be treated by auto-suggestion, the use of mantras such as "God is great"* and "Serve God not self." He added: "The trouble is ultimately spiritual and amounts to an attack on the spirit by the powers of evil." Expanding on this theme, he spoke of the "spiritual vertigo" of his increasingly godless generation:

> With the loss of the old beliefs it is as inevitable as the sequence of day and night. . . . Wherever there is intellectual activity today there is this trouble. It is hereditary [only] in so far as intelligence is hereditary. It is a weakness of strength.

During his initial period at corps headquarters and on routine visits there later, Wingate made a mixed impression on his fellow officers. From the top down they were predisposed in his favor as the bearer of a family name much honored in the Sudan. His performance as a company commander was well regarded, too.

But his generally scruffy appearance, his habit of lounging about his quarters in the nude, and the "bolshie" views that he seemed unable to repress did not go down at all well. Eventually, as one of his contemporaries would recall, the colonel in command of the East Arab Corps sent for Wingate and told him to curb his tongue. "I don't like the things you say and I don't like you. A young officer should be seen and not heard," said the colonel, warning Wingate that he would be returned to his regiment in disgrace if he did not smarten up and keep his views to himself.

This was painfully reminiscent of the reprimand he had been given by his commandant at Woolwich and seemed to Wingate to be just another example of the blinkered pomposity shortly to be epitomized by the cartoonist David Low's invention, the immortal Colonel Blimp. But he swallowed hard and bit back the indignant response that rose to his lips, even though he considered the CO's admonition to be an outrageous denial of his right to free speech.

---

*The oft-repeated creed of his Muslim soldiers.

To trim and compromise was not in his nature and would become even less so in the future, but Wingate realized that to be sent home under a cloud might be the effective end of his army career. He was convinced that he was divinely destined for greatness and that, despite the small minds in high places, the army was his route to that destiny. "I cannot be a nobody. I cannot be nothing!" as he said in a letter to Peggy.

One of Wingate's operational tasks as a *bimbashi* in Kassala Province was to suppress an epidemic of ivory poaching by gangs coming over the border from neighboring Ethiopia. And it was while leading an antipoacher sweep in April 1931 that he was brought face to face for the first time with the inevitable consummation of the profession of arms: violent death. A gang of nine poachers had fled at the approach of his patrol, but one of them stood his ground and opened fire on them with his ancient rifle. Returning fire, one of Wingate's men shot him dead. Wingate viewed the corpse, an old man wearing a ragged djellaba and a cast-off SDF jersey, and was overcome by a sense of terrible responsibility for the death of this obviously impoverished wretch. "He only possessed one thing of any value or importance," he would recall later, "and that was his life, and we took it away."

While Wingate and his men continued their sweep over difficult terrain between the Blue Nile and the Dinder, the fate of the old poacher played on his mind, setting off a train of thoughts and speculations about the fear of death and the meaning of life. He set these thoughts down, not always very coherently, in a weeklong series of journal entries, which he addressed to Peggy Jelley soon after returning to his post from an annual leave in England, which he had spent with her.

April 12: . . . Death is no respecter of persons and we should not live so that the death of another is the death of ourselves. . . . I have, I think, loved mercy and justice but I have yielded too much to my own desires and lusts because I wanted to. And to this extent my house is built on the sands of self. . . . I feel I can now cast aside this self-love and that, should it please God to take my life, I shall know that my love for His creation lives on, and that my own self is a small part of me. If it should please Him to spare me, why then I hope that all my life after I may be more careful of God's creatures and less indulgent of self. . . .

April 14: These last months, instead of living where God has placed me, I have lived entirely in England. . . . The effect is as though my body in an English drawing room were to see its stomach wandering among African forests and about to be torn to pieces by wild beasts. The feeling is "What has this danger to do with me? By what rule of common sense or common justice am I exposed to risks so totally unrelated to my whole way of life?"

I must learn to love God's creation wherever I am and not to shut myself up in a world of dreams that the world of reality can so pitilessly shatter. . . . We cannot wholly live either here and now or in an imagined future, but we must have just that touch with the ideal that will enable us to work with a blessing upon reality.

Literally overnight, Wingate's mood of philosophical introspection changes and his continuing diary entries read like a boys' adventure story.

April 15: Now right out in the wilds. No human being within an hour's march and civilization's outposts four days away. . . . There is no water either way for a day's march. . . .

April 18: . . . The men began to go down in their tracks, and eventually I had to halt the column and adopt the very risky expedient of taking a few camels to fetch water from the Dinder, which I believed to be only a few miles away. . . . The heat has been extraordinary. Literally, one can hardly stand it lying in the shade. Imagine walking all day without a scrap of shade and now on over iron-hard, cruelly rough, chopped-up soil, bursting through long grass and thorns, thorns, thorns. . . .

Today (18th) I've had my fill of adventures—have shot two buffalo, two lion and I don't know what else. . . . Now we are just off to El Oowad, about twelve miles north. I hope, please God, to sleep tomorrow at Galleger or Ras Amen, and the next night to be on my way home to Singa.

April 19: We're now at El Oowad and I've just got back from an unsuccessful lion hunt. I must tell you that yesterday we imprisoned a lion in a belt of dense scrub. I'd shot him somewhere, so he was probably ill-tempered. However, he got away by a most ingenious ruse which I'll tell you some day.

Wingate's seemingly insatiable urge to kill lions, purely for sport, so soon after his pious resolve to be "more careful of God's creatures" shows how rapidly and completely he could switch from being a man of somber introspection to being a man of unthinking action. And his gift for swift and effective action was displayed when he shot dead a seven-foot spitting cobra that rose up at him out of the bush. He sent the skin to Peggy, who had it made into a pair of shoes.

On returning to base at the end of his *idara*'s long and grueling sweep, in which they killed one more poacher, wounded two, and captured eleven, Wingate wrote a detailed official report on the operation. It was read by, among others, the governor-general, Sir John Maffey, who commended Wingate's "very interesting narrative of a most successful expedition conducted with great dash and judgment." Added Sir John: "His account of his adventures has taught me a great deal."

British officers serving with the SDF were allowed three months' home leave every summer as an antidote to the harsh conditions, brutal heat, and loneliness of service in the outstations of the Sudan. During those leaves Wingate divided his time between Peggy's parental home in Fareham and his own in Godalming. The Jelleys remained less than overwhelmed at the prospect of their daughter's marriage to "that rude young man," but as Wingate neared the end of his five-year stint with the SDF, and while on home leave in August 1932, he and Peggy announced their formal engagement through a notice in *The Times*.

Back in Kassala for his final tour of duty, Wingate's thoughts turned toward one final adventure before leaving the Middle East. His imagination had been fired by one of the enduring legends of the region— that of a fabulous lost oasis named Zerzura, deep in the uncharted Sea of Sand that straddles the frontier between Egypt and Libya.

The legend described Zerzura as a place of sweetness and delight, the abode of thousands of songbirds, fluttering about a gleaming white city, where a sleeping king and queen and an army of marauding black giants had their abode. The approaches to Zerzura were guarded by djinn, who whipped up a sandstorm to hide it whenever travelers approached.

Like many legends, the story of Zerzura may have had a basis in fact. Many respected geographers and explorers believed that the oasis itself might exist, if not the white city and its magical inhabitants. The desert-traveling Hungarian adventurer Count Ladislaus Almasy (real-life protagonist of the 1997 Oscar-winning film *The English Patient* and the novel on which it was based) had theorized that it was located somewhere amid the dry riverbeds, or wadis, that run north and south from the Gilf Plateau, 450 miles due west of Aswan.

For a while there was a suggestion—brokered by Cousin Rex—that Wingate and Almasy might stage a joint expedition in motor vehicles, but in the end Wingate decided he would rather go it alone and arranged to hire a caravan of thirteen camels and four cameleers for the trek.

An unexpected last-minute obstacle almost aborted the venture: when Wingate made what he thought would be a routine application to SDF headquarters for permission to make the expedition during his six-weeks' end of secondment leave, he was refused. The powers that be felt, perhaps not unreasonably, that it was too risky an undertaking. Determined to press on, Wingate turned to Cousin Rex for help, and once again it was forthcoming. Sir Reginald made a tactful intervention through the old-boy network and the War Office gave Khartoum the green light for Wingate to proceed, providing he waived his right to any benefits or compensation should he die or be invalided during his quest.

With that problem out of the way, and with the receipt of surveying instruments on loan from the Royal Geographical Society in London, Wingate left Khartoum for Egypt by train on 28 January 1933, alighting four days later at a junction 350 miles south of Cairo. From there he traveled 220 mile due west by truck to the desert outpost of Qasr Dakhla, where his camels and their attendants awaited him.

From there they followed an ancient road west to the wells of Bir Abu Mungar, and thence along the same crumbling track toward Kufra, deep inside the otherwise trackless Sea of Sand. "The desolation of this high and ghostly waste of grey rock has a powerful effect on the imagination," he wrote in an account of his journey for the Royal Geographical Society. "Suddenly to be translated here one would suppose oneself to be on the moon. Everything looked as though it had been falling to pieces forever."

It was desperately hard going, made even more so by the extra hardships that Wingate had devised, true to his habit of testing himself and those under him to their limits. Spurning the usual routine of desert travel, he made his protesting men and complaining camels plough ahead through the heat of the day, instead of traveling through the night. Conceding that this "would scandalise the military experts of the camel corps," Wingate nevertheless maintained, "Once get your beasts thoroughly hardened and you can ride roughshod over most of [the rules]." It was a maxim he would apply equally, and with great success, to the men who came under his command later in his career.

He wore a long Arab jibba over his service shorts and bush shirt, with a turban on his head and open sandals on his feet. And to observe the effects of a feeding regime he had worked out for himself, he subsisted on a diet of biscuits, oranges, cod-liver oil, and dried dates "as hard as cardboard."

He did not find Zerzura, or any trace of it, only the carcass of a camel, the skeleton of a bird, an egg, and a prehistoric flint tool. But in retrospect Wingate considered the experience to have been worthwhile:

> I recalled all the abortive effort, the vain expense of strength of the enterprise, now rapidly receding into the past, and wondered whether I regretted it; whether I would do it again were the chance to offer. Before I considered it I knew that the experience was real, and that therefore I would always treasure it.

Back at the rail junction where he had begun his desert journey, Wingate caught the next train north to Cairo, stayed a few days with a friend, and then went on to Port Said, where he boarded the P&O liner *Cathay*, bound from Sydney to Marseilles.

Chapter 4

*I*T WAS THE BRIGHT YELLOW SHOES that caught the attention of Ivy Paterson as she sat in a deck chair in the shade of the *Cathay*'s bridge and watched the new passengers coming aboard in Port Said. The shoes were of the kind one might expect to see on the feet of an Alexandrian pimp or an Armenian rug merchant, not on a young Englishman of the officer class, as their owner appeared to be.

The rest of his outfit was conventional enough, if a trifle scruffy— shabby gray flannel trousers, a leather-elbowed tweed jacket over an open-necked shirt, a scuffed camel-skin briefcase under one arm—and his brown hair was plastered down with some kind of cream or grease. He looked lean, tanned, and weathered.

Ivy Paterson, together with her husband, Walter, a retired Ceylon merchant, and their daughter, Lorna, a schoolgirl just sixteen, had been at sea for over two weeks, on their way back to their home in Scotland from a family visit to Australia. Having noted the yellow-shoed young man and the other new arrivals, Mrs. Paterson returned to her book.

In conversation later, as the *Cathay* headed due west toward Malta, its next port of call, she discovered the reason for the garish footwear. The good-looking and intense young Englishman, having introduced himself as Lieutenant Orde Wingate, Royal Artillery, explained that his feet were so swollen and painful after an arduous desert trek that he had been obliged to find a pair of extra-soft shoes. And unfortunately the only such shoes he had been able to find in Port Said were these, he told her. He glanced down at his garishly shod feet with a quick self-deprecating smile that fleetingly revealed a couple of missing teeth.

The well-to-do and sophisticated Mrs. Paterson found that smile, and the young man's general demeanor, quite appealing:

He had a fine skin [she would recall], unusually fair for a man, though tanned where exposed to the sun. His eyes were . . . remarkable. . . . Rather deep set and of perwinkle blue. . . . He had a salient sort of nose—side-face rather like Wellington—and a wide and well-shaped mouth. . . . His speaking voice was of a most pleasant quality and intonation.

That quite factual description of Wingate at age thirty was larded with insights into his character and personality that Mrs. Paterson can scarcely have entertained at first sight; it was written almost three decades later, and consequently owed a good deal to hindsight. His eyes, said Mrs. Paterson, were those of "a prophet and a visionary" and it was "fascinating to listen to him when he talked or 'held forth' . . . on almost any subject under the sun. He spoke brilliantly. But he could be very quiet and silent for long periods."

However retrospective those perceptions might be, there is no question that Wingate did make an immediate and deep impression on her—and even more so on her adolescent daughter, Lorna, who, or so the girl would recall later, "marched up to him and said, 'You're the man I'm going to marry.' We both felt the same way about it."

Her mother remembered events rather differently. "It is true," she wrote, "that on the deck they looked at each other" and "it may be they both felt the pull of fate." But Wingate seemed shy at first and, according to Ivy, hovered in the background for a couple of days:

> Lorna had formed a firm friendship on this voyage with a retired elderly General, and they used to spend most of their time together discussing the affairs of the universe. . . . [Orde] was in the habit of drawing up his chair unobtrusively to within earshot while pretending to read his book. . . . At last he plucked up courage and spoke to her.
>
> Well, after that there was never such a talking. They were both of them prepared to talk about everything under the sun and both of them had equally definite opinions and not always the same by any means.

When the *Cathay* docked at Malta, Wingate went ashore with the Patersons, took Ivy aside to a coffee shop, and told her what he had already told Lorna herself: that he was in love with Lorna and wanted to marry her. "If anyone had told me that this would happen to me with a girl of sixteen I would not have believed them," Ivy remembered him saying. In reply, she reminded Wingate pointedly that when they reached Scotland Lorna had to go back to her boarding school in St. Andrews to prepare for entrance into Oxford University. He replied, "Yes, I know, but if there is any chance for me I will wait for her as long as I have to."

Feeling a little sorry for him, I then said something which was strange, but quite true. "Well, you know, a fortune teller read Lorna's hand a few years ago and said she would marry a very famous soldier, so you never know—why, Mister Wingate, it might be you!"

When the ship reached Marseilles, Wingate and the Patersons disembarked and caught the train to London, where Orde and Lorna bade each other an emotional farewell and went their separate ways— he to a difficult meeting with the fiancée he was about to jilt, and thence back to his regiment, she to her matriculation studies at St. Leonard's School for Girls in Fife.

Ivy and Walter Paterson no doubt imagined—and certainly hoped—that this shipboard romance would soon be forgotten. They wanted Lorna to finish her education and were not at all sure that a penniless, thirty-year-old subaltern, however interesting a personality, was a suitable husband for their adolescent only child. But two years later, a day short of her eighteenth birthday, Lorna Paterson cast aside all thought of higher education and a career, or of a "brilliant" marriage, and became Mrs. Orde Wingate.

It certainly sounds odd: "love at first sight"—culminating in marriage—between a teenaged schoolgirl and a man almost twice her age. Sixteen-year-old girls do, of course, often have wild crushes on older men, but few would dare to blurt it out, as Lorna says she did, on first acquaintance. Mature men do, of course, often feel strongly attracted to girls half their age, but they generally stifle the feeling, especially if married or about to be.

What was going on here, then? Wingate was scarcely the kind of inadequate male who needs a pliable "little woman" he can dominate. Lorna, for her part, was a far from typical teenager and anything but pliable. Well read, intellectually precocious, and with a lively mind of her own, she was neither intimidated nor overawed by the charismatic and disputatious Wingate. Indeed, she would quite soon prove to be his equal in argument.

One easy assumption might be that she was unconsciously looking for a father figure. She had a living father, of course, in Walter Paterson, a successful businessman and, in his youth, an outstanding sportsman, who had made his fortune early and retired at fifty. But as both parent and spouse it was Ivy who was the dominant partner in the Paterson household, and it may be that Walter was just not assertive enough within the marriage to satisfy the willful Lorna's need for a strong male presence in her life. This, after all, was a time long before feminist ideas altered people's perspectives on the roles of the sexes.

As for Wingate's existing engagement, the alacrity with which he had fallen for Lorna is alone evidence of his ambivalence about marriage to Peggy. And she herself would concede later that during their six-year relationship he had often expressed doubt about the rightness and wisdom of the match.

He would tell her ruefully that he had nothing to offer her but the cramped life of a garrison wife, but coming from a man who was sure he was destined for greatness that may have been no more than a convenient excuse. A deeper reason for avoiding marriage to Peggy seems, paradoxically, that her gentle intelligence reminded him too much of his mother's. Orde had come to realize that Peggy's qualities of calm and patience would not be good for him in a wife and, as Peggy would concede some years later, "It would have been futile to marry. He needed argument and independence from his partner."

This appears to have been a remarkably shrewd judgment. If Wingate was to fulfill the God-ordained but as yet unknown destiny that he was certain awaited him, he would need the Sturm und Drang of a relationship more combative than the one that Peggy felt was "so complete, so perfect." He now saw that he was more likely to find it with the feisty young Lorna Paterson. In all things the maverick, Wingate was about to turn Freudian dogma onto its head, and reject instead of marrying the woman who reminded him of his mother.

And yet, casting around for an entirely rational explanation of why Orde Wingate, mature soldier, fell so hard for Lorna Paterson, adolescent schoolgirl, and vice versa, does not really lead anywhere. As philosophers, scientists, and poets down the ages have found, there is no explaining the phenomenon of romantic love, in any of its guises. Nor, for that matter, is there any explaining why, in the matter of choosing a mate, Wingate should have followed so closely in his father's footsteps. Neither Lorna nor Ethel Wingate were Lolitas; neither Orde nor George Wingate were Humbert Humberts. Can there be such a thing as an innate predisposition to follow one's father in seeking a wife in the schoolroom?

As Wingate neared home, Peggy Jelley was anticipating a joyful reunion. A friend had given her the loan of her flat in Belgravia so that she and Orde could be alone together. But when she went to collect him at the Army and Navy Club in Pall Mall she realized instantly that something was terribly wrong. He was haggard and "looking like death." She demanded to know what was the matter and, as they walked in Green Park, she questioned him until he admitted the truth.

Devastated but dignified, Peggy told him their engagement should be broken off immediately. Wingate, burdened with guilt and wracked by indecision, tried to delay a final break. They drove to Godalming to seek his mother's advice. Peggy waited in the car while Orde went inside alone to talk to Ethel. She told him that if there was any doubt in his mind it was his duty to himself and to Peggy not to go ahead with the marriage.

From Godalming they drove to Hawkestone, where they went in together to face Peggy's parents. After Orde had left, alone, her father said, "I could kill him." Peggy's older sister Mary was implacably unforgiving. "What man can be forgiven," she demanded of Derek Tulloch many years later, "for having ditched a girl after all those years of keeping her tied to him with such a long engagement, including intimacy that should not have been unless marriage was to follow?"

For her part, Peggy felt her whole world had collapsed. "I was in a daze for years. He took my mind with him," she would tell Orde's sister-in-law Judy Wingate, with whom she struck up a remarkable friendship a couple of years before her death, aged eighty-eight, in 1996. She never married. "After Orde all other men seemed uninteresting," she said. But she insisted that she never felt any bitterness at his rejection of her. Indeed, she refused to call it rejection: she was "set aside," she said.

Of course, it was hateful at the time, but never so dreadful as it would have been had we torn each other into shreds in our human efforts to keep the love we had known between our two souls.

A feeling of guilt over his treatment of Peggy and uncertainty over his future with Lorna did nothing to make Wingate's return to life as a gunnery officer in England any easier. Reduced to his substantive rank of lieutenant, where he joined a long line of frustrated subalterns awaiting promotion to the next rung of the ladder, he joined the Ninth Field Brigade RA at Bulford Camp in Wiltshire—a dismal conglomeration of corrugated iron and wooden shacks, where he had to share living accommodation with three other single subalterns in a draughty and poorly furnished hut divided into four by partition walls of canvas.

But the mechanization of the Royal Artillery, then under way, and his elevation to the position of the brigade's senior subaltern, gave him plenty to occupy his mind and keep his depressions at bay. He had to absorb a lot of technical information to get himself up to speed on the latest innovations in artillery equipment. He was the brigade's messing officer, too, which gave him the opportunity to try out his advanced—for the time—ideas on diet, such as less meat and starch and more fresh fruit and vegetables.

He also tried out, with some success, an unconventional way of preventing fellow junior officers from overspending at the bar. He kept a few bottles of watered-down gin in reserve and "any officer who had a fourth drink would be given the doctored variety."

And he had the pleasure of renewing his friendship with Derek Tulloch, who, back from India and now married, was once again based at Larkhill, just a few miles away. Soon they were out tallyhoing again with the South and West Wiltshire Hunt.

None of Wingate's letters to and from Lorna from this period survive. Separated by five hundred miles and the respective demands of army and school they saw very little of each other. But Ivy Paterson made frequent visits to London, leaving her husband behind at The Place of Tilliefoure, their country estate in Aberdeenshire, and whenever he could Wingate went up to town to see her and press his suit. "We had many pleasant and happy times together, for we had much in common," Ivy would recall. "We both loved music and frequently went to concerts, also the occasional film and theatre."

She observed approvingly that he "always met women as his intellectual equals" and never talked down to them. "He admired a people or a nation where the women were real partners with their menfolk." On the other hand, "he expected a great deal from women and was sometimes surprised if they could not keep up with him."

Mrs. Paterson's recollections of that time seem somewhat saccharine. She makes no mention of her and her husband's misgivings about Wingate as a prospective son-in-law. Lorna had led a sheltered childhood and they felt, not unreasonably, that she was too young to be thinking of marriage. And although Wingate was their social equal, his financial standing and prospects were far beneath theirs. Although he had by this time been promoted, how could he possibly keep Lorna in anything like the style she was accustomed to on a captain's pay?

Ivy makes no mention of a furious row that brought matters to a head when she made a fuss about his being alone with Lorna in his car one evening while they were all three in London at the end of September 1934. Wingate gave Ivy the rough edge of his tongue and, back at Bulford the next day, wrote her an extraordinary nine-page letter of reproof. "It was imperative," he insisted, "that I should have a long uninterrupted talk with Lorna then and there and nowhere else and at no other time."

> What you suppose can be done in a car in lighted streets I can't think. Ivy, if you really cannot trust us there is just as much danger in two hours out of your sight as in two hours in a car together—in fact much more if we're devoid of decency. Such a supposition is so intolerable that we must regard you as an implacable foe if you persist in it.

Declaring that "I love Lorna utterly. My love for her is stronger than yours," Wingate went on to accuse Ivy of stifling her daughter:

> I've watched you with horror time out of number—little words and acts of hers—the most harmless, Ivy—you turn and rend her. I swear that the most impartial of spectators would condemn you for it as I do. For example, why always and inevitably a tight-lipped scene when she loses her glasses? What in God's name does it matter if

she loses every pair ever made? Why your perpetual refusal to re-
spond to her affectionate advances? . . . Ivy, as God sees me, I tell
you I am frightened for her—you'll have her on your hands a nervous breakdown. . . . If that happens Ivy I shall curse you from the
bottom of my soul.

After several more pages in similar vein, Wingate expressed his and
Lorna's determination to be married come what may and then had the
cool nerve to suggest that if Ivy and her husband were concerned
about his relative poverty they should make Lorna an allowance equal
to what they currently spent on her, as "an act of love and generosity."

I am writing to Paterson by this post asking his approval to our marriage, the sooner the better but within a year at latest. It depends on
you what his answer will be. This is an extraordinary letter to write
to you Ivy, a woman of the world, and most people would think me
mad so to approach you. But I believe in speaking the unvarnished
truth on important occasions and I know you are sincere enought to
appreciate my motives. Ivy dear, be merciful unto us and generous.

Ivy and her husband capitulated, although they had legal grounds
to prevent the marriage. But it was a cold peace. Eleven days before the
wedding, Orde felt it necessary to urge his sister Sybil to abandon her
plans to have tea with Ivy and Walter Paterson. "Affairs are in such a
state at present," he said, "that your visit would almost certainly do
harm. I could easily satisfy you of this in conversation but hesitate to
do so on paper. I do beg you to cancel it." She did.

On 24 January 1935, the day before Lorna's eighteenth birthday and
almost two years after their first meeting, she and Orde were married
in Chelsea Old Church, London. Instead of a prayer book, she carried
a white vellum-bound copy of *Wuthering Heights*—one of Orde's favorite novels. Another of Orde's favorites, the hymn "To Be a Pilgrim," words from Bunyan's *Pilgrim's Progress,* was sung, as was
Parry's "Jerusalem," words by William Blake. Lorna's mother would
recall that the church looked lovely, "with masses of mimosa, flown
from the south of France." Yet altogether, it must have been a tight-
lipped occasion, with the Paterson parents—who presumably paid for
the mimosas—stifling their lingering disapproval of their new son-in-
law and the Wingate parents stifling their dour Nonconformist mis-

givings at finding themselves inside an Anglican church. Only close family were present; none of Wingate's fellow officers—not even his dear old friend Tulloch—had been invited. There were no wedding photographs and there is no record of a wedding breakfast of any kind.

The newlyweds motored off to Devonshire in Wingate's battered old sports car for a fortnight's honeymoon and then returned to Bulford to start their life together in married quarters, a rather ramshackle house on the edge of the camp, overlooking Salisbury Plain. They quickly filled the place with books and records and the minimum necessary amount of furniture. But although they had two batmen to tend them—one to cook, the other to wash and clean—the Wingates were scarcely model householders. She had always had someone to pick up after her and, anyway, had the same bohemian temperament as her husband. Once, when both batmen were on leave at the same time, the newlyweds went a whole fortnight without washing up. Having sullied their entire stock of cutlery and dishes, they simply ate straight out of cans until the wash-and-clean batman returned to tackle the plates that had accumulated in the kitchen sink. Tulloch recalled that

> Lorna heard the batman bemoaning the pile which met his eyes and tore into him like a fury and told him he should be only too glad to have some work to do.* I think she made him believe it too.

The Wingates also had original ideas about household pets. They kept a goat, and because as a child Lorna had always wanted to own a monkey, Orde bought a small Barbary ape from Harrod's pet department. As Tulloch would recall:

> The monkey was NOT a nice monkey. . . . It was un-housetrainable, had a passion for beer and used to get extremely drunk. . . . On one occasion we returned from a weekend leave to find a curt note attached to the monkey's cage saying we had been honoured by being chosen to look after it for a fortnight while Orde and Lorna were away. I shall remember that fortnight until my dying day. The little brute made messes everywhere.

---

*This was a time of high unemployment in Britain, though the army was still finding it difficult to get recruits.

And naturally the Wingate household became famous for conversation since, as Tulloch observed, "Orde was always a great talker."

He would speak very fast indeed and quite frequently hold up a dinner party for considerable periods; at other times he would talk and eat at the same time, which sometimes had disastrous results. Lorna was far from being an echo of his views. She had very strong views of her own and was as well read as Orde. Consequently, on occasions a duel would ensue which was both entertaining and frequently instructive.

Tony Simonds, another officer who was a close friend and colleague of Wingate's in the 1930s, remembered Lorna as "very pretty, very young, very good figure, very passionate, very fiery, very argumentative—not an easy person to talk to. Whatever she did, she did with enormous enthusiasm."

She used to lie on the floor and do yoga and nobody was allowed to speak to her. I shall never forget one time when she got her legs behind her head and couldn't get it out again. So for a joke I left her there, just as she was. Eventually, Wingy came along and untangled her. She was a very unusual woman.

In the autumn of 1935 Orde and Lorna's life at Bulford came to an end when Wingate was posted to the Yorkshire steel town of Sheffield as adjutant of a Territorial Army field brigade. It was the kind of posting he had been dreading for some time. "I am at a dangerous age," he had told his father. "One is liable to be sent on all kinds of unpleasant jobs, like territorial adjutancies and such like."

To be deposited among the dark, satanic mills of the industrial north to look after a bunch of part-time soldiers was a far from glamorous appointment for one who had served in the Sudan and explored the Libyan Desert. To make matters worse, Wingate had to leave Lorna behind at Bulford until he could find suitable accommodation for them in Sheffield. In such depressing surroundings he had to struggle hard to fend off the depressions to which he was subject. He was able to respect and sympathize with the gritty northcountrymen he found himself among, but the grim steel town was "alien country" where he could never feel at home. "I hated the life and the neighbourhood," he would tell his mother.

Early in the new year he found rooms for himself and Lorna in a country pub ten miles out of Sheffield, but it was a strange existence in which he alternated periods of intense activity with periods of lethargy. As Lorna recalled:

> At these times he preferred to go to bed and stay there as long as possible, eating very little and drinking enormous quantities of weak tea; having two or three hot baths a day and going back to bed to sleep, wake up and talk or read for a few hours, and then throw down the book and go to sleep again.

Seemingly becalmed in his career, and aghast at the prospect of three more years in Sheffield, Wingate became keener than ever to qualify for a place at the Staff College in Camberley. Without the initials "PSC"—"Passed Staff College"—on his official record, his chances of attaining senior rank would be slight. He passed the written examination to qualify for a place at his second attempt in February 1936, but he had to clear another hurdle to obtain one of the eight places available to gunners.

Unsure that he would be given due credit for his service in the SDF and his one-man expedition to Zerzura, he turned once again to Cousin Rex, hoping he would put in a word for him with the Army Council "if you would like to see me treading in your footsteps (somewhat tardily!) and the name of Wingate with fresh prospects of greatness in the service of the country." Wingate had no doubt that he had the right stuff, but there is more than a hint of desperation in his letter to Sir Reginald:

> It would be false modesty in me to say that I have a poor opinion of my abilities. I have a very high opinion of them. . . . Given the opportunity . . . I see no reason why I should not reach the highest rank. . . . But if I fail now in this, my last chance to get to Camberley, I shall not waste any more time in the Army.

This time Sir Reginald's intervention did not manage to turn the trick, and Wingate was crushed when his name was not among the Staff College nominations listed in *The Times* of 24 July 1936. But before resigning his commission as he had threatened, he decided on one last, bold throw of the dice.

He was with his weekend warriors, taking part in a Territorial Army exercise on the North Yorkshire moors ten days later, when the newly appointed chief of the Imperial General Staff, General Sir Cyril Deverell, came on an inspection visit. Surrounded by his red-tabbed retinue, the CIGS was standing on a hilltop overlooking the scene of mock battle when Wingate strode up to him and saluted. Startled by this abrupt intrusion by a junior officer, Deverell demanded to know what Wingate wanted.

The general's entourage looked on in amazement as Wingate proceeded to ask whether Deverell, as chairman of the Staff College selection committee, had been aware of his desert exploits. When the general replied, somewhat tersely, that he had not, Wingate said he thought the committee should have been informed and handed him a copy of the *Royal Geographical Society Journal* containing his article on Zerzura.

Taken aback by Wingate's effrontery—but clearly impressed by it—the supreme commander promised to look into the matter. A few days later, Wingate received notification that although no place could be found for him at Camberley just then, he would be considered for the first available staff job appropriate to his rank and experience.

Only days later, word came through from the War Office: he was to proceed immediately to Palestine for posting as staff intelligence officer to Fifth Division headquarters in Haifa. A few days before he was due to embark, Wingate received an urgent telegram from Godalming: his father, who had been ailing for some time and was in his eighty-fourth year, was on the point of death. Orde rushed home, arriving in time to be recognized and exchange a few last words with his parent.

Book Two

PALESTINE

*The Jews are loyal to the Empire. The Jews are
men of their word. . . . You can have no idea
what they have already done here.*
—Orde Wingate

*Lucky for us that Wingate's fanatical Zionism
gets the better of his sense of duty.*
—Blanche (Baffy) Dugdale

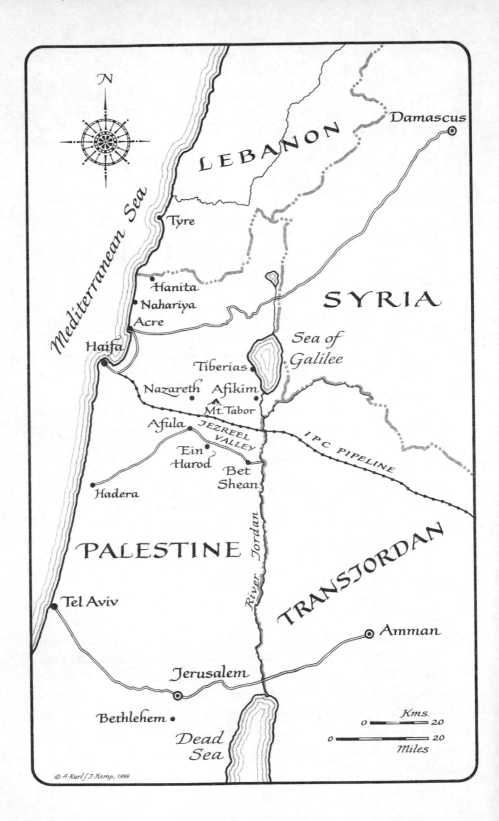

N

LEBANON

Mediterranean Sea

Tyre

Hanita
Nahariya
Acre

Haifa

SYRIA

Sea of
Galilee

Tiberias

Nazareth Afikim

Mt. Tabor

Afula JEZREEL
VALLEY

Ein
Harod

Bet
Shean

Damascus

I P C PIPELINE

Hadera

PALESTINE

River Jordan

TRANSJORDAN

Tel Aviv

Amman

Jerusalem

Bethlehem

Dead
Sea

Kms.
0   20
0   20
Miles

© A·Karl / J·Kemp, 1999

Chapter 5

B Y SEPTEMBER 1936, when Wingate arrived to take up his duties in Haifa, Palestine was in turmoil and its British rulers, struggling to retain control, were realizing to the full what a bed of nails they had made for themselves by attempting to pursue mutually contradictory policies in the Middle East. Wingate had not been at Fifth Division headquarters more than forty-eight hours when the bodies of four young British Palestine Police officers were discovered around their ambushed vehicle in the hills of northern Galilee, near Rosh Pina. Dozens of spent .303 cartridges around them testified that they had put up a desperate fight before being picked off by Arab rebels in the high ground above them.

Under the Balfour Declaration of November 1917, Britain had promised that once they had cleared the Ottoman Turks out of the Holy Land they would "use their best endeavours" to bring about "a national home for the Jewish people" in Palestine. In the next breath of the same document they had undertaken to do so without prejudice to "the civil and religious rights of existing non-Jewish communities," as they termed the territory's overwhelming Arab majority. That majority was now in open revolt against its British rulers.

The declaration, named after Foreign Secretary Arthur Balfour, who signed it on behalf of Lloyd George's war cabinet, was a product of both sentiment and calculation. It made its appearance at a moment when—although a British expeditionary force was advancing steadily on Jerusalem—things were at a particularly difficult point in the global conflict against Germany and its allies. There was bloody stalemate in France; the Russians were crumbling on the eastern front; and the kaiser's U-boats were draining Britain's lifeblood in the Atlantic. True, the Americans were now engaged, but it still seemed that the war could go either way.

In this context, the Balfour Declaration was a calculated pitch for the moral and financial backing of international Jewry, especially American Jewry, whose most influential members were of German origin and inclined to be proud of it. It was also in the nature of a reward to the British-naturalized Zionist leader Dr. Chaim Weizmann, a brilliant industrial chemist whose invention of a process for making acetone from maize had proved vital to British production of high explosives. To a certain degree, Britain's promise to the Jews also fulfilled a romantic notion, long felt in British ruling circles, that it would be an act of historic and poetic justice to help the ill-used people of the Bible return to their ancient homeland.

In short and simple terms, the Balfour Declaration had seemed like a good idea at the time. To the perennially insecure and imperiled Jews of eastern Europe it came as a deliverance. "We saw in Britain the saviour of our people," Menachem Begin, the Israeli prime-minister-to-be, then a boy in Poland, would recall. But little thought was given to what the declaration would look like to the Palestinian Arabs and the Arab world in general.

In Cairo, Wingate's Cousin Rex was one of many highly placed British officials to express alarm. In a cable to Sir Mark Sykes,* one of the principal architects of British Middle East policy, he warned that both Muslim and Christian Egyptians viewed "with little short of dismay prospect of seeing Palestine and even eventually Syria in hands of Jews."

The provisions of the Balfour Declaration were incorporated into the terms of Britain's League of Nations mandate to rule postwar Palestine, and it did not take the "non-Jewish communities" long to conclude that its two promises were irreconcilable and to act accordingly. If the Arabs were to achieve the independent state their leadership desired—and that they thought had been at least implied when Britain called them to arms against their Turkish rulers—the British would have to be driven out, and with them the scores of thousands of Jewish settlers who, beginning to arrive in numbers after the end of the war, had been buying up Arab-owned land as fast as funds would allow.

---

*And father of Christopher Sykes, Orde Wingate's future authorized biographer.

Initially, those settlers came mainly from Russia, Poland, and elsewhere in eastern Europe, the traditional centers of Jewish habitation and native anti-Semitism. With the coming to power of Hitler in 1933 the flow increased dramatically as foresighted German Jews fled the horror to come. Total immigration, which had numbered ninety-five hundred in 1932, rose to almost sixty-two thousand in 1935, the year in which the Nazis enacted their notorious Nuremberg Laws against the Jews. The Jewish population of Palestine now numbered some four hundred thousand, and the proportion of Arabs, which had been 90 percent of the total at war's end, had now been reduced to 70 percent. If the Jews continued to come at the present rate, the Palestinian Arabs believed, they would be at best outnumbered, at worst swamped.

Up to the mid 1930s Arab resistance to Jewish immigration had expressed itself in savage but sporadic raids on Zionist rural settlements and British police posts and in spontaneous anti-Jewish pogroms in urban locations such as Hebron and Jaffa. In mid-1936, the situation burgeoned into full-scale Arab revolt, under the inspiration of Haj Amin al-Husseini, the grand mufti of Jerusalem, and the military leadership of Fawzi el Kawaukji, a fair-skinned, blue-eyed Lebanese Druse who had been an officer in the Ottoman army during World War I. Kawaukji became a ringleader of the 1925 Druse uprising against French rule in Syria, territory that had come under French control through the postwar Sykes-Picot Agreement, when France and Britain had divided the spoils of the defunct Ottoman Empire. When the Druse revolt was bloodily put down, Kawaukji fled to Saudi Arabia to escape a death sentence and was eventually hired by the mufti to bring some cohesion to the Palestinian revolt. In a piquant manifestation of the colonial rivalry that still existed between Britain and France, the French allowed that uprising, with its Islamic fundamentalist overtones, to receive strong backing from the puppet Syrian government. With such support Kawaukji did his work so effectively that the British would eventually have to send two divisions of troops to restore some semblance of order.

But although the security threat came from the Arab side, British attitudes vis-à-vis the two Palestinian communities were, to say the least, ambivalent. When Wingate arrived to take up his job on the intelligence staff, he found more sympathy for the Arabs than the Jews. Whatever the statesmen and politicians might have decided in the heat of the Great War, powerful factions in Whitehall and the War Office, and individual soldiers, policemen, and civil servants on the ground, were now being driven by other calculations and different sentiments.* Those sentiments included a widespread, if not particularly malignant, form of social anti-Semitism common among Britons of all classes. In working-class circles this would be expressed in beery "Thank God I'm an Englishman" terms; at higher social and educational levels it was more a matter of snobbery—"They're a bit pushy, aren't they?"—even though a baptized Jew, Benjamin Disraeli, had been a popular prime minister in Victoria's day, even though her son Edward VII had had many Jewish friends, and even though Britain's doors had been opened wide to refugees from the Russian pogroms of the late nineteenth century. In short, British attitudes toward the Jews, though frequently frosty, were in no way comparable to the bred-in-the-bone racism of eastern and central Europe, let alone to the institutionalized Jew-hatred of Nazi Germany.

Like Rex Wingate, most senior officials during the British mandate over Palestine held to the view that Britain's best interests throughout the Middle East—and in turbulent India, with its large Muslim minority—lay in supporting the Arabs. The Arabs could be "guided," as the Jews could not, and the Arabs were sitting on vast reserves of oil, which the Jews were not. As well, many of the Jewish migrants to Palestine were seen to be bringing unwelcome Marxist ideas with them from eastern Europe.

Beyond all this, the foreign policy establishment was dominated by Orientalists who felt a romantic affinity for Arabic culture, especially that of the Bedouin—the "noble savage" who in his various guises throughout the empire (the Masai of Kenya, the Gurkha of Nepal, the Fuzzy-Wuzzy of the Sudan, the Sikh of the Punjab) represented some ideal of manly courage, spartan simplicity, and courtly charm. As the future Israeli prime minister Shimon Peres, an immigrant from Poland to Palestine in the early 1930s, has pointed out, "The Arabs—and espe-

---

*The Anglo-Jewish philosopher Isaiah Berlin used to liken the Palestine Mandate to a third-rate English public school in which the British were the teachers and the Arabs and Jews were the pupils, but in separate houses. The Jews won all the prizes but the teachers preferred the Arabs because the Jewish boys were insubordinate, disrespectful, no good at games, and constantly complaining to their parents, who in turn complained to the governors.

cially the Bedouin—were famous for their hospitality and their winning ways. They had been wooing and winning the hearts of British imperial officialdom for decades. . . . Against such wiles we had no chance."

This was true enough. As a subject people, the Zionist Jews, although practicing a policy of *havlagah,* or self-restraint, were a prickly proposition as compared with the Arabs—appreciative of the opportunities opened up by the Balfour Declaration, yes, but irritatingly nondeferential; as technologically adept and culturally advanced as their rulers (perhaps more so, which was quite intolerable) and unlike the Arabs altogether impossible to patronize. In short, "too clever by half," as the British officer class would say, which made the Jews at best the recipients of grudging respect instead of the condescending affection accorded to the Arabs.

One NCO described the views of the common British soldier this way: "Certainly, the Jews were white, but they didn't speak English. Yes, they worked like hell—few of us had ever seen Jews work like that before and they turned great sandy deserts into beautiful green oases with oranges, lemons and, yes, even fresh vegetables. But give me the Arab every time, said Tommy Atkins."*

Wingate, as an Arabist by training and one who had thoroughly mastered the language and, with it, absorbed much of the culture of the Arabs, might have been expected to share the majority sentiment of Palestine's British rulers. But, as we have seen, Wingate never accepted received wisdom and never followed the crowd. Some who knew him in those days take the view that as a born maverick he was bound to stake out a contrary position. Colonel (then Lieutenant) Tony Simonds, who worked closely with him in military intelligence, says that Wingate told him shortly after arriving, "Everyone's against the Jews, so I'm for them." No doubt Wingate did say something of the kind, but there was far more to it than that.

Until his arrival in Palestine in September, he had had little if any contact with Jews. The first one he knowingly encountered, a fellow pupil at Charterhouse, seemed to him "a small, pale nondescript-looking boy," and Wingate had thought, "How extraordinary, there is somebody who is a descendant of David!" The comment was without

*The generic name for the British private soldier of World Wars I and II (and the Boer War before that).

malice. Unlike many Englishmen of his class and generation, Wingate had not been brought up to disdain the Jews. On the contrary, as the child of dissenting Christian radicals he had been taught to have a particular regard for them as the children of the Old Testament, rather than to despise them as the betrayers of Christ. Wingate's father, for instance, believed that it was Russia's "wicked persecution of the Jews through the centuries" that had brought divine punishment, in the form of communism, down upon the Russian people.

On a purely pragmatic level, Wingate had become enormously impressed within days of his arrival in Palestine by the pioneering spirit of the Zionist settlers. He was struck by the vigor and scale of their achievements in agriculture, industry and commerce, medicine, education, the arts, and the sciences, and by their willingness to endure physical hardship and personal danger to build up their *Altneuland*, their "old-new land," as Theodore Herzl, the founder of political Zionism, had characterized it. As Wingate saw things, the Zionist pioneers' achievements were in telling contrast to the sloth and backwardness of the Arabs, leading him rapidly to the conclusion that it was the Jews and not the Arabs who were Britain's natural allies in the Middle East and that a Jewish state, joined to Britain through membership in the Commonwealth, would be a major strategic and economic asset.

Within four months of his arrival in Palestine—by which time he had been moved from Fifth Division headquarters in Haifa to GHQ in Jerusalem—he was telling all this and more to his cousin Rex. In a lengthy memorandum, sent by hand for reasons of security, and regardless of the fact that Sir Reginald had never shared his enthusiasm for the Jews, he skewered one by one the arguments of the Arabists in terms that would have done credit to the most ardent Zionist. Which in fact Wingate already was.

On the Arab Revolt: "We need only a) arm the Jews, b) proclaim martial law and arrest and exile every Arab notable to find ourselves able to master the revolt with no more than the eight battalions already here. . . . Interference by Trans-Jordan will provide the excuse for the removal of the corrupt and slovenly [Emir] Abdullah and the reclamation of the country for Palestine. The military strength, past, present and future, of the whole Arab group is quite negligible. . . . The potential military strength of the Jews . . . is equivalent to at least two British army corps."

On Arab unity: "Islam in reality cares little about the Arabs of Palestine, and although concerned in the preservation of the Holy Places and finding the thought of the Jews in Palestine distasteful, would be prepared to accept a fait accompli. In any case, Islam today has no strength."

On the Mandatory administration: "We seem to send only the worst type of British official to Palestine. They hate the Jew and like the Arab who, although he shoots at them, toadies to them and takes care to flatter their sense of importance. The truth of the matter is, Sir, that the whole tribe of officials out here are third rate."

Although a mere captain, Wingate—with Lorna, who had arrived from England to join him in November 1936—had enjoyed the hospitality of Government House, thanks to a letter of introduction from Sir Reginald to the British high commissioner, Sir Arthur Wauchope. But this did not prevent him from criticizing Sir Arthur in the most scathing terms. He had "my sympathy and admiration for his fine qualities," Orde told his cousin, but he was "past his work by common consent and should be removed."

> He does not know what to do, asks and takes anyone's advice, pays his suit to the rebellious Arabs, begs their minor leaders to help him, and generally betrays that he has lost all grasp of affairs. . . . Owing purely to the vacillations of H[is] E[xcellency] and the pro-rebel sympathies of the entire civil service, what might have proved a mere riot developed into an armed rebellion.

By contrast Wingate had only the most fulsome praise for the Jews, who, as a consequence of the Arab Revolt, "had to witness their work destroyed, their families threatened, their blood spilt, and the blame for all laid on their shoulders."

> The Jews are loyal to the empire. The Jews are men of their word. . . . You can have no idea what they have already done here. You would be amazed to see the desert blossom like a rose; intensive horticulture everywhere—such energy, faith, ability and inventiveness as the world has not seen. . . . [T]he Jews will provide better soldiery than ours. We have only to train it. They will equip it. Palestine is essential to our Empire—our Empire is essential to England—England is essential to world peace. Islam is out of it.

As Wingate penned what he called "the low-down" to his influential cousin, a royal commission of enquiry headed by Lord Peel was concluding two months of hearings into the Palestine situation with a view to finding a way for Britain to extricate itself from the mess it had stumbled into. Saying that the commission "appears to be pro-Arab" and "in all probability has no idea what to think or what to do," Wingate put forward his own unabashedly partisan proposals.

Britain must assume full responsibility for the protection of legitimate Arab interests, he urged, but should then "ruthlessly suppress any attempt at opposition . . . recognise the right of the Jews to emigrate to Palestine as the absorptive capacity of the country admits [and] advance the foundation of an autonomous Jewish community with all the means in its power." Relating the solution of the Palestine problem to the world war that he saw to be inevitable, Wingate concluded: "For pity's sake, let us do something just and honourable before it comes. Let us redeem our promises to Jewry and shame the devil of Nazism, Fascism and our own prejudices."

It was an extraordinary document, showing not only Wingate's early and total commitment to Zionism, and consequent disdain for the Arabs, but a characteristic tendency to see affairs in terms only of black and white. Shades of gray were not to be recognized. As postwar events would confirm, Wingate's assessment of the military potential of the Jews and the cohesion of the Arab world was shrewd enough. But he displayed a sublime disregard for diplomatic realities and, especially in his references to Transjordan and its Hashemite ruler, Abdullah, an almost Machiavellian ruthlessness. And he never mentioned the three-letter word that was at the heart of all British Middle East policy—oil.

For Wingate, whatever the problem at hand, there were never to be any grounds for compromise, which to him signified weakness if not betrayal of principle. When a fellow officer once pointed out to him, mildly enough, that there were "two sides to the Palestine problem," he replied, "I know that. I just happen to be on the right side."

Within a few months of his arrival Wingate had been accepted among the Zionist leadership, from Chaim Weizmann down, as a staunch supporter whose sincerity was beyond doubt. They dubbed him "Hayedid"—The Friend—a sobriquet by which he was still remembered among Israelis more than half a century after his death. But friendship seems altogether too pallid a term for Wingate's attachment to the Jewish people and to the idea of Zion. More Catholic than the pope, more royalist than the king—such threadbare phrases hardly begin to convey the depth, scope, and durability of his passion. In the words of Bunyan's hymn, Wingate's favorite, "One here will constant be, come wind come weather."

Wingate's Old Testament upbringing, his particular perception of Britain's imperial interests, and his contrarian nature go only part of the way toward explaining so close an identification with a people to whom he did not belong and an ideology that could only set him apart from his fellows and—running counter to the received wisdom of his superiors—could only damage his career prospects. As one who felt he had been persecuted in his youth for being "different," he had a natural affinity for the Jews. As a patriot, he clearly believed that in serving Zionism he would also be serving British interests. But that may have been an unconscious rationalization, providing cover for a more complex motivation. It is tempting to believe that by serving Zionism he was, at some profound level, resolving the uncomfortable contradictions within his own psyche.

Clearly, mainstream Zionist ideology spoke powerfully to both sides of Orde Wingate's dual personality—to the twentieth-century humanist as much as to the seventeenth-century theist. Pragmatic and secularist on one hand, poetic and God-haunted on the other, combining "progressive" social and political ideas with mystic notions of return and redemption, Zionism was an ideology that might have been devised for Wingate and he for it: thesis, antithesis, synthesis. One might say that when he arrived in Palestine his emotional, spiritual, and intellectual receptors were already primed to lock on to Zionism. All his adult life, as he had told Peggy Jelley and others, he had been seeking a cause to fight for. Now he had found it, and although war, fate, and officialdom would subsequently send him to the far ends of the earth, he would remain committed for life to the political idea that made him spiritually whole.

It was at a Government House dinner, soon after his arrival, that Wingate made the acquaintance and won the confidence of Chaim

Weizmann—"a truly great man," he told his cousin, "and I am proud to say, our friend." The Zionist leader, on one of his frequent visits from Britain, was the governor's principal guest. At table, Weizmann's wife, Vera, was seated next to Wingate, who must have been in sparkling conversational form. She found him "one of the most interesting men I have ever met," she told her husband when, in proper colonial fashion, the men "joined the ladies" after cigars and brandy.

For his part, Weizmann, who had an eye for a pretty woman, had noticed the vivacious Lorna, and as the party broke up he invited the Wingates home for a nightcap. They talked well into the small hours, the Wingates captivated by their host's legendary charm and breadth of interests, the Weizmanns deeply impressed by the patent sincerity and enthusiasm of this unusual Englishman and his sparkling young wife. Any suspicions Weizmann might have entertained that Wingate had ulterior motives—for he had not concealed that he was in military intelligence—were soon dispelled.

A few days later the Weizmanns invited the Wingates to join their party at a memorable series of concerts in which Arturo Toscanini conducted the newly formed Palestine Symphony Orchestra, an event that was a cultural high point in the life of the embryonic Jewish state.* So began a long, intense, and at times turbulent friendship between Wingate and Weizmann, in which Lorna played considerably more than a secondary role. She was by now as ardent a Zionist as her husband. "In fact, more so," said Tony Simonds, "more noisy, more vociferous."

With Weizmann's endorsement Wingate was accepted as a trustworthy friend of the cause by other Zionist luminaries, including Eliahu Golomb and Emmanuel Wilenski, two senior commanders of Haganah, the Jews' underground army in the making. Other early friendships were with David Hacohen, the chief of the trade union contracting organization Solel Boneh, and political leaders such as David Ben-Gurion and Moshe Shertok (later Sharett), both future prime ministers. Wingate's "deep-set eyes and suppressed passion" made an immediate and profound impression on Shertok in particular.

---

*Surprisingly, Toscanini's first concert included excerpts from Wagner's opera *Lohengrin*—this despite the composer's well-known anti-Semitic sentiments and Toscanini's refusal to perform at the Nazi-patronized Wagner festival at Bayreuth. To this day Israeli orchestras will not play Wagner.

A rather different kind of impression was made on another prominent Zionist named Eliahu Epstein, who later (as Eliahu Elath) became Israeli ambassador in London. When he visited the Wingate residence one hot afternoon, his host met him at the door, stark naked. Without a word of explanation, let alone apology, Wingate led Epstein into the sitting room, where he initiated a lively discussion of Persian literature, Epstein's specialty. Then they discussed Wingate's special passion, Zionism. He was still naked when he showed his guest politely to the door some hours later.

The Wingates' home was a flat in the Talbieh district of Jerusalem, looking across the Kidron Valley to the Old City, its massive gray Ottoman and Crusader walls capped by the golden Dome of the Rock, and beyond that to the Mount of Olives. Lorna found it "delightful," although she thought the landlord, a Christian Arab, was "a scoundrel." Perhaps, but he was no match for the feisty Lorna. "I designed the furniture and he paid for it," she told her sister-in-law Monica, "but so enormous was the expense . . . that he, at any rate, will never again sign such a contract."

> When, after spending £250, I made him buy a large desk and we sat trembling with fatigue, he paid me a compliment. He said 'Mister Captayne [Orde] leaves all the business to you, for you may be young but you are clever.' This was balm to the sore heart of one who has always been chidden for absent-mindedness and helplessness.

Soon after moving in, Wingate informed his mother that he was busy learning Hebrew and that already "I can speak in a halting fashion with our Jewish servant, who hails from Hungary. I should say that we are about the only British in Palestine who have Jewish and not Arab servants." Within a few weeks Wingate reckoned he was also about the only British army officer in Palestine who could speak serviceable Hebrew as well as fluent Arabic. In a letter to Weizmann, who was at that point in London, he boasted that "I have learned about 1,000 millim Ivrit!"—a thousand Hebrew words—and that "it is a great pleasure to me to read the Old Testament in the original."

He was captivated by the biblical countryside. "It always seems alive," he told his mother. "The spring has been very lovely. We made an expedition up the Jordan at Easter. . . . The whole of this area [at the base of the Sea of Galilee] was a mass of golden flowers, shoulder high. Elsewhere one found delphiniums, stocks, tulips, poppies, hyacinths, marigolds and hollyhocks."

In Jerusalem, Lorna threw herself into the cultural and social life of the Jewish elite. Ruth Dayan, then newly married to the future Israeli military hero Moshe Dayan, recalls their first meeting at the home of a mutual friend. "She was very young and very beautiful. People couldn't take their eyes off her. She was slim, petite, almost oriental looking in a Chinese-style blouse with buttons down the front and a high collar. She looked like a porcelain doll." Ruth Dayan's parents had already met the Wingates, who were well known and well liked as a couple who, apart from their pro-Zionist sympathies, had intellectual interests that were also not common in British army circles.

On duty, Orde applied himself to his intelligence work with an innovative zeal that both impressed and irritated his colleagues and superiors. His office was in the run-down Fast Hotel, near the Jaffa Gate, which had been the headquarters of Imperial Germany's military mission to the Turks in World War I. Ivor Thomas, a corporal who ended his military career as a lieutenant colonel—a notable achievement in the class-conscious British army—has left an intriguing account of his days there as Wingate's clerk in the 1930s:

> I knew at once that we had taken on a personality, a character and someone who was going to be entirely different. . . . He had very blue penetrating eyes, aquiline features and a faraway, wild ascetic look with a distinct scholarly air. He was far removed from the usual run of officers. . . . He asked me to tell him all about myself and to give him a rundown on my complete Service Record, qualifications and, what was most unusual for an officer of those days, my aspirations.

As for Simonds, who shared an office with Wingate, Thomas said he "played polo, had money, was young, keen, a romantic, not many brains but had a good knowledge of the country. . . . He became a very great friend of Wingate, and was the perfect foil for Wingate's scholarship."

Capitalizing on his language skills, Wingate personally supervised the translation of the Hebrew and the Arabic press and built up detailed, cross-indexed personal files on the leading figures of both communities, down to local level. "Between us," Thomas would recall, "we worked like beavers in that little office and built up a system which was at first ridiculed by everyone but which finally became the information bureau for the most obscure information . . . and over the years must have been a godsend to newcomers to the Middle East."

Despite this, Wingate's outspoken pro-Zionism, his dismissive manner toward those he considered "military apes," his slovenly turnout—not at all the crisp Sandhurst look—and his general contempt for military orthodoxy made him enemies among many of those very officers who made use of his files and dossiers. Not content with making no secret of his preference for the Jews, Wingate also scarcely hid the fact that he was passing on sensitive information to his friends in the Jewish Agency. As an intelligence officer it was within his discretion to use information as an aid to establishing contacts, but how far it was legitimate to go is another matter. Tony Simonds told the authors that during 1937 he discovered that Wingate was passing on raw military intelligence reports to the Jewish Agency.

"He took them off my desk," said Simonds. "They were written on thin bits of paper called flimsies. He handed the bloody lot to the Jewish Agency. I objected and there was a hell of a row. He said, 'You won't be able to stop me.' I said, 'I'm going to lock them in my drawer,' and he said, 'All right, I'll force the lock.' " Simonds, in failing health at age eighty-six,* chuckled as he recalled the confrontation almost sixty years after the event. "He was very fanatical. I liked him very much. I got on very well with him. But I must admit he was a fanatic."

There is no documentary or other evidence to support Simonds's allegations concerning the intelligence flimsies. He cannot have reported the matter or Wingate would surely have faced a court-martial. He might, of course, have remained silent out of friendship, but Simonds's account must be considered doubtful. What is beyond doubt, though, is that at the time Wingate was leaking some sensitive political information to the Jewish Agency. A letter he wrote to Weizmann at the end of May 1937, dropping broad hints about the main recommendations of the still-secret Peel Commission report, confirms this.

The commission had decided to recommend partition and, getting wind of this, Wingate sent a letter to Weizmann in London by hand of

*He died in February 1999.

his mother-in-law, Ivy Paterson,* who had been visiting Jerusalem. "In my position I see a good deal of what is going on," he wrote, "and I cannot but be aware that some solution on the lines of cantonisation is far from improbable." Although the Peel Commission report would soon be made public, this was at the very least an indiscretion that could have gotten Wingate into serious trouble if known of at the time.

In a further indiscretion, Wingate, assuming that any partition agreement would grant the Jewish ministate the right of self-defense, offered his services and those of "another officer who is in Jerusalem and has an unrivaled knowledge of Palestine"—obviously Tony Simonds—to command and train a Jewish military force. He ended this letter with the words "May God bless you and your work." Weizmann replied, also by hand delivery, that he would be "proud and happy" to accept Wingate's offer.

Shertok, who was number two in the Zionist hierarchy, was equally receptive to Wingate's offer but not so keen about Simonds, whom he regarded as a lightweight. For his part, Simonds has never claimed that his commitment to the Jewish cause was anything but pragmatic. "I wasn't pro-Jewish per se," he told the authors, "I was anti-Arab. We were fighting the Arabs, so the Jews were our friends. I really became interested through Wingate. And I had a Jewish girlfriend. That's all."

On another occasion, in January 1938, when Wingate gave the Jews information about a confidential message concerning Palestine conveyed from the Foreign Office to King Ibn Saud of Saudi Arabia, another notable English pro-Zionist, Blanche "Baffy" Dugdale—niece and biographer of Arthur Balfour—noted in her diary: "Lucky for us that Wingate's fanatical Zionism gets the better of his sense of duty as Intelligence Officer. He is clearly one of the instruments in God's hand."

The Peel Commission report, published two months after Wingate's letter to Weizmann, proposed giving the Jews a statelet compris-

---

*Mrs. Paterson's delivery of Wingate's letter was the precursor of an unusually warm correspondence between her and Dr. Weizmann. Between June 1937 and August 1938, a period of intense activity for the Zionist leader, he found time to write her no fewer than nine letters, in many of them referring to Orde and Lorna in the most affectionate and solicitous terms. For instance: "It makes me literally sick with indegestion [sic] at the very thought that two such wonderful people might be victimized because of their views and sympathies. . . . Just think of the probability of your children safely installed in the Jewish state. What a dream!"

ing Galilee, the Jezreel Valley, and the coastal plain to a point midway between Gaza and Jaffa—about 20 percent of the total land area, or as Weizmann pointed out less than one fifth the size of Wales. The Arabs would get the rest, minus Jerusalem, Bethlehem, and a corridor linking those towns to the Mediterranean at Jaffa, all of which would remain under British mandate.

The Arabs rejected this proposal outright; the Jews, with grave misgivings, decided to accept it as a basis for negotiations. Although vehemently opposed by the Zionist Revisionist minority under Ze'ev Jabotinsky* and by many mainstream Zionists too, the Peel proposals would at least give the Jews what they most desired, a state of their own, and could be used as a launchpad for later expansion. "The Kingdom of David was smaller," observed Weizmann in a letter to Wingate's mother-in-law. "Under Solomon it became an empire. Who knows? *C'est le premier pas qui coûte.*"**

At this point, the Arab Revolt, which had been dormant since the Peel Commission had begun taking evidence, flared up anew and more fiercely than before. Agents of the well-financed rebel headquarters in Damascus began buying up arms and distributing anti-British propaganda leaflets around the Middle East. They drew up hit lists of British officials to be assassinated and made sure these were leaked into Palestine to create a jittery atmosphere. They made an unsuccessful attempt to kill Roy Spicer, the inspector-general of the Palestine Police, but did not fail a little later when they murdered the Australian Yelland Andrews, the district commissioner for Galilee, as he went to church in Nazareth. Andrews had ridden into Palestine as a member of the Australian Light Horse during Allenby's 1917–18 campaign against the Turks. An Australian friend, another Light Horseman, was so distraught at Andrews's death that, blind drunk and in full evening dress, he staggered about the Old City of Jerusalem with a brace of revolvers shooting at every Arab he could see. The Australian was sent home and the matter hushed up.

---

*Vladimir Jabotinsky (1880–1940). Brilliant Jewish journalist and novelist born in Odessa whose Revisionist Zionist Organization encouraged Jews "to gather iron" and is the inspiration for Israel's right-wing Likud party, with its uncompromising attitude toward the Arabs. In Wingate's day the more extreme Jabotinskyites had begun to turn terrorist, targetting left-wing Jews as well as Arab civilians.
**"It's the first step that counts."

British officials everywhere—Wingate of course included—began to take special precautions against assassination, carrying a personal weapon at all times, varying their routines, searching under their cars for explosives: all the now globally familiar anti-terrorism measures. On his trips to visit Jewish kibbutzim Wingate used to practice an anti-ambush drill he had devised himself. Thomas was his armed escort on one such journey:

> He suddenly decided to stop, threw his arms literally around the driver's neck, opened the car door, and then went charging up the nearest bank, hiding himself away in some nearby nullah and then yelling to find out where we had got our heads down.

In October 1937, the British arrested five members of the Arab Higher Committee and deported them to the Seychelles. But not the grand mufti; he took sanctuary in the Haram El-Sharif, the sacred plateau on which stands the Dome of the Rock and the Al-Aqsa Mosque and which no British soldier or policeman might enter. From the Haram Amin escaped to Beirut and ultimately to Berlin. There he was welcomed with open arms by Hitler and there he spent World War II, greatly to the future detriment of the Palestinian cause. Rarely has the old maxim, much quoted in the Middle East, that "the enemy of my enemy is my friend" been rewarded with such disastrous consequences.

Chapter 6

FROM THE WATCHTOWER of the embattled Jewish settlement of Hanita, on high ground near Rosh Hanikra in northern Galilee, lookouts could spot an approaching vehicle a mile or so before they could make out exactly what it was. The lookouts were especially curious about the one they saw coming their way one afternoon in April 1938. It might belong to the Palestine Police, but did not look quite boxy enough to be one of the locally made armored cars in which the police patrolled the new Tegart Wall* along the border with French-controlled Lebanon. Nor did it appear to be a British army vehicle. And yet civilian cars, whether Jewish or Arab-owned, had become very much a rarity. So had unexpected visitors—at least, those of a friendly kind.

If the Haganah had given permission for somebody to visit Hanita, a warning would have come in a series of Morse flashes made by car lamp fitted with a shutter from the signal station that the Jewish Agency maintained on Mount Carmel, overlooking Haifa some twenty miles to the south. Hanita also had a concealed radio transmitter in direct touch with Haganah headquarters in Tel Aviv, but this was only for emergency use and its existence was a closely guarded secret; most of the younger volunteers had no idea it existed.

Once the Hanita garrison—about ninety strong, including ten women—had been notified, there was a well-established procedure for receiving visitors. They were expected to wait at Nahariyya, the nearest Jewish community, about ten miles away on the Mediterranean coast, while a detachment from Hanita went down to collect them in

---

*Named after Sir Charles Tegart, a former commissioner of police in Calcutta, who persuaded the Mandate authorities to erect an eighteen-foot-wide barbed-wire entanglement guarded by concrete blockhouses along what is now Israel's northern frontier with Lebanon and Syria.

the armored truck—boiler plate welded onto a Chevrolet chassis—that was kept for this purpose. On the way back, the stench of diesel would cheat visitors of a first sniff of the pine-scented slopes on the Rosh Hanikra range. And the growl of the engine as the truck crawled around the bends in low gear would drown the soft cooing of the wood pigeons among tall conifers where Arab snipers lurked.

Hanita was more than just one more Jewish settlement: it was a paramilitary stockade-and-watchtower outpost located at the sharpest end of what the Zionists called Eretz Israel, the land of Israel. The Zionist leadership was particularly anxious to establish more Jewish settlements in the Galilee before Sir John Woodhead's Palestine Partition Commission had decided how the Peel Commission's grand plan to divide the land between Arab and Jews should be implemented. Among the dozens of people the Woodhead Commission had interviewed was Wingate—flattering attention for a junior officer. They had been sufficiently impressed with his views to ask him to put them in writing, which he promised to do as soon as he had a moment.

Hanita had been under siege for two weeks by the time it was approached by the mysterious lone vehicle and had become a symbol of Jewish resolve to claim the land and hold on to it. Beyond that it was living proof, at a time when the Jews of Germany and Austria were being savagely oppressed, that some Jews fought back.

By now, the lookouts could see through their binoculars that the approaching vehicle was a black, open-topped Studebaker, with a lone occupant. As it turned off the road onto the dirt track toward the stockade, a young, Polish-born, American-raised volunteer named Zvi Brenner yelled out a warning for it to stop. The other volunteers took up position with rifles, submachine guns, and an Austrian-made Schwarzlose heavy machine gun.

The car pulled up and out stepped a man wearing a light-colored suit and a wide-brimmed hat of the type that Israel Carmi, a young German-speaking Jew from Danzig,* thought of as a Borselino. The

---

*Danzig, nowadays known as Gdansk, was at that time an ethnic German town located within Poland but designated a Free City by the League of Nations. Its Jewish minority, sandwiched between German and Polish anti-Semitism, was enthusiastically pro-Zionist.

man who was wearing it looked to Carmi "like the kind of lowlife you saw hanging around certain dubious cafés in Tel Aviv." But Brenner recognized him immediately as Captain Orde Wingate, an oddball British officer he had met once before in the company of David Hacohen, the trade unionist leader, at a Jordan Valley kibbutz called Afikim.

As Brenner and Carmi reached the car they saw that its seats were littered with an assortment of weapons and other equipment. These included a British army canvas pack, a Lee-Enfield rifle, a large revolver with a double lanyard in a leather holster, and, mixed casually among the clutter, some metal objects shaped like small pineapples, which they recognized from their Haganah training as Mills grenades. There was also a small, leather-bound Bible, a canvas map case, and several loose Ordnance Survey maps, held in place by a British army steel helmet.

Brenner knew from their previous encounter that Wingate, unlike most British officers, was considered by the leadership of Haganah to be a friend. "He claims the government is not doing enough against the Arab gangs," Hacohen had said.

And Wingate had shown a gratifying interest in the everyday life of the kibbutz, more like a visiting Jewish fund-raiser from the Diaspora, Brenner thought, than a passing Englishman. He had been particularly interested in their diet, contrasting it with the unhealthy stodge served to the British troops and congratulating them on the perfection of their fresh vegetables, as evidence of which he had sunk his teeth with relish into a raw onion, as if into an apple.

So Brenner was not entirely surprised when Wingate, on arrival at Hanita, claimed to be carrying letters of introduction from Chaim Weizmann and the supreme Haganah commander, Eliahu Golomb. He ushered Wingate over to meet the camp commander, Zvi Ben Yaakov, who, despite the letters, remained ill at ease. His dilemma was understandable. The settlement was visibly equipped with weapons banned by the British authorities, who only permitted the kibbutzniks to defend themselves with shotguns and a few rifles.

Could he keep his machine gun and other automatic weapons ready for instant use in the presence of a British officer—and an intelligence officer at that—no matter how well disposed? Perhaps it was a trick and the letters elaborate forgeries. Ben Yaakov decided to use his secret radio link to check this Englishman out. Meanwhile, he told

Wingate that he should spend the night in Brenner's tent. While his belongings were being removed from the Studebaker, Yaakov whispered to Brenner, "Zvi, you're in charge of this meshugener. Don't let him out of your sight."

His use of the Yiddish word for a madman—as in English, often a term of affection, even admiration—was justified enough. Only three days after Wingate's solo visit, three young Jews from Nahariyya who tried to make the same trip were ambushed and killed. But for the past three months Wingate had been blithely wandering all over Galilee and the central Jezreel Valley—sometimes alone, sometimes driven by the faithful Corporal Thomas—to visit the network of settlements that he had begun to perceive as the launchpad for a daring and innovative campaign. His plan was to penetrate rebel territory by night, stop the smuggling of weapons across the Lebanese border, and rout the elusive Arab gangs that were causing both the British authorities and the Jewish settlers so much trouble.

Wingate realized that the Jewish kibbutzim offered a string of bases that rebel intelligence would be unable to monitor, unlike the regular army and police posts, virtually none of which were without potential spies in the shape of Arab servants or locally recruited policemen. He had already sent his superiors a memorandum urging them to use the settlements:

> The great advantage of staying in a Jewish colony is that one can disappear. Entrances and exits are not watched. By night Arabs keep well clear of them unless intending to attack. The consequence is that, although it might be known that one has gone there, no one can say that one is still there.

The well-defended kibbutzim would also provide a pool of tough, resourceful young men as well as some Great War veterans as potential recruits for offensive action against the gangs, though Wingate was not yet ready to suggest this to headquarters. He had already learned a lot in his peregrinations around the biblical countryside of which he had heard so much as a child. While visiting kibbutz Tirat Tzvi in the Jordan Valley he had ridden on horseback with the headman, Gershon Ritov, to inspect ancient fords across the Jordan River, which Tony Simonds, in an enciphered message from Jerusalem, had warned him were now being used by gunrunners:

According to a most reliable source, the great majority of arms and ammunition is coming by car to Der'ah* from Damascus. It is then transferred to camels and mules and packed into cereal bags or poultry cases. These convoys then cross the Jordan into the Ghor area after dusk.

Wingate spent several nights crouched uncomfortably on the river-bank at likely crossing places, waiting for the sight or sound of a gun-runners' caravan and hoping to set up an ambush. But he had to give up the idea when he discovered that "the tremendous din of frogs, to-gether with the pipes of shepherds, the bells of their flocks and the continuous barking of dogs made the hearing of passage of fords im-possible."

Sometimes British troops were as surprised by Wingate's sudden appearance at their positions as the Haganah volunteers had been at Hanita. Lieutenant Rex King-Clark, a wealthy young officer in the Manchester Regiment—so wealthy that he had piloted his own light aircraft from England when posted to Palestine**—was in command of a fifty-man garrison in an unoccupied Jewish hotel on the three-thousand-foot summit of Mount Canaan. From this magnificent posi-tion, a few miles northwest of the Sea of Galilee, the Manchesters could see both the snow-topped peak of Mount Hermon in Syria's Golan Heights and the shimmering waters, six hundred feet below them, where Saint Peter had fished and Christ had walked.

The Manchesters were occasionally sniped at by rebels and had set up one of their Vickers heavy machine guns on the flat roof of the hotel. They were hoping, in particular, to end the career of one sniper who was using something akin to an elephant gun. It could penetrate several brick walls, but so far had failed to hit any human target. Below their position, at the junction of the hotel driveway and the twisting road that led to the ancient town of Safad a couple of miles away, they had set up a roadblock. One afternoon a sergeant reported to King-Clark that a strange civilian motorist had been arrested at the road-

---

*The southern Syrian town where T. E. Lawrence famously lost "the citadel of my integrity" when, disguised as a Circassian youth, he was subjected to the homo-sexual advances of the local Turkish bey.

**His great-grandfather had made the family fortune in Glasgow manufacturing cotton thread. His relatives included art historian Lord (Kenneth) Clark, host of the TV series *Civilisation*.

block after a rifle and a number of grenades had been found in his car. Their prisoner claimed to be a British staff officer, but though he sounded like one he certainly did not look the part.

In those days British army officers were not issued with or required to carry any form of identification, unlike Other Ranks, who were always expected to have their paybooks with them. An officer's accent and appearance were supposed to be identity enough.* King-Clark went down to the hotel entrance where prisoner and escort were waiting:

> There, standing in the foyer, was this extraordinary figure in an uncertain Panama hat and creased Palm Beach suit, set off by the zigzaggy blue and red Royal Artillery tie. When he saw me coming down the stairs—and before I could speak—he asked in a coldly furious tone "Are you the officer in command here?" Taken aback a bit, I replied in a rather cagey way that I was, whereupon he announced that he was Captain Wingate, a staff officer at GHQ . . . and was to be released immediately.

King-Clark went out to examine his prisoner's car, noting that it was "a new but rather ill-used 1937 Studebaker four-seater convertible with the hood down." In the back, "lying higgledy-piggledy over the seats and the floor," were an assortment of items similar to those the Haganah volunteers had found at Hanita—a bolt-action Lee-Enfield service rifle, a bandolier of ammunition, two or three No. 36 Mills bombs, and a quantity of maps and papers. King-Clark soon concluded that his prisoner was what he claimed to be and released him with what he later recalled as "quite unnecessary apologies." He could not understand why Wingate should not have been better humored with soldiers who were merely doing their duty, especially looking and acting the way he did:

> Officers in Palestine during the Troubles didn't drive around the country in private cars and they were not allowed to wear plain

*More than half a century later, little had changed in this respect. Although officers had long since been issued with ID cards, British reporters covering the Gulf War of 1990–91 and wearing odd items of military uniform soon discovered that the right kind of accent was often the only password needed to talk their way into forward positions.

clothes. . . . Moreover, though Wingate was not Jewish . . . he had a high-bridged nose and narrow face, which particularly when in severe repose, could give a Semitic cast to his features—and this, I gathered afterwards, had added weight to the picket's decision to bring him in.

An example, perhaps, of the beholder's eye seeing what it wants to see. Jews who were close to Wingate at the time never for a moment thought he looked anything other than the Gentile British officer he was, albeit one of the more eccentric kind. Still, as Brenner would explain many years later, they did not all yet entirely trust him:

> After all, he was a British intelligence officer, and we were used to the fact that the British liked the Arabs. That was especially true for those officers who spoke Arabic—and Wingate spoke fluent Arabic. . . . The way in which Wingate travelled about freely in an area which we considered extremely dangerous made people even more suspicious of him.

Nor were the Hanita garrison the only ones to have such doubts. Ruth, the new bride of Moshe Dayan—at that time an auxiliary Settlement Police sergeant, but eventually to become Israel's most famous soldier—was living in Shimron, a small experimental kibbutz in the Jezreel Valley, when Wingate turned up. This time he was wearing a khaki drill uniform, though without badges of rank, and carrying his usual jumble of kit in the back of the car. Although his reputation had gone before him, the kibbutz secretary was one of those who thought it was too good to be true. As soon as their visitor was separated from his luggage, the secretary ordered Ruth Dayan to search it. She was reluctant, but did as she was told. "I opened his suitcase with great misgivings," she recalled, "but there was only a Bible in it and maybe a pair of underpants, but no pajamas: I understood from others that he always slept in the nude."*

If Wingate suspected that his bag had been searched he chose to say nothing about it. His passion for Zionism was such that he was prepared to accept what he might otherwise consider a slight or a humiliation from the people he so admired, even perhaps to welcome it.

---

*Speaking sixty years after the event, General Dayan's widow confessed, "It's funny, but I still have a guilty conscience about searching his things."

Consider, for instance, the contrast between his behavior toward King-Clark's troops and his reaction when he paid an unexpected visit to Brenner's old kibbutz, Afikim, at the southern end of the Sea of Galilee.

It was sunset and the main gate was locked. Finding no one there, and considering himself well-enough known by now, Wingate climbed over it. On the other side he was confronted by a young woman, a newly arrived American-Jewish volunteer who did not recognize him. She was on guard duty and demanded to know, at the point of a shot-gun, how he had got in. When he told her and explained who he was, she ordered him to climb back over again and wait while she opened the gate. He meekly obeyed and would often repeat the story with rel-ish as an example of the soldierly qualities of both sexes in the Jewish settlements.

After his first visit to Hanita, Wingate made many more, finding it a supreme expression of the pioneering Zionist spirit he so much ad-mired. The deliberate establishment of such settlements in exposed and dangerous locations was part of the campaign of "creating facts," by which the Jews were extending and consolidating their grip on the land in the face of furious Arab resistance. If its presence was madden-ing to the Arabs it was deeply irritating to the overstretched British, who refused to protect it, leaving that job ostensibly to the poorly armed Jewish Settlement Police, but in practice to the officially banned but unofficially tolerated Haganah. At Hanita, their arms were the best and latest that money could buy, including an Austrian heavy machine gun and several Finnish copies of the famed American Thompson submachine gun. And within twenty-four hours of their establishing Hanita they had urgent need of them when, reacting with unaccus-tomed speed, Arab rebels launched a night attack on this latest Zionist effrontery.

When it started most of the defenders were trying to sleep in wind-lashed bell tents, their stockade half completed around them. Both sides fired at shadows and muzzle flashes. At one point the Arabs tricked the defenders into squandering their shots on the scattered em-bers of an untended fire. Two Jews died in that first attack. Came a cold, eye-watering dawn, and Zvi Brenner examined the tired-looking faces around him and concluded that if the Arabs had been willing to get really close the settlement might well have been overrun. It was the beginning of a siege. By the spring of 1938, when Wingate paid his first visit, the name of Hanita had become a rallying cry for the Jews of Palestine and many others in the Diaspora.

Beneath the minor peak on which it sat was a substantial flat-roofed stone house, shaded by conifers, that had once been the home of an Arab tenant farmer and his family, dispossessed when their absentee landlord in Beirut had sold the land to the Jewish National Fund. The JNF had paid much more than the land's agricultural worth—enough to outweigh the owner's fears of being tracked down by a gunman sent by the mufti to punish those who sold to the Jews. As soon as the deeds were in Jewish hands, Haganah had taken possession, erecting one of its prefabricated forts, which looked like something out of the Old West.

From the outside it had the appearance of four plain log walls, each about one hundred feet long, enclosing a watchtower. On top of the tower was an item not to have been found at Fort Laramie—a searchlight, powered by a gasoline-driven generator. Nor were the palisades quite the stuff of the Great Plains: they were double walls, the cavity between them filled with gravel, making them the next best thing to solid stone and easily capable of stopping a rifle or machine gun bullet.

These solid defenses, and the settlement's withering firepower, did not deter the Arab enemy and their attacks often coincided with Wingate's visits. On a particularly bad day, when Brenner was on guard duty at a post rigged up just outside the perimeter, two Haganah pickets were killed by Arab sharpshooters. One of them died alongside Brenner; the other lay mortally wounded in the open. Frantically working the bolt of his Lee-Enfield rifle, Brenner gave covering fire to a young woman volunteer who ventured out to drag the wounded man to safety.

Then, to his astonishment, Brenner spotted Wingate, leopard-crawling out of the killing zone toward him. As Arab bullets *zizzed* and cracked above them, Wingate muttered to him, "Zvi, all of you are doing something great here. You can be proud of yourselves."

Without authorization from his superiors, and at the risk of severe condemnation if they found out about it, Wingate began to take out small patrols at night. He wanted to break the Haganah volunteers of their defensive mentality, getting them to go "beyond the fence" to carry the fight to the enemy. This notion was doubly controversial: it contradicted the Zionists' own policy of restraint while flouting British determination not to allow the Jews to take offensive action against the Arabs.

The first time Wingate proposed to venture out at night to reconnoiter the countryside around Hanita, Ben Yaakov, the settlement commander and one of Haganah's best men, tried to dissuade him. Such a thing was unheard of. When Wingate insisted, Ben Yaakov demanded that he take an escort of fifty men. Wingate demurred and after much haggling they settled on seven. One of them was Brenner, who recalled how Wingate had explained in a few words how he expected them to behave at night and then led them out of the settlement at a furious pace:

> From the very first moment he walked unwaveringly, like one who knew the area well. For us—who didn't know anything further than ten yards from the fence, who had never gone out at night and had never even left during the day except for the most urgent of tasks—it appeared to be somewhat miraculous. . . . From time to time Wingate would stop us for a short while, walk forward and disappear. He would shield himself behind a bush or rock, turn on a dim flashlight for a few seconds, and read a map. He would then return to us and we would continue walking. . . . We had complete trust in the man leading us.

To Wingate, the men he led out into the night where the Arab enemy lurked were not so much Diaspora-born Russians, Poles, and Americans as descendants of his Old Testament warrior-heroes, Gideon and Joshua, and he was determined that they should think of themselves as such. During the first patrol he led out of Hanita, the exhausted Haganah volunteers, sprawled beneath the stars during their first break after a grueling uphill slog, were startled to hear Wingate's strangely accented Hebrew emanating from the darkness with a terrible authority. "You are the sons of the Maccabees," spoke this strange prophet, who had come among them in the guise of Captain Wingate. "Why do you fear the Arabs? Each of you is worth twenty, thirty, or even a hundred of them."

Some of the Haganah had rather more battle experience than their leader, having served in various First World War hellholes with the Russian, German, or Austro-Hungarian armies. Yet this intense, Bible-haunted Englishman, whose own combat experience consisted of chasing bandits in the Sudanese bush, exuded such confidence that they were almost mesmerized by his presence. Moshe Dayan felt that he affected them all with his fanaticism and faith:

> Before going on an action, he would read the passage in the Bible relating to the places where we would be operating and find testimony to our victory—the victory of God and the Jews.

The patrols that Wingate led out of Hanita in the spring of 1938 were the forerunners of the officially sanctioned Special Night Squads, the mixed Anglo-Jewish units that would locate, demoralize, and defeat the hitherto elusive Arab gangs.* Wingate was never impressed by the guerrilla prowess of Fawzi el Kawaukji and his henchmen. "They are quite unable to face any sort of change or surprise onslaught," he wrote in an official assessment. "This is their character and they are quite unable to change it. In person they are feeble and their whole theory of war is cut and run. Like all ignorant and primitive people they are especially liable to panic."

A harsh, some might say deeply prejudiced verdict and not one shared by most of Wingate's fellow officers. They tended to express a sporting admiration for the rebels, who were surely motivated mainly by native patriotism and some of whom, whatever their crimes, fought bravely and were uncannily able to vanish into thin air when cornered. At least one such gangster went to the gallows with a firm tread and a cheery greeting for the British policeman who had captured him.** And assuredly Wingate's choice of language in an official report, even when applied to the king's enemies, seemed calculated to offend the Arabists of the army and the Colonial Office. It was the kind of nose tweaking he could rarely resist.

Even so, Wingate retained his backers in high places. General Sir Archibald (later Viscount) Wavell, who became general officer commanding, Palestine, in September 1937, soon had his eye on Wingate as a promising young officer. Wavell was a clever, poetry-loving soldier who had served under Allenby in the First World War campaign that

---

*A word, *ursabi* in Arabic, which the Arabs themselves used to describe the rebels and which appears to have no derogatory connotations, unlike the official "bandit" or "terrorist." The plural of *ursabi* is *ursabat,* which the Tommies corrupted to "oozlebart," a term that was used in army signal traffic.

**According to the memoirs of Inspector Geoffrey Morton of the Palestine Police, who in 1942 shot and killed the Jewish terrorist leader Avraham Stern.

ended five hundred years of Turkish rule over Palestine and, fortunately for Wingate, was a great admirer of Cousin Rex:

> His name at once caught my attention. . . . I was not then aware of
> the connection with T. E. Lawrence, whom I had known well, but I
> had realised at once that there was a remarkable personality in the
> rather untidy young officer with the piercing eyes who was obviously no respecter of persons because of their rank and had no hesitation in putting forward unorthodox views and maintaining them.

There is a possibly apocryphal story that Wingate convinced Wavell to accept his idea for the little Anglo-Jewish guerrilla army that became known as the Special Night Squads by a piece of calculated cheek, or as his Jewish friends would say, chutzpah. He is supposed to have found out that Wavell was visiting a certain outpost by car and, having reconnoitered the route, to have stood at a bend in the road, wearing his trademark Wolseley solar topee, and flagged Wavell's car down as it slowed. Having inveigled his way into the car, so it is said, he then proceeded to talk Wavell into agreeing to his demands for the establishment of the Night Squads.

True or not, the story is certainly in character. Though austere in many ways, Wingate had a decidedly flamboyant streak and to the end of his life was frequently accused of exhibitionism, as witness that unorthodox headgear, which, like Montgomery's funny hats and Patton's ivory-handled revolvers, was calculated to attract attention to himself. And no doubt "ambushing" Wavell in his car would have appealed to him far more than merely applying for an audience through some possibly supercilious aide-de-camp.

Whatever the circumstances, it is clear that Wavell was first intrigued and then convinced by Wingate's plan to defeat the Arab Revolt by taking back the night from the rebel gangs with countergangs—mixed patrols of British troops and Jewish fighters, operating from Jewish settlements, who were willing and able to confront the rebels up close and on their own ground. As Wingate declared in his seventeen-page assessment:

> There is only one way to deal with the situation: to persuade the
> gangs that in their predatory raids there is every chance of them running into a government gang which is determined to destroy them,

not by an exchange of shots in the distance but by bodily assault with bayonet and bomb.

Wavell was the man to give him permission to raise and deploy his countergangs—just as, again and yet again during Wingate's career, it was Wavell who would provide the opportunity for this maverick officer, the loosest of all the Royal Artillery's cannons, to show his true mettle. And if Wingate often stretched his mentor's patience until it twanged, ultimately he never let him down.

Chapter 7

*I*N THE SPRING OF 1938, Rex King-Clark, the wealthy young subaltern whose men had been bold enough to arrest Wingate on Mount Canaan, opened his campaign diary with some first impressions of soldiering in Palestine. To date, he grumbled, there had been "no very large battles, although many alarms."

> Our fighting has not gone beyond one ambush, in which we fired a large number of rounds but without, I fear, doing any damage, as the trucks we were in did not stop, it being against orders to do so, and shooting at a man five hundred yards away from a lurching vehicle does not lead to good results, particularly if in the heat of the moment one forgets to put one's sights up.

The style and all it signifies was a celebration of exactly the kind of amateur tradition that Wingate so despised among the British military. But for King-Clark, at least, all this was about to change. He would soon find himself leading a detachment of Wingate's Special Night Squads, much closer than five hundred yards from rebel gunmen and rarely on a moving vehicle.

Yet for several weeks it looked as though the Night Squads might be stillborn. Wingate lost his most important supporter when Wavell was called home as Britain began to make reluctant preparations for a new war against Germany. His successor was Lieutenant General Sir Robert Haining, who was nobody's fool but not so independent-minded as Wavell, more inclined to listen to Wingate's pro-Arab detractors and to do without the countergangs that Wavell had thought worth a try.

But the next obstacle in Wingate's path came from an entirely unexpected quarter—from inside the Jewish leadership. An influential faction within the Zionist hierarchy did not like the idea of Jews fighting alongside the British against the Arabs; they remained wedded to the belief that those Jews who chose to settle in Palestine should practice restraint and learn to live in peace with their neighbors, resorting to the gun only when all other options had been exhausted. Wingate was coldly furious when he learned of this opposition to his plans. He went to Jerusalem to confront Shertok at the Jewish Agency. It was a classic Wingate performance in which, having prepared one carefully honed line, he delivered it to maximum effect. "Shertok," he said, "why do you spend so much time with your enemies and ignoring the help of your friends?" Then he walked out. The next morning a chastened Shertok phoned Emmanuel Wilenski, the architect who was the head of Haganah intelligence for northern Palestine, and told him he had decided to support the Night Squads idea. "Your friend shouted at me," he said, "but all the same he impressed me."

Then came another setback. At the end of May 1938, Wing Commander Alan Ritchie, the new intelligence chief at GHQ, decided on a far-reaching reorganization and designated three additional intelligence centers—one in Haifa; one in Nablus, north of Jerusalem; and one in the predominantly Christian Arab town of Nazareth. Wingate was ordered to take charge at Nazareth. He dragged his feet. His plans did not include manning a desk in Nazareth or anywhere else. But Ritchie insisted, and away went his disgruntled subordinate, determined that his own agenda should take precedence. Which it very soon did, as events outside his or Ritchie's control played midwife to the birth of the Night Squads.

The summer of 1938 was the time of the Czechoslovak Crisis, and in Whitehall the War Office became preoccupied with contingency plans to send a British Expeditionary Force to France for the second time in twenty-five years. In that context, Palestine seemed very much the sideshow of a sideshow, a bottomless pit that swallowed up troops who were badly needed elsewhere. As Colonel Henry Pownall in the Secretariat of the Committee on Imperial Defence complained: "Sending troops to Palestine is like pouring water onto the desert sands."

So the reinforcements Haining had been promised never materialized, and he was forced to make do with an infantry strength of six battalions, or about five thousand men. With the Arabs in full revolt not a rifle could be wasted and that included those of the part-time Jewish policemen, or Ghaffirs, on the settlements. Consequently, Haining gave the go-ahead for the Night Squads, telling Brigadier John Evetts, commander of the Sixteenth Brigade at Haifa, to give Wingate all the assistance he could.

A priority for the squads was to be the protection of the Palestine stretch of the Iraq Petroleum Company's pipeline, running from Kirkuk to the refinery at Haifa. The rebels were shooting holes in it almost nightly and then igniting the little geysers of oil that ensued so that they lit up the night sky in a most satisfyingly dramatic way.

Wingate had been coming in and out of Evetts's area of operations for almost a year now and the brigadier was already a fan. "You chase them by night and I'll chase 'em by day," he enthused. From each of the three infantry battalions in his brigade—the Manchesters, the Royal Ulster Rifles, and the Royal West Kents—the brigadier ordered that one adventurous junior officer and a dozen volunteers from the ranks should be seconded to Wingate's new unit. Wingate believed that regular British soldiers and Haganah volunteers would make a formidable fighting combination, each having qualities that the other lacked. Not that he wanted his Jews to emulate their new comrades in all things. "Don't imitate the British Tommy," he warned. "Learn his calmness and discipline, but not his stupidity, brutality, and drunkenness."

Judging by the caliber of the officers he got, Evetts seems to have made it clear to his battalion commanders that they were not to unload their duds on Wingate. Above all, they had to be superbly fit. Lieutenant Michael Grove of the West Kents was skipper of his battalion's soccer team and brought most of them with him for a one shilling a day "special duties" bonus, while King-Clark had recently completed a physical training instructor's course at Aldershot.* And Humphrey "Bala" Bredin from the Ulster Rifles, who would have the most distinguished career of the three—retiring with two DSOs and the rank of major-general—was a first-class rifle shot.

The British infantry contingents were quartered in three separate Jewish settlements. The main one, where Wingate had his headquar-

---

*King-Clark celebrated his secondment by visiting a Haifa gun shop and buying a 9-mm Mauser machine pistol, capable of firing a twenty-round magazine in two seconds. The British army was still more than a year away from acquiring any kind of submachine gun.

ters, was at Ein Harod, in the Jezreel Valley and named after the spring of Herod where, as told in the Old Testament, Gideon selected the three hundred warriors who would scatter the Midianite host: "And the number of them that lapped, putting their hand to their mouth, were three hundred men . . . And the Lord said unto Gideon, By the three hundred men that lapped will I save you" (Judges 7: 6–7).

Gideon was Wingate's special Old Testament hero. He originally wanted to name the Night Squads Gideon Force, but his superiors found that altogether too partisan. He was less admiring of the military qualities of King Saul, who also campaigned in the vicinity of Ein Harod and lost a battle there against the Philistines. When Wingate's friend David Hacohen came to visit him in 1938 Wingate launched into a description of the battle, as recorded in the Old Testament. "Saul was a bloody fool," Wingate told Hacohen. "Why did he make a direct frontal assault? He should have sent a small detachment by night to take the Philistines from the rear." To Wingate, it seems, those ancient battles were as real as if they had happened yesterday.

It was mid-June when King-Clark and his dozen Manchesters arrived at Ayyelet Hashahar, a settlement near the Syrian frontier, to commence service with the Night Squads. On meeting again, neither mentioned their previous somewhat prickly encounter, and King-Clark noted in his diary that he found Wingate "an odd gentleman, but one of great determination and the courage of his convictions." He was unhappy over Wingate's decree that his twelve men should be spread between two squads with an equal number of Jews, which he thought would "detract from the superiority of the Manchesters." Also, he noted: "I don't imagine the Arabs are going to enjoy having a bunch of Jews wandering through their villages at night." But after only forty-eight hours he was beginning to have second thoughts.

The Jewish Ghaffirs' sergeant is a "brave type"—ex–German army and has the right idea. . . . I don't feel so badly now about having mixed night squads as the Jews are getting the hang of the idea.

Training had started, with particular emphasis on the use of the seventeen-inch bayonet. Wingate was very much against "peppering the night with shots" against unseen targets and wanted to inculcate the habit of a swift grenade followed by a charge and the awful intelligence of cold steel. King-Clark and his NCO, Corporal Fred Howbrook, a sandy-haired Lancastrian, were determined to instill "a little ferociousness" in their Jewish recruits and set up some straw dummies for practice. "They love Corporal Howbrook's exhibitions!" King-Clark enthused. But not all of them did. One of the Haganah men was so overwhelmed by Howbrook's bloodcurdling yells, the punctured sacking, and the dancing bayonet that he fainted clean away.

A couple of nights later King-Clark's squad had their first taste of action when they exchanged fire with a group of rebels and took three prisoners. "Not bad for the first night out," noted King-Clark, "and the Ghaffirs have gained a lot of confidence from it."

The West Kents were stationed at Hanita, and Wingate drove there to lead them and their Jewish squad mates in a raid on the border village of Jurdieh, the springboard for repeated attacks on the Jewish outpost. From the Palestinian side of the border Jurdieh was inaccessible, so Wingate led his squad by way of a shortcut on the Lebanese side of the frontier. This was a risky thing to do. Had he been detected, the subsequent row with the French might have had him sent home in disgrace. Zvi Brenner, marching directly behind Wingate with a satchelful of grenades, was impressed by how he "was able to adjust to the terrain in a most extraordinary way."

> In fact, he was so sure of himself that we began to suspect that this wasn't the first time he had walked here. From time to time he would stop, examine the map by the light of his special flashlight, and move on. . . . Wingate didn't follow any paths but walked in straight lines. . . .

At about 2 A.M., when they reckoned to be close to Jurdieh, they stumbled on a shepherd sleeping out with his flock. Questioned by Wingate, he confirmed that they were in the vicinity of the village. Wingate let him go "and a few minutes later we heard his cries in the direction of the village."

> He was shouting "Jews" and "guns". . . . People woke up in seconds. From all the homes they began firing in our direction. We lined up along a brick wall and began to return fire. Wingate stood by us and showed us where to shoot, as he shouted "Here! Here! Here!"

Both sides had little more than sounds and flashes and the occasional suggestion of a silhouette to take rough aim at. At one point, Wingate dashed forward into the village with Brenner and a second grenadier to lob grenades among the tightly packed mud-walled houses before running back to cover. The Arabs had the high ground and the better field of fire. Even the British squadsmen, who were trained to husband their ammunition, were beginning to get to the bottom of their fifty rounds each. Wingate began to make plans for a withdrawal when firing from the high ground ceased: Wingate and his men did not know it, but the sheikh in charge had taken a leg wound and his followers had lost heart. Seizing the opportunity, Wingate gave the order to get out, leaving two dead Arabs.

> And again Wingate led us swiftly, climbing up hills and down into valleys, forging his way through the forest with supreme confidence. . . . We were amazed. . . . Only he was capable of leading us in such territory with such confidence.

> But the most important lesson that Wingate was teaching the Jewish settlers was as much psychological as tactical and was to form the basis of strategic doctrine in the future Israeli army. "He taught us to go beyond the wire," says Brenner, "not just to defend our settlements but to go out and confront the enemy in his lair."

The squads began to increase their patrolling of the oil pipeline to Haifa, whose contents so regularly illuminated the night sky over the Jezreel Valley and lower Galilee. "Look, someone has lit the menorah,"* the Jewish settlers would joke. But the flames were a constant reminder that after dark most of the land beyond their fences was enemy territory.

Often Wingate would go out with squads other than the one based at his headquarters in Ein Harod. He was with the West Kents and their Jewish fellow squadsmen from Hanita when there was a brisk exchange of fire, and Lieutenant Grove was again impressed by Wingate's apparent indifference to the shots *zizzing* about his head

*The Jews' seven-branched ritual candelabrum.

while he directed the men to their positions as if he were on an exercise. "Wingate was walking along saying, 'No, you point that way and you point that way.' . . . He took no notice of the bullets whatsoever. . . ."

King-Clark was surprised at the knowledge Wingate demonstrated of the finer points of infantry fighting. After all, he was a gunner, "a species the infantry tended to view with a degree of supicion—maybe because they were cleverer." Never before had he encountered a commander who was so painstaking, who drove himself quite so hard, who was so determined to expunge the devil from the smallest of details. There were instructions on everything from tactics to clothing—how formations should march at night and maintain contact, what weapons were most effective, what kind of boots and socks to wear. He stipulated that bayonets were to be sheathed in dark cotton cloth to ensure they did not flash in the moonlight. He also had corks stuck on the ends of the bayonets to prevent accidental wounding while his squads were on the march. And the physical demands were unrelenting; squads were expected to cover at least fifteen miles in a night and be fresh enough to fight at the end of it. On one occasion, King-Clark's men walked twenty-two miles before going into action.

Wingate was never one of those British officers innately suspicious of technical innovation. On the contrary, he welcomed new ideas. Nevertheless, he demonstrated a positively Victorian relish for the rifle and bayonet, though later in his career he did argue that the British should have a semiautomatic rifle like the Americans. Curiously, he showed no interest in acquiring submachine guns, though these were infinitely more suitable than rifles for night patrols, when the chance of an aimed shot is rare.

No detail was ever beneath his consideration. "Be painstaking," he urged his squad leaders, though few could ever match him in this respect. Particular attention was paid to teaching the tactics he had devised to disguise his squads' true intentions. He assumed that almost any intended movement that became known to any Arab was likely to reach the rebels, if only through innocent gossip. It would be rare for a British patrol to pass through an Arab village without having its numbers and direction noted and reported. That being so, Wingate ordered his squads to attach themselves to regular army or police convoys, so that they could drop from their slow-moving vehicles, a

couple at a time, and assemble silently off the road before proceeding
to their true objective.

If proceeding from a settlement on foot they were to leave singly or
in pairs and then gather at an agreed rendezvous, not less than half a
mile away. Other dos and don'ts included never walking down a track
for more than half a mile, but zigzagging across it to avoid counteram-
bush, and never going back to base by the route on which they had set
out.

On one seriocomic occasion an innovative idea of Wingate's led to
considerable confusion. When Ephraim Krassner, his Haganah liaison
officer, thought he heard him ask for some chauffeurs he objected on
the grounds that the army must surely have plenty of drivers. "Not
chauffeurs," snapped Wingate, "shofars, as in Jericho." It had seemed
to him that they could unnerve rebel villages at night by copying
Joshua's tactics at the siege of Jericho and blowing the rabbinical ram's
horn. But suitable rams' horns were in short supply and the rabbinate
were reluctant to allow their shofars to be taken out of the synagogues.
For a while there was some halfhearted experimentation with army bu-
gles, but eventually Wingate dropped the Joshua gambit.

Similarly dropped was an experimental signaling system. For communication with brigade headquarters in Haifa, Wingate had been
given a radio transmitter mounted on a small truck. With scant regard
for the perils of hubris, Wingate gave himself the personal call sign
"Winner." But small walkie-talkies were not yet off the drawing board,
and for internal communications he devised a signaling system employing a flashlight wired to the end of a three-foot pole, the extra
length a precaution against the operator being felled by an enemy
sharpshooter. One flash would mean halt and get into battle formation.
Two flashes meant form ambush to the right, three flashes form to the
left, and so on. But flashing lights were essentially incompatible with
Wingate's doctrines of stealth and concealment. The Haganah men
felt uncomfortable with them, and soon the poles and torches were
abandoned and low whistles, emulating the sound of night birds, were
used instead.

By now, Wingate was beginning to feel that his Jewish squadsmen—
in particular his stars, people such as Carmi, Brenner, and Dayan—
were metamorphosing from enthusiastic amateurs into dependable
soldiers, living proof to him that they really were the descendants of

the Maccabees. This had not been achieved entirely by kindness and sympathy for Zionism. If Wingate was admired, he was also feared. In the British army it was a court-martial offense for an officer to strike an enlisted man, but the Special Night Squads existed in a misty limbo beyond the frontiers of military law. Wingate did nothing to lengthen his short fuse and did not hesitate to use his fists, or at least the open palm of a hand, on anyone who did not follow an order to the letter or otherwise fell short of his exacting standards.

When he saw one of his Jewish junior leaders drink at a well before his men had slaked their thirst he struck the mug from his hand; when a man he had entrusted with a pair of wire cutters did not have them readily at hand he pushed him into the barbed-wire fence that was holding the squad up; if he was leading a squad over rough ground and the silence was broken by a tired foot rattling a loose stone, some humiliating slapping or punching would follow.

Brenner would recall that the worst offense of all was to be trigger-happy. Gershon Ostrovski, one of the founding fathers of kibbutz Ein Harod, first incited Wingate's wrath by turning up for his first patrol without a hat to cover his baldness, which was oddly luminous by moonlight. Then he made things worse by firing at a shadow. Brenner watched in horror as Wingate pinched the cheeks of this venerable pioneer, demanding in Hebrew: "Why without an order, why without an order?"

At first, some Jewish squadsmen deeply resented this kind of treatment. Brenner himself once remonstrated with Wingate after he kicked a young man who had collapsed after a grueling night march. It would be hard to imagine any other British officer getting away with this kind of behavior. There would have been complaints and the Jewish Agency might have withdrawn all cooperation unless the officer were replaced. Yet in the way of soldiers who are learning to regard themselves as an elite, the Jews of the Special Night Squads began to take a special pride in being Wingate's men. "He was our father," said Brenner years later. "When he became angry and reprimanded us we knew it was because he loved us and we loved him."

While admiring Wingate for his physical endurance, his capacity for hard organizational work, his seemingly casual bravery, and his uncanny ability to navigate in the dark across featureless terrain, they also recognized a quality the Jews usually admire but the British often suspect: cleverness. His inventive mind seemed to devise an answer to every problem that arose. Carmi was especially impressed by Wingate's extraordinarily retentive memory: "He had only to see a map once and he had learned every feature on it."

For their part, the British enlisted men regarded Wingate with a mixture of awe and amusement at his eccentricities, which were perhaps more apparent to them than to their Jewish comrades-in-arms. At one point the Manchesters started their day trying to guess on which legs the odd socks worn beneath Wingate's uniform shorts would appear. Corporal Howbrook, the virtuoso of the bayonet, liked Wingate's style from the start—the twin revolvers he had taken to wearing cowboy style, the unpressed uniform, the way he looked you in the eye. It was good, he thought, to meet an officer who knew what he wanted and how to get it.

Perhaps it took the young British officers a little longer. The three SNS subalterns were precisely the kind of young men Wingate could never manage to be—indeed, would never want to be: clubbable, sports-minded, not at all introspective, and instinctively anti-intellectual. King-Clark, probably the most broad-minded and widely traveled, who had perhaps seen Wingate at his worst at the Mount Canaan roadblock, soon realized that his new commanding officer came out of a very individual mold. For his part, Grove was convinced that Wingate was brave as a lion. He just wished he could learn to like him more.

But likability was not an essential quality for command; efficiency was and leadership and courage, and no one could deny Wingate had all those. What none of his men yet realized was just how lucky Wingate could be as well.

Chapter 8

B
Y THE MIDDLE OF JUNE 1938 the squads had yet to fight a major action with the gangs, but the constant night patrols in the vicinity of the pipeline—Wingate preferred to call them "moving ambushes"—had led to several skirmishes and sabotage was definitely on the wane. The raid on Jurdieh had also paid an unexpected dividend. The *mukhtar* of that village had sent a delegation to the Jewish settlement at Hanita suing for peace. Thereafter, apart from the occasional sniper, the siege of Hanita was over.

Recognition of Wingate's achievement came from both sides. Haining, Wavell's successor, sent a message to Brigadier Evetts in Haifa saying how impressed he was with SNS "and all concerned with them." Wingate had also made his mark with Fawzi el Kawaukji, who put his name on a hit list with a thousand pounds on his head, the kind of fortune that would mean an Arab peasant might never have to work again. But still there had been no major clash, something that would really make the rebels' eyes water. Michael Grove, the Royal West Kents subaltern, was coming to accept that SNS operations were rather like a tedious country walk with the only consolation that they were about as dangerous.

Then came the encounter at Dabburiya, a small town at the foot of the olive-covered slopes of Mount Tabor* about five miles southeast of Nazareth. It is named after Deborah, the prophet and first woman judge of Israel. Showing uncharacteristic initiative, one of Fawzi's bands moved away from the pipeline and hit the British where they least expected it. They made a night raid on Nazareth itself, killed some Christian Arabs they deemed to be collaborators, and more or

---

*Mount Tabor is where the New Testament sets the Transfiguration, Jesus's revelation to three of His disciples that He is the son of God.

less took over the town, apart from the police post, for the hours of darkness. Shortly afterward Wingate went out in person to investigate a tip passed on to him by the local district commissioner that the rebels were using a forester's hut on a wooded hillside, but when he got there he found no signs of recent occupation.

Then came another tip that confirmed what Wingate had always suspected, namely that the rebels, confident that the British would rarely venture farther than the pipeline at night, preferred the comfort of staying in a village within easy walking distance of Nazareth rather than live in primitive cabins in the hills. His informant had narrowed the possible targets down to two. One was Ein Mahil, a hill village east of Nazareth, and the other its neighbor Dabburiya in lower land about two and a half miles away to the southeast. Dabburiya had a police post nearby, so both Wingate and the intelligence center in the police compound at Nazareth agreed that the rebels were most likely in Ein Mahil.

By now the SNS were about 140 strong. Wingate collected over half of them—thirty-two British soldiers and fifty-five Jewish volunteers—and gathered them at Afikim, Zvi Brenner's old kibbutz just below the Sea of Galilee. From there they set out in a fleet of seven trucks, three of them civilian vehicles from the kibbutz. There were two Lewis-gun teams, one of them from the Ulsters under a Corporal Mac Mac-Conville, a big man who carried the machine gun alone and prided himself on being strong enough to fire the weapon from his hip.

Wingate's superiors had urged him not to take armed Jews into Arab villages at night if he could avoid it, and for once he did not find doing what he was told difficult: it obviously made better tactical sense to draw the rebels out into the open than blunder about a village's narrow lanes in the dark. Wingate decided to surround the suspect village by establishing ambushes on all the obvious escape routes. Then he would cause the rebels to panic and run into the ambushes.

There was only one problem. The rebels were not at Ein Mahil. They were at Dabburiya, where, as a nod toward the proximity of a police post, a few sentries cloaked against the cold were staring out through the light mist. Wingate eventually conceded that his men were approaching the wrong place when King-Clark, as planned, fired a couple of white Verey flares in the hope that the gang would rush out to investigate. Nothing happened.

At midnight Wingate's eighty-seven men moved south toward Dabburiya in their separate squads, walking in column with some squads well ahead of the others and nobody quite certain where the others were, let alone the enemy.

What exactly happened next has always been, at least from the British viewpoint, a matter of controversy. "As an operation everything went without a hitch," wrote Wingate, but King-Clark always remembered it as "a cock-up of the first water."

Dabburiya was a dirt-poor place of flat-roofed houses whose mud walls would hardly stop a stone, let alone a rifle bullet. Most of the village was surrounded by high ground except to the south, where the land fell away in a rough dirt motor track that meandered toward the main Afula–Ein Harod road. At the western edge of the village, surrounded by haystacks, was the village threshing floor.

Wingate, having at last found his rebels in strength, was clearly unable to launch a properly coordinated assault. Instead, all surprise was lost when the first squad to get to the outskirts of Dabburiya went immediately into action. These were Grove's men, who encountered two armed Arabs among the haystacks around the threshing floor. One was shot dead and the other ran away.

Once the alarm was given the wakened rebels grabbed their rifles and climbed onto the flat rooftops from where they began some brisk firing in the general direction of Grove and his men. The amount of return fire told the Arabs that they outnumbered the intruders, and they stood their ground. Both sides used grenades.

Then Private Chapman, Grove's batman who in action switched from officer's valet to grenadier, was hit in the stomach. Grove decided to pull his squad out and helped get Chapman back to the threshing floor, where they covered him with one of the blankets abandoned there by the Arabs they had disturbed. The lieutenant then fired a red Verey light to call for a truck in order to evacuate his batman.

It was now about two in the morning and cold. A couple of the West Kents discovered some more Arab blankets in the straw and draped them around their shoulders poncho style. Wingate turned up and saw to it that Chapman, who was in considerable pain, was loaded onto a truck and taken away. Corporal MacConville of the Ulsters and the Lewis-gun teams arrived. Carmi noticed that the big corporal was carrying one of the Lewis guns himself. Its round drum magazine, like a thick plate, was already fitted.

By now it had become obvious to the rebels that they were dealing with much more than a small British patrol, and they began to scatter in all directions. Some ran uphill through the cover provided by the olive groves on the lower slopes of Mount Tabor. Wingate decided to pursue this faction. "Cover me in and cover me out," he ordered Corporal MacConville and the Lewis-gun teams. Then he told the rest to follow him:

> I was advancing through some olives at the foot of the mountain when firing broke out in the rear; this was from a few bandits who were escaping westwards. I opened fire on them and appeared to have silenced them. I was moving on again when a burst of fire came from the rear, again at close quarters, killing one supernumerary and wounding two soldiers and myself. Unfortunately, this put a stop to further advance by me. I despatched the wounded at once and silenced the enemy fire.

At this point there was no enemy fire, something Wingate must have been only too aware of by the time he came to write his report. He and his men had been hit by MacConville, who had been firing his Lewis gun from the hip and would almost certainly have inflicted even more damage had he been issued with one of the new Brens, which were much lighter and easier to control from this position. It seems that at first Wingate's party was attacked by Arabs escaping westward, and among those who turned with Wingate to face them and return the fire were the West Kents who had picked up the blankets against the cold and whose silhouettes, under the star-filled Palestinian sky, were no different from the rebels. MacConville thought Wingate was driving the Arabs right onto them and couldn't believe his luck.

It was a classic nighttime "friendly fire" incident. In the early hours of 11 July 1938 Corporal MacConville came within inches of robbing Zion and the British army of Orde Wingate before he had properly got into his stride. Wingate was hit five times in the arm and legs. Luckily, all the wounds were caused by the Lewis's .303 rounds ricocheting off the flinty ground, and the bullets had lost much of their velocity. Even so, it was entirely a matter of luck that no vital organs were penetrated or bones broken. The Jewish supernumerary had been hit several times in the stomach and had died quite quickly.

Shouting at MacConville and his gun teams to hold their fire, the squadsmen carried their casualties back to the grain-threshing area, where Carmi dressed Wingate's injuries. Just as it was getting light King-Clark, having left Zvi Brenner in charge of the Jewish part of his squad, took his Manchesters into Dabburiya. The heavy firing had stopped though there was still the occasional shot, for Bredin and the rest of the Ulsters were now on the scene, and Wingate had urged him to take up the pursuit of the tardier rebels up the mountainside.

King-Clark found Wingate sprawled on the threshing chaff, the centerpiece of the kind of gallant tableau nineteenth-century painters usually composed in their studios:

> Though Wingate's face was white as a sheet and very taut, he was sitting there, in the hay, covered in blood and giving orders in English and Hebrew quite calmly.

It was a sight that banished any lingering doubts King-Clark may have had about Wingate. A few hours later, he found himself writing in his diary, "He is the most extraordinary man."

The Jewish half of King-Clark's squad under Zvi Brenner walked through the deserted streets of Dabburiya, fingers on the trigger, noting several bodies as they did so. Despite his injuries Wingate refused to leave until he saw that Brenner and his men were safe. For once, Brenner thought Wingate appeared somewhat less than heroic:

> He looked very pale and frightened and sorry for himself. He hated pain and the first thing he said to me was: "I hope I'm not going to die because of you. I refused to leave until I made sure you were all right. Now take me to hospital quickly."

Private Chapman had already gone with the other seriously wounded to the military hospital at Haifa. There he died, making the Night Squads' total casualties two dead and five wounded. The rebels lost at least nine dead.

Despite the elements of fiasco Wingate could rightly claim that much had been achieved. They had gone out into the night, surprised a large rebel force in its insolent hiding place, scattered it before it could get up to any more mischief, and in the process inflicted considerably more casualties than they had suffered themselves. Wingate estimated that a total of fifteen rebels had been killed and twenty wounded. Certainly, toward the end, and it probably lasted no more than an hour, the killing became one-sided.

Brigadier Evetts evidently agreed with Wingate's general assessment for he recommended that he should be immediately awarded the Distinguished Service Order, only below the Victoria Cross in the pecking order of British medals for bravery in the face of the enemy. The citation not only mentioned the Dabburiya action and the wounds Wingate sustained there but also the raid on Jurdieh on the Lebanese border and the dramatic reduction in sabotage along the oil pipeline. "Captain Wingate has throughout displayed gifts of leadership and personal gallantry of a very high order."

From hospital, on the day he had been told to expect a visit from General Haining, Wingate wrote to King-Clark: "My leg goes on well but has been carved up a bit to get some deep splinters out so may take a few days more than I hoped." Meanwhile, he caught up with his paperwork. To an army stenographer he dictated a report of the Dabburiya action that was an epic of evasion when it came to the circumstance of his own injuries:

> We learned, however, that however unpleasant it may be for the enemy village fighting at night is both dangerous and difficult. More deliberation and care is called for than is suitable to an encounter in the open. All this is obvious but the personnel concerned have now learned it.

A couple of days after Wingate was admitted Bala Bredin came in to have some flesh wounds on his forehead examined, the result of a long-range sniping duel that ended when a round hit the breech of his Lee-Enfield and almost blinded him with splinters. But not before Bredin had ambushed, near the village of Bira, the remnants of the band scattered at Dabburiya and killed fourteen of them, the SNS's greatest triumph to date. Then King-Clark exacted a small revenge for an old humiliation of Western arms. In 1187 Saladin had routed the Crusaders on an extinct volcano known as the Horns of Hittim. On a bright moonlit night, King-Clark took his Manchesters there and killed four rebels without loss.

The continued success of Wingate's men was one of the few bright spots in a generally depressing picture for the British in Palestine. In Haifa on 25 July 1938 Jewish terrorists from Irgun Zvai Leumi, disciples of Jabotinsky's Revisionist Zionism, which called for the expulsion of all Arabs, exploded a big bomb in a packed Arab marketplace. Forty-three people were killed and over forty more wounded. Short of troops, Brigadier Evetts had to ask the visiting battleship HMS *Repulse* to land armed shore parties to enforce a curfew and help clear up the mess.

While the sailors were putting crippled market donkeys and mules out of their misery, at Haifa railway station two luckless Jews were discovered by a vengeful Arab mob and stoned to death. In Jerusalem another Irgun bomb killed ten Arabs near the Dome of the Rock.

Wingate probably had the Haifa marketplace atrocity in mind when he recalled his promise to the Woodhead Commission to put his views in writing, and he delivered a prescient warning:

> Should the time ever come when the Jews have reason to believe that they have been betrayed, or that their best hope lies in a complete reversal of their policy, we shall find that we are facing something very different from the Arab revolt.

Ten years later, fighting a losing battle to curb illegal immigration and tormented by ruthless Jewish terrorism, the British quit Palestine.

On 2 August 1938, a few days after he had been discharged from hospital, Wingate wrote to his mother:

> I am quite well again and back at work. Gunshot wounds is the War Office way of saying bullet wounds. They have to do it differently. These were only flesh wounds and healed at first intention—much to my surprise as they were caused by ricochets and the soil was filthy. However, I must have pure blood or something. My enforced rest in hospital could not have happened at a better moment. I had some important memos to write and at last got time to do so.

"Back at work" was a modest description of the events of the previous week. Wingate had returned to the fray with the alacrity with which he once remounted after a fox-hunting fall. He got back to Ein

Harod on 27 July, where he was met by Chaim Sturmann, the leader of the settlement and famous for being a man of few words. Sturmann once held serious doubts about the wisdom of recruiting Jews for the Special Night Squads, for he belonged firmly to that part of the Zionist camp that was convinced that they must not merely coexist but have the most cordial relation with the Palestinian Arabs. But Wingate had won him over, and a friendship had evolved between the British officer and this taciturn man so that they were often to be seen silently pacing the perimeter wire together. "Chaim's silences are worth other men's conversations," Wingate once observed.

Now Sturmann organized a dinner to mark his friend's return, interspersed with frequent toasts from his hosts in the Russian and Polish tradition in which most had been brought up. Wingate concluded his own speech with a few words in Hebrew. "God gave it to us to slay the enemies of the Jews," he told his breathless audience. "For the enemies of the Jews are the enemies of all mankind."

The next morning Wingate had a word with the man who had accidentally shot him. "MacConville," he said, "at Dabburiya we all made a great many mistakes. The needful thing is for us to learn from our mistakes." And Corporal MacConville was dismissed to finish his military career some twenty years later a much decorated regimental sergeant major.

Wingate's wounds were far from healed. At times it was obvious he was still in some pain. One leg was bandaged from his knee to his ankle, and on the other leg a bandage started beneath the long shorts and ended at his knee.

But when an informer codenamed "The Otter" came through with the news that, after crossing the Jordan, some gun- and drug runners would be gathering at Um Mejadea in the Wadi Tubas, the valley that leads from Beisan to Nablus, Wingate did not hesitate. "It's not his legs that cope with it," said Bredin, who shared a room with Wingate at Ein Harod and probably knew him better than any of the other officers. "It's his mind."

All the SNS available were mobilized and, with their founder and commanding officer at their head, taken on a grueling trek across some of the hardest countryside Palestine had to offer. First Wingate led them on a compass bearing over flinty hills and then descended into valleys where they waded, almost waist deep in places, through stinking, sulfurous marshes. After he got through them he called a halt and changed the dressings on his wounds.

They reached Um Mejadea at three in the morning, a few minutes after the arrival of the smugglers with their Mausers and Lebanese hashish on a string of camels and donkeys. Wingate waited for first light. After the confusion at Dabburiya this became an increasingly common tactic: march at night to fight at dawn. As soon as it was light enough to see their targets they ambushed the Arabs as they moved out of the hamlet with the rising sun behind them. Eleven were killed and four captured in the first few minutes. The remainder, who numbered about thirty, dispersed and were pursued into the hills, where more shots were exchanged. Wingate's attempt to lead the hunt were defeated when he discovered that his damaged legs would no longer support him and, almost speechless with fatigue, he had to be carried to one of the trucks where it was discovered that some of his healing wounds had reopened.

Two days later, on Sunday, 31 July 1938, having made some recovery from his exertions, Wingate was driving through Haifa in his Studebaker after visiting the city to make a personal report of his latest success to Brigadier Evetts. When he slowed at a road junction three Arabs sidled up and one dropped a grenade into the open-topped car. It failed to explode. Revolver drawn, Wingate left the car and ran off in pursuit, but his legs had not mended sufficiently and his would-be assassins soon disappeared.

The Times reported the incident and noted that Captain Wingate had had a "remarkable escape." Wingate obviously thought so too. Coming at the end of the most exhausting and tumultuous month of his military career to date, his second close shave left him badly shaken. He went to see his friend Emmanuel Wilenski, had several whiskies with him, and then collapsed into a deep sleep and spent the night there. In more cosseted times, somebody might have informed Wingate he was suffering from post-traumatic shock disorder, an idea that even his open mind is likely to have considered the most puerile indulgence.

There were several shootings and bombings in Haifa that day, and whether Wingate was merely another target of opportunity or his assailants were hoping to collect the thousand-pound reward Fawzi el Kawaukji had put on his head was never known. Wilenski preferred not to take any chance with The Friend. Zvi Brenner, the cheerful little Polish Jew who had been raised in Chicago, was appointed Wingate's permanent bodyguard.

Haganah had more reason than ever to look after their unusual benefactor. Building on the success of the Special Night Squads, Wingate was about to lay down the second of the foundation stones that would help provide an underground citizens' militia with the trained cadre of a regular army.

When General Haining paid Wingate the honor of visiting him in hospital he must have known that he was dealing with a clever and ambitious officer determined to exploit to the hilt the laurels he had recently received. Wingate had already proposed to Brigadier Evetts that the SNS be expanded by two more British subalterns and twenty soldiers and at least another hundred or so supernumeraries with the appropriate arms, including eight Lewis guns. This would have effectively brought SNS's ration strength to about three hundred strong—a considerable independent command for a thirty-five-year-old captain in Britain's peacetime army. Haining, probably on Evetts's advice, said no. But he did give Wingate permission to intensify his training program at Ein Harod with the proviso that the Jewish Agency provide the funds for it.

But when he went to the agency to ask for their assistance to start a Jewish NCOs' course, Wingate again encountered unexpected opposition just as he had when he first mooted the idea of the SNS. The right wing Zionists had become increasingly disturbed by the success of the Night Squads and the military talent they were producing. They accused the kibbutzniks and the rest of the Zionist left of hijacking the Jewish army before the state was even born. While this internal bickering went on Wingate quietly went ahead and recruited, "surreptitiously almost" according to King-Clark, more Jewish supernumeraries so that Jews began to outnumber British soldiers in the SNS.

At about this time he also began to flaunt more of the visible appurtenances of the eccentric. He grew a beard, a naval affectation the British army generally despises, though it could hardly be denied to an

Arabic-speaking intelligence officer who might need to move about in disguise. He also began to put aside his flat service cap for his venerable Wolseley cork-lined pith helmet, which, combined with the facial hair, gave people the impression they were dealing with someone who might have fought the *mahdi* and was certainly much older than thirty-five. Invited to a wardroom party on a warship at Haifa harbor he arrived in a filthy uniform bearing a bag of grenades over one shoulder.

When at Ein Harod, to stress the need for punctuality among the supernumeraries, he took to wandering about the place dangling from his wrist a large alarm clock set to ring at the time of his next task. Even the kibbutzniks, no prudes, found his casual nudity intriguing, and the young women vied with one another to find the best spots to view the living quarters of this naked ascetic who had come to stay. King-Clark noticed that, though he was always perfectly polite to them, Wingate never seemed to allow himself to be distracted by a pretty face.

King-Clark was allowed to bring his monoplane up from Egypt to a dirt landing strip he had discovered near Kibbutz Afikim. Most of his squadsmen, British and Jews, had never been airborne, and from here he gave them joy rides disguised as reconnaissance trips and the like. Wingate always turned down his invitations, and King-Clark concluded he was one of those people for whom the thrill of flying held no allure at all.

King-Clark had already discovered that unorthodox and eccentric officers were more common in the British army than outward appearances might suggest. Even so, at times he and the other two subalterns were undoubtedly embarrassed by their leader's increasingly outlandish manners and appearance, which were not what their public schools and Sandhurst had taught them to expect. Theirs was a reluctant admiration for a superior whose bravery, cleverness, extraordinary capacity for hard work, and ultimate effectiveness they found undeniable. Even so, at times they would have preferred a commanding officer with a more obvious élan.

Outside his command Wingate's DSO had stirred the kind of debate among his brother officers that would dog him for the rest of his career. Opinion was divided between those who thought he was a complete fraud and those who conceded he was a brilliant officer though a bit of a poseur. John Hackett,* a captain in the Transjordan Frontier Force who sometimes liaised with Wingate over pipeline security, was among the latter:

> He was a sort of circus comedian who couldn't stop being a comic even off the stage. I don't think he regarded it as an act. He had built himself up into this puritanical, fire-eating, dedicated, Round Head type Cromwellian soldier with a Bible in one hand and an alarm clock in the other as it were. . . . It was possible to laugh at him but not when he was there.

Certainly, the SNS were not giving the rebels any laughs. Although the squads were never more than one hundred and fifty strong, Wingate's tactics, direction, and the quality of the intelligence he was getting began to produce successes that were out of all proportion to their numbers. The painful lessons learned at Dabburiya had been fully assimilated, and after that night they did not take another fatal casualty. By the high summer of 1938 the squads were at the peak of their performance, well-oiled killing machines. When they did make contact with the enemy, the conclusion was rarely in doubt.

Some of the rebels switched from direct engagement to planting land mines, homemade affairs but surprisingly lethal. The explosive was often unwittingly provided by sloppy army engineers who had failed to detonate all the charges they had placed in the houses of known rebels blown up by court order.** It was then discovered by the newly destitute as they explored the rubble of their homes. King-Clark lost a subaltern friend in the Manchesters to a mine, and they were regarded, even by these professional soldiers, as underhand weapons and bitterly resented.

Otherwise, most of the British in Palestine, military or civilian administrators, still tended to have more time for the Arabs than the Jews. In action Wingate's young officers generally displayed all the compassion of tigers. Even so, they rarely seemed to have felt any hatred for the Arabs they killed. Their feelings toward them were a mixture of pity and contempt lit up by occasional flashes of frank

---

*Later General Sir John Hackett GCB, CBE, DSO, MC—Arnhem veteran and author.

**A practice the Israelis continue *con brio* on the occupied West Bank and Gaza Strip.

admiration for the style of these untutored partisans with whom, as Wingate had predicted, their clashes became increasingly one-sided. After a while, the murderous fun of ambush sometimes left the squads appalled by their own virtuosity.

About half a century later, former squad commander Mike Grove, by then a retired lieutenant colonel and of a generation mostly untroubled by notions of political correctness, recalled an encounter with rebel horsemen in a wadi:

> [T]hey appeared at dawn with the sun just coming up, galloping across the plain into the mountains. And they looked magnificent with their rifles strapped on their back and their cloaks flying, and horses galloping . . . it seemed a bloody shame to kill them. . . . But when we had killed them . . . I don't know if you've ever shot squirrels but they look rather fine up a tree, when it falls down at the bottom it just look[s] like a dead rat—that's roughly what they looked like.

On that particular occasion, Grove was acting on intelligence supplied by Wingate, who had given him strict instructions regarding the time and place and the way to get there:

> I suppose I had to walk about twenty miles. . . . The maps were fairly good but in the dark it's awfully difficult to tell what counts as a wadi and what doesn't. . . . We used to go by the stars and by time. . . . So many miles to the hour and so on. . . . Just about dawn, to our amazement, coming straight at this wadi was this party of horsemen. . . . How he discovered that they were going to be there I've just no idea.

Sometimes it was not so much good intelligence that brought the SNS their double-figure body counts but Wingate's creative ability to improvise and then exploit a situation with all his usual perfectionism.

There was no better example of this than the action that took place in early September at a Bedouin encampment near the village of Beit Lid on the Plain of Esdraelon, long suspected to be a transit point for rebels crossing from Galilee into Samaria in what is now known as the West Bank.

Wingate sent for a battered open farm truck he had borrowed from Ein Harod, crewed in its cab by two soldiers dressed in the blue flannel shirts favored by Jewish agricultural workers. In the back of the truck, lying flat on their bellies so that they were invisible behind its low sides, were fifteen British soldiers and Jewish supernumeraries, whose weapons included a couple of Lewis machine guns.

The truck was to be a Trojan horse to lure the rebels into the open. His squads made their normal circuitous nighttime approach and came in from different directions to seal all the obvious escape routes. Then, in the first gray light of dawn, after a wet night that had left the surrounding land a gluey bog, the driver of Wingate's truck trundled right into the waking village.

Bredin, some of whose Ulsters were on the truck, thought it worked like a dream. By the time it had come to a halt broadside to the village, its apparently panic-stricken crew tumbling out of the cab and running for the edge of the road, the lieutenant estimated that forty or fifty exuberant rebels were gathering around the honeypot. Then the wooden sides were dropped to reveal the prone figures behind the Lewis guns and the Lee-Enfields. As they opened fire, the squads began to close in.

King-Clark was on his last operation for the SNS before four days' leave and rejoining his battalion. Convinced that nothing would come of the Beit Lid search, he had gone dressed for leave rather than battle in freshly starched shorts and shirt, suede desert boots, and his best Sam Browne belt.

> As we advanced across the flat dusty ground in nice, extended order towards the Bedouin tents, the village on the hillock to our left, the rising sun in our front, someone began to shoot at us—spaced single shots which kicked up the dust in front of us . . . then we were treated to an extraordinary spectacle. . . . An Arab on horseback, his kheffiyah headdress pluming out behind him, galloped out of the tents and across the plain . . . we saw puffs of smoke rising around him and heard the stutter of a light automatic in the distance; it was the Ulsters' Lewis gun. . . . The Arab reined his horse onto its hind legs, turned and galloped back towards the village, disappearing from our sight.

King-Clark led his men through the low black Bedouin tents where they saw a figure with a rifle dash from one of the tents and crouch below a low wall on their right flank. The subaltern turned to his nearest Jewish soldier and made bayonet-fighting gestures. The man's eyes widened and he pointed incredulously to the seventeen inches of Sheffield steel attached to the end of his rifle. King-Clark nodded and watched as the Jew climbed onto the wall and made repeated and un-ambiguous downward thrusts at something they could not quite see.

> A minute later he was back at my side, an old Mauser rifle in his free hand, his own bayonet blooded to the hilt, his eyes wild with the shock of what he had just done.*

As the fight continued Corporal Howbrook killed Sheikh Tahir, the gang's leader, who was hiding behind a pile of brushwood. He was the horseman whose bid to escape Wingate's net had so aroused King-Clark's admiration a few minutes before. Howbrook recalled:

> He was trying to reload his rifle. . . . He had the bolt open and I could see the yellow cartridge cases shining in the magazine . . . so I shot him twice with my pistol. But Lieutenant King-Clark didn't think he was killed, didn't think he was dead. There were nervous twitches. . . . So I shot him twice again.

By now the rebels were running in all directions. Wingate, rifle in hand, fought his way through the village itself at the head of a squad. His transport then joined him, including the command truck equipped with a heavyweight wireless set on which "Winner" exuberantly passed on the SNS bag to brigade headquarters in Haifa. The final tally was fourteen rebels killed and two captured for no SNS losses. Battalion sweeps of eight hundred men rarely netted that many.

They also recovered sixteen rifles. Captured weapons were highly prized by both British soldiers and Jewish supernumeraries because the Mandate authorities paid a bounty of four pounds apiece. When they passed through Afula on the way back to Ein Harod, for the first time that anybody could remember Wingate permitted them to stop off at a café and spend some of the bounty money while the bloody bayonet was passed around for inspection.

Wingate had not slept properly for at least twenty-four hours, and his legs wounds had reopened again. But he could not bring himself to

---

*Despite Wingate's enthusiasm for cold steel this appears to have been the only time the bayonet was used by the SNS.

rest. He drove immediately to brigade headquarters at Haifa to report his latest success and hand over documents discovered at Beit Lid indicating that the Arab mayor of Tantura, a fishing port about twenty miles south of Haifa, was allowing gunrunners' caiques to land there from Syria up the coast.

It was a Sunday morning and Major Leslie Wieler, Evetts's brigade major, was having a lie-in when Wingate appeared at his bedroom door looking, not surprisingly, "thoroughly dishevelled." Having told Wieler the joyful news of Beit Lid and informing him that he had deposited the captured rifles in the guardroom, Wingate left to get his leg wounds dressed.

Rebandaged, Wingate reported to Evetts in his married quarters on the slopes of Mount Carmel overlooking the sweep of the Bay of Haifa. While he was explaining the captured documents the stress and lack of sleep of the last forty-eight hours finally overwhelmed him. He collapsed on the brigadier's sofa, where he lay in a semicomatose state all day, occasionally being spoon-fed by a motherly Mrs. Evetts. The next day Wingate personally led a raiding party to Tantura but, to his great rage, a Jewish squadsman shot the mayor dead as he made a run for it and there was no chance to interrogate him.

The Jewish Agency finally sorted out the wrangle with the right wing and provided the wherewithal for the Jewish NCOs' course at Ein Harod. Nearly 120 trainees attended the first and, as it turned out, the only course. It lasted for three weeks and started on 13 September 1938, just as the Czechoslovak Crisis moved to its climax* bringing war in Europe closer than ever.

"You are the first soldiers of the Jewish army," Wingate told the candidates in his halting Hebrew. This turned out to be no more than the truth because many of them went on to achieve high rank in the Israeli army, often after World War II service in British uniform.

But for Wingate personally, the most important outcome of the course would be the remarkable friendship he struck up with a young Jew named Abraham Akavia, who became his official interpreter.

*Britain was about to mobilize its fleet and France its army reserves.

Akavia was born in December 1916 at Kolno near Poland's border with East Prussia, where his father was a wealthy timber merchant. In 1925, after his father's death, his mother brought him to Palestine, where she had Zionist relatives living at Petah Tikvah.

He took a civil engineering degree at Haifa's Institute of Technology and immediately found employment with Haganah translating military texts from English into Hebrew. Since demotic Hebrew was still a new and evolving language this involved coining Hebrew words and phrases for contemporary military items.

None of the NCO trainees had served in the SNS but all had been selected by Haganah because they were considered the brightest and the best of their volunteers. The Jewish SNS members almost instantly began to refer to them as "the college boys." They were divided into squads of twelve each with a British NCO and a translator. Akavia was sent to help the translators by preparing them for the military terms they would encounter in the next day's training program.

Wingate barred his audience from taking notes at his lectures, arguing that it interfered with concentration. It was one of Akavia's tasks to go to Wingate's room every evening and receive a precis of the talk he would deliver at Ein Harod's half-completed theater the next day. Akavia would translate it, cut a stencil, mimeograph and distribute it. Later, following complaints that his predecessor had been embellishing Wingate's lectures, Akavia took over the job. His first translation gave a good indication that Wingate was thinking beyond the kind of guerrilla warfare the SNS were fighting. It was a lecture on "Co-operation between Infantry and Artillery." This was the beginning of a working relationship with Wingate that a few years later would take Akavia on an extraordinary adventure when they campaigned together in a faraway land.

On the second day of the NCOs' course, Wingate's lecture was disrupted when somebody came into the theater to announce that Chaim Sturmann, the taciturn leader of the settlement to whom Wingate had become so close, had just been killed when his car went over one of the rebels' new land mines. Wingate might well have been court-martialed for what happened next. His bodyguard Zvi Brenner gives a vivid description:

He gave out a cry, which was more a scream than an order: "Everyone into the cars!" . . . We grabbed our rifles and within a few seconds were all in the cars. Without any plan of action or any preparation, with Wingate at our head, we entered the Arab part of Beit Shean, which swarmed with gang members, and began to beat and trample anyone in our path. Wingate himself went out of control, entering stores and destroying whatever was in them. An hour later we returned to Ein Harod.

There, Wingate was almost immediately overcome by remorse. It seems that more than shops were broken up. According to Akavia, who was not present, two or three people may have been killed. The next day, after attending Sturmann's funeral, Wingate went back to his podium and started lecturing his disciples on what he called the "morality of punishment."

The irony is considerable. On Sturmann's wreath card Wingate had written, "A great Jew, a friend of the Arabs, who was killed by Arabs."

Sturmann, who died while reconnoitering the site for a new settlement, strongly believed it was quite wrong to inflict collective punishments because, apart from being immoral, they were the best recruiting sergeant the rebels had. Wingate, on the other hand, wanted the villages to become more frightened of the British than they were of the rebels, who often themselves terrorized those they considered uncooperative. He had frequently argued with Sturmann over this.

Wingate would not be the first or last soldier to lose his temper with civilians suspected of shielding the guerrillas who torment them. Compared with the horror of the 347 Vietnamese civilians slaughtered by U.S. conscripts at My Lai or the 14 unarmed Irishmen picked off by British paratroopers at Londonderry, what happened at Beit Shean was a minor affair. More have died over a football match. But Wingate knew that by behaving like one of his avenging Old Testament warriors he had set an awful example. Zvi Brenner tells how he agonized over it:

> The problem of punishment, and in this context the broader problem of the morality of battle, was something which concerned Wingate greatly. On the one hand, he demanded that the innocent not be harmed. On the other hand, he knew that he faced a dilemma: can one observe this rule in a battle against gangs which receive assistance from the residents of the villages?

Wingate had always stressed that the squads must not mistreat Arab prisoners or civilians. Beit Shean seems to be the most glaring example that he did not always practice what he preached. Brenner describes him forcing oil-soaked sand into the mouths of some Arab men suspected of breaching the pipeline.*

Undoubtedly the Beit Shean incident, however much Wingate might have regretted it, marked the crossing of a moral Rubicon by the Night Squads and gave ammunition to their critics within the British army and civil administration. Not that there were any rebukes at the time. On the contrary, Wingate appeared to have got away with it. "Some of the things we did you could not do today because the media would be watching you, it would be on TV," recalled Israel Carmi over half a century later.

Perhaps in direct reprisal for the Beit Shean raid the rebels now committed one of the worst Arab atrocities of the uprising. On 2 October, a couple of days before the Jewish NCOs' course was due to finish, Kawaukji's men raided Kiryat Shmuel, the ancient Jewish quarter of Tiberias on the Sea of Galilee. Eleven of the nineteen Jews they killed there were children. To make matters worse a fresh British infantry battalion, the First Staffords, had just taken up garrison duties in the town and had done virtually nothing to prevent the massacre.

The rebels shrewdly decided to infiltrate the town on a Sunday when they had observed a good many of the British soldiers were usually off duty and unarmed and enjoying the resort's facilities. When the gang produced their hidden weapons and the killing started, some of the bewildered infantry, to whom Palestine had so far seemed reassuringly like a weekend at Blackpool, were seen cowering beneath café tables or behind cinema seats.

The remainder were easily pinned down in the old gray stone Turkish fort where they were quartered, allowing the rest of the gang to go about their butchery. Some of the child victims were stabbed and then tossed into a burning synagogue. Then, having already broken so many of the tenets of their faith, the rebels decided to break another and open their looted liquor. This caused them to linger long enough

---

*Leonard Mosley, Wingate's first biographer who met him as a journalist in the years after Palestine, enlarges the occasion into the summary execution of one of the Arabs concerned for failing to answer questions. There has never been any independent confirmation of this story, and Mosley's very readable book is flawed by irritating errors on things that could easily have been checked. It is possible that Mosley is confusing it with another incident at which Wingate was not present, which is dealt with in the next chapter.

for Wingate, who had squads patrolling nearby, to receive radio reports that all was not well in Tiberias and snap into action.

He placed his main ambush to the northwest of the town where the road switchbacks up the hill as it leaves the Jordan Valley and passes through the village of Lubia. It appears there was also a patrol, or moving ambush as he would prefer to call it, beyond it to catch those rebels who somehow got through the first one and grew careless in their relief. Fuddled with drink and, in some cases, also staggering with the weight of looted furniture, between forty and fifty of the rebels were killed with no losses to the SNS.

Two days later Wingate and Bredin pursued the remnants of the gang to Dabburiya after the keen-eyed Wingate recognized a rebel leader named Naif Zobi traveling in one of two taxis on the road to Nazareth. More rebels were gathered in the vicinity of Dabburiya, the village where Wingate had been wounded, and Mount Tabor behind it. As the squadsmen closed in a rifle duel developed between Bredin and Naif Zobi around the hillside monastery affiliated with the Church of the Transfiguration on Tabor's summit.

It soon became apparent that the squadsmen were outnumbered, and Wingate, who had his radio truck with him, called in the RAF to give them support. This was rather innovative thinking for 1938, when many senior RAF officers, unlike their Luftwaffe equivalents, were still insisting that there was absolutely no tactical role for aircraft on a battlefield. Unfortunately, this incident gave weight to the naysayers. The Hawker Hart biplanes that promptly answered Wingate's call (thanks to King-Clark's interest in aviation SNS relations with the RAF were good) dropped their bombs much closer to Wingate's men than to Naif Zobi, and the surviving rebels were able to escape in the confusion. Nonetheless, the bodies of fourteen "oozlebart" were found. This turned out to be the last time Wingate would lead his Night Squads into battle.

The SNS had been the only British unit to inflict any casualties on the Tiberias raiders. Their success was to have a curious sequel. Visiting Palestine at that time was General Sir Edmund "Tiny" Ironside, governor of Gibraltar and, more important, general officer commanding-designate for all the British troops in the Middle East.

In British army circles, Tiny Ironside was a legend for his intelligence work in South Africa during the Boer War, when he wandered the veldt disguised as a Boer trader.* He had served with distinction in France during World War I and was regarded as almost certainly a future chief of the Imperial General Staff. At six feet four inches, the barrel-chested Ironside was at least ten inches taller than Wingate, but, despite outward appearances, they had quite a lot in common. Both had started their careers in the Royal Artillery and both demonstrated an irascible nature that lived up to that corps' reputation for producing officers who were "proud and prejudiced." Both were accomplished linguists—Ironside is said to have spoken seven languages quite fluently.

The morning after the massacre of the Tiberias Jews, Ironside had visited the town with Brigadier Evetts and been so disgusted by the dismal performance of the Staffordshire regiment that he had sacked its commanding officer on the spot. The general, in a thoroughly foul mood, then departed Tiberias the same way some of the raiders had taken along the switchback road to the west.

Ironside's temper was not improved when he encountered a crumpled-looking captain sporting a perfectly dreadful beard and on his head the kind of awful Wolseley-pattern helmet that Lord Kitchener had favored in the Cape. There were a couple of small trucks parked nearby and the bearded officer seemed to be supervising some equally scruffy-looking soldiers who were struggling to place some heavy objects on them.

Before Brigadier Evetts could introduce them Ironside inquired, "And who are you?"

"I'm Wingate," came the prompt reply.

For the first time the general realized that the "heavy objects" being placed on the trucks were the bodies of Arab males. It was quite obvious who they were because a number of rifles were being thrown in after them.

Years later, Ironside used to tell people that what left a lasting impression was the way Wingate answered him as if his name alone were enough, as if he were already famous. It was not the way captains normally spoke to generals even if they did wear the mauve-and-blue-edged ribbon of the DSO above the left pocket of a grubby shirt.

---

*He was thought to have been the original inspiration for the novelist John Buchan's hero Richard Hannay, the Boer War veteran who solves the mystery of *The Thirty-nine Steps*. In real life this master of disguise was almost given away in South Africa by his faithful terrier, having forgotten to remove the metal plate from his collar that read, "Edmund Ironside, Royal Artillery."

Chapter 9

*I*N EARLY OCTOBER 1938, Wingate applied for and was granted home leave. Two years of exploits with the Night Squads, his wounds during the battle at Dabburiya, the attempt on his life in Haifa, the launching of the NCOs' training school at Ein Harod, and his frequent conflicts with his military superiors had left him drained, physically and mentally. He badly needed a period of rest and relaxation.

It was also almost six months since he had seen Lorna, whose departure from Palestine to avoid the hot weather had also removed the only likely distraction between his formidable concentration and the task at hand. But these were not the only reasons why he wanted to get to London so urgently. Appeasement was in the air. Chamberlain had sold out the Czechs at Munich, and Wingate had no doubt that he and his cabinet were about to do the same to the Jews.

It would probably have been in Wingate's better interests to remain in Palestine and defend his corner in the face of mounting evidence that his superiors wished to be rid of him and the Night Squads, even though events like the massacre at Tiberias showed that the Arab Revolt was rising to new heights of intensity. But Wingate thought he could do more for the Jewish cause at the center of imperial power.

His decision to absent himself astonished his faithful bodyguard Brenner, who asked Wingate why he was leaving Palestine at such a crucial moment. Wingate told him in confidence that he was going in response to a cabled summons from Weizmann in London.

Can this be true? We know that Wingate was always ready to put himself at the beck and call of the supreme Zionist leader, but no documentary evidence of such a summons exists either in the Weizmann Archive in Israel or in Wingate's own papers. More to the point, much as he valued Wingate as a soldier, as a personal friend, and as a passionate pro-Zionist, Weizmann—a shrewd, seasoned, and cautious diplomat—had no great respect for his political and diplomatic skills: Hayedid was altogether too much of a firecracker.

Weizmann had just received a reminder, if he needed one, of Wingate's propensity to combine shrewd analysis with reckless advice. Writing from Palestine, the prominent Zionist Dov Yosef described a conversation in which Wingate said that Weizmann should confront Chamberlain and tell him not to believe he could sell out the Jews as he had the Czechs. "We know now that we cannot trust you any longer," he should say, and walk out.

When Yosef disagreed with Wingate, saying that it would be madness for the Jews to break off relations with the British, Wingate insisted that "your only chance is to act as I suggest."

The vehicle for the British government's next step in the abandonment of its commitment to the Balfour Declaration was to be the report of the Woodhead Commission to which Wingate had supplemented his verbal testimony with a written statement from his hospital bed after he was wounded at Dabburiya. The Woodhead Commission had been set up to work out the practical details of the Peel Commission's recommendations for partition, a formula that the Jews had reluctantly accepted and the Arabs had rejected. In the event, Woodhead was to revise Peel almost beyond recognition.

Wingate had made his usual strong pitch for the Zionist case while claiming disingenuously that as a rule he "scrupulously observed" his obligation as a serving British officer not to take sides. Forestalling any possible accusation of partiality, he had written, "Nowadays people seem to imagine that impartiality means readiness to treat lies and truth the same, readiness to hold white as bad as black and black as good as white. . . . I believe that righteousness exalteth a nation and righteousness does not mean playing off one side against the other while you guard your own interests."

Wingate's homily fell on deaf ears. When the Woodhead report was published on 9 November 1938, the statelet that had been offered to the Jews by Peel had shrunk from one fifth the size of Wales to less than that of an average English county—a coastal strip measuring forty miles by ten.

The sense of shock and betrayal these proposals caused in the Yishuv and throughout international Zionism was compounded by the truly horrible irony that their publication coincided with *Kristall-*

nacht, the notorious "Night of Broken Glass" during which the Nazi leadership unleashed the mob on Jews and Jewish property throughout the Third Reich. Hundreds of synagogues were put to the torch. Thousands of Jews were beaten up, raped, or murdered. Twenty thousand were bundled off to concentration camps. The community was fined one billion marks, then worth some $250 million.

Malcolm MacDonald, the British colonial secretary, had been a pro-Zionist before assuming cabinet responsibility for Palestine. Now the exigencies of office had persuaded him that Britain's interests lay with the Arabs. On 24 October he told Parliament, "The problem of persecuted Jewry must be dealt with outside Palestine."

He paid tribute to the achievements of Jewish settlers in Palestine but argued that the architects of the Balfour Declaration could not have foreseen the present situation. Then, striking a note of pious awe over his feelings for the Holy Land, he recalled how as a child he was "told stories about Nazareth and Galilee, about Jerusalem and Bethlehem where was born the Prince of Peace."

"I always thought the prince of peace was born in Birmingham," the backbench Tory MP Winston Churchill is alleged to have murmured to a colleague. Birmingham was the birthplace of the arch-appeaser, Chamberlain.

Wingate had returned to a London obsessed with the threat of world war and little conscious of the exploits that had won him the DSO in Palestine. He and Lorna rented a furnished flat in central London and, with the assistance of Cousin Rex, set about arranging meetings with the great and the good. Ben-Gurion was also in London, and Wingate met with him and Weizmann to work out a plan of action. They dreamed up a new partition scheme, giving the Jews less territory than Peel but more than Woodhead, and took it to Lord Lloyd, an influential member of the upper house whom Wingate had met some five years before. Although opposed to Zionism, Lloyd was a fair-minded man and scrutinized the plan respectfully, although he balked at the idea of a Jewish army, Wingate's favorite hobbyhorse, as too provocative of Arab opinion.

Trading on the family name, Wingate secured a one-on-one meeting with Malcolm MacDonald. The colonial secretary also listened politely but gave no ground. And in career terms the meeting was definitely not a good move for Wingate. When word of it reached Palestine, as was inevitable, his superiors were outraged at the intervention of so junior an officer in affairs of state. The War Office also heard of it, of course, and Wingate was unofficially warned to desist.

"I have been ordered to shut my mouth and I intend to shut it as noisily as I can," he told Rebecca Sieff, wife of the wealthy British Zionist Israel Sieff, of Marks and Spencer fame.

Wingate also tried without success to influence the media. He secured interviews with Geoffrey Dawson, editor of *The Times,* and Lord Beaverbrook, proprietor of *The Daily Express,* both of them apostles of Chamberlain's appeasement policies and little concerned about Jewish claims to the Holy Land. Both sent him away with a flea in his ear. The only eminent Englishman on whom Wingate's ideas seem to have made a really favorable impression during that hectic autumn in London was one who was already sympathetic to the Zionist cause—the out-of-office Chamberlain-baiter Winston Churchill. Through their Zionist connections Wingate and Lorna were invited to a birthday dinner party for Churchill given by the elegant Anglo-Jewish socialite Venetia Montague. After the last course had been served Mrs. Montague drew Wingate and Churchill together and a discussion ensued on the subject of Palestine.

As always on this topic, Wingate was in vivid form. Dialogue turned into monologue and England's greatest orator listened in silence while the intense young officer lauded the martial qualities of the Jews of Palestine, their achievements in settlement and reclamation, their loyalty to Britain, and their potential value to the British Empire. When a frivolous female guest rashly tried to change the subject, Churchill turned on her—"slowly, like the gun turret of a tank," as Lorna would recall—and shut her up with, "Here is a man who has seen and done and been amid great actions, and when he is telling us about them you had better be quiet."

Shortly after that Wingate received orders to return to Palestine—not to Ein Harod and his Night Squads and NCOs' school, but to intelligence analysis duties at GHQ in Jerusalem. His boss in military intelligence, Wing Commander Ritchie, and the force commander, General Haining, had become "apprehensive of the lines on which the SNS organisation was developing."

The Night Squads' days were numbered. The end of the Czechoslovak Crisis had released massive reinforcements, bringing

Haining's total strength to eighteen infantry battalions. Haining was happy to conclude that the SNS would soon be "surplus to requirements." He put the unit under Lieutenant Bredin and dispersed the headquarters camp at Ein Harod as a prelude to the eventual disbandment of the SNS itself.

Meanwhile, in a tense face-to-face meeting, Ritchie told Wingate he had acted improperly in obtaining an interview with MacDonald. Wingate replied that he had acted in accordance with a higher loyalty—to his conscience. Despite these sharp differences of opinion, Ritchie penned a fair-minded if schoolmasterly official appreciation of Wingate, describing him as "fundamentally an individualist [who] possesses an exceptionally strong character which accounts for his success when working alone but is a handicap to him as a member of a team."

> As an intelligence officer he has many of the most useful qualities; he is a first class linguist, speaks reads and writes Arabic and Hebrew fluently. He has a methodical brain and has shown ability in organising the section of the intelligence branch under his control. His judgment, when not obscured by preconceived ideas, is good and he is capable of very hard work when his interest is engaged, but is inclined to be impatient of control if he does not think his views are being accepted. . . . Usually he is a good mixer, talks well and is interesting company. Although he plays no games he is a good horseman and has a good physique. He keeps himself very fit and has great physical endurance. To sum up, Captain Wingate is an exceptional officer who, provided he finds the correct employment, will make a name for himself.

"Provided he finds the correct employment" seems to be the key phrase here. The decision had surely already been made that Wingate should be transferred out of Palestine. General Haining wrote a postscript endorsing Ritchie's opinions, predicting that in future Wingate would find the opportunity to "make a name for himself" and adding this piece of advice: "In the interests of the Service he must subordinate self at times to the common good."

Having been shown these reports, which he conceded were "scrupulously fair," Wingate nevertheless insisted that his maverick behavior was not due, as he felt Ritchie and Haining had implied, to "personal qualities and personal ambition," but "to a sense of duty." A month later a conference of Eighth Division intelligence officers in Haifa, to which Wingate as a GHQ staff officer was not invited, produced a comment on the Night Squads that, when it crossed his desk a few days later, threw Wingate into a rage.

> The conference [it said] is generally opposed to the dressing up of Jews as British soldiers; in particular, it is considered undesirable to have a proportion of Jews in SNS detachments; these should be entirely British. . . . [I]f it is desired that we should conciliate the Arab, we should not provoke him by using Jews in offensive action against him.

Refused permission to visit division HQ to put the record straight, Wingate wrote to the divisional chief staff officer expressing the indignation of "one who has fought beside 'Jews dressed up as British soldiers' in no less than fifteen engagements with rebels in superior numbers." Men of whatever race or creed who fought bravely under British officers against rebels should not be so described, wrote Wingate. "The statement of fact made in these minutes is untrue, the conclusion is erroneous and the terms employed are improper." Wingate concluded his lengthy memorandum, which recorded in detail the origin, development, and battle experiences of the SNS, with the words, "If we in this country pursue a policy of favouring our enemies at the expense of our friends, what fate may properly await us?"

The divisional commander, Major General Bernard Montgomery,* saw Wingate's memorandum and let him know that he, too, disapproved of the intelligence conference's offensive language. He ordered it to be changed and offered to make what amends he could by recommending certain Jewish SNS men for decorations. Wingate remained unmollified by this minor moral victory. For the next three and a half months he tried in vain to be allowed to return to service in the field, either with his beloved Night Squads or in some other role. The final fate of the SNS remained uneasily in the balance as Bredin, not yet

---

*Later Field Marshal Viscount Montgomery of Alamein who defeated Rommel in North Africa and became Britain's most popular general, though his arrogance and overweening conceit often soured Anglo-American relations.

twenty-two and glorying in his first independent field command, determined to show that they would be as effective under him as they had been under Wingate.

As the nights grew longer and colder in northern Palestine so the war there became more vicious and the restraint Wingate had preached but not always practiced became rarer. The bomb in the Arab market in Haifa, the Tiberias massacre, and the Beit Shean reprisal set the tone. In mid-October SNS troops visited the village of Sila el Daher after a nearby stretch of the pipeline had been breached. Afterward, Haganah intelligence intercepted a message to the grand mufti's representative in Damascus:

> [They] chose three persons as follows: Lufti el Youssef, Mohammed el Youssef and Rashid Ibrahim el Kassem and took them out 30 metres from the village. There they were tied, shot and they are dead.

Among the Mandate's civil administrators the first murmurs against the Night Squads' activities were fast becoming roars of protest, with accusations that the SNS were driving the previously uncommitted into the arms of the rebels. Gawain Bell, a bright young colonial administrator, had known and admired Wingate in the Sudan, where he thought him a refreshing change from most of the army officers he encountered. But when he transferred to Palestine toward the end of 1938 he found the fruits of Wingate's original mind disturbing.

> Wingate's extreme pro-Zionism . . . had caused him I think to go over the top in the way in which he was determined to crush these Arab gangs. He had a great deal of success in doing this . . . but I didn't like what I heard on the Arab side, considerable casualties from time to time . . . led to a feeling of bitterness between the Arab villagers who may or may not have been instrumental in acts of terrorism.

Even if innocents were not being killed, there was considerable distaste for the tactics being employed by the Night Squads, a feeling that training Jews to bushwhack unprepared Arabs was somehow unsporting and demeaning to the Crown. Hugh Foot, a contemporary of Bell's who went on to become Lord Caradon and Britain's last governor of Cyprus, felt that the Night Squads "forfeited our general reputation for fair fighting."

On 11 May Wingate got his marching orders. A message from the War Office assigned him to the post of brigade major with a newly formed Territorial Army anti-aircraft unit headquartered in London. This was not entirely the military backwater it might appear half a century later. In the last months of peace, as the appeasers of Britain and France became increasingly aware that being nice to Herr Hitler had failed, the obsession with air defense reached almost hysterical proportions.

Franco's victory in the recent Spanish civil war had been partly due to the Luftwaffe support Hitler had provided, and the destruction of the Basque town of Guernica had come as an awful warning. In their conquest of Ethiopia the Italian air force had dropped mustard gas on Emperor Haile Selassie's troops. In the war they were fighting in China, the Japanese had ruthlessly bombed Shanghai and Canton, killing thousands of civilians. For the last two years Leslie Hore-Belisha, Britain's dynamic secretary of state for war, who had the unenviable task of trying to upgrade the services after years of neglect, had become obsessed with the danger of air attack.

If war came, would Britain be able to prevent enemy bombers, perhaps laden with poison gas, from reaching its centers of population? Until 1938, when the British army, for years the Cinderella of the three services, at last began to be reequipped, anti-aircraft measures were the only thing successive British governments had been prepared to spend heavily on. Public opinion demanded nothing less.

Hore-Belisha had recently increased the Territorial Army to a war strength of 170,000. But even though there was a growing realization that Britain might once again have to field an army on the continent of Europe, much of the TA was still manning searchlight batteries and anti-aircraft guns. So Wingate had been appointed to what, in the spring of 1939, was the elite arm of his corps. Nonetheless, in an extraordinary display of loyalty to the Zionist cause, he sought Weizmann's advice as to whether he should accept it. Via Jewish Agency headquarters in Jerusalem he sent a cabled message to Weizmann and Shertok, who were in London for an abortive Colonial Office–sponsored roundtable conference: OFFERED IMMEDIATE TRANSFER GOOD STAFF APPOINTMENT IF REFUSE RISK BEING SENT ANYWHERE STOP WILL ACCEPT YOUR VIEWS AS TO ACTION.

One can only conclude from this that if urged to do so Wingate was ready to resign his commission and remain illegally in Palestine to work for the cause. He had already told his friend David Hacohen that he was prepared to take so drastic a step. "The time for self-restraint is past," he reportedly said. "You will have to go underground and I will come with you." Pointing to his DSO ribbon, he added, "This does not matter, nor does my future as a British soldier."

Hacohen showed better sense than Wingate, urging him forcefully to do no such thing. It would be of no benefit either to Zionism or Wingate himself, he said. In the same spirit, Weizmann and Shertok disregarded Wingate's impulsively cabled request for advice.

Before leaving for England, Wingate was allowed to travel to the new SNS headquarters at Kadurie to say good-bye to his men, both British and Jewish. He addressed the general company first in English and then added in Hebrew, "I am sent away from you and the country I love . . . because we are too great friends. They want to hurt me and you. I promise you that I will come back, and if I cannot do it the regular way I shall return as a refugee."

He knew that a British government White Paper setting out future policy on Palestine was due to be published within a few days, and he had good reason to fear the worst. Arriving in Haifa, Wingate went to visit his friends, the Wilenskis. According to Wilenski's wife, he appeared somewhat the worse for drink and was carrying a paper bag containing four bottles of whisky. He handed these to his host and said, "In the next few days you are going to need all the whisky you can get."

The following day, 17 May, the MacDonald White Paper duly appeared. It was disastrous to Zionist interests. All idea of partition had been abandoned; Jewish immigration would be restricted to fifteen thousand a year for five years, then stopped altogether unless the Arabs allowed it to continue; all land transfers from Arabs to Jews would be prohibited; and at the end of five years an undivided Palestine would be granted independence under a two-thirds Arab majority.

That night Wingate attended a gathering at the Wilenskis'. Most of the local Zionist hierarchy—principally senior Haganah officers—were present. What was said at this occasion remains a matter of controversy. According to Wingate's first biographer, the British journalist Leonard Mosley, Wingate told the company, "The time has come to declare war on the English," and—his face pale and eyes burning—he urged them to blow up the strategically vital Haifa oil refinery, offering to lead the operation himself. According to Mosley, the Haganah men gave this sensational proposal short shrift and turned it down, arguing that the eve of war between Britain and Nazi Germany was "no time to embarrass the British, even for the sake of a Jewish state."

Can this story possibly be true? Would a British officer, even one so impulsive and fanatically dedicated to a cause as Wingate, actually propose a treasonable act of such magnitude?

Tony Simonds, who remained a lifelong admirer of Wingate, believed it. "He told me he had done it," he told the authors, "and I think he meant it seriously. He said that something had to be done to wake them [the British government] up." Against this, it must be recorded that Simonds was in advanced old age and uncertain health when he spoke to us, and that his recollection of other events did not always prove reliable. And it was impossible to find other corroboration for the story, which Akavia, Wingate's translator at the NCOs' school, for one, flatly rejects.

Mosley cited no source for his allegation, first made in an article in the *Sunday Express* of 6 March 1954 and repeated in his book *Gideon Goes to War*. Some matters of simple fact, such as the date of the meeting, are clearly mistaken, and others clouded. For instance, was the gathering some kind of Haganah council of war or merely an impromptu farewell dinner in Wingate's honor?

Researching his authorized biography of Wingate in 1956, Christopher Sykes interviewed the Wilenskis (who had meanwhile hebraized their name to Yalan) and one other surviving eyewitness, the retired Israeli chief of staff, General Yaakov Dori, who had been one of Wingate's pupils at the NCOs' school. All three insisted it was a social occasion, not a council of war, and strenuously denied that Wingate made any such proposal. Indeed, Wilenski said that Wingate specifically warned the company against any kind of military action against the British.

"If you ever resort to violence," he reportedly said, "if you kill one British soldier or one British policeman, you may so shock people in England, who think better of you, that you may throw away a great and priceless asset." For her part, Lorna Wingate was unable either to refute or confirm the story, saying she had not been present. Although also not present, other Haganah and Jewish Agency insiders, such as David Hacohen, Chaim Laskov, Israel Carmi, and Moshe Shertok, denied all knowledge of such an incident, telling Sykes they would surely have heard of Wingate's proposal had it been made.

At six decades' distance, in the absence of documentary or persuasive oral evidence, and with all the principals long since deceased, it is impossible to reach a firm verdict on the truth or otherwise of this allegation. But the story seems improbable, even given Wingate's fanatical attachment to the Zionist cause and his taste for hyperbole, plus the evidence that he had been drinking under the stress induced by the White Paper.

After Haifa, there were more farewell parties in Jerusalem before Wingate and Lorna entrained on 26 May for Port Said to board the troopship *Dorsetshire* for home. Once aboard, they learned that, true to the military's traditional talent for mishandling transport arrangements, they might have remained in Palestine a few days longer: the ship was to call at Haifa before proceeding westward. In Haifa once again, Orde and Lorna had time to go ashore and say farewell to members of the Weizmann family, who regarded the Wingates almost as their own: Chaim's brother Chilik, his wife, and his young son Ezer—who was destined to become an RAF fighter pilot, chief of staff of the Israeli air force, Israeli defense minister, and finally president of Israel—and the Zionist leader's aged mother.

She pronounced a blessing on Orde, laying her hands on his head in benediction as he departed, never to live again in the land of his heart and his dreams.

Chapter 10

*A*s THE *Dorsetshire* steamed westward, Wingate shut himself in his cabin and, forgoing the end-of-term social shenanigans of fellow officers and their wives, began writing a twenty-seven-page memorandum that he entitled "Palestine in Imperial Strategy."

This was an extraordinary document, tapped out on a typewriter borrowed from the ship's purser. In it Wingate set out, no less, to change the whole course of British Middle East policy and, in so doing, revealed much of his own complex and contradictory personality. As might be expected, he energetically skewered the prevailing racial prejudice of his day, anti-Semitism. At the same time, however, he displayed rather less generosity of spirit toward the Arabs.

As a rhetorical device, he first summarized the well-known arguments, both overt and concealed, in favor of a pro-Arab strategy:

> We must foster Arab gratitude and co-operation by opposing Jewish settlement and supporting Arab national aspirations, especially in Palestine. . . . The Jews are a peculiar people whom nobody likes, and for this there must be a good reason. Their manner is unpleasant. We do not trust them. . . . They are not a military race. Their fighting value in war would be small. . . . All the cards are in our hands and provided we proceed with proper tact and deliberation we have nothing to fear from the Jews.

Then—after trashing "that unfortunate masterpiece," T. E. Lawrence's *Seven Pillars of Wisdom,* and those "distinguished Britons who found it amusing and convenient to live among and write about the Arabs"—he proceeded to demolish the straw men he had put up:

> The united [economic] strength of all the Arabic speaking communities . . . is equivalent only to that of a fourth class power. . . . The

military potential of the Arab world is very far below that. . . . Any country that was in earnest in its desire to quell the feeble kind of rebellion we have witnessed in Palestine would find little difficulty in doing so. . . . The Arab is lazy ignorant, feckless and, without being particularly cowardly, sees no point in really losing his life.

In another dig at his remote kinsman, Lawrence, Wingate discounted the importance of the Arab Revolt of World War I:

The vanity of the principals plus a great amount of romantic dust has been allowed so far to obscure what really did happen. A ragged horde of at most a few thousand and often only a few hundred Bedouin, paid in gold for approximately two days' fighting per month . . . caused the Turks a certain amount of embarrassment and anxiety. . . . In return for the highly paid assistance of this small rabble of Hedjazi Bedouin, we have handed over to the "Arabs" the whole of Saudi Arabia, and the Yemen, Iraq, Trans-Jordan and Syria. A more absurd transaction has seldom been seen.

As for the "so-called" Arab population of Palestine, they had "fought against us throughout the war until the utter defeat of the Turk made it wise and profitable to desert him." Wingate went on to deny the validity of promises made to the Arabs in World War I by Sir Henry McMahon, Cousin Rex's predecessor as high commissioner in Egypt. "When we turn from the Arab cause to the Jewish, what a contrast!" wrote Wingate:

Instead of the ambiguous letters of a plenipotentiary making promises to unrepresented third parties in the enemy's camp, we have the united war cabinet giving an undertaking [the Balfour Declaration] to a principal. We have the Jews making services to the allies which, however lowly they are rated, must have been many times as valuable as those of the Hedjazi Bedu. Finally, we have the League of Nations granting us the Mandate on condition that our promises to the Jews be fulfilled.

As for the sanctity of Palestine to the Arabs, Wingate asserted Jerusalem to be many times as holy to Christianity and Judaism as to Islam: "Low be it spoken, but the whole claim of Islam even to the Dome of the Rock rests upon a tale that today is regarded as at least as incredible as the Arabian Nights by all but the most fanatical of Moslems." This was a reference to the Muslim belief that the Prophet Muhammad, astride his horse Burak, ascended in a dream to heaven from a spot in Jerusalem that was later enclosed within the Dome of the Rock, Islam's most ancient and beautiful shrine.

Wingate enthused, as usual, about the successes and the potential of the Zionists in Palestine. No one who had not thoroughly inspected their settlements could readily believe the extent of their achievements, he said:

> The natural character of the Jew is that of a creative individualist. He is obstinate, but a tremendous worker, capable of great enthusiasm. All over the world today are homeless Jews with not only excellent natural facilities but also a high degree of training. . . . The industrial potential of the Jews now in Palestine is high. Capital is available if the word is given. The industrial potential of the Jews waiting to come to Palestine is even higher. . . . It will be at once evident what a powerful accession of strength such a development will mean to us. Instead of having in Palestine an army without striking power . . . holding down a despairing Jewish community . . . we would have an army which could be absolutely secure of its base, with excellent facilities for repair and local supply, with an army of technicians ready to hand . . . leaving it free to fight the real enemy.

Wingate summed up by recommending that the 1939 White Paper be shelved ("we can easily have it declared illegal"); that the Mandate should continue, with large-scale Jewish immigration authorized and illegal immigration winked at; that the Jewish development of Palestine should become the cornerstone of imperial policy; that a Jewish army should be raised at once and the Arab rebellion extinguished by the expansion of the Special Night Squads or similar formations throughout Palestine. Such a Jewish state, Wingate concluded, "will of course become a member of the British Commonwealth of Nations."

There was no mention throughout this document of the all-important three-letter word Wingate so often overlooked when considering Middle Eastern policy: oil. Nor, less characteristically, was there a single biblical reference.

When the *Dorsetshire* reached Gibraltar, Wingate took unusual steps to bring his opus to the attention of the highest possible military authority—General Ironside, governor of Gibraltar, commander in chief designate for the Middle East, and at the outbreak of war to become (if only briefly) chief of the Imperial General Staff. The *Dorsetshire* was to stay in port only a few hours and no shore leave was allowed. Ignoring this, Wingate slipped ashore just after dawn, passed unchallenged through the dockyard, and hitched a lift to Government House.

There, with characteristic audacity, he sent up a message to Sir Edmund, who was still in bed, requesting an immediate interview. Ironside had no difficulty recalling the battle-grimed officer in the old-fashioned Wolseley helmet who had given him his name on the heights above Tiberias and sent word that he would meet Wingate in his dressing room. There, Wingate handed over his memorandum and exchanged a little inconsequential chat before returning to the ship, his absence unnoticed.

In London a couple of weeks later Wingate received a letter from Ironside expressing "complete agreement with your paper." The general also agreed with Wingate about "that unfortunate charlatan Lawrence," with whom he had had some dealings in Iraq in 1920—"He was such an impossible creature that I cannot understand how this wretched myth has sprung up around him." Ironside also expressed "the profoundest admiration" for the Night Squads' achievements and said that "to hear that these activities have ceased is sad." He said that if the situation had worsened in the autumn of 1938 he had "made up my mind to arm the Jews and to withdraw most of the troops." About the Jews as a people, he seemed somewhat ambivalent.

> I do not know the Jews, except under the worst conditions of oppression in Russia and Germany, but I must confess that I have been a little frightened of the strength and sincerity of Zionism. To see Jews in such numbers is somewhat terrifying. I must confess that Tel Aviv was an extraordinary experience. I wondered what would happen were the country to become very prosperous—as I am sure it would under the Jews. I wondered if the Jews would not radiate once more from their new home in Palestine back into the world of Gentiles. Would that be good for the British Empire? It is very perplexing.

As Wingate should have known, soldiers do not set policy in the British political system, and Ironside's "complete agreement" with his memorandum counted for nothing. Britain's politico-military Middle East strategy remained unaffected.

———

While on leave in London Wingate received copies of the confidential reports written by his superiors at the conclusion of his service in Palestine. He was outraged. Ritchie alleged that he had carried out his duties "indifferently" and said that despite Wingate's "many exceptional qualities [his] ardent nature often obscures his judgment and distracts his sense of proportion. . . . [H]e has given his sympathy so wholeheartedly to the Jewish cause that his success in the intelligence branch has become valueless."

General Haining concurred:

> The tendency . . . to play for his own ends and likings instead of playing for the side . . . has become so marked, and a matter of such general comment, as to render his services in the Intelligence Branch nugatory and embarrassing. His removal to another sphere of action has been timely.

From the headquarters of his new brigade in Chelsea, Wingate struck back in a formal complaint, accusing Ritchie of bias. "The views he held contrary to my sympathies [have] invalidated his proper appraisement of my qualities," he wrote.

> I left Palestine in the belief that I should not receive an adverse report. . . . I had ample means in Palestine of producing evidence to rebut every adverse comment. . . . Much of the evidence on which I could then lay my hands is not available here.

Requesting that Ritchie's report be withdrawn in favor of one by Brigadier Evetts—"the officer who alone could estimate fully the value of my work"—Wingate stressed that "neither I, nor my wife, nor any member of our families has a drop of Jewish blood in our veins." But, "I am not ashamed to say that I am a real and devoted admirer of the Jews. . . . Had more officers shared my views the rebellion would have come to a speedy conclusion some years ago."

In formal terms Wingate's rebuttal took the form of a Complaint to the Sovereign, in accordance with any officer's right to appeal, under the terms of the Army Act, against an adverse report. This was a serious and solemn proceeding. First his appeal would be considered by the Army Council. Then the council would send its recommendations to the secretary of state for war. After consideration, the secretary would convey the matter to the king himself, with his own recommendations. Wingate put his case for redress in a fifteen-page document, claiming inter alia that in carrying out his duties he had displayed "creative ability; judgment of men, military problems and political realities," and—rather less credibly—"tact."

The matter dragged on for months, while Britain and Germany stood on the brink of war and beyond. Wingate's complaints were relayed to Ritchie and Haining in Jerusalem. They replied to them, point by point. This inspired a further lengthy "annexure" from Wingate to his original memorandum. In October the Army Council decided that his appeal should be denied and advised the war secretary, Leslie Hore-Belisha, accordingly. This meant that unless Hore-Belisha felt otherwise, or Wingate withdrew his appeal, the complaint would have to go before the king. That would put Wingate's army career at great peril, for unless the king found in his favor his commission would be forfeit.

Fortunately for Wingate, Ironside—by now chief of the Imperial General Staff—intervened at this point, with a note to Hore-Belisha commending Wingate's "very valuable qualities" and suggesting that "had [he] been handled better, I think that he might have stopped his supreme crime of favouring the Jews too much." This was a shrewd thrust: Hore-Belisha was himself Jewish. He took Ironside's point that there was "nothing in the report which prevents Captain Wingate being employed for the good of the Army" and that "his merit is thoroughly known" and suggested to the Army Council that Wingate be given the opportunity to drop his appeal.

The Army Council gave Wingate that opportunity, in writing, on Christmas Day 1939. On Ironside's private advice, Wingate wisely agreed to back off and drop his complaint, and the matter was formally closed. As would occur more than once, the career of Wingate the rebel had been saved by an exalted member of the very hierarchy with which he so often found himself at odds. From Cousin Rex through Archibald Wavell to Winston Churchill, the names of his admirers and sponsors were a roll call of the Great and the Good. Orde Wingate may have been an outsider, but he was an insider's outsider, just as the

Zionists themselves, for all their outsider status, had powerful insider connections within the British establishment.

Six decades on, it seems almost bizarre that, with Britain at war with Germany from 3 September 1939, so picayune a matter as the future of a junior officer should have been allowed to occupy even a moment of the Army Council's time. But this was the period of the so-called Phony War (not so phony, of course, for the Poles, who were overrun within days) and an almost eerie atmosphere of "business as usual" prevailed, at least on the surface, in Whitehall.

The feared immediate aerial onslaught against London and the Home Counties did not materialize, so Wingate's duties as brigade major of the Fifty-Sixth Light Anti-Aircraft Brigade, headquartered at Duke of York's Barracks, Chelsea, and later at Sidcup, in Kent, were not particularly demanding. Nor were his material circumstances. Thanks to Lorna's allowance, the couple were able to rent a flat at 49 Hill Street, Mayfair—an address well beyond the salary of a major without private means.

This was close to the Dorchester Hotel in Park Lane, where Weizmann and other Zionist luminaries held weekly court when they were in London. Wingate, still passionately involved in Zionist affairs—and particularly in the campaign to raise a Palestinian Jewish legion as part of the Allied forces—was one of the regulars at these meetings, where he was able to expand his circle of influential acquaintances. These, apart from the indefatigable diarist Baffy Dugdale and her husband, included the likes of Leo Amery, MP, soon to become secretary of state for India; Robert Boothby, MP, a close associate of Winston Churchill's; Victor Cazalet, MP, who as a Territorial Army major also happened to command one of the anti-aircraft batteries in Wingate's brigade; the celebrated historian Professor Lewis Namier; and Walter Monckton, MP, another future cabinet minister.

At about this time Wingate also made the acquaintance of two influential journalists—Frank Owen, who was editor of Lord Beaverbrook's *Evening Standard,* and Michael Foot, the *Standard*'s assistant editor and chief leader writer. Foot, a brilliant left-wing gadfly who was many years later to become leader of the British Labour party, had come to know Wingate through the latter's sister Sybil, herself a Labour party activist on the left wing of the party.

Foot recalls that Wingate "had a kind of mystical belief" that all the failures of prewar British policy in the face of Axis aggression "had to be put right." Such failures of course included Palestine, but also the appeasement of Hitler and Whitehall's inaction over the Spanish civil war and the Italian conquest of Ethiopia, then more commonly known as Abyssinia. Although Palestine and Zionism were his main preoccupation, Wingate spoke passionately on all such issues. "He told us how he intended to have a part in restoring Haile Selassie to his throne, and lo and behold he eventually did just that," said Foot.* "He had a kind of belief, I suppose, that God was guiding him, though he expressed it in an amusing manner. He had a streak of zealotry, but it was also with a sense of humour."

Foot and Owen had two or three all-night talking and drinking sessions with Wingate in Owen's Lincoln's Inn flat. Owen, who was something of a military expert** and employed a stable of top-flight military analysts, including J. F. C. Fuller and Basil Liddell Hart, was particularly impressed by Wingate's innovative ideas on how the war should be conducted. Foot was impressed by his political ideas, unusual for a career officer, and his capacity for alcohol. "Despite his puritanism and his Plymouth Brethren upbringing—they're teetotallers, I believe—Wingate was very good at drinking," Foot recalled. "We sat up all night bibbing red wine and I think we took him to Henekey's [a well-known London bar] once or twice, too. His sister Sybil was a flaming left-wing socialist and I assume that Wingate was something of a socialist too."

During this Phony War period, with the Luftwaffe providing little to keep his anti-aircraft batteries busy, Wingate had free time to devote to the Zionist goal of persuading the British to sanction the creation of a Jewish fighting force, which he hoped to command. The Chamberlain cabinet, including the Jewish war minister Hore-Belisha, had so far been distinctly cool toward Weizmann's offer to raise a Jewish legion, analagous to the Free Polish, Free Czech, and later Free French armies. "Your public-spirited assurances are welcome and will be kept in mind," Chamberlain had notified Weizmann stiffly. The prevailing

---

*Wingate's mother-in-law, Ivy Paterson, also recalled a prediction by Wingate, as early as 1936, that one day he would put Haile Selassie back on the throne.

**Owen subsequently became editor of *SEAC,* a newspaper produced in Delhi for the troops of Southeast Asia Command—a post in which he would once more come into contact with Wingate, not always amicably.

official view at the time was that if the Jews of Palestine wished to fight
the Nazis they should do so as individual members of the British
armed forces. In Palestine, the Haganah—its status always ambiguous—was being treated as a purely illegal organization. And Wingate
had been incensed to learn that forty-three of his Night Squadsmen
and NCO candidates, including Zvi Brenner and Moshe Dayan, had
been arrested for drilling with unauthorized weapons. As Baffy Dugdale recorded in her diary, "Victor [Cazalet] and Wingate beside
themselves with rage."

At their trial, Dayan and his comrades protested that they had been
training solely to defend Palestine against a possible German invasion,
but they were nevertheless sentenced to varying terms of imprisonment in the Crusader fortress at Acre. General Ironside seems to have
been as appalled as Wingate, calling the sentence "savage and stupid"
and telling Weizmann, "The idea of condemning one of Wingate's
boys to imprisonment! They ought to have given him a DSO." But the
wheels of military justice grind slow, and despite Ironside's strictures,
the Haganah men remained prisoners for eighteen months until they
were pardoned* by the anti-Zionist but fair-minded Lord Lloyd, by
then colonial secretary.

David Ben-Gurion, who was one of the Zionist leadership in 1940
London and would become Israel's first prime minister, believed that
the formation of a Jewish army to fight alongside the Allies was "more
than a right; it is a necessity of the moral strategy of this war, which is
waged not merely for national self-interest, but for human justice and
freedom." But Wingate, who wanted passionately to lead such a legion
himself, felt that Ben-Gurion and Weizmann were not pushing the case
vigorously enough and told them so in terms so blunt that he and they
temporarily fell out over it.

When Churchill replaced Chamberlain as prime minister on 10 May
1940, hopes rose among the Zionists. But sympathetic though he was
to their cause, Churchill did not feel he could break ranks with his new
colonial secretary and other cabinet members, who held to the view
that by arming the Jews Britain would make enemies of the Arabs.

---

*On his release, Dayan volunteered to fight alongside the British against the
Vichy French in Syria and received the wound that left him with his trademark eye
patch.

A memorandum headed "Palestine 1940," which Wingate submitted privately to Churchill through the great man's acolyte, Brendan Bracken, perhaps did not help matters. Churchill himself might not have thought so, but some in his entourage felt its language was needlessly provocative. "Our government's policy over the past twenty years of toadying to any and every enemy, eagerly offering as a peace-offering the lives and interests of avowed friends, is still continued," Wingate wrote. "It makes us greatly despised—and disliked."

This document was interpreted by many as a personal attack on the new high commissioner in Palestine, Sir Harold MacMichael. Baffy Dugdale, for one, "was much upset by Vera [Weizmann] blabbing out, before half a dozen people, that Orde Wingate had written eight pages to the PM accusing the High Commissioner of being a Fascist." Mrs. Dugdale added: "Wingate is an able man but an irresponsible lunatic, and I only hope Lewis [Namier] is right in saying that such action will do no harm to anyone but himself."

By this time the war was entering a phase of acute danger for Britain and calamity for France. On the day Churchill assumed office, 10 May, Hitler launched his blitzkrieg against western Europe. Within three weeks his Wehrmacht outflanked France's supposedly impregnable Maginot line, swept through the neutral Netherlands and Belgium and into northern France. The 300,000 strong British Expeditionary Force was forced onto the beaches at Dunkirk, where they destroyed their heavy equipment and, under relentless attack by the Luftwaffe, began their epic evacuation across the Channel. Among these evacuees were two of Wingate's SNS subalterns, Bala Bredin and Rex King-Clark. France's collapse was imminent,* and Britain was threatened by the very real possibility of invasion.

The debacle in France was being partly explained by the presence of hundreds of saboteurs the Germans had infiltrated behind the Anglo-French front lines. These stories were exaggerated but widely believed. The best one had German paratroopers fluttering to earth disguised as nuns. On 1 June 1940, three days before the Dunkirk evacuation ended, Wingate went to the War Office to see General Ironside, whom Churchill had removed as CIGS and put in command of Home

---

*German troops entered Paris on 14 June and France signed an armistice eight days later.

Forces. Wingate proposed the formation of a unit similar to his Special Night Squads. Its task would be to hunt down the sabotage units the Nazis were expected to insert before their main invasion force.

The idea was initially well received. Preliminary arrangements were put in hand for Wingate to command a special guerrilla-type unit of 10 officers and 150 men, all of whom would be drawn from the anti-aircraft brigade he was attached to. At first, it was decided to deploy them in Northern Ireland, where it was feared the Germans might exploit Republican sentiments as they had done farther south in 1916. Wingate flew to Belfast to see the general in charge.

But the plan was quashed by Wingate's old nemesis General Haining, now vice chief of the Imperial General Staff, who for once was perhaps right as far as Wingate was concerned. He feared that if the Germans were not stirring the IRA up Wingate certainly would. "It is not thus that nations win wars," despaired Wingate on his return.

Tiny Ironside came to his rescue.* There had been reports of "fifth columnists" in Lincolnshire, which the general considered a likely area for a German landing. Wingate and his 150 men were posted to Northern Command headquarters at York.

By this time, however, the circumstances of war had changed somewhat and, unknown to him, Wingate's name was being mentioned in connection with a different project, far from the home front. On 10 June, four days before the Germans entered Paris, Mussolini had perpetrated his notorious "stab in the back" by declaring war on France and Britain. "With the courage of a jackal at the heels of a bolder beast of prey, Mussolini has now left his ambush," declared *The New York Times* in an America sounding less neutral by the day.

Determined to grab some of the spoils of victory, one of Mussolini's first acts was to try to expand his colonies in Africa, where Libya in the west and Ethiopia in the east were separated by British controlled Egypt and Sudan. From their strongholds in Ethiopia, Italian forces lunged against the surrounding British colonies, which were all weakly garrisoned. British Somaliland became the first to fall after it was invaded from neighboring Italian Somaliland.

By then the British cabinet was already contemplating operations

---

*This was the last time. A month later Ironside, who was sixty, was sacked as CIC Home Forces and retired with the rank of field marshal.

against the Italians in Abyssinia. First discussions took place in July, when Wingate's name was put forward by Leopold Amery, now secretary of state for India, as the "ideal man" to lead a guerrilla force to operate inside that Axis-occupied African kingdom while regular Allied forces attacked from neighboring British East Africa. Amery saw in Wingate "a much more virile and solidly balanced Lawrence, but with much the same sort of power of inspiring others."

Had he known of it, Wingate would no doubt have been excited by this recommendation, not just because it was an indication that, despite evidence to the contrary, his stock was high in influential circles, but because of his particular concern for the fate of Abyssinia. Despite his previously expressed ambition to help restore Emperor Haile Selassie to his throne, however, Wingate had by this time conceived somewhat different ideas for action against the Italians. Driven by his desire to lead Palestinian Jews into battle, he had devised a plan to command a Jewish long-range desert force in an attack from the south on the Duce's forces in Libya.

This plan, incorporated by Weizmann in a proposal he sent to Churchill on 3 September 1940—exactly a year after Britain had gone to war against Germany—seemed to turn the tide of governmental reluctance to arm the Jews. Ten days later, on Friday the thirteenth, Lord Lloyd and the foreign secretary, Anthony Eden, informed Weizmann that His Majesty's government agreed in principle to the raising of a ten-thousand strong Jewish fighting force in Palestine. "A lucky day. A great day!" Mrs. Dugdale recorded in her diary:

> The walls of Jericho have fallen, fallen! I looked in at the Dorchester and found Chaim just back from his interview, elated and solemn. He said "It is almost as great a day as the Balfour Declaration." Orde Wingate was there, too, radiant. It may be the beginning of a great future for him, too.

The next day, Mrs. Dugdale went to the Wingates' flat, where she found Orde and Namier enthusiastically discussing plans for recruiting, training, and deploying the proposed Jewish fighting force. "[Orde] said without conceit that no-one could carry out these ideas except himself, failing himself General Evetts." But the British had apparently made Weizmann aware that they wanted someone other than Wingate to command the force. Unwilling to provoke a clash with the government just as they were coming around to accepting his proposal, Weizmann was proceeding cautiously. Wingate sensed this and accused the Zionist leader of dragging his feet over setting up an appointment for him to see the new CIGS, General Sir John Dill. "He lost his temper very badly when he thought Chaim had failed to be straightforward with him," wrote Mrs. Dugdale, ". . . and nearly smashed the teacups. Afterwards, he apologised, but he is a most ungovernable character."

Three days later Wingate was summoned to the War Office for his meeting with Dill, expecting that at last he was to fulfill his ambition to lead a Jewish army into battle. For a while they talked at cross-purposes. Then Dill made it clear that Wingate was destined not for Palestine but for Abyssinia. He was to report forthwith to Middle East GHQ in Cairo, where he would receive his orders. And he was not on any account to go to Palestine, either on duty or on leave; his passport was to be endorsed accordingly.

Wingate was dumbfounded. He drove straight to Zionist headquarters in Great Russell Street, Bloomsbury, where he sputtered out his fury and frustration to Weizmann. He begged Weizmann to intervene with Churchill to change his orders. Weizmann said this was impossible and sensibly counseled Wingate to swallow his disappointment and seize the opportunity to win fame and battle honors in Abyssinia.

Wingate refused to be mollified, convinced that Haining and other enemies in the War Office were punishing him by denying him the job he most coveted. The prohibition on his entering Palestine or Transjordan seemed to him to be proof of that and put him into what Mrs. Dugdale described as "an awful state of mind." The truth was that he had been earmarked for the Abyssinian campaign and his appointment endorsed by Wavell, the Middle East commander, before the plan for a Jewish legion ever received serious consideration. Dill told Weizmann as much in a subsequent interview, but Wingate refused to be convinced. His undoubted zeal to see the Italians driven out of Abyssinia was as nothing to his longing to command a Jewish army. Right up to the moment of his leaving for Abyssinia via Cape Town, Cairo, and Khartoum on 19 September, Wingate went on badgering Weizmann to intervene personally with Churchill on his behalf. But Weizmann was determined to keep his powder dry for matters of greater importance, and they parted in anger.

Even after Wingate had gone, Lorna kept up the pressure. As late as January 1941, by which time she was anticipating her husband's return from his Abyssinian adventure, she was criticizing Weizmann for his lack of vigor in the matter, prompting him to reply that while he had "tried my best" the problem was partly due to Orde's "differences with some of the high and mighty." The crux of the problem, he said, was "the real disparity between our views and those of the people with whom we have to deal and who are in control."

> You and Orde are suffering from it, as you put it, for four years. I can boast of fifty years' work, disappointment, frustration and achievement and those fifty years are merely a tiny fraction of the age-long suffering of my people.

Weizmann's exasperation is evident. But he retained a fatherly fondness for this sometimes uncomfortable young couple. "I knew in what spirit [Wingate's] reproaches had been made," he would say. "My wife and I both loved and revered him."

In the event, all the frustration and tension were for naught. Differences within the British cabinet kept the issue of a Jewish fighting force in suspension for nineteen months. Then, within inches of a final agreement, Whitehall put the project on ice. "Our readiness to serve has earned us only rebuffs and humiliations," Weizmann protested to Churchill. ". . . Ten thousand Palestinian Jews have fought in Libya, Abyssinia, Greece, Crete and Syria. But our people are never mentioned; our name is shunned; all contact or co-operation with us is kept dark as if it were compromising. . . . Even in Palestine our people . . . are permitted to serve only under humiliating limitations and conditions."

Perhaps at that point Weizmann thought back to Wingate's headstrong advice in that hectic autumn of 1940, before he left for Abyssinia: "You ought to go into Winston's room and demand a Jewish army. You ought to bang the table!"*

---

*In 1945 a Jewish Brigade, far less than the promised ten thousand men, did eventually go into action with the British army in Italy during the last three months of the war. Included in its ranks were Israel Carmi, Zvi Brenner, and Avraham Akavia. Brenner was badly wounded and never able to walk properly again. Apart from this, as Weizmann said, Palestinian Jews who volunteered on an individual basis saw action in British units all over the world. His son, Michael, was killed flying with the RAF.

Book Three

ETHIOPIA

*Abyssinia was one of the most thrilling cam-
paigns you can imagine, far more so than my
long walk in Burma.*
—ORDE WINGATE

*Wingate should have got a knighthood for what
he did in Ethiopia.*
—WILFRED THESIGER

Chapter 11

KHARTOUM WAS, of course, familiar ground for Wingate,
though no longer the imperial backwater he had known in the
late 1920s and early 1930s. With Italy now an active ally of Nazi Germany, the somnolent Sudanese capital had become the planning
headquarters for a British assault on the centerpiece of the Duce's
"new Roman Empire" in the Horn of Africa—occupied Ethiopia, or
Abyssinia as it was then more commonly called.

Wavell, Britain's farsighted commander in the Middle East, had
begun to think about prising Abyssinia loose from Italy's grasp even before the outbreak of war with Germany and ten months before Mussolini had brought Italy into the war. In August 1939 Wavell had called
an old Abyssinia hand named Dan Sandford out of retirement in England—where he was implausibly employed as secretary of the Guildford Cathedral Appeal Fund—and appointed him his intelligence
adviser on the subject of Haile Selassie's occupied kingdom. And by the
time Wingate arrived in Khartoum on 6 November 1940, Sandford was
already filling the role Wingate had assumed would be his—that of leading a clandestine mission to foment and direct a popular rising against
Italian rule. Wingate's allotted task, rather, was to act as liaison between
British military headquarters, Sandford's Mission 101,* and the emperor, and to supervise the recruitment and training of Abyssinian volunteers, or Patriots as Haile Selassie insisted on designating them.

At the time, headquarters opinion in Cairo and Khartoum was divided on the prospects for taking Abyssinia from the Italians. Wavell
thought of the country as "a plum ripe for the picking," its occupiers
isolated and dispirited, its population rebellious and resentful. But

---

*So named after a type of fuse commonly used in the British army to detonate artillery shells. Sandford was an ex-gunner.

Major General Sir William Platt, commander of the heavily outnumbered British forces in Sudan, believed the Italian grip was too strong and the native population too divided for the fruit to be plucked. Also, he did not like the idea of his command becoming cluttered with young romantics looking for glory as guerrilla heroes. "The curse of this war," he liked to say, "is Lawrence in the last."

Wingate, for all his lack of regard for his distant cousin, had views of his own on that subject, and, after a meeting with the exiled emperor, who was being lodged under the unlikely pseudonym of "Mr. Smith" in a villa near Khartoum, he resolved to visit Sandford as soon as possible at his headquarters on the wild Gojjam plateau, deep inside Abyssinia. Overcoming an innate fear of flying and discarding the idea of parachuting in—not so much because he was afraid but because it would take too long to walk out again—Wingate prevailed on the RAF to land him at his destination. On 20 November, accompanied by Dejazmatch Makonnen Desta, a young Ethiopian of princely blood who spoke a little English, he drove to a landing field at Roseires, about fifty miles from the Abyssinian frontier, to embark on his hazardous flight into the interior.

At first sight his pilot, Flying Officer Reginald Collis, thought that Wingate looked "more like a Baptist missionary than a British Army officer" in his crumpled and ill-fitting tropical uniform and outsize pith helmet of the kind that, as a badge of empire, had long since become a music hall joke. Wingate's preparations for their journey seemed equally risible. Collis had devised a thoroughgoing survival kit for himself and his navigator, Sergeant Frank Bavin-Smith, which included strong walking shoes, jackknives, water bottles, and plenty of ammunition for their service revolvers. All Wingate had brought in case they were forced down was a large piece of cheese, an onion, and an old-fashioned alarm clock with a bell and carrying handle.

The four men clambered aboard the RAF Vickers Vincent, a sturdy but obsolescent single-engine biplane bomber with three open cockpits. Wingate and Desta shared the middle cockpit with Collis solo in front and Bavin-Smith behind with his maps and a Lewis gun. The Vincent had played a useful role keeping unruly elements in order in distant parts of the empire, bombing the Kurds of northern Iraq among others. But the Kurds and other rebellious tribesmen lacked an air force; the Vincent would be easy meat for an Italian interceptor.

Up front, Collis had more immediate concerns. He needed to gain height to get over the nine-thousand-foot escarpment ahead of them, and the lumbering biplane's Bristol Pegasus engine was not noted for its rate of climb. Also, the Vincent was designed to carry three, not four, people. Collis thought of lightening his load by jettisoning Bavin-Smith's radio or, even worse, dumping the sacks of gold coins—fifteen thousand Maria Theresa dollars,* fresh from the imperial mint in Bombay—that they were to deliver to Sandford.

In the end, Collis vaulted over the escarpment using the glider pilot's technique of riding the standing waves of warm air ascending its face. But soon he had another problem: his oil temperature gauge was registering ninety-five degrees centigrade. Reaching for the speaking tube that connected him to the other cockpits he told Wingate what was happening.

> His only comment was that "we have to keep going." Clearly, the problem did not mean much to him and such trivia as a greatly over-heated aero engine was not going to stop him pressing on. . . . I then kept a very close eye on the temperature readings; they rose slowly further to an alarming 97 degrees and then remained constant, prob-ably because we were in cooler air.

Collis would have found Wingate's insouciance in the face of rising oil temperatures and manifest pilot alarm even more surprising had he realized exactly how afraid his passenger was of flying. At a time when few people had flown and routine commercial flights often lurched about the sky in stomach-churning fashion, Wingate definitely pre-ferred horses to aircraft.

Collis was now well inside Italian-occupied territory and hoping that even if the enemy—not yet equipped with radar—saw or heard them, they would imagine that the Vincent was one of their own planes. Through gaps in the cloud Wingate could see the color of earth changing from desert brown to green as, having crossed the es-carpment, they began to fly over the verdant uplands of the Gojjam plateau, stronghold of the Patriots. They had been airborne for a little over two hours when Bavin-Smith notified Collis that they were near-

---

*Despite Rome's attempts to introduce the lire, the Maria Theresa was still com-mon currency in rural Ethiopia.

ing journey's end. Over the district known as Sakala, fissured with chasms and canyons, they began to look out for the smoke signal they had been told to expect. Finally, "a column of smoke rose up from a hillside dead ahead of us. . . . I could see people below jumping about and waving their arms furiously. Clearly, we had arrived!"

The Vincent may have been outdated, but its slow speed and robust frame made it ideal for landing on short stretches of rough ground. Collis made several low passes to get a better view before throttling back and landing. According to his altimeter they were 9,700 feet above sea level.

This plateau, to which Abyssinia's Amhara aristocracy traced its roots, was a part of the country the Italians had never tried to conquer. Rather in the manner of their Roman ancestors confronting the Scots, they had sealed it off with roads and forts—though unlike Hadrian not literally with a wall. The nearest settlement of any note on the map was a huddle of huts called Faguta, where Sandford had established his headquarters.

Collis thought most of their reception party looked straight out of a Hollywood adventure epic—a bunch of noisy, wild-looking tribesmen with leather shields, spears, and the occasional ancient musket. They were led by a big, bearded native warlord, beside whom stood a stocky European, incongruously bald and bespectacled, with a toothbrush moustache, though tanned and hard-muscled for all his fifty-eight years. This was Colonel Sandford.

He was uniquely qualified for his role as Wavell's Abyssinia expert. As a young army officer before World War I, he had fallen in love with this strange, wild country—christianized fifteen hundred years before and the only African nation never to have been colonized by the white man—and had gone on to the army reserve in order to become a British vice consul in Addis Ababa. A decade or so later, having emerged from the war with the scars of one serious wound, two DSOs, and a Légion d'honneur, he had returned to Abyssinia to farm. In the years that followed he had become a friend and confidant of Haile Se-lassie, the "Conquering Lion of Judah," who claimed direct descent from King Solomon's one night of love with the Queen of Sheba. Such was the young emperor's trust in Sandford that he eventually made him a provincial governor. After the Italians invaded in 1935, shred-ding the ragtag Abyssinian army with high explosives and mustard

A handsome family: (left to right, back row) Rachel, Monica, Orde, Sybil, and (front row) father, "Tossie," Granville, mother, and Nigel. Orde appears about sixteen in this picture, and it is difficult to see how a schoolmate could have described him as "rat-like."

The parents:
Col. George Wingate and his
wife, Ethel, raised their children
in the fear of God and "the
sincere milk of the Word."

Wingate the horseman: Although he had no time for team sports or ball games, Wingate was a dashing steeplechaser and an avid rider to hounds.

On leave from the Sudan: The late developer had matured both physically and intellectually and was in search of a cause.

The love he lost: Wingate with Peggy Jelley, the girl he discarded after years of courtship and a formal engagement.

The match he made: Lorna Paterson was barely sixteen when she and Wingate—twice her age— met and fell in love.

*The young bride: Lorna Wingate, photographed the day before
her marriage. There were no wedding photographs.*

PALESTINE

In the Holy Land: Orde and Lorna Wingate by the wall of Jerusalem's Old City.

Mourning and reprisal:
Wingate (Moshe Shertok to his left)
at the funeral of Chaim Sturmann,
whose death he avenged by
the raid on Bet Shean.

Comrades in arms: Zvi Brenner (second from left) with three British Tommies,
members together of Wingate's Special Night Squads.

The bodyguard: Zvi Brenner, appointed Wingate's bodyguard after the Arab rebel leadership put a price on his head.

On the march: One of Wingate's Night Squads returns to base after a nocturnal patrol. Note the variety of uniforms and headgear.

gas, Sandford was forced to flee to Britain, settling in Surrey. There he remained in close contact with the emperor who, despite Britain's appeasement of the Italian aggressor, had set up his exile court in England, close to the ancient spa town of Bath.

By the time Wingate arrived Sandford had been inside Abyssinia for ninety-nine days at the head of a mission comprising seventy Abyssinian Patriots and porters; four British officers, one of them a doctor; and two British signallers equipped with heavy suitcase radios. It was a modest beginning. They were armed only with thirteen Lee-Enfield service rifles, three revolvers, and thirty antiquated single-shot Martini-Henry breechloaders.*

For the first few weeks of his mission Sandford had observed radio silence, maintaining contact with Khartoum by means of typed dispatches, sent by cleft stick and runner through Italian lines to the Sudanese border 150 miles away. Very few messages came back. Sandford's pleas for more money, more rifles, and some show of air power to counter Italian propaganda that Britain was finished were all ignored. The news they were barely able to hear through the static on BBC shortwave bulletins was not exactly morale boosting, either. Every time they tuned in they expected to hear confirmation of a Nazi invasion of Britain. But by the time of Wingate's arrival the Luftwaffe had been defeated in the skies over southeast England and the 1940 invasion scare had evaporated.

And Sandford was beginning to make a little progress of his own. He had made peace between two rival Abyssinian warlords, persuading them to take a public oath to fight the Italians instead of each other. And his number two, Captain Ronnie Critchley (a six-foot-eight Hussar who liked to say that he had joined Sandford's mission because he was too tall to get into his regiment's new tanks), had successfully carried out several long and hazardous reconnaissances of the Gojjam by foot, one of them a trek of ninety miles.

Wingate's arrival itself was an event. Collis's Vincent was the first British aircraft Sandford's Patriots had ever seen and a heartening

---

*An adventurous Australian rancher called Arnold Weinholt, a Boer War veteran and big-game hunter who was an old friend of Sandford's, had tried to bring them more arms. But the weapons were lost when he was murdered by the stark-naked warriors of a xenophobic Stone Age tribe whose capacity to wage war the Italians had advanced a couple of millennia by teaching them to use firearms.

demonstration of outside support. As soon as he had passed on Haile Selassie's greetings to the notables present, Wingate contrived to get Sandford alone to tell him all the good things arising from a visit to Khartoum at the end of October by Anthony Eden, the British secretary of state for war. After three months of neglect, Sandford was delighted to learn that Eden had told Platt to treat the exiled emperor as an asset whose presence in Sudan was no longer to be regarded as a provocation of the Italians.

Wingate told Sandford that the Patriots were to be reinforced with British cadres, known as operational centers, which would normally consist of one British officer and four NCOs, all volunteers. These centers would be equipped with mules and radios and Ethiopian interpreters appointed by Haile Selassie. Working in the name of the emperor, they would stiffen Patriot forces in the Gojjam by providing leadership and fire support with machine guns and mortars. They would have with them detachments of the Sudan Defence Force and regulars of the Ethiopian army who had crossed the southern border as refugees into British-ruled Kenya. Most important of all, as soon as they had established a safe base the emperor was to return, providing a rallying point for his people.

Internal revolt would be coordinated with a major offensive from without. Platt with twenty thousand men, mostly from the British Indian army, would attack from northern Sudan into Eritrea and Tigre province; while a larger force—comprising forty thousand British-officered African troops and twenty-seven thousand white South Africans—would attack from Kenya under Lieutenant General Alan Cunningham. They would still be significantly outnumbered by the men under Mussolini's viceroy, the duke of Aosta. He commanded a force 340,000 strong—a quarter of a million of them Italian-officered *ascari,* or native troops, and the rest Italian grenadiers, carabinieri, and Blackshirt militiamen.

Sandford's mission would be expected to divert as many of these as possible to the Gojjam. Or was it to become Wingate's mission? As in Palestine, Wingate had found a cause he believed in passionately. Indeed, Haile Selassie's claimed descent from Solomon, his title of "Conquering Lion of Judah," and other biblical connections to some extent linked the two causes in Wingate's imagination. Also, Wingate believed that success in Abyssinia would greatly strengthen his case for subsequent command of a Jewish force in the Middle East. So although Sandford outranked him, and had far greater knowledge of the country, Wingate was determined that the Patriot campaign would be run his way; Sandford's role would have to be political rather than military.

Sandford was an amiable man, delighted by Wingate's arrival and pleased to find they were of like mind in admiring Haile Selassie and intent on his early return. Unlike Wingate, Sandford also had the fault of liking to be liked, so at this first meeting they got on well together, even though they had a difference of opinion. Sandford believed that the best and most obvious way of fomenting rebellion was to arm the populace—the more guns the better—and encourage them to get on with it. Wingate thought otherwise. As he would say in his report on the campaign, composed some months later: "To raise a real fighting force you must send in a corps d'elite to do exploits and not peddlers of war material and cash. Appeal to the better nature, not the worse. . . . We can hope that the rare occasional brave man will be stirred to come to us and risk his life to help our cause. This is what is of value to us. All the rest—the rush of the tribesmen, the peasants with billhooks—is bugaboo."

Despite a late night and the consumption of a potent mixture of native *tej* and Scotch whisky, dawn the next day saw Wingate, Collis, and Bavin-Smith preparing for takeoff. At first attempt it became obvious to Collis that even with one passenger less, the ground was too rough for the Vincent to work up enough speed to get airborne. At the end of their improvised runway there was a deep chasm, into which they would surely disappear like a pocketed billiard ball if they were not flying when they reached it.

On the brink of destruction, Collis revved down and stopped. Wingate tapped him on the shoulder and demanded to know why, saying they couldn't possibly remain where they were. Collis taxied back and started a second run and was just about to reach the point of no return again when Wingate suddenly saw sense and called out "Stop—stop!" Collis did so "with alacrity."

> My passenger now muttered words about the Will of God and the perils of flying; and this was followed by asking me what I now intended to do. Well, that made a nice change, the aircraft captain making decisions rather than his passenger.

Collis decided to lighten the Vincent's load by jettisoning everything that was not absolutely necessary and also to smooth the takeoff strip by filling in potholes and removing rocks. They concealed the Vincent under some trees while Collis supervised a Patriot labor force to do the necessary work. Then the pilot set to work with a pipe wrench and adjustable spanner to remove the long-range fuel tank from its bracket beneath the undercarriage. Bavin-Smith's bulky radio was also unbolted and discarded. The rear cockpit Lewis gun was spared, however; it might at least keep an Italian fighter at bay long enough for them to hide in a cloud.

Next morning, Wingate again made his good-byes to Sandford while Collis hand-cranked the Pegasus engine into life and the three of them boarded the Vincent. The precise direction of the improved strip had been marked with strips of white cloth running down the center, and Critchley had agreed to stand with his back to the edge of the chasm waving a colored umbrella to indicate the point at which they should be airborne. Collis cleared the brolly with inches to spare.

Once safely aloft, Collis reduced height to lessen their chances of being spotted by the nearby Italian garrisons. Nearing an enemy airfield at Dangila, Bavin-Smith spotted three CR-42 biplane fighters on the ground with their engines running. Collis took the Vincent even lower, reaching the edge of the escarpment at almost zero feet, "and then slid downhill as fast as I could for the 150 miles back to the comparitive safety of the frontier."

According to Collis, once on the ground at Roseires, Wingate lost no time in telling the area commander, an unnamed colonel, what his transportation requirements would be for the coming campaign: "I want twenty thousand camels and I want them right away." When the astonished colonel pointed out that there were not that many camels in the entire province, Wingate reportedly snapped, "Don't bore me with the difficulties—just get on with the job." Collis and Bavin-Smith* tiptoed out of the room before the colonel could explode at being thus spoken to by a mere major.

Later, at Khartoum, the two flyers' commanding officer, Squadron Leader James Pelley-Fry, could not contain his curiosity and asked this strange army officer who had very nearly lost him a plane and crew,

*They were both decorated for the Gojjam flight.

why he was carrying an alarm clock. "Because wrist watches are no damned good—they never work," replied Wingate.

Before he took the flight to Faguta, Wingate had been in Khartoum for exactly two weeks, arriving there from Cairo by flying boat, which landed on the Nile not far from his accommodation at the Grand Hotel. During that short space of time he had already begun to make himself thoroughly unpopular around Platt's headquarters. "Wingate lost no time in applying his ruthless energy to his new task," commented the senior officer who wrote the British official history of the East African campaign.

At first Wingate had continued to resent the Ethiopian assignment, seeing it as a miserable substitute for what he should be doing, which was leading his Night Squad veterans into battle behind enemy lines in Libya. Despite the sympathy* he had expressed for Haile Selassie and his cause to the left-wing journalist Michael Foot, his sense of victimization, his disgust with all those in authority, consumed him.

But he warmed to his mission on finding that many colonial officials in Khartoum, starting with Governor-General Sir Stewart Symes, who had an Italian wife, frequently exhibited the same sort of prejudice toward the only country in Africa that had never been colonized as his coevals in Palestine had toward the Jews. Symes, who would shortly be replaced, had even delayed Haile Selassie's progress to Khartoum by insisting the emperor's party come no farther south than Wadi Halfa, the first Sudanese town after crossing the Egyptian border.

Most of the resident British administrators reiterated that having anything at all to do with Haile Selassie would only provoke the Italians and make a bad situation worse. They pointed out that on the Libyan-Egyptian border and the Sudanese-Ethiopian border British troops were greatly outnumbered. If Mussolini had the nerve to attack from both directions at once it would be all they could do to avoid being crushed by a gigantic Italian pincer movement whose points

---

*It has been suggested that Wingate met Haile Selassie briefly before the war at an anti-Fascist protest meeting he attended with his sister Sybil in London, but no documentary evidence has surfaced that might confirm this.

would close on Khartoum itself. Some underlined their argument by quoting Count Mazzolini, the Italian ambassador in Cairo,* who in a touching farewell to his Egyptian servants had promised to be back in about two weeks.

Most of the reinforcements Wingate had told Sandford about were still on the high seas or sorting out their kit in South African transit camps. Sudan was virtually defenseless. Its RAF presence was little more than a token gesture, and the Sudan Defence Force was never intended to be more than the gendarmerie Wingate had served in. There was not a single armored vehicle in the entire colony, and the only artillery was a brace of ancient Turkish cannon outside the governor's residence.

But the antipathy displayed toward Haile Selassie was not only because his presence was felt to be a grave provocation. Some of the Sudan Political Service openly admired the funding and energy their Italian counterparts had brought to their colonial enterprise in Ethiopia. Nor was their admiration confined to the splendid roads the Italians had built. They also appreciated the Fascists' efforts to stamp out the Ethiopian bandits' age-old pastime of raiding the Sudan for female slaves.

Furthermore, they could point to Ethiopians who felt the same way. Haile Selassie was a popular monarch, but he had his rivals among the aristocracy, some of whom had put themselves and their followers at the disposal of the Italians. And collaboration had undoubtedly been made easier when the gallant duke of Aosta replaced the treacherous Marshal Rodolfo Graziani, whose crimes were said to include feeding his Ethiopian dinner guests live to the crocodiles in Lake Tana.

Leonard Mosley, a correspondent for Kemsley Newspapers, who came to Khartoum shortly after Haile Selassie, recalled the complacency of the Khartoum establishment with obvious contempt:

> They would regret being conquered but there were many of them who felt that, if conquered they must be, they could not be in better hands. They had a great admiration for the work of the Italian Governor-General in Ethiopia, the Duke of Aosta, and he was known to

*Egypt was nominally independent and did not declare war against Italy. In reality, its defense and foreign affairs were entirely in the hands of the British, who controlled the Suez Canal.

have sent personal, if unofficial, assurance of civilized treatment for the natives of the Sudan if and when the Italians arrived. They sincerely hoped that this atmosphere of goodwill would not be curdled by the presence in their midst of a dethroned Emperor.

The same people saw Haile Selassie, a dapper, bearded little man with the fine-boned features of his race, as a joke figure, an emperor without an empire,* an amusing little wog whom they dubbed "Highly Salacious." Nothing could have been better contrived to arouse Wingate, to dull the ache he felt at being diverted from his true purpose in life, which was to harness the forces of Zion to the British cause.

Once again, just as in Palestine, it was his destiny to rescue potentially valuable allies from the clumsy and prejudiced hands of the "military apes," Wingate's usual description for all superiors who failed to share his vision. Here again was a worthwhile cause, another David against Goliath, about to be squandered by insensitive handling. "He had found an ideal scabbard for his sword," noted Mosley.

While others mocked, Wingate made it his business to take "Mister Smith" very seriously indeed. He visited him regularly in the Pink Palace, a villa in the village of Jebel Aulia about thirty miles south of Khartoum, closely guarded against the possibility that Aosta might send a hired assassin. At their first meeting Wingate found Haile Selassie to be as depressed as only an exiled monarch can be so close to what he believed to be his birthright. He had come to Sudan expecting the British to put an army at his disposal. This may have been naïve so soon after Dunkirk, when everything was in short supply and London's museums were handing over their pikestaffs to the newly raised Home Guard. Nonetheless, the emperor was justified in complaining that little had been done toward making the Patriot campaign a reality.

Wingate told him that the liberation of Ethiopia was "an indispensable part of British war aims" and it was of great importance that the Ethiopians themselves should play their part. This was, of course, the diplomatic thing to say, but Wingate meant every word of it.

*The concept of "empire" in Ethiopia is there because the ancient land is occupied by many different peoples of whom the main groups are the Amharas, who are Coptic Christians, and the Muslim Eritreans and the Tigreans.

I told him . . . that he should take as his motto an ancient proverb found in Gese, "If I am not for myself, who will be for me?" and trust in the justice of his cause. It was vital for Ethiopia's future that the Patriots should fight a successful campaign under their Emperor, and if the aid he had hoped to get from us was not forthcoming, then he must go to war without it.

However, Wingate was determined to see that His Majesty's government honored all its pledges to Haile Selassie and rarely failed to show his displeasure, regardless of rank, if he felt this enthusiasm was not reciprocated.

If he could not get satisfaction in Khartoum he would hitch a ride with the RAF up to General Headquarters Middle East in Cairo and demand satisfaction there. This was not always productive.

"My dear Wingate," wrote a harassed officer on Wavell's staff after one such visit, "I saw Brigadier Barker the other day about your signals personnel . . . the brigadier complained rather bitterly about your 'vague demands' and also that you left grubby bits of paper on his desk while he was out of the room. What the truth of the matter is I do not know but it did not leave him in a very co-operative mood."

On 2 December Wavell presided over a conference in Cairo to discuss the forthcoming offensive in East Africa. Cunningham and Platt were there and so was Wingate, the most junior officer present. Wavell probably knew that the chances of Wingate being seen but not heard were slim and allotted him ten minutes to tell of the rebellion he intended to raise in the Gojjam. He took thirty. Even worse, he strayed into the history and justice of their cause, of ideals as well as ideas, all territory into which British officers rarely trespassed. Wingate lectured the generals that it was vital that the world should see that Britain was being generous as well as just to Ethiopia, that one of the great crimes left unpunished by the Appeasers was about to be dealt with. And he told them how they should address the Ethiopian people:

Fifty-two nations let you down in 1935. That act of aggression led to this war. It shall be the first to be revenged. We are not, as your exploiters the Italians say, merely another imperialism. We offer you freedom and an equal place among nations. But what sort of place will this be if you have had no share in your liberation? Fight under your Emperor against odds.

They must, Wingate said, overcome the Ethiopians' innate suspicion of all white men. And offers of money and second-rate equipment would not be enough. They not only had to fight alongside the Ethiopian but in front of him. "His contact with our young officers must convince him that he had been misinformed, that we were not only brave soldiers but devoted to the cause of his liberties."

Wingate ended his discourse on an even loftier note, moving from Ethiopia to Middle East strategy in general. He suggested that, if they only retained a few troops in Kenya to keep Ethiopia's southern border sealed, the bulk of the forces under Platt and Cunningham would be better employed sweeping the Italians out of North Africa, leaving Ethiopia to him and the emperor. They would "cause the Italian Empire to waste away from within" and oblige Aosta to surrender by May. It was a bravura performance, and even Platt, who had been telling everybody who would listen that the Patriot effort would amount to no more than a "mosquito bite," did not have the heart to interrupt it. Cunningham was particularly impressed. Wavell's views are unrecorded, but, as Wingate's mentor, perhaps it is fair to imagine a certain pride in his protégé.

Five days later Wingate was back in Khartoum. Working with him as a staff officer at headquarters was a Captain Douglas Dodds-Parker of the Grenadier Guards, formerly of the Sudan Political Service. Dodds-Parker, who would become a Tory MP and parliamentary undersecretary, spent much of his time smoothing feathers ruffled near vertical by Wingate.

In one notorious incident over breakfast on the Nile veranda of the Grand Hotel, Wingate accused two young staff officers of being cowards who had found themselves safe jobs. The officers concerned, who were valued and hardworking, declared that they had had quite enough of this sort of thing and would request to be assigned elsewhere. Dodds-Parker told Wingate that, obviously, he would have to do the same because he was doing similar work and therefore these accusations must equally apply to him. "Then Wingate laughed at himself and good humour was restored," wrote Christopher Sykes, his authorized biographer. Whether this laughter included an apology is not made clear.

Dodds-Parker was constantly fulfilling the same function between Wingate and General Platt. The staff at GHQ found Wingate and

Dodds-Parker an odd pair, the one tall and smart, polite and agreeable, the other short, crumpled, and cantankerous. They seemed living proof that opposites sometimes attract.

There was a more logical explanation. Dodds-Parker was the Khartoum representative of a new and very secret organization that was bankrolling all of Wingate and Sandford's efforts in Ethiopia. This was the Special Operations Executive, hurriedly set up with Churchill's backing in July 1940 to organize resistance in the countries that had fallen under enemy occupation. Dodds-Parker worked under an old acquaintance of Wingate's, Terence Airey. The two had first met during Wingate's stint with the Sudan Defence Force when Airey had been serving in Khartoum. Now a colonel, Airey mostly worked out of Cairo, and, like Wavell, he thought that Wingate had talent.

In the empire-building way of Britain's intelligence services, SOE had somehow finessed it so that Wingate's war chest came from its coffers. Abyssinia was, after all, the first country to be formally occupied by an Axis power. But in no way can the extraordinary campaign that was about to unfold in the Gojjam be properly counted as an SOE operation, though they did learn from it. Collis's magnificent flight was SOE's first insertion and pickup by air. In Europe the SOE would eventually have entire squadrons at its disposal.

But Wingate always made it plain that what he had in mind was quite different from the licensed terrorism SOE would practice with its trained assassins and saboteurs. What Wingate preached was regular warfare but behind enemy lines, something he was beginning to call "long-range penetration," and he was very aware of the distinction:

> While it's not denied that great results can be achieved by fifth-column sabotage . . . we are not discussing sabotage here, but something far more effectual; actual war and rebellion on the enemy's lines of communication and in his back areas.

Wingate did play a part in quashing a misconceived attempt by MI6, Britain's secret intelligence service, which was already becoming jealous of SOE, to initiate operations in East Africa. A Lieutenant Colonel Courtenay Brocklehurst, a Kenyan settler who had worked as a game warden, wanted to encourage the mainly Muslim Galla to rise against their traditional overlords, the Coptic Christian Amhara. Both Wingate and Haile Selassie regarded this as an outrageous piece of British meddling in the internal affairs of the country, even proof of Italian allegations that Britain had a secret agenda to add Ethiopia to its empire.

"On sighting a certain Colonel Brocklehurst you will shoot him," Wingate instructed Tony Simonds, his old friend from Jerusalem who was now a staff officer at Wavell's Cairo headquarters. Simonds had agreed to join him on the Ethiopian adventure as long as he could walk rather than parachute into the Gojjam as Wingate had originally suggested. Simonds was frightened of parachuting and didn't mind admitting it. Wavell canceled the Brocklehurst plan to the great relief of Simonds, who was never quite sure when Wingate was joking. But it continued to rankle with Wingate.

Simonds's arrival in Khartoum was important for Wingate's own morale for, despite Dodds-Parker's lubrication, his abrupt and abrasive manner was making him fresh enemies around Platt's headquarters by the day. Another familiar face from Palestine who joined him at about this time was Abraham Akavia, his Haganah translator for the NCOs' course at Ein Harod.

Before leaving England Wingate had received written orders that on no account was he permitted to enter Palestine. His response to this was to get Palestine to come to him. By contacting the Jewish Agency, and by dint of a tremendous amount of string pulling through a sympathetic brigadier at Wavell's headquarters, he got permission to start recruiting Jewish doctors for his force and for the immediate dispatch of Akavia, who had agreed to work as his clerk.

"A clerkless officer is an impotent officer," declared Wingate, an odd remark from the lips of a fighting soldier. Yet it was true that, off the battlefield and even on it, probably the best example of Wingate's ability to think on his feet was demonstrated by the fluency of his dictation. Almost sixty years later Abraham Akavia still remembered it with awe. Ideas, arguments, and reprimands were assembled into lengthy letters and memoranda without any umms and ahhs, indeed with hardly a pause to draw breath. Wingate set great store by this and believed that—"as long as he can dictate"—a staff officer could quadruple his workload providing he had available a competent clerk.

There was another reason he wanted the twenty-four-year-old civil engineer with his self-taught Gregg shorthand. Wingate needed much more than a clerk. He needed somebody who was a combination of personal secretary, a gofer, and an executive officer. In the British army such a person was sometimes found filling a post called brigade major. And though Wingate was not a brigadier but still a major himself, it was now accepted that Wingate not Sandford would be field commander in the Gojjam. Christopher Sykes, who was in Cairo as a captain on Wavell's staff, found this curious acquiescence to Wingate's seizure of command quite typical of the post-Dunkirk mood, which saw at least the temporary deflation of the Blimps.

> The time was an odd one; heroic, generous, irresponsible in one sense, and exaltedly responsible in another. . . . In such a time any man who believed, and could convey his belief that he knew the way out of the disaster into victory, was sure of a respectful hearing, and was more likely than at any other time to obtain a following.

Akavia came to Cairo from Haifa by train and then traveled by riverboat up the Nile to Khartoum. They met at the headquarters Wingate had established in Gordon College,* where his office was as chaotic as the one he had kept at Ein Harod, with a jumble of kit on the floor. Ethiopia, Wingate explained to Akavia, was going to be good for Zionism. If he succeeded there it would further his career, and promotion would put him in a better position to help his friends in Palestine. Meanwhile, there was much to do and not enough time to do it in. As Akavia was taking this in he realized for the first time that among the clutter on the floor was a wooden camel saddle.

This was Akavia's introduction to Wingate's transport problem, something he had started to come to grips with almost as soon as he stepped out of Collis's Vincent at Roseires. Trucks, like everything else, were in short supply in the Sudan. Undoubtedly the most suitable animal transport for Ethiopian mountain trails was the mule. But the Italian army and various Ethiopian *banda* working with them had done a good job of rounding up mules before they could be smuggled to any British expedition forming up across the frontier. Wingate's re-

---

*In Khartoum many buildings and institutions commemorate this God-fearing Victorian general, who was slain by the *mahdi*'s Dervishes. Wingate's cousin Rex, then an intelligence officer, participated in the British revenge at Omdurman in 1898, where an army of medieval fanatics met Kitchener and left eleven thousand dead on the field.

sponse was to use camels, which were plentiful in the Sudan though almost unheard of in the higher parts of Ethiopia. At that moment Captain William Allen, a travel writer and former Tory MP who became Wingate's paymaster, was busy buying camels as fast as he could find them. He had been given permission to acquire up to twenty-five thousand.

By now Wingate had worked out the first stages of his plan of campaign. While Platt attacked from the north and Cunningham from the south he would take the emperor back into his kingdom in a series of staged moves. First they would cross the frontier along the river Dinder and then set up an advanced headquarters on Mount Belaiya, a massif rising six thousand feet off Ethiopia's western lowlands about one hundred miles from the Sudanese border. Reconnaissance indicated that the Italians did not occupy Belaiya and their patrols along the border were infrequent. Once Haile Selassie was safely ensconced there, Wingate, his men, and his camels would find a way up the Gojjam escarpment. As soon as they could they would establish another stronghold for the emperor on the Gojjam, which would serve as a magnet for all the Patriots in the area. The camels would be carrying arms and ammunition and some rations, though it was Wingate's intention to supplement these off the land and with captured Italian supplies.

Meanwhile, Wingate continued his personal guerrilla war with Platt and his staff. Simonds was astonished to find exactly how acrimonious relations had become:

> They didn't like Wingate, they didn't approve of his mission, and even more, they didn't believe it had any chance of success. . . . Indifference, incompetence, apathy . . . it says volumes for Wingate's energy, determination and relentless drive that he surmounted the obstacles and barriers put in his way.

At this time, Simonds was preparing to go to Faguta to take over Mission 101 from Sandford, who in turn was going to join the emperor at Belaiya as his "political adviser." When Wingate discovered his old friend had been supplied for his hazardous journey with three brand-new trucks that had not been broken in properly and were without spare tires, tow ropes, or the shovels and sand tracks necessary to get out of loose sand, he flew into a rage.

That evening General Platt, while seated at a dinner, glanced up to see a red-faced colonel in the Ordnance Corps, the supplier of Simonds's vehicles, being pushed unceremoniously into his presence. Behind him came Wingate who announced, "Here is a traitor—shoot him." Three hours later Simonds was delivered three trucks in good condition "complete with every kind of spare and petrol."

Wingate was impossible and everybody knew it. Whispers of powerful backers made him even more loathed, and they were true. SOE had allotted one million pounds to the campaign, and Dodds-Parker saw that he had an open checkbook. This did not stop Wingate complaining that he had been given nothing but "sick camels and the scum of the cavalry division."

But the rudeness quickly stopped if Wingate sensed somebody was worthwhile. He soon forgave Allen, for being both an Old Etonian and a cavalry officer from an exclusive regiment, the Life Guards, when he learned he was also the author of four travel books and a novel. Nonetheless, there were times when Allen wished that Wingate would not inflict on him a page by page analysis of his current reading: the American historian John Motley's erudite account of sixteenth-century empire building, the *Rise of the Dutch Republic.*

As Christmas 1940 approached, there was an upsurge in British fortunes in the Middle East. On 9 December Wavell gave General Richard O'Connor permission to attack the 250,000 Italians who had invaded Egypt's Western Desert from Libya. O'Connor had no more than 30,000 men under him, but he achieved compete surprise and in a matter of days had pushed the Italians back across the Libyan frontier. An even greater humiliation had been inflicted on Italy by Greece, which Mussolini had invaded in October, expecting it to be a pushover. But the Greeks had first held the Italians, then sent them reeling back into Albania; winter had set in and they were now freezing to death in mountain blizzards.

In Khartoum everybody knew there was going to be a British offensive in Ethiopia: the only question was when. Simonds's idea that he was engaged in a mission of enormous secrecy was knocked sideways from the first day he arrived in Khartoum, when he walked into the bar at the Grand Hotel to be greeted by a crowd of journalists who cheerfully demanded to know what part of Ethiopia he was heading for. Nor was press interest by any means confined to Fleet Street. The romance of restoring an emperor to his throne had particularly caught the imagination of the Americans, who were looking for fresh angles on the war now that the Battle of Britain was over. Among them was Edmund Stevens of *The Christian Science Monitor,* who had made a name for himself covering the Russo-Finnish War and the German invasion of Norway. Stevens already had one advantage over most of his colleagues: he spoke fluent Italian.

It was now six months since Italy had declared war, and the officers and journalists under the propeller fans at the bar of the Grand Hotel, or sitting at the veranda tables watching boats and debris drift down the Nile, were getting impatient. Nor were American reporters the only romantics. William Allen, Wingate's newly appointed camel master, noted the mood:

> Everyone was milling around, talking, listening, hoping and intriguing to get up into Ethiopia. . . . On the one side was what appeared to be the ghastly fate of being detailed to train Ethiopians . . . on the other was the chance of maneuvering for a place with one of the Operational Centres . . . obscure subalterns dreamed of wandering as new Lawrences over the face of Ethiopia.

Upstairs in his room Wingate still liked to shock his guests by receiving them stark naked, sometimes while applying a brush to his body or lashing out at flies with a knotted hand towel. Startled visitors found themselves being mercilessly flogged because an unnoticed insect had sought sanctuary about their person.

One temporary subaltern who was not much seen in the bar at the Grand was Wilfred Thesiger, an Oxford boxing blue whose grandfather, Lord Chelmsford, had broken the power of the Zulus in South Africa. Thesiger had been born in Ethiopia, where his father was consul, attended Haile Selassie's coronation, and like Wingate believed passionately in the emperor's cause. Tall and big boned, he had the lean face of an ascetic. People who did not know him sometimes thought he would look more at home in an Oxford common room. But Thesiger was as tough as nails, a fearless hunter of big game, and already an explorer of Ethiopia's Danakil Desert. Like many of his contemporaries, he had transferred to the Sudan Defence Force from the Sudan Political Service, which considered itself to be the elite of all

Britain's colonial services.* He increasingly preferred the company of primitive people, preferably nomads, to most Englishmen, never drank whisky, and confessed to Tony Simonds that he had reached the age of thirty without ever kissing a woman—something he never felt inclined to remedy. He knew Dan Sandford well and was cooling his heels in Khartoum waiting for Wingate to give him permission to join him.

One day Wingate asked him if he was happy. Thesiger carefully replied that, generally speaking, he was. "I'm not happy," said Wingate, "but I don't think any great man ever is."

Where others saw outrageous egotism, people who got to know Wingate well often detected a sly, straight-faced sense of humor. But there is no doubt that by now Wingate's belief in the righteousness of Haile Selassie's cause was only exceeded by his belief in himself, his overweening sense of destiny. He knew what he was fighting for and loved what he knew. Cromwell was about to be unleashed on Fascist Italy.

On New Year's Eve, while others spent the day celebrating not only the arrival of 1941 but more British successes in Libya, Wingate was dictating to Akavia a two-and-a-half-page letter to a certain Colonel MacLean at GHQ Cairo on the urgency of his requirements:

> Finally, I would like to emphasise that every weapon, every round, every vehicle, gallon of petrol, pound of gelignite, that comes now is going to its destination under the enemy's ribs. The Ethiopian campaign is . . . a matter of hand to mouth improvisation. It is also very much a matter of time. If we push on at all speed the indispensable part of the campaign . . . can be completed by May. This done, in a sense, all is done.

The first casualty was the code name Mission 101. Wingate decided to change it to Gideon Force after his favorite Old Testament warrior. He had wanted to call his Night Squads something similar, but there had been objections. This time there were none. In all, with its Sudanese and Ethiopian battalions and its British operational centers Gideon Force numbered about two thousand men.

---

*It was said they only accepted entrants with first-class degrees from Oxford or Cambridge and a "blue" for representing their university at rugby, boxing, or rowing.

Chapter 12

O N 20 JANUARY 1941 Wingate stood at attention by the side of Haile Selassie as the emperor tugged at the lanyard on a flagstaff planted a few yards inside Ethiopian territory. When he had finished, the royal standard, which shows the Lion of Judah against the national colors of green, yellow, and red, was flying over his kingdom for the first time in almost five years.

As the standard was unfurled Michael Tutton, recently a district officer in Tanganyika and now commanding a company of the Second Ethiopian Battalion, was relieved to hear his company bugler blow a general salute "without a single mistake." The only military training Tutton had ever received had been in Eton's Officer Training Corps (Eton was at least as well represented in Ethiopia as it was at Waterloo) and his experience of honor guards was limited. The rest of his battalion, which was about a thousand strong including six British officers and four sergeants, had already gone ahead with their camel and mule transport to the advance base on the Belaiya massif.

The ceremony took place in a dry riverbed near the camel stop of Um Idla about two hundred miles southeast of Khartoum, where the river Dinder sets the border between Sudan and Ethiopia. The emperor was flown down there from Khartoum with an escort of two Hurricanes of the South African air force and emerged beneath the traditional royal umbrella while his courtiers struggled behind him with the state war drums. Wingate had reservations about these props, feeling that they lent an archaic air to the proceedings, and failing to share the enthusiasm of romantics like Thesiger, who "felt that the sound of the war drums, audible for miles, would have disturbed the Italian garrisons more than the loudspeakers Wingate used for propaganda."

Despite his doubts about the drums and the regal parasol, Wingate had stage-managed the whole affair with due regard for pomp and circumstance, insisting that a proper flagpole be provided—"the Emperor proposes to haul the flag up himself so we don't want anything to go wrong." He also organized press coverage and sent a wireless message to GHQ reminding them to ensure that the journalists "Mosley, Matthews and Monckton" had confirmed seats on the Valencia aircraft going back to Khartoum, from where they would telegraph their dispatches.

It was not a bad color story, though it had to compete on the foreign pages with Franklin D. Roosevelt's inauguration for his third term as president. The crown prince and the duke of Harar—the emperor's adult sons—were both there, uniformed and on horseback. So were Ras Kassa, his cousin, the Dejazamatch Makonnen Tafara Worq, the emperor's secretary, and the *echege,* the chief monk of the Ethiopian Coptic church and second only in rank to its spiritual head, the *abuna.*

Also in attendance were several senior British officers, including Air Chief Marshal Sir Arthur Longmore, the air commander in chief for the Middle East. Around them turbaned Bren gunners from the Frontier Battalion of the Sudan Defence Force, dug into foxholes and their weapons mounted on stands, scanned the sky for any sign of the Italian air force.

As Haile Selassie, who was wearing the uniform of a British officer with an ivory-handled revolver on his belt, saluted the flag a photographer employed by Captain George Steer's propaganda section took his picture. Steer, a former correspondent of *The Times* in Addis Ababa during the Italian invasion, was a confidant of the emperor and editor of the Amharic language news sheet *Banderachin* ("Our Flag"), which had a color print of the Ethiopian flag incorporated in its title.

Wingate had some firm ideas about the line Steer should be taking and objected when he and some other officers wanted the photographer to take a picture of the emperor, a small man, standing on an armored car as he reviewed his troops. "Are we going to have tanks and armoured cars for our battles?" Wingate demanded. "And besides, the Negus'* smallness is symbolic. The battle to be fought here will be like the battle of David and Goliath and David shall triumph."

To which the immaculate Dodds-Parker said that this was all very well, but it would be nice if they could give David some more elastic for

---

*The Amharic title for "emperor."

his slingshot. And it was true that, as Tutton's company brought their sandaled feet together and presented arms, the Ethiopians hardly looked a match for the thirty-five thousand enemy troops British intelligence reckoned they would be up against.

Nonetheless, David and Goliath victories were already being scored against the Italians in Libya, where on 5 January forty thousand of Graziani's troops had surrendered to one-third that number of Australians at Bardia. When, immediately after the ceremony, the emperor and his retinue boarded a convoy of trucks for the journey to Belaiya, the mood was resolute. But their immediate plans were foolhardy: Wingate was determined that the royal progress should be on wheels. It was considered far too risky to send the emperor by air so it was proposed to follow what was known as the "White Route," named after the American corporation that, before the Italian conquest, had been commissioned to survey a road in the area.

This was an example of Wingate at his stubborn worst. He knew that a similar attempt by Simonds in the trucks he had procured from the humbled Ordnance Corps colonel had failed. The vehicles had been sent back, and most of Simonds's journey to take over Sandford's old Mission 101 headquarters at Faguta had been completed on foot or by mule.

Not to be put off by this, Wingate insisted that it was perfectly possible to get trucks through the thick acacia scrub and along the rocky, thorn-spiked, and sunbaked wadis that lay between them and Belaiya. Eventually, toward the end of the campaign, and with a lot of sweated labor on road-making, this was done with a gratifying improvement in the supply situation. But at this stage, Wingate's belief that everything was possible as long as you tried hard enough was to be proved wrong.

Soon after they had left the dusty Muslim border villages and driven through the Shankala Desert region, they began to get into serious trouble. Even the official account of the campaign published the following year by the Ministry of Information, Britain's wartime propaganda arm, made no attempt to disguise the emperor's inauspicious start to the reconquest of his kingdom:

The lorry carrying the Emperor itself rolled over at one point, and on several occasions he and all his lords had to turn out to build stone and bush tracks over the almost impassable dry river beds. Days were passed without water and the heat was very great.

It did not help matters that Wingate was also determined to adhere strictly to compass bearing and cut across country in straight lines as he had done with his Night Squads in Palestine. The essential difference was that Palestine was accurately mapped and Ethiopia only crudely charted—Flying Officer Collis had discovered that the heights of most of its mountain peaks were wrongly recorded.

As it happened, they were in no danger of getting lost, for the trail to Belaiya was blazed in a way those who trod it would never forget—by the reeking carcasses of Wingate's camels.

Unlike the Sudanese, the Ethiopian troops from Tutton's battalion who had gone ahead of them were no good with camels—an animal so unknown to Ethiopians that when they did get among the villages of the Gojjam they were greeted like a traveling circus.

Now started the great camel massacre, which would reach its peak ascending the escarpment to the plateau, where the poor stubborn beasts starved because, deprived of their thorn bushes, they refused to try grass and, malnourished, then caught terminal chills in the thinner, cooler air. For the weakest camels the dying started even earlier. The Ethiopians overloaded them or made them march at the wrong time of day and soon a compass was unnecessary, for the way ahead was signposted by the clatter of vultures and the stench of burst camel. In a single day the emperor's party counted fifty-seven carcasses.

About fifty miles from Belaiya they gave up and sent the trucks back. Mules and horses were provided for them by Tutton's company, who had easily caught up with them though with the loss of thirteen out of forty-eight camels. Tutton watched them move off on the last stretch. Wingate and the emperor were mounted on mules pursued by the *echege,* "with his venerable beard, gallantly padding along on foot through the African bush with his black robes flapping and his prayer book in hand."

Riding an Abyssinian mule, which according to Akavia was no bigger than a Palestinian donkey, astride a wooden saddle under a hot sun often almost eclipsed by clouds of black dust was an uncomfortable business. Later in the campaign Akavia's saddle sores would at least temporarily dismount him. As they approached Belaiya, relations between Wingate and the emperor sometimes showed signs of strain. At one point Wingate forgot himself and urged the little monarch on by giving his mount a firm thwack on its hindquarters. "I hope when we meet my people," snapped the Lion of Judah as he was borne away, "they will know which one of us is their emperor."

Their arrival at Belaiya, exhausted and disheveled, was watched with some glee by Lieutenant Colonel Hugh Boustead, who commanded the Sudan Defence Force's Frontier Battalion. Boustead had not known Wingate long, and he already disliked him. No doubt, this had a lot to do with resentment that Wingate, a mere major with a DSO won in minor skirmishing in Palestine, had somehow become de facto commander of an expedition that should have been Sandford's or even his own. Wingate might have overcome this with tact, but tact was rarely Wingate's way.

It was not that Boustead himself was some stiff-necked Blimp. In a campaign that would involve far more than its share of British eccentrics, he was one of the stars, with a pedigree in adventure that was second to none. His service life had begun as a midshipman in the Royal Navy, but finding that tame and wishing to play a more active part in the First World War, he had deserted his ship in Simonstown to enlist as a private in a South African Scots regiment bound for France. There he had been commissioned in the field, won the Military Cross for bravery, and received the king's pardon for his desertion. After the war he had served for a while in the Gordon Highlanders, fought against the Bolsheviks with the White Russian general Anton Denikin, then participated in Britain's 1924 Everest expedition.

Afterward, he joined the Sudan Defence Force, which he left in the late 1930s to transfer to the Political Service, returning to the army shortly after war was declared. Having spent a few months in England being "polished up" with other reserve officers, he was chosen to command the newly raised Frontier Battalion, an elite unit drawn from the rest of the SDF and including sergeants who had served under Wingate as young soldiers.

Curiously, Wingate does not appear to have met Boustead during his own prewar service with the SDF and it did not help that their first encounter occurred when Wingate received Boustead sitting in his bath, having reluctantly set aside his reading of *Pride and Prejudice*.

Even if Wingate had tried harder, the temperamental gulf between them was enormous: Boustead's fun-loving Cavalier to Wingate's Bible-thumping Roundhead, both exaggerating and flaunting their extremes of character. Like Wingate, Boustead was physically tough despite his forty-six years but he had been in enough hard places to know that any fool can be uncomfortable. Whenever possible he kept a civilized table, with a cloth and decent utensils and a bearer pouring captured Chianti. Wingate frequently ate on the hoof and, according to Thesiger, on one memorable occasion disdained a place at Boustead's table to sit on the ground and tear a boiled chicken apart with his bare hands.

In his book *Guerrilla War in Abyssinia*, which he wrote close to the events, William Allen of the Life Guards, who became Boustead's transport officer, produced thumbnail sketches of both men as he observed them in the field. Allen had a good eye as well as a pen that reveals a sense of historical continuity. He saw in Boustead "that average combination of spirit and of qualities of a certain class of Englishman which we may call greatness and which has made and which maintains the British Empire. . . ."

> To me Hugo Boustead seemed to personify this peculiar English type. Slight, wiry and nervous, he had the quality of the rapier in his character. His looks, his movements, and his mannerisms belonged somehow to the eighteenth century. Put a tricorn hat on that lean, wrinkled face, add a sparse pigtail and a high tight collar and he might have been one of Clive's or Nelson's officers.

Like most of the officers in Gideon Force, Allen appears to have preferred Boustead to Wingate when it came to picking his company around the campfire. But writing before Wingate had reached the height of his fame, when his Ethiopian adventures were not well known, the author nevertheless detected the potential for greatness within him, the coiled spring locked in the modest frame:

> Wingate's tactics, if exhausting to the troops employed, were not extravagant in lives. He never spared his own body . . . he had a thirsty passion for battle as others have for gambling. His pale blue eyes, narrow-set, burned with an insatiable glare. His spare, bony, ugly figure with its crouching gait had the hang of an animal run by hunting yet hungry for the next night's prey. . . . His big nose and shaggy beard could recall, as he proclaimed the glories of Israel, the ghost of some harassed hill prophet; but the bony structure of the face, the thin, high-bridged line of the nose and the gleam of the

deep blue eyes declared some old Norse blood soured through Covenanting centuries.

Thesiger was another of those who preferred Boustead's company and noted that when Wingate joined other officers around a fire in the evening, conversation tended to dry up and people drifted away. But he got on better with Wingate than most people, which, apart from their shared enthusiasm for Haile Selassie, was hardly surprising. Thesiger was only seven years younger, had already spent a lot of his young manhood in mountain and desert, and was physically just as tough. Once he asked Wingate why he was such a fervent supporter of the Zionists. Wingate explained to him that his sympathy for the Jews dated from the bullying he had suffered as a small boy at his prep school, from the solace he found in the Old Testament and from reading about the persecution of Jews and the way they never gave up. In the summer of 1997, almost sixty years after that conversation, Sir Wilfred Thesiger told one of the authors over lunch that in his view Boustead, delightful man though he was, never amounted to much more than a good battalion commander. "He lacked Wingate's vision," he said.

Boustead devoted a lot of his energy to proving just how wrongheaded Wingate could be. He had, for instance, been quite adamant that it was silly to think of building an airfield at Belaiya. When, before the advance party took possession of the massif, a likely patch of greensward had been spotted, he had insisted that the RAF fly him over it and returned triumphant having positively identified it as a bamboo clump that would have been suicide to land on. Yet a suitable place was eventually found and an airfield was laid at Belaiya under the supervision of Major Ted Boyle, a fortyish Kenyan settler. Boyle was one of those whites—and there were many—who thought he knew how to treat Africans. As commanding officer of the Second Ethiopians he had the reputation of a martinet and was not above using his fists on them.

By contrast, Boustead had the highest regard for the mainly Muslim Sudanese under him, who, like himself, were proficient regular soldiers. Despite their small numbers and the lack of heavy weapons, they had been preparing for a possible war with Italy ever since Mussolini invaded Ethiopia in 1935. In short, his battalion were undoubtedly the best troops Wingate had, which made his lack of a good relationship with Boustead even more unfortunate. If anything, his relations were even worse with Boyle, whom he thought inexperienced and unfit for command. Even so, these two battalions were the hard core of Gideon Force—two thousand men versus almost twenty times that number left by Aosta to guard the Gojjam plateau while he dealt with the main British incursions from north and south. It was true that there were also thousands of Patriots running about with a variety of weapons, but Wingate never regarded them as serious military allies. Their main value to him was that, as long as they believed that the emperor was winning, he could be certain that Gideon Force would exist within the embrace of a friendly populace. They would ensure that they never starved and that the enemy never surprised them.

In addition, the first of the operational centers were in action. Simonds and the five tough Australian gunners* who made up Number One Operational Centre had already gone beyond Belaiya and ascended the escarpment to the green expanses of the Gojjam plateau. The Australians were now directing Patriots in operations in Beghemder Province to the north of Lake Tana.

Another brigandish crew already engaging the enemy was commanded by an aristocratic Coldstream Guards officer, Viscount Arthur Bentinck. After being lamed by a leg wound in the First World War, Bentinck, who came from a prominent Kenyan settler family, had served under Thesiger's father as vice consul in Addis Ababa and learned Amharic. Aged about sixty, he had persuaded Sandford, who was in no position to hold his age against him, to give him a job and soon established an independent command known as Mission 101 North. Accompanied by a band of twenty-five Ethiopian Patriots, six Yemeni mercenaries, and four Sudanese soldiers, Bentinck had last been sighted limping off into the bandit country of the Gondar region bent on persuading its unruly residents to put aside their cherished feuds and wage war against the Italians.

Commanding Number Five Operational Centre was a South African–born captain in the Rifle Brigade named Laurens van der

---

*These Australians had wanted to get involved in Ethiopia even before the call went out for volunteers, having encountered an Ethiopian priest while sightseeing in Jerusalem's Old City who moved them with an account of the plight of his country.

Post, a practicing Christian whose father had fought the British in the Boer War. Van der Post, who would later survive Japanese captivity to become a writer of popular philosophy and ultimately personal guru to Prince Charles, commanded the only center to get all its camels from the Sudanese border to the Gojjam plateau without losing a single beast. Other centers were still training their Patriot volunteers in the Sudan, and some of these were not ready in time to see any action. Some, like Bentinck, would never come directly under Wingate's command. And Platt himself, despite his earlier objections to irregular warfare, poached some centers to operate behind the lines of the Italians he was facing in Eritrea.

On 10 February, as Haile Selassie began to recover from the rigors of his trek in one of the underground bomb shelters that had been prepared for him, Wingate left Belaiya from Boyle's new airstrip and was back in Khartoum a couple of hours later. Such was Wingate's impatience to get the emperor back onto Ethiopian soil that it never seemed to occur to him that, after almost five years away, the fifty-year-old monarch probably would not have minded waiting another two or three weeks and being flown to Belaiya in reasonable comfort.

But Wingate never could abide delay, and when they raised the flag at Umm Idla nobody was sure whether it was feasible to construct an airfield at Belaiya. Boustead's discouraging report had certainly not helped matters. As it was, the first RAF pilot sent to collect Wingate gave up after two attempts to find the landing ground, which was at the foot of the massif. It was Flying Officer Collis, the hero of Faguta, who brought him out.

Wingate found that morale had never been higher at Platt's headquarters. In Libya the number of prisoners taken now totaled about 130,000, and O'Connor's armor continued to advance. Things were going so well that Wavell had pulled out the Fourth Indian Division and given it to Platt, who had already ventured well into Eritrea but had now come up against formidable Italian defenses in the Keren Mountains. Rome had ordered a reluctant General Luigi Frusci, the commander in Eritrea, to withdraw from the plain and make his stand at Keren. By doing so it was hoped that he would entice British troops into a protracted battle and prevent them being sent to Libya, where it was feared that all the Italian settlement along the old Phoenician coast, including the colonial capital of Tripoli, would soon fall.

The British knew this because of a more clandestine victory than the one celebrated in newspaper photographs of the acres of prisoners being harvested in the North African desert. The secret Code and Cypher School at Bletchley Park in England had cracked the Italian army's high-grade cipher in East Africa. Bletchley, whose decrypted treasures would eventually be sourced to the cover name ULTRA,* had outstations in Cairo and Nairobi. They were reading all the wireless traffic between Aosta and Frusci. Once he was certain of the Italian plans, Wavell gambled on reinforcing Platt in the hope that an immediate investment in East Africa of his limited resources would result in a swift victory and the opportunity to concentrate all his assets in Libya for a final push that would drive the Italians out of Africa altogether.

In this heady atmosphere Wingate had some personal good fortune to celebrate. It was officially confirmed that he had been promoted to the rank of acting colonel and made commander of British and Ethiopian forces in the Gojjam. Sandford had been given the rank of brigadier and made the emperor's political adviser. In theory at least, he was to have no more say in military affairs, and it was now up to Wingate to raise what hell he could in the Gojjam in the name of the emperor.

Intelligence, most of it probably provided by the Bletchley intercepts, had already given Wingate a good idea of what he was up against. His opponent was General Guglielmo Nasi, who commanded in the Gojjam and was reckoned to be one of the better Italian generals—he had taken part in the original invasion in 1936. Nasi's forces now outnumbered Wingate's by thirty-seven thousand men to about three thousand—that was assuming Gideon Force could rely on keeping one thousand Patriots in the field. Otherwise Gideon Force had a ration strength of about two thousand.

Apart from odds in the Italians' favor, they possessed some forty artillery pieces of various calibers, mortars, fifteen armored cars, and regular local air support from about ten bombers and six fighters. Gideon Force had four locally made mortars without range calibrators, no artillery, no armored cars, and the RAF had already warned them that

---

*ULTRA's main meat was the decryption of intercepted German messages enciphered by ENIGMA machines, which the Germans thought unbreakable.

while they would do their best their main task would be supporting
Platt's and Cunningham's divisions.

Nor were the Italians entirely without friends in the Gojjam. In December, Aosta had shrewdly restored Ras Hailu, a septuagenarian aristocrat who had long been a rival of Haile Selassie, as governor of
Gojjam. Despite the news of the emperor's return there were reports
that many of the Gojjam peasantry were visiting Debra Markos, the
provincial capital, to pay homage to Ras Hailu. Aosta had also allowed
the old collaborator to raise a militia, or *banda* as they were known, of
about fifteen hundred men. It looked like the Ethiopians might be
going into a civil war.

For Abraham Akavia the Ethiopian campaign began, gently enough,
on 14 February 1941 when Wingate returned to Belaiya with him in a
Wellesley bomber. There had been a last-minute hitch about a civilian
clerk accompanying an officer behind enemy lines, but Colonel Airey,
Dodds-Parker's SOE boss from Cairo, was visiting Khartoum and
when he saw how desperately Akavia wanted to go he smoothed things
over.

It was Akavia's first flight. He sat behind the pilot in the seat normally occupied by the navigator or aerial photographer while Wingate
occupied the rear gunner's position behind him. The engine was
much too noisy to talk over. When they flew over landmarks of interest
such as the Silwar Dam on the Blue Nile Wingate passed him notes.

The Wellesley, successor to the Vincent, was a single-engine monoplane with covered cockpits that had broken a world record for long-
distance flying in 1938. As a warplane it was less successful, being not
all that much faster than the Vincent and unable to carry as many
bombs. Space was cramped. The only way Akavia could look out was
through a Perspex cover in the floor of his cockpit, and every spare
nook and cranny on the Wellesley was either occupied by bundles of
the latest issue of Steer's *Banderachin* showing pictures of the emperor at the flag-raising ceremony or various items of kit Akavia had
been procuring for Wingate and himself in Khartoum. Among his pur-
chases was a wristwatch Akavia had bought to replace Wingate's em-
barrassing alarm clock.

SOE allowances were generous, and Akavia had been entitled to buy a tent and a folding camp table and chairs, but there was not enough room to stow them in the Wellesley. In any case, Wingate despised such comforts, so Akavia made do with sleeping bags and a few cooking utensils. He was also advised that the only warm clothing he needed was a raincoat and not to bother with a heavy overcoat. He came to regret this for, as soon as the sun goes down, the Gojjam plateau can get very cold, and Gideon Force would do much of its work in the dark.

Their pilot got lost and took four and a half hours instead of three to find the landing ground at Belaiya. Until then, Collis had been the only one to make a successful landing there. They stayed for one night and dined on *durra,* the Ethiopians' maize porridge, which, Akavia confided to the campaign diary he was keeping, "looks (and tastes) like earth."

After dinner Akavia took notes at Wingate's first "Orders Group" conference for the officers still at Belaiya. Among those present were Boustead, Bimbashi (Major) Peter Acland, his forty-year-old number two, and Major Donald Nott, a regular from the Worcestershire Regiment who had been in Palestine at the same time as Wingate. Nott had left a safe staff job among the "Gabardine Swine"* in Cairo to join what he called Sandford's "Scallywag Show" as quartermaster, though he was hoping for a more active role. The Orders Group was the first indication of what a firm grasp the commander of Gideon Force already had of Italian intentions and, being an intelligent young man, Akavia soon concluded that the British must be able to read coded Italian radio traffic. The names and pecking order of the enemy commanders were as familiar to them as their own.

Wingate explained that the Italians were continuing to remove themselves from any garrison that could be easily isolated so that they could concentrate their forces and make various strategic points very hard nuts to crack. It was for this reason that Colonel Adriano Torelli, a First World War veteran in his early fifties, had moved from Dangila—which had been bombed by the RAF in one of their rare excursions over the Gojjam—to Bahar Dar on the shore of Lake Tana. There were now two other enemy garrisons in the Gojjam—at Burye and

---

*So called because Egypt's better tailors specialized in running up officers' uniforms in this material.

Debra Markos, the provincial capital—with smaller forts on the hill-tops around them, rather in the way medieval barons protected their estates.

These garrisons were under the command of one Colonel Leopoldo Natale, who had been told by General Guglielmo Nasi, overall commander of the Gojjam region, on no account to withdraw from them. Nasi realized that it was imperative to demonstrate Italian determination lest their Ethiopian supporters, especially the *banda* loyal to Ras Hailu, went over to the emperor.

It was Wingate's objective to cut the road between Debra Markos and Addis Ababa, isolate the Gojjam from the rest of Ethiopia, besiege the garrisons, and force them to surrender. Wingate told his officers, whenever possible, to avoid attacks against Eritrean and other native troops. "It is my intention to undermine the Italian morale by delivering attacks at night against Italian nationals whenever possible." However, officers were to prevent "outrages" against Italian prisoners.

Wingate and Akavia left Belaiya in the late afternoon of Saturday, 15 February. They had with them a caravan of nine camels and one horse and were escorted by ten men of the Sudan Defence Force under Oubashi (Corporal) Jawanil, who gave Akavia his one and only lesson in the art of camel riding. It occurred to Wingate that although Akavia was a civilian it was improper for him to go unarmed. So he loaned him his service revolver, a .38 Enfield, which Akavia was to carry for the rest of the campaign—an act that was to have crucial and quite unexpected consequences. Wingate himself carried a rifle and sometimes grenades, which he used whenever he had the opportunity.

The first night they camped not far from Belaiya. It was cold and Wingate gave Akavia his winter service dress trousers to sleep in, which he continued to use as pajamas for the rest of the campaign. Next day they went through some thick clumps of bamboo, and much to the disappointment of Akavia, who could still hardly believe the adventure he was having, they did not spot any elephants. Still, there was plenty of other game about, including zebras, giraffes, and gazelle. They followed the Belese River against its flow as it came down from the escarpment and made their camp among some trees on its bank. That night it was both cold and damp, and they huddled around their fire, eating tinned fish and hardtack from their ration boxes, washed down with hot tea.

For the first time Wingate began to tell Akavia something of himself and his upbringing, the taut childhood Sundays with readings from the Old Testament and brawn instead of a roast joint on the table because his father donated so much of his army pension to missionary funds. And against a chorus of digestive rumbles from the aloof and recumbent camels, Akavia found himself listening to Wingate reciting all of Psalm 126—from memory and in Hebrew: "When the Lord restored the fortunes of Zion, we were like those who dream. . . ."

The next afternoon, they reached the Second Ethiopians' forward camp at the foot of the escarpment, which Major Boyle and most of his officers had now moved up to. Here their escort was expanded with the addition of about thirty of Boyle's Ethiopians. Wingate and some of the escort, including an Ethiopian cadet officer who was acting as his interpreter, went on ahead, and Akavia followed with the camels and their Sudanese minders. Strung out behind them, between Belaiya and the escarpment, were the main elements of the SDF Frontier Battalion and the remainder of the Second Ethiopians plus some more British officers and NCOs of the operational centers that were gradually coming on stream. The camel caravans moved at an average speed of about two miles an hour and stretched for miles, looking like a whole army on the move rather than a couple of battalions, although mercifully hard to bomb from the air because in the parched land before the escarpment the camels' beige-colored hides provided a natural camouflage. But if they were hard to spot, they were easy to stampede and could take a long time to round up.

Soon, Italian agents were picking up gossip of a very large British force heading their way. General Nasi's intelligence staff estimated that they were at the very least facing two regular British brigades with artillery support—a comical overestimate, being at least seven thousand more men than Wingate had at his disposal. As for artillery, Gideon Force was the proud possessor of four mortar tubes, courtesy of the Sudan Railways maintenance workshops.

Akavia's nine camels were the first to reach the top of the escarpment—probably the first ever, judging by the reaction of the first villagers they encountered on the plateau with its tall elephant grass, lowing cattle, and clusters of *tukuls,* the round grass and reed huts of the Amhara.

For Wingate this was a moment of vindication, for without camels he would have been without transport.

As Gideon Force straggled in, and the first curious Patriots came to inquire whether it was true the emperor was close by, Wingate dictated to Akavia an order of the day for his British personnel. It was short and although its inspiration might have been Churchill's admission that he had nothing to offer the British nation but "blood, toil, tears and sweat," it was pure Wingate:

The comforts which we now lack and the supplies which we need are in possession of our enemies. It is my intention to wrest them from him by a bold stroke which will demand all your energies and all your devotion. I expect that every officer and man will put his courage and endurance to the severest tests during the coming decisive weeks.

Chapter 13

After all Mussolini's bombast, Wingate, along with most British soldiers in the Middle East, had expected that the Italian army would be a formidable fighting machine second only to the Germans. General O'Connor's stunning victories in Libya had changed all that.

Over half a century later even the grandchildren of the generation of British and Commonwealth soldiers who fought them will recite jokes about the number of reverse gears to be found in Italian tanks. Wingate himself was the first to admit that, if he had directed a similar campaign against the Germans, it would have proved "a very different matter."

As it happened, the men Gideon Force were about to take on were generally of a much higher caliber than the Italian troops in Libya. There the enemy were mostly disillusioned Italian conscripts. One of the reasons they were disillusioned was because their tanks were even less battleworthy than the undergunned British armor.*

In Ethiopia it was a different story. For the first weeks of the campaign the Italians had air superiority, and in most places the terrain made it impossible for Platt and Cunningham to make much use of their few tanks. As for Wingate's command, the kind of nineteenth-century punitive expedition his father might have led would probably have had more firepower. Moreover, the Italian national units—the Savoia Grenadiers, the ardent Fascists in the Black Shirt battalions, and the fighting gendarmes of the carabinieri—could be resolute and formidable opponents. In the mountains of Keren they made Platt's troops bleed for every yard gained and held up his advance for almost two months.

---

*Not until 1942 when the Americans gave them Shermans did the British really possess a tank capable of taking on Rommel's panzers in the desert.

But undoubtedly the most outstanding Italian soldiers were the officers and sergeants in the colonial battalions where the rank and file were Ethiopian—Eritrean, Amhara, or Tigrean. These men seem to have found themselves in the same somewhat challenging position of British officers in Gurkha regiments, where the routine courage of their men demanded the highest standards of leadership. Officers who led from anywhere but the front lost all respect and those who commanded Mussolini's colonial battalions sometimes displayed an upright gallantry rarely glimpsed on the battlefield since the American Civil War—and often paid the inevitable price. It is true they were rarely as professional as the Germans. But nor were the British most of the time.

The Italian plan in Ethiopia was to hold Eritrea on the coast, Gondar in the north, and Gojjam between them in the center until such time as the British were pushed out of Libya and needed the men they had in East Africa to shore up their defenses in Egypt again. Nor, by the time Wingate got Gideon Force onto the plateau and started his operations, did this seem so fanciful. Hitler had decided that the British could no longer be allowed to humiliate his Fascist partner. A few days before, on 12 February 1941, German armored units had begun to arrive in Libya under the command of a panzer general named Erwin Rommel. Soon Africa Orientale Italiana would not seem such a lost cause.

One of Wingate's first acts was to visit Simonds at the old Mission 101 headquarters at Faguta. He set off with an Ethiopian guide, both mounted on mules. Akavia, with another guide and also on muleback, followed him. On his solar topee the clerk had pinned a paper Ethiopian flag torn from a copy of *Banderachin,* for he was understandably anxious not to be mistaken for one of the Italian occupiers. The Ethiopian peasantry were almost invariably armed even if it was only with a copper-studded leather shield and a spear.

Akavia greeted them all with *"Ingliz"* and *"Tena yistaliyie,"* which meant "May you be given health in response to my prayers." This was met with great delight, and he later discovered that, in this very hierarchical society, it was a greeting used only to those of superior rank and, coming from a European, truly astonishing. There was more than an air of Don Quixote and Sancho Panza about the travels in Ethiopia of Orde Wingate and his faithful clerk.

As Akavia soon learned, he had little reason to be nervous. Although the *banda* of the renegade aristocrat Ras Hailu did make occasional punitive sorties, the days when individual Italians would wander about the Gojjam had long gone, if they ever existed. And, as it was intended, news of the emperor's arrival supported by British troops had spread. As far as the Italians were concerned it was a rough neighborhood and the only way they would leave their forts was in very large numbers.

Simonds was supposed to have Patriot sentries around his camp at Faguta, but they tended to take their duties lightly. Wingate entered like a ghost and took Simonds by surprise.

> I was lying, rather tired, on a "bank" by my "office"—when I suddenly felt a brooding and sinister influence. I looked up to see Wingate squatting beside me.

His unchallenged entry put Wingate in a filthy mood, and he and Simonds, who had recently returned from an abortive attack on an Italian fort, had a stand-up row about it. Wingate decided that Simonds's command, which included Thesiger and a notional control of the Australians of Number One Operational Centre, was slack. The next person he rounded on was one of the other members of the British team, Staff Sergeant George Grey, the incredibly hard-working Signals NCO whose formidable workload, a round-the-clock business of sending and receiving Morse messages between Faguta and Khartoum then enciphering and deciphering by candlelight, had doubled because his corporal assistant had become quite seriously ill.

Grey's response was dramatic. He collapsed and went blind. For two days, "a remorseful Wingate," according to Simonds, helped to nurse him so that his sight partially returned. Grey was then evacuated by mule and camel to the Belaiya airstrip and flown out to Khartoum for two weeks' rest before returning to Ethiopia, where he continued to serve with distinction.*

Wingate closed down the Faguta camp and went off to an abandoned Italian fort at Engiabara, where Simonds joined him the next day, not without incident, for his native mules took one look at the

---

*Grey was commissioned in the field, in the British army the best way to cross the chasm between NCO and officer, and retired with the rank of lieutenant colonel.

camels Gideon Force had gathered there and bolted at the sight. Simonds, who was tired and still full of resentment over Wingate's tantrum at Faguta, had another row with his commanding officer, whose epaulettes now carried the crown and two pips of a full colonel, albeit a temporary one.

But Wingate counted few men as close friends, and those he did he remained loyal to. Simonds was given another independent command, which became known as Beghemder Force after the northern province it operated in. Originally, it consisted of four Northern Irish Territorial Army artillery sergeants (one of whom Simonds would recommend for a posthumous VC), the tough Canadian-Scot lieutenant who commanded them, about one hundred Sudanese detached from Boustead's battalion, and some Patriots who varied in number according to distraction. Later it would be reinforced with another operational center of one British officer and four NCOs, who turned out to be of dismal quality.

Wingate gave Beghemder Force two main tasks. The first was to protect his northern flank and spoil any chance of Colonel Torelli falling on him from his new base at Bahr Dar on the southern shore of Lake Tana. The second, which was afterward thought to be quite inspired and an example of Wingate's ability to think strategically well ahead of events, was to block all northern exits and trap thirty-seven thousand enemy troops who could have been used elsewhere. Meanwhile, Wingate had to persuade the Italians in the Gojjam that his tiny force was at least as big as anything they could deploy, if not bigger.

> I would divide my force into two parts, in the proportion of one to three. The weaker force should contain the Northern Italian force until reinforced and strong enough to go out and cut the Dessye-Gondar road. [This was Simonds's Beghemder Force.] The stronger force, under my own command, I would direct upon the Nile bridge at Safartak, thus cutting the enemy's retreat, and then proceed by a process of night attack plus fifth column penetration to reduce the various garrisons.

It was a good plan, easy to understand. You could grab a stick and mark it out in the dust: seize the vital bridge (Safartak), cut the enemy off from his capital (Addis Ababa), dispatch part of your force to block and distract the most likely source of any relief column coming to his rescue (Simonds), and then "reduce the various garrisons" at your leisure. Providing, of course, those garrisons did not become aware of exactly how puny their besiegers were and sally forth and reduce them.

Serious war gamers employ a die to make their tabletop exercises more realistic. They recognize that warfare has so many imponderables it rarely goes completely to plan. Wingate's war was no exception, though one would hardly credit it from his own summary of the campaign:

> On 25th February I marched from Engiabara with 1500 men of 2nd Ethiopians and Frontier Battalion [Sudanese regulars] . . . All marches were made by night owing to Italian superiority in the air. We passed Burye, making a reconnaissance in force against it the following day and laid siege to the Italian posts of Mankusa and Dembecha.

What really happened was nowhere near as easy as Wingate makes it sound, and if disaster was averted it was more by luck than judgment. Fifteen hundred men with camels, mules, and the few horses used to carry the heavier weapons such as the Boyes anti-tank rifles and Lewis guns made a straggling column over three miles long. Although he had emphasized the need for silence, Wingate soon realized that these men were hardly the caliber of his beloved Special Night Squads.

"First night march proved Gideon Force has still much to learn: noisy; apt to lose the way," noted Akavia in his campaign diary.

The Ethiopian battalion, in particular, had not been trained for night maneuvers. Now, for all his emphasis on the need for the British cadre to project themselves as humble servants of the emperor, Wingate began to lose his temper with them and Boyle. Tutton was soon filling the pages of his dairy with his concern over the way that Wingate was dividing his small command:

> We could see that Wingate and Boyle were becoming less and less reconcilable—the trouble was their enmity reflected on us and split the whole force into two camps. On one side Wingate, the Sudanese and one or two of our officers who Wingate was inclined to favour, on the other side the CO [Boyle] and all those who were determined to support him. . . . Nerves were sorely strained by fatigue

and physical hardship, savage thoughts and unbecoming hatreds divided us in a highly dangerous and explosive manner. Yet at the very worst, underlying all their discords there was a grim determination to bring the enemy to action and to rout him.

Orders were given for the advance parties to gather wood and start guiding beacons on the small hillocks that punctuated the plain. There was considerable enthusiasm for this and soon an entire hillside of dry grass was ablaze, illuminating the long snake of the column for miles around. Men got lost in the dark. There was marching and counter-marching along mountain tracks. It was very cold. Tutton wrote that it was a scene he would never forget:

> The milling camels. The whistling wind. The black slopes of the mountain lit up by the fire . . . men fell asleep on their feet, teeth chattered.

Wingate tried to switch to the low whistles and flashing lights regularly used as recognition signals by his Night Squads. It was then that he discovered that the average Ethiopian, while often pleasing on the reed flute, considered whistling to be flying in the face of nature. The use of lights was even worse, for it almost proved fatal. One of the SDF's young British officers, a *bimbashi,* was told to go ahead of the main party with the camels and find a campsite for the night. When he could not be found, Wingate, Akavia, and Dr. Clifford Drew, Gideon Force's medical officer, eventually found the camels but no sign of the *bimbashi.* Akavia and the others moved a little way off the main road.

> Wingate now borrowed my electric torch and gave our recognition signal. As if in answer, fire was opened upon us by machine guns from two directions and from the flashes it looked as if they were only 200 yards away. We quickly fell flat on our bellies and crawled backwards to the head of the column. Here we met the Bimbashi who had had difficulty in finding a suitable camping place and so continued on his way, oblivious to the fact that he was getting nearer and nearer to Mankusa fort all the time.

Akavia does not record what Wingate had to say to that *bimbashi.* However, he does note his own relief that the Italians had not been taught some of the Wingate rules for night fighting, which included not shooting until you can see the enemy, "and if you can see them you can also get them with the bayonet so don't shoot."

If the Italians had been disciplined enough to hold their fire Akavia was convinced that Gideon Force might easily have camped on the hill below the fort and been slaughtered in their bedrolls as soon as the machine gunners had light enough to see. It would have been a devastating blow to the morale of the Patriots, many of whom would probably have gone over to the renegade Ras Hailu.

As it was, Wingate continued to demonstrate that he possessed the one quality that Napoleon demanded of his generals above all else: luck. The blazing hillsides, the long camel caravans, a lost British sergeant who unwittingly bivouacked in the lee of an enemy fort as if he had a regiment of artillery behind him all helped to convince the Italians that the British were among them in great strength. Wingate, like all great illusionists, soon saw how he could exploit the situation:

> The vivid imagination of the enemy was always ready to picture a company as a division for the first two days following its appearance. . . . It was essential to maintain the momentum of surprise, if benefit were to be obtained from his credulity and cowardice.

Wingate did this by harassing almost every Italian military establishment along the good tarmac road their engineers had built between Burye and Debra Markos, the regional capital, with one pinprick raid after another. Most of these occurred at night and were designed to keep the Italians on edge.

Sometimes they were no more (and no less) than moonlit sniping at silhouetted sentries, the chilling crack of a single aimed shot followed by the crumpled body his comrades were reluctant to approach. Or the muffled cough as it came out of its tube that was the only warning of a mortar bomb landing in the compound itself, leaving the defenders bracing for more bombs that often never came: mortar ammunition was precious. Every bomb had to be brought up the escarpment on the backs of the camels, which continued to die at a much greater rate than any of the humans involved in the conflict. "A camel Calvary" the saddened transport officer William Allen called it.

But mostly they were the equivalent of First World War trench raids, with bombing parties crawling close enough to machine gun nests to be able to launch a shower of grenades before melting into the night. The Sudanese became particularly adept at these raids once their British officers had taught them the mysteries of the Mills 36 grenade. Sometimes the Italians, goaded beyond belief, would try to catch their tormentors unaware. Bill Harris, in his late twenties and one of the few Sandhurst-trained regular officers with the Sudanese battalion,* found himself trying to hold off an Eritrean cavalry charge by firing a Bren gun from the hip. They came at his platoon through the smoke of blazing elephant grass, yelling their war cries before wheeling and hurling grenades from the saddle. When the smoke had cleared Harris and his men found about twenty dead and dying horses, the nearest forty yards away from their positions. Meanwhile, the RAF bombed Burye and caused some panic when they hit a *banda* camp—the first of only two appearances they made over the Gojjam, for Platt, still struggling to dislodge the Italians from the Keren, had the lion's share of the air support. One of the slow-moving Wellesleys engaged in the raid was shot down and its crew taken prisoner.

Wingate, the gunner, had to rely on his artillery, which consisted of his four homemade mortar tubes, though later on Gideon Force acquired a couple of Italian cannon of Garibaldi vintage. He soon discovered that even some of his regular infantry officers had never been taught how to lay a mortar and had to give them on-the-job training. During one of these occasions, when he was imparting his black arts to Makonnen Desta, the aristocratic emissary from the emperor who had flown in with him and Collis the previous November, the Italians began to mortar them back.

As the explosions got closer, Wingate ordered his companion to take cover while he continued to load and fire the mortar. The British army, he insisted between shots, had many officers, but Ethiopia needed its few educated people. More showmanship? When Wingate wanted to he could produce it in spades, and it undoubtedly helped morale. Bravery, like fear, can be infectious.

But there is no doubt that other motives were at play here. Wingate, unlike most of his brother officers, did not subscribe to the belief that the sun would never set on the British Empire. In a letter to Hugh Boustead, following the death of a young officer named Colin MacDonald in one of the night attacks, he revealed he was looking forward to a time when all of Africa, not just Ethiopia, would be free:

*The rest were "hostilities only" subalterns from the Plantation Syndicate and the Political Service.

MacDonald died to put right a wrong done in 1935 [Italian invasion of Ethiopia] and also, which is probably more important, to give the black races of Africa a chance to realise a free civilization. This is a worthy cause for which to die and more worthy than a mere defence of one's own midden.

MacDonald had died when some promised Ethiopian support failed to materialize, leaving the young officer and his Sudanese to their own devices. Boustead was, understandably, furious and could hardly have been mollified by Wingate's sanctimonious advice in the same letter: "[I]f the failings of others are to be a justification for our own, there will be no virtue."

And virtuously enough, Wingate continued to lead from the front with all the attendant risks. Shortly after his thirty-eighth birthday, which he spent camped in a wadi outside Burye, he divided his force.

The Second Ethiopians under Boyle were sent ahead to begin hit-and-run raids on Dembecha fort while he remained behind with Boustead's battalion of Sudanese and a Vickers machine gun detachment from Boyle's Ethiopians to try and capture the fort of Mankusa, which lay off the tarmacadam highway between Burye and Dembecha. Wingate was accompanied by Azaj Kabada Tessema, an emissary from the emperor's court who was there to assist in liaison with the locals and stir them up.

After three days of siege all was going well. They had established a headquarters near a hilltop church, where a certain amount of comfort was provided by the presence of their cooks and grooms since, for all its leanness, there was an element of safari about Gideon Force. The church, surrounded by a high wall, was just under a mile from the fort, which was therefore easily in range of their Vickers machine gun. From there they had gone forward with their single mortar until, from about one thousand yards, they managed to set most of the fort's buildings alight. A couple of times Italian aircraft bombed the area of the church, but Gideon Force were well dug in and suffered no casualties. The resident Patriots had joined in the attack and they were constantly replenishing their ammunition from captured stocks of Mannlicher and Alpini they had brought with them from Engiabara. Akavia, who was rarely far from Wingate's side, expected that the fort was about to fall to them "like a ripe fruit."

Then Wingate received a radio message from Khartoum and all was utterly changed. Platt's headquarters were "reliably informed" that shortly after dawn the Italians were going to attack Wingate "in force" from the direction of Burye. "Reliably informed" usually meant that a coded Italian radio message had been intercepted and deciphered.

Wingate rightly surmised that Colonel Natale, convinced that the night raids were the prelude to a major British offensive in the same league as the ones Platt and Cunningham had launched, had decided to get out before Wingate assembled his "divisions." Natale's plan, which was contrary to General Nasi's orders, might be best described as a "surprise retreat." He would abandon Burye and fall back on Debra Markos, knocking aside any opposition he encountered en route. There was little doubt that he could do this, for he had at least five thousand troops at his disposal, including armored cars, cavalry, and artillery as well as close air support.

Wingate's initial reaction was to sidestep smartly out of the way "and smite the hindmost of them." But Tessema, the emperor's representative, demurred. He pointed out that they would lose a tremendous amount of face among the populace if they retreated now, and the young men were likely to turn *banda* and put on Italian uniforms again. Wingate listened and decided on a compromise. Most of the Sudanese battalion under Boustead, plus the Ethiopian-crewed Vickers gun detachment from the church, would take up a position north of the highway and then return to it at 7:00 A.M. the next day in time to attack Natale's column as it went by. At the same time Wingate dictated to Akavia a warning for Boyle to keep his camel transport off the road until the Italians had gone by. The note, tapped out on Akavia's Imperial portable, was sent off in the cleft stick of a runner.

Wingate decided that he would remain on what they had come to call Church Hill with two of Boustead's Sudanese platoons. Since he was short of officers he appointed Akavia to command one of the platoons and later co-opted a third platoon under a young British officer named Desmond Creedon. As a contingency measure all heavy kit would be packed for rapid withdrawal. His idea was that if the Italians had really decided to evacuate Burye and marched down the road in force, a small number of men could get away quickly. If the Italians were not coming it would appear that the British had never left.

This failed to fool the Patriots and others of the emperor's subjects hanging around Wingate's headquarters. They noticed the thoughtful way the Sudanese were loading their mules and decided to make themselves scarce. Boustead, true to form, was skeptical about the plan from the start, pointing out that by sitting on territory that was about to be attacked Wingate was going against his own standing orders to conceal their weakness in numbers by always operating in the dark. Whether Wingate explained about the objections raised by Tessema is not clear.

The Italian attack on Church Hill began at about 7:00 A.M. the next day—the time Boustead was due to show up on the road—with a continuous and terrifying hail of heavy machine-gun fire from the direction of the Mankusa fort. Fortunately, the high stone wall around the church protected Wingate's men from most of it. The Italians, who were slightly below them, also appear to have been firing high. But it was obvious that the fort had been reinforced with the vanguard of Natale's column. Wingate replied with the nine Brens he had available, and though the range was extreme on at least one occasion he was observed working a rifle himself. There was no sign of Boustead and the rest of his battalion. About an hour after the attack began Wingate's men started to come under increasingly accurate artillery and mortar fire and Wingate decided to get out while they still could. Akavia crawled over from his position outside the wall to Wingate's headquarters dugout to receive his orders. It was to be a staged withdrawal. First the cooks and the grooms would go with the mules. Then Wingate would take out the center platoon first because it had the most exposed route. Akavia would keep firing for another three minutes and follow him. Creedon's men, who were nearest the road, would provide covering fire before making their own escape.

The camp followers got clean away, their only casualty being the mule carrying all Wingate and Akavia's food, cooking utensils, and blankets, which, understandably, they did not pause to salvage. Wingate went next, running at a crouch. The Italian fire intensified and Akavia kept his men shooting back, one eye on his watch, which seemed to be recording the slowest three minutes in the history of the universe.

Then I ran over with the Sudanese platoon across the main road, making first off to the east so as to get further way from the enemy's machine-guns which never let off for a minute. I fail to understand

how none of us was hit by this continuous fire, though I actually saw
the bullets raising little clouds of dust a couple of yards from us. . . .
Only by a big detour and fleetness of foot did these platoons extricate themselves from the Mankusa church position.

Before they split up Wingate had instructed him to rendezvous "at
those hills over there" and waved in what might have been a northerly
direction. Akavia had to make a large detour, and it was some hours before they were reunited. "I thought I was going to lose the only other
Zionist I have here," said Wingate, obviously much relieved.

Boustead, who had singularly failed to smite the hindmost or any
other part of Natale's column, had been greeted in a far less cordial
fashion. Harassed by low-flying aircraft, he had noted the size and firepower of the retreating Italians, decided it would be suicide to meddle
with them, and returned to his last campsite, where Wingate discovered him enjoying his breakfast. "Wingate had reached Boustead's
camp at 10:30 and he was simply furious when he heard what had happened," noted Akavia.

This hardly does justice to what occurred. Wingate called
Boustead, the man who had once run away from sea to get closer to the
action, a coward. In any circumstances it would have been an outrageous suggestion and, according to Thesiger, Boustead never forgave
him for it. Wingate would later estimate that Natale had ten thousand
with him, which he might have done including the *bandas'* families. By
all accounts he had at least five thousand fighting men compared to
Boustead's nine hundred or so. Even so, the fire-eating Bimbashi Harris, the young officer who had repelled a cavalry charge with a Bren
gun, had been disappointed when Boustead would not let him attack
it. Wingate immediately set about reversing all this, and Boustead's
Sudanese were soon skirmishing with Natale's rearguard, who made
sure they got nowhere near the main body of the column.

The scene was now set for one of those military accidents where
both sides have blundered and the outcome must depend largely on
luck. In this case the dice rolled in Wingate's favor, though later, at a
time when he feared he might never get another field command, he
would try to give the impression it was carefully planned.

Boyle, the commander of the Second Ethiopians, remained bliss-
fully unaware of the approach of Natale's column. Without a radio, he

had last heard from Wingate four days before and had never received the cleft-stick message dictated to Akavia at Mankusa, warning him to get his animals off the road.

With the three hundred men remaining after various units had been detached, Boyle had continued to stage night raids on the Dembecha fort. In this he was assisted by Wilfred Thesiger, who was involved with a band of Patriots led by a man named Haile Yusuf, known to his British allies as "Highly Useless," though Thesiger was fond of him. Meanwhile, convinced that the local initiative remained firmly in their hands, Boyle had encamped where the highway to Dembecha crossed a river, an area of shoulder-high elephant grass and forest. Later, an incredulous-sounding Wingate would write:

> [T]he 2nd Ethiopian Battalion . . . returning tired from a night attack on Dembecha, sat down in the line of the enemy's retreat along a river bank crossing the motor road, in what must have been one of the worst tactical positions for defence in history.

The river was called the Charaka, and Boyle had placed his battalion so that the river's banks were between it and the Italian garrison they were tormenting at Dembecha. They were on the same side of the river, more of a muddy stream in most places, as Natale's column, which they no more expected to collide with than a London bus. Their camels, lightly guarded, were grazing on one side of the road and the men camped on the other.

Michael Tutton's D Company were bivouacked farthest away from the river, and Tutton, who took out a dawn patrol, was one of the first to get involved. He came scampering back through the long grass, bending double because Sergeant Dick Luyt* already had his company—"yelling with excitement"—firing at the advance guard of the Italian Eleventh Colonial Battalion.

Natale was convinced he had walked into a rather badly laid ambush intended to block his passage to Dembecha until his pursuers caught up with him. He must have been thanking his lucky stars that the enemy were so inept that they were not all on the far bank behind a blown bridge. Even so, Boyle and another Kenyan settler, a second

---

*A South African Rhodes scholar and Oxford rugby blue who ended his career with a knighthood as vice chancellor of Cape Town University.

lieutenant named Sydney Downey, did somehow manage to get two of the Vickers guns manhandled to the other side of the river, from where they could cover the bridge. Boyle's Sudanese servant also knew where his duty lay and ran off to guard the major's kit.

For the next four hours Natale tried to smash his way through. Thesiger, on a ridge behind the river with Haile Yusuf's men, heard continuous small arms fire and some shelling from the Italian pack artillery, then watched the battle unfold from his ringside seat:

> The Italians halted in dense formations, and their battalions moved forward in turn to engage Boyle's troops. From our hilltop the scene resembled a battle fought in Napoleonic times.

Below him the participants were not finding things quite so orderly. Sergeant Luyt had placed the barrel of a Lewis gun over a fallen tree and was firing burst after burst at the *ascari,* pausing only to prise jammed cartridge cases from the breach with a penknife every time the ejector mechanism failed. Standing by his side with a rifle was Tutton, who was picking off the Eritrean NCOs, betrayed in the long grass by the scarlet flashes on their epaulettes. When he brought his journal up to date Tutton wrote:

> At one time I saw an Italian officer driving on his men with sjambok and shot him through from side to side. Yet he only stiffened and stumbled out of sight.

Already streaming blood from minor wounds to the leg and arm, Tutton was hit squarely in the right thigh by a grenade which "mercifully failed to explode." It was picked up by his Ethiopian company sergeant major, who pulled out the pin and threw it back.

Incredibly, despite the odds, the Ethiopians were holding their ground. The Italians brought up their two armored cars, each one equipped with three Breda machine guns now trained on the Ethiopian troops on the left side of the road. This was formidable fire support. Lance Corporal Wandafrash Falaka picked up a heavy Boyes .55 anti-tank rifle, dashed across the road, and flopped into the long grass on the other side. A few seconds later the Italian armor was about one hundred yards away. The Boyes had become perhaps the most despised weapon in the British armory. But if it was rarely capable of penetrating a panzer it did very well in the hands of Lance Corporal

Falaka. First he emptied one five-round magazine and then, ignoring the Breda fire desperately trying to seek him out, changed magazines and fired five more spaced single shots. Both the lightly armored vehicles came to a halt, their Italian crews maimed by the remains of the big bullets ricocheting wickedly around the cars' insides. Falaka ran back into cover, abandoning the cumbersome Boyes, though not before he had spiked it by removing its bolt.

The Savoia bomber that had accompanied the Italian column bombed and machine-gunned the Ethiopians, but after Falaka's display they put up such a barrage of small-arms and Lewis-gun fire that soon a great cheer went up when the plane was seen rapidly losing height and heading for Dembecha. Patriots observed it making a forced landing there.

While this was going on the *banda* cavalry came around the right flank and herded away Boyle's camels. From his hilltop Thesiger watched the enemy begin to cross the Charaka downstream from the bridge and work their way behind the Ethiopians. He sent Boyle a note by runner warning him what was happening, but he need not have worried. Natale called his men back, fearing that they might be cut off by the Patriots who were easily visible along the ridgeline. He was not to know they had no desire for a more active part in the proceedings. Instead he sent for his rearguard, the Sixty-fifth Colonial Battalion under Colonel Antonio de Mandato, who were only lightly engaged with Boustead's Sudanese, who had yet to catch up with them in strength. De Mandato was ordered to launch yet another frontal assault, supported by mortars and artillery. Captain Allen Smith, a New Zealander who had worked in Ethiopia as a missionary before the Italian occupation and who was Boyle's adjutant, told Wingate what happened next in a long handwritten account of the action he sent the next day.

> A strong force appeared marching down the road headed by an Italian Colonel in a full uniform and the Italian flag. This force marched steadily forward towards the bridge across the Charaka, protected by flank guards who kept up a continuous fire on the Ethiopian positions. Everyone who saw this column advancing was struck by the splendid bearing of the Colonel at its head and the courage with which he led them on. He proved, however, too good a target to miss, and fell to a bullet.

Lieutenant Downey's Vickers jammed, one of the crew was dead, and the other had disappeared. He fired his revolver at the mass of soldiery on the bridge and then dived into the elephant grass. Some weeks later Downey told his friend Michael Tutton what happened next:

A wounded Italian officer staggered up holding in his intestines having been shot through the stomach. The wounded man cried, "Non tirare!" threw up his hands and collapsed over Downey who was covered with his blood. Downey did what he could for him. While he was attending him Downey heard some movement and a camel strolled past. Then he felt something hard in the small of his back.

The *ascari* were in no mood to take prisoners, but Sottotenènte Marchetti made sure his men spared the life of the enemy who had tried to help him. Now the battle was almost over. The Ethiopians began to fall back into the woods behind them. Natale broke through, taking his wounded and the captured camels with him, leaving behind the wrecked armored cars with their working Breda guns, scattered papers from a smashed field office, dropped rifles, ammo boxes, knapsacks, and the dead. One hundred and twenty-two Ethiopians were killed fighting on the Italian side and twenty-one on the British. Five Italian nationals, including three officers, were killed, and Natale had just over two hundred wounded, ten of them Italian officers. Boyle's battalion had forty-eight Ethiopians and two British wounded and Downey was captured.[*]

After the battle, the cleaners, feathered and otherwise, began to descend. Haile Yusuf's Patriots at last left their ridge, stripped the bodies of both sides, and seized anything else that was portable. They discovered the hiding place of Boyle's loyal Sudanese servant and murdered him when he refused to hand over his master's possessions. Later Thesiger tried to excuse the Patriots' behavior by saying that they looted in case the Italians should return and were reluctant to fight lest, after six

---

[*]Casualty figures for the Charaka River action come from considerable research in Britain, Ethiopia, and Italy undertaken by Judge David Shirreff MC, a veteran of the Abyssinia campaign though not with Wingate, whose book *Bare Feet and Bandoliers* must be the definitive account of the Gojjam expedition. Shirreff makes the valid point that the high number of Italian officer casualities indicates that they led from the front. Downey was released when Addis Ababa surrendered and gave Tutton the account of his capture.

years of unaided struggle, they should be killed on the eve of their liberation.

Boyle and his officers took a less charitable view and said much the
same thing about the Patriots as the Italians did, which was that they
were not Patriots at all but no better than bandits, *"vile shifta."* Despite
their anger, their admiration for "their own" Ethiopians knew no
bounds. Tutton, a classical scholar at Eton, likened his battalion's fight
to the stand the three hundred Spartans made against the Persian
horde at Thermopylae.

Wingate claimed later that the enemy were "much impressed" and
that "over one thousand casualties" had been inflicted on them. Presumably this exaggeration came from Boyle, whom, for once, Wingate
was quick to praise. "It is quite evident from the remains on the
ground that your men put up a great fight."

Natale's casualties, though much greater than the Second Ethiopians', were relatively small. Even if the number of real combatants he
had with him was as few as five thousand, his casualties would have
been no more than 6 percent. But he was undoubtedly shaken up—the
Italian official history refers to "a violent battle against huge forces,"
which they wrongly believed included a large contingent of Sudanese.
There is no indication that Natale had any idea that he outnumbered
his opponents by at least twenty to one. Thesiger, while full of admiration for the conduct of the Second Ethiopians, called this clash Boyle's
Blunder. But after Charaka River the rot began to set in fast for the Italian forces in the Gojjam.

In the late afternoon, when they were burying the dead and Tutton
was insisting that his men redig the grave of an *ascari* whose foot was
sticking out of his resting place, Wingate and Akavia followed
Boustead's battalion to the Charaka bridge on muleback. One of the
first people Wingate encountered was young Bimbashi Harris, who,
along with some other walking wounded, came staggering down the
road covered in blood, propped up between a couple of his Sudanese.

Harris had pursued Natale's column to the outskirts of Dembecha
and had then been hit in the arm and chest by machine-gun fire. Some
of his men had been killed. Having been rebuked by Boustead for mak-

ing too much noise—an effective ploy, for it made him believe he was not as badly hurt as he was—Harris had walked several miles more or less unaided. Wingate dressed his wounds and managed to persuade him to eat a little canned tunafish, but they did not hold out much hope for him.*

All next day there was skirmishing around the Dembecha fort, which looked like a very tough nut to crack because its defenses were well sited and the garrison was now reinforced by Natale's column. Then Wingate was informed that explosions had been heard from inside the fort, from where columns of smoke were rising. It was obvious that Natale was preparing to depart and, as at Burye, was trying to destroy what he could not take with him.

A few hours later Wingate and Akavia moved into the abandoned fort, where for the first time in the campaign they slept on beds, which they dragged outside the main building because there was so much unexploded ordnance in the fort. In keeping with his doctrine of living off the enemy, Wingate tried to salvage what he could.

Thesiger discovered him "scrambling about on a great pile of burst tins, mostly of meat." Their contents stuck to Wingate's "rather hairy" legs, for he was in shorts. Supplies were already being flown into Burye, where the emperor had now moved his court, in a captured Italian aircraft and some South African air force transports. Now Wingate organized local labor to clear a landing strip at Dembecha. In the process, Thesiger witnessed Wingate's darker side when he saw him slash his Ethiopian interpreter across the face with a stick at some transgression, though the man practically worshiped the ground Wingate stood on.

They stayed at Dembecha for four days, partly for what later armies would call "rest and recuperation," while Haile Yusuf's Patriots harassed Natale's departing column with some long-distance sniping. Wingate knew the value of praise and awards. He had the Second Ethiopians on parade and thanked them for their performance at Charaka for which he later tried and failed to get Lance Corporal Wandafrash Falaka a medal. Among the men who received Wingate's

*After an agonizing muleback journey over the thirty miles to Burye, Harris was evacuated by air. He made a complete recovery, dropped in Normandy as second in command of a parachute battalion, was wounded again, and after the war retired to farm in Kenya.

personal congratulations was the South African sergeant Dick Luyt, who had done such execution with his jamming Lewis gun*. Shortly after this Luyt was commissioned and received the Distinguished Conduct Medal.

Their time at Dembecha was marred by one terrible accident. While Wingate was out of the fort one morning, Onbashi Ajawanil, the commander of his Sudanese bodyguard, the Ethiopian interpreter, and another Sudanese soldier were playing cards in a room containing at least one can of petrol. Somebody's cigarette or match caused an explosion that sent them, as Wilfred Thesiger put it, "like living torches staggering about the yard."

Thesiger, who immediately took charge, found some morphia in the abandoned Italian dispensary and, since the men were in great pain and obviously beyond medical help, gave all three what he imagined to be a lethal overdose. The interpreter, who kept asking for Wingate, died in a captured Italian car en route to the field hospital that Dr. Drew had established at Burye. The *onbashi* also lingered on, tended by Akavia, who managed to get a bottle of whisky to his blistered lips. When Wingate turned up, it seemed to Akavia that the Sudanese was trying to lie at attention before his commanding officer:

> He never uttered a complaint or even a sigh when we were near him. In answer to Wingate's questions he stated: "No, I'm not suffering at all, your highness the Pasha; With God's help I shall get better, your highness the Pasha." It was a real hero's death.

Thesiger told Wingate that his interpreter had been asking for him. "God, it makes me feel a brute," said Wingate.

After the fall of Burye and Dembecha many of the *banda* who had previously given their allegiance to the renegade Ras Hailu began to see the error of their ways and rallied to the emperor. Bolstered by these defections Wingate began to close in on Debra Markos using the same tactics of hit-and-run night raids as he had around Burye. In "Campaign Operation Instruction Number 19," dictated to Akavia, he

---

*Shortly after this Luyt was commissioned and received the Distinguished Conduct Medal.

stressed the importance of keeping up the momentum of their attacks, not resting on their laurels:

> Although enemy morale is obviously shaken . . . his communications are becoming shorter as ours are becoming longer. It is therefore essential to continue guerrilla operations, avoiding being pinned down by him.

Wingate repeatedly requested air support, as much for its effect on Patriot morale as its military contribution. "The lack of bombing on Mar[k]os is impossible to explain away and is having a disastrous effect," Thesiger, still operating with Haile Yusuf's Patriots, warned him in a hand-carried dispatch. But faced with competing demands from Platt in Eritrea and Cunningham coming up through Italian Somaliland, all the RAF could spare was a single sortie from a Blenheim bomber.*

This did little harm to the elegant white-painted colonial architecture of the provincial capital, now the last Italian outpost in the Gojjam and under new command. Natale had been sacked by General Nasi, who was outraged by his precipitous flight and replaced him with Colonel Saverio Maraventano, a Sicilian who had trained as a violinist as a young man and was decorated for valor against the Austrians during World War I when he had been taken prisoner.

General Nasi told the inflated garrison at Debra Markos that "it was a long road to Rome" and they had run out of places to flee to. Nor did Nasi seem to believe for one moment that they were facing the same kind of regular British imperial divisions as were the men who were holding up Platt's advance on the cliffs of Keren. It was, he reminded them, a disgrace to be defeated by the forces of Haile Selassie.

Maraventano took heed. Among the smaller outposts Natale had abandoned during his "surprise retreat" was a fort named Emmanuel about halfway between Dembecha and Debra Markos. Wingate had garrisoned it with a thirty-strong Sudanese platoon from Boustead's battalion under a British officer. On 19 March 1941 Maraventano followed up an air attack on the fort with an artillery barrage and an assault by two infantry battalions that killed two, captured eight, and

---

*Some days later a single Free French aircraft from Djibouti dropped some propaganda leaflets in the right place but then went on to bomb Burye, where the emperor was encamped, by mistake. Fortunately, there were no casualties.

put to flight the rest of its meager defenders. One of the prisoners managed to escape, but at least two were apparently shot in cold blood in obscure circumstances. This is the only recorded Italian atrocity throughout the campaign and was never explained.

Nor were the British entirely blameless in this respect. A few days later a patrol led by Tutton machine-gunned some Italian *ascari* as they played or watched a soccer match outside one of the forts around Debra Markos. "Hence the slaughter," Tutton noted in his diary after a deserter brought them the news that they had killed or wounded forty-three men. The newly commissioned Lieutenant Richard Luyt, who had replaced the captured Downey, was disgusted by the incident.

In the Gulit Hills on the approach to Debra Markos, which stands at a height of some eight thousand feet, the Italians had built a semicircle of small forts. Wingate's response to the loss of Emmanuel was to surround the position with the Ethiopian battalion while he continued with his night raids against the Gulit forts. On at least two occasions he led these raids himself, crawling up to the Italian wire, waiting for the single mortar bomb that would announce their attack, throwing grenades, and then leading the rush with fixed bayonets that drove the enemy out. Once in possession, Wingate's tactic was to stay until a couple of hours after dawn then pull out before the Italians had started a counterattack. Once, forewarned by a radio intercept that the Italians intended to attack them in strength, Wingate roused his force a couple of hours before dawn and led them off into the Chokey Mountains. Akavia was given the task of hurrying the camel and mule minders up a very steep hill:

> As usual, Wingate demanded fast movement . . . and he rushed from one place to the other goading everyone to superhuman effort. He also told me to stand by the side of the track and hurry everybody up. . . . [H]e was shouting in Arabic to the Sudanese who claimed, "the road is impassable," and his shouts seemed to have an immediate effect on the soldiers who admired so much this strange Britisher, who had led them successfully to battle and had shared all their perils and discomforts throughout the fighting.

In a radio message Sandford congratulated him on the success of the Gulit raids but added a plaintive "I do not think a man in your position should have taken such a close up share in such an operation."

His severest critics like to imply that Wingate was a bloodthirsty glory hunter who would never delegate if he could squeeze a trigger himself. Akavia denies this and maintains that for Wingate, fighting was "always just a means to achieve a higher aim." As for the raids in the Gulit Hills, Akavia explains Wingate led them himself both to raise morale and because "the chances of success were much higher whenever Wingate personally took part."

Certainly, his involvement in these will-o'-the-wisp operations made him an elusive commander. The despair, fatigue, and irritation Sandford often felt is only too apparent in a handwritten note he left after he arrived at Wingate's headquarters in Dembecha to discover his quarry was out making war against the Italians again:

> I came out here this afternoon to find out what the situation is, if possible to contact you. I find you are too far off to make that possible—in fact I've taken so long by the road (one car broke down) that I must make a night journey back as it is . . . for goodness sake keep in better touch with everybody. . . . It is very difficult to help you 100% if you don't keep us in the picture.

Relations with Sandford were deteriorating badly and not just over keeping in touch. Wingate blamed the brigadier for exposing his real strength to the Italians and encouraging Maraventano's attack on Emmanuel by not keeping up the highly visible supply columns that had initially led the enemy to number Gideon Force in terms of brigades rather than battalions. Nor could Wingate understand why Sandford had retained some of the officers and sergeants of the operational centers that were now coming on stream, two of which had been absorbed into the emperor's bodyguard. Even worse, Sandford had done the very thing Wingate had always preached against and distributed hundreds of rifles to various Patriot leaders who had come to pay their respects to the emperor regardless of their military effectiveness. (Some of these late ralliers were no more than bandits, and there were instances of them sniping at and raiding Wingate's own supply columns.) Wingate sent a message to Colonel Airey, the SOE liaison man in Khartoum, complaining that Sandford did not understand the first thing about guerrilla war:

> The value of Patriot fighting is very small; the value of Patriot support is great. . . . These Patriots hold the district for the regular

force, giving it security against surprise and cutting the enemy's communications.

Airey suggested that Wingate go down to Burye "to sort things out," and he departed with Akavia and a small escort, leaving Boustead to continue harassing the Gulit forts and mine the roads in between them. The "sorting out" took about five days, during which time Wingate upset Sandford sufficiently for him to complain to Platt, who was then at a very crucial point in the Battle of Keren. Platt rebuked both of them for the squabble, pointing out, reasonably enough, that he was trying to fight a battle and had better things to do than adjudicate between bickering members of his team elsewhere. A few days later, Wingate sent a reply that by his standards was positively groveling though not without a dig at Sandford for bothering the general with such trivia:

> I was more than sorry that news of disputes in our small company reached you at a critical stage of the vital battle. This was not my doing—I was in favour of washing my linen at home! In fact the storm in a teacup was all settled before the news reached you. I think you can depend on me to do my upmost to prevent any recurrence.

Wingate's presence in Burye did to some extent help free the logistical bottleneck, which was beginning to unclog anyway, mainly because some small Ford trucks had been pulled and manhandled up the escarpment. This was the work of SDF Bimbashi Henri Le Blanc, a French Canadian and noted pioneer of African truck routes. He had served in the Royal Flying Corps during the First World War and wore his old wings on the tunic of his SDF uniform.

For some of the British personnel in the operational centers the prolonged absence of all creature comforts, particularly alcohol and tobacco, combined with the monotonous Ethiopian diet had a devastating effect on morale. The worst cases, according to its commanding officer, occurred in Simonds's Beghemder Force, the most farflung of Wingate's command. An entire operational center—a lieutenant whom Simonds would describe as "a coward and a disgrace" plus four sergeants—began to walk toward an Italian fort with their hands up. Simonds changed their minds by picking up a Lewis gun and sending a burst above their heads. "Fortunately, despite being a bad shot I didn't hit them."

Poor diet inevitably led to poor health. Jaundice and dysentery were common. Simonds had jaundice and almost all the British had malaria at one time or another. Wingate, along with many of the Sudanese civilians who looked after the camels, became infected with jigger fleas. The female of this unpleasant parasite lays its eggs, which grow to about the size of a pea, in the feet of its host. They cause a maddening itch, the feet begin to swell, and the eggs have to be cut out individually. Ethiopians had a certain amount of immunity to these things or had lived with them so long they regarded the infestation as normal.

There was also a crisis in the morale of the Second Ethiopian Battalion, the heroes of the Charaka River, when over one hundred men mutinied. They claimed that even after they had proved themselves in battle, Boyle and Smith, his adjutant, continued to knock them about and treat them with disdain. The mutineers were particularly incensed that Smith had insisted on burying an Italian in a grave they had prepared for one of their own comrades. Wingate sacked both officers and wrote to Airey saying that Boyle had "no tactical knowledge, no judgment." This did not stop Boyle finishing the war commanding the Somali Scouts. Wingate evidently regretted his own readiness to lash out from time to time and strongly disapproved of Boyle and Smith's reputation for doing the same, though the Ethiopians seemed to think this was perfectly normal conduct and adopted exactly the same attitude as some of the Palestinian Jews had in the Night Squads. "Wingate was our father. If he struck us it was to correct us so that we would not err again," said a Patriot leader named Nega Selassie.

Certainly Boyle's successor had men flogged before the paraded battalion for squandering ammunition in celebratory fusillades, and the gallant Sudanese could also be caned across the buttocks by their sergeant major, just as their British officers had been at school. Neither Ethiopians nor Sudanese, or for that matter the British, found anything strange in this. Patriot warlords routinely meted out floggings, and Thesiger records the whipping of a female camp follower who had accidentally fired her revolver. On at least two occasions he himself ordered Patriots under his command to be flogged for looting.

Before he left Burye—an ugly little town of corrugated iron shacks amid mounds of festering garbage—Wingate visited the tented imperial court, which, forever careful of its dignity, had arranged itself under an ornate display of canvas walls and carpeting in the shade of some trees. He found the emperor anxious to advance farther into his king-dom.

When Wingate returned to Dembecha he found that he would not have to keep Haile Selassie waiting long. In the five days he had been away the Italians had decided to evacuate Debra Markos and get out of the Gojjam altogether. The decision had not been made by Maraven-tano, who had been quite happy to soldier on, but by his commander, Aosta. It followed Platt's long-resisted breakthrough at Keren, which together with Cunningham's liberation of British Somaliland and ad-vance on Aosta's headquarters in Addis Ababa from the south had ut-terly changed the military situation. Nor did the Italians continue to enjoy air superiority after a South African air force strike against their main airfield at Addis, which wrecked thirty aircraft before they could take off.

Maraventano was ordered to take his column across the Blue Nile gorge, north through the Muslim-dominated Shoa region, which had always been well disposed toward the Italians, and then on to the mountains around Gondar. Addis Ababa, which was of political but no tactical value, was also to be evacuated. The Italian plan was to concen-trate in Gondar, where the British would soon be hampered by the start of the rainy season, and to hold out there until the German offensive in Libya obliged the British to leave the fighting to the Patriots and with-draw their divisions to defend Egypt. Rommel had started his attack there on 24 March, and the British, who had sent some of the best units in their desert army to reinforce the Greeks, were already reeling back.

The only Italian to remain in Debra Markos was a doctor who stayed to look after those hospital cases who could not be moved. Wingate, on taking possession of the town, was happy to advertise his success. Among his entourage was the Italian-speaking American jour-nalist Edmund Stevens, one of the war correspondents who were now hitching lifts on aircraft to Burye. Stevens had been amusing Wingate by translating some of the graffiti the Italians had left behind—"En-glishmen you have always been cowards and pimps. We'll be back in three months"—when a field telephone that the British suspected was linked to one of the forts on the Blue Nile started ringing, then stopped. Wingate had an idea. "Call them back," he told Stevens, "and tell them that a British division ten thousand strong is on its way up the road. If they ask who you are, say you're Dr. Grigorio."

The United States was still officially a neutral country and would be for another eight months, but Stevens did not hesitate:

> I gave the handle of the field telephone a vigorous crank, lifted the receiver and yelled *Pronto*. . . . After I had repeated the call several times an answering *Pronto* came from the other end. It was the Italian army switchboard operator. . . . I then delivered Wingate's spurious message. "What shall we do?" shrieked the operator. I answered, "Clear out quick as you can." . . . A few hours later Wingate dispatched 700 Ethiopians to take over the once strongly held Italian post of the Blue Nile Crossing.

It was a small consolation for a much larger disappointment. Wingate had been hoping to cut off Maraventano's column, now at least twelve thousand strong, as it crossed the Blue Nile gorge where it was most vulnerable. Thesiger and two other British officers were negotiating with a highly regarded local warlord named Belai Zelleka to attack them. But Ras Hailu—"the old fox" Wingate called him—had one last card to play for his Italian friends before he submitted to Haile Selassie.* He bought Maraventano's passage through the gorge by offering Zelleka one of his daughters as a bride—an irresistible bribe for a commoner among a people who cherished notions of class even more than the English. Thesiger did not realize it had happened until Maraventano was across and well into the Shoa territory. With some trepidation, for he fully expected to get the blame, Thesiger rode to Debra Markos to tell Wingate what had happened and found him "unexpectedly understanding."

Boustead's Sudanese and several thousand Patriots went after the slow-moving Italian column, snapping at its heels like terriers. The rearguard *ascari* chased them away only to have them return the next day. Some of the Sudanese were under the command of Major Nott, who had at last managed to extricate himself from his quartermaster's duties back at Burye. Wingate, his task almost done, stayed behind in Debra Markos. The town was now surrounded by Patriots, who were preparing to both honor their emperor and to celebrate the end of their Lenten fast with the best Easter party for years. The

---

*Ras Hailu was swiftly forgiven, for the Lord of the Gojjam was too influential to be disposed of like some common traitor.

Jewish doctors Wingate had recruited from Palestine—all had temporary commissions in the Medical Corps—now began to arrive in force. One went to Simonds's headquarters, where the sight of his cap badge was greeted by the British personnel with cries of "A doc! A doc!" Most of the others set up a clinic below the citadel's walls at Debra Markos, where their patients included Wingate, who sat patiently while Dr. Wohlman cut out his jigger fleas but insisted on treating himself for his malaria. It was just before Passover and Akavia and the doctors had organized a seder meal with its reading of the Exodus narrative. The local unleavened *injara* bread was considered an ideal substitute for the matzo required by Hebrew tradition. Wingate accepted Akavia's invitation to attend "and made a moving Zionist speech."

The doctors were concerned that the foul conditions that prevailed in the crowded Patriot camps around the town would lead to an outbreak of cholera. With characteristic attention to detail Wingate turned his efforts to improving its sanitary arrangements:

> The best type of latrine to prevent the breeding of flies, is a narrow trench about a foot wide, and about two-and-a-half feet deep, which is filled and redug daily, the length of the trench depending on the number using it.

The emperor entered Debra Markos on 6 April 1941. On the same day the leading armored cars of Cunningham's South Africans drove into Addis, much to the relief of the large number of Italian civilians, who, unable to leave with Aosta's troops, feared they might be massacred by vengeful Ethiopians. While he was receiving submissions from Ras Hailu and lesser chiefs and impatiently awaiting General Cunningham's tardy permission to enter his own capital, Haile Selassie gave a party for Wingate, Sandford, and the other British officers. "I rise to propose the health of Your Majesty, which will be drunk in the wine of the discomfited aggressor," said Wingate, raising his glass of captured Spumante. "Until the liberation of Ethiopia the big wrong which brought this war in its wake had not been put right."

The immediate restoration of Haile Selassie to his throne was another matter. Wingate was asked by Cunningham to do all he could to delay Haile Selassie's arrival in Addis because until they were firmly in control the British feared that his presence there might excite its citizens to rape and murder the Italian community.* Both Wingate and Sandford rightly thought there was little danger of this—Haile Selassie was sensitive about accusations of barbarity.

Wingate began to suspect that this delay was part of some Foreign Office plot to marginalize Haile Selassie now that he had fulfilled his purpose and that Ethiopia was about to be turned into a Palestine-style British protectorate. The memory of Courtney Brocklehurst's mission to get the Galla to rebel against the Amhara still rankled. All this, so typical of Wingate when he had little else to do but brood about the vital statistics of latrines, turned out to be nonsense.

Mounted on a gray charger, Wingate led the emperor into Addis Ababa on 5 May 1941, exactly six years after the Italians' own triumphant entry. The horse had originally been procured with the emperor in mind, but Haile Selassie was saddle weary and preferred to ride in a black Ford convertible, driven by Bimbashi Le Blanc.

The order of procession began with Wingate, who had been persuaded to wear shorts because the gabardine drill trousers he had worn for three months had completely changed color below the knee. Behind him on foot, led by Lieutenant Luyt and Mr. Akavia, came a company from the Second Ethiopians, who had been issued with new long-sleeved khaki sweaters. They were followed by a detachment from Boustead's Frontier Battalion in their khaki turbans. Next came the motor cavalcade with the emperor's Ford. Ethiopian mounted policemen and motorcyclists from one of the South African divisions protected the flanks.

As soon as they spotted the emperor's car the crowd lining the route prostrated themselves then rose and threw flowers and surged around the convertible. This frightened the horses, and three of the mounted policemen were thrown off. The Weedon-trained Wingate only kept his seat with difficulty. Patriots formed up and marched alongside them. Not everyone was impressed. Michael Tutton, who took part in the parade with the recently released Sydney Downey, had obviously still not got over the way the Patriots had looted his battalion's dead at the Charaka River:

---

*In the end an armed guard did have to be put on some of the Italian women, but, according to Shirreff, this was to shield them from the more persistent British junior officers, who had spent several months in the field.

[There were] many ferocious looking savages with huge mops of filthy black hair. . . . The majority of the men's faces appeared to be stamped with every vice under the sun, cruelty, greed, cowardice, cunning, lechery and ignorance. . . . It horrifies me to call these brutish savages our allies against a white race for whom I once had some affection.

Akavia thought the "brutish savages" were behaving well. For the moment his main concern was the direction he was headed. He knew that only senior officers were supposed to enter the palace grounds to take part in the ceremony there. But as they approached the palace gates Wingate turned in the saddle and commanded, "Follow me, Akavia!"

So I followed Wingate into the Palace grounds where a guard of honour of the King's African Rifles was lined up waiting for the Emperor to make his appearance. Wingate moved off to the left to find a place for his horse. . . . I was greatly embarrassed and wished that the earth would open up. . . . So I quickened my step and walked up to the verandah of the Palace where scores of senior officers were standing and waiting for the Emperor. There were only a few majors among those present: all others had higher ranks. I felt quite naked, since I was without any badges of rank, and found an inconspicuous place behind one of the columns.

Thus Wingate procured a place for Zion when the South African artillery fired a twenty-one-gun salute, the honor guard presented arms, and Haile Selassie, Lion of Judah, was returned to his throne.

There was one more act. Maraventano's column was still at large with Nott constantly nipping at its flanks with a growing force of Patriots, for Nott's success was proving a good recruiting sergeant.

Gideon Force had now been officially disbanded. Wingate came under Cunningham, who had made him the responsibility of Lieutenant General H. E. Wetherall, commander of British forces in the capital. Wetherall wanted Wingate to replace Simonds, who, under protest, had been ordered to a staff job in Crete.* Wingate had other ideas.

He knew that Haile Selassie, for domestic reasons, yearned for a famous victory where the victors were mostly Patriots and not British imperial troops. The emperor placed two thousand of his best Patriots under Wingate's command, sending along Ras Kassa, the elderly viceroy of Ethiopia, as their titular head. Their task was to catch Maraventano.

Wingate left Addis Ababa on 10 May 1941 accompanied by Akavia,** some wireless operators, British and Australian sergeants from the operational centers, a platoon of Sudanese, and various cooks and servants. Ras Kassa was following. On this occasion Akavia was traveling separately in a captured Fiat car while Wingate went ahead with the signalers in one of Le Blanc's battered trucks. Five days later, after both vehicles had broken down and they had switched to mules, they found Nott's harassing force near the village of Addis Derra. Thesiger saw him arrive:

> Now for the first time I really appreciated his greatness. Bearded and unkempt, he had got off his mule, stared about him with searching eye, set face and jutting jaw, then called us together. He wasted no time. He told us that he intended to make the Italians surrender and that in a few days time.

So far Maraventano was doing very well. He commanded an unwieldy column of about twelve thousand people, of whom perhaps eight thousand were truly combatants, with some four thousand pack animals. He had about a thousand sick and wounded with him, was short of medicine, and was treating an outbreak of dysentery with potions made from local herbs. He was determined that none of his column should fall into the hands of the Ethiopian "rebels," who were

*He never got there; the Germans captured the island first.
**Akavia was particularly glad to be leaving the capital. For the first time he had been exposed to Wingate's driving, which was accompanied by some revealing remarks about the moral dangers inherent in Britain's road-safety campaigns. "We're building a race of cowards," he informed Akavia. "Our young men should be taught to take chances."

said to castrate their prisoners before killing them.* On a couple of occasions he had tried to turn on his tormentors, whom he outnumbered at least ten to one. But though his tough *ascari* could usually be relied upon to scatter the Patriots, they did not do as well against Nott's detachments of Sudanese and Ethiopian regulars from the Second Battalion. A dashing daylight assault came up against machine guns sited in textbook manner on ideal defensive turf—Nott was a professional in his early thirties—and proved beyond even the courage of the Eritrean NCOs, whose cries of *"Avanti"* only mocked their dead.

Yet Nott knew that, even with Patriot reinforcements, they were not strong enough to stop Maraventano, who had almost achieved his aim of getting into rough country where he could hold out through the rains in the hope that British reverses elsewhere might completely alter the picture.

In coded high-speed Morse Wingate's "appreciation" of the situation was sent to Wetherall at Eleventh Division headquarters. To the dismay of all concerned the next day a message came back ordering Wingate to proceed at once to Debra Tabor and Nott to Addis Ababa. Wingate sent back: "Read the appreciation I have sent you. Stop." This followed some playing for time during which Wingate twice ordered Akavia to claim that Wetherall's message was "corrupt" (garbled). Eventually an exasperated officer at divisional signals got Akavia to repeat what he was receiving letter by letter. "I intended, as far as possible, to comply with orders," he would later explain. "But thought it legitimate to get to Debra Tabor by moving in the enemy's direction instead of away from him."

Below him he could see Maraventano's column as it moved out of Addis Derra toward Agibar and Amba Alagi, where Aosta had taken the garrison from Addis Ababa and was now once more facing siege. Wingate guessed that Maraventano intended to climb the massif to the north as a first step toward Agibar:

Joining this massif to Agibar was a panhandle. . . . I organised my force into two columns. The smaller was to proceed without a single animal, carrying only two days rations and seize the panhan-

*"Now they can't participate in any form of grind, for they're back from Ethiopia with their organs left behind," sang British troops to the tune of "The British Grenadiers."

dle. . . . The larger column was to pass up the heights round the enemy's west flank by night, and then push him up against the pan-handle.

The Italian was running out of places to run to. The smaller column was to be commanded by Thesiger. He would have under him a full op-erational center of a lieutenant, four sergeants, and forty-three trained Ethiopians, Lieutenant Rowe and forty men from the Second Ethiopi-ans, and about three hundred of the better Patriots. They would take with them an old Hotchkiss machine gun. Ken Rowe, a Rhodesian, in-sisted on coming, though for some time now he had been suffering from badly blistered feet. He was popular among his Ethiopians, who called him Jiggsa, "the Strong One." Before he left, Wingate told The-siger to make sure he inflicted at least two hundred casualties. "Their morale is bad and we're damned well going to make them surrender."

The plan almost failed. Three days later it was a seriously wounded Rowe, shot through the chest, who was prisoner of the Italians, while Thesiger was hobbling about after a shell from one of Maraventano's pack howizters had blown him off his feet. He thought at the time that his knee had been hit by a stone, but a quarter of a century later a slither of shrapnel was discovered. His small force had been subjected to a cavalry attack in which Wandafrash Falaka, the hero with the anti-tank rifle at Charaka River, had been killed and Rowe, who could not move fast enough on his bad feet, had been shot and captured. The-siger had been forced out of the fort they had seized on the panhandle but turned and stood at another good position a bit farther north. And, against all the odds, an increasingly desperate Maraventano was still unable to push them aside.

Meanwhile, Wingate's column was squeezing the Italians from the other direction. "The Patriot forces on this occasion displayed great courage and frequently ran in among the enemy's troops," reported Akavia.*

On the second day of this battle, when it seemed that at any moment Maraventano must break through Thesiger's lines just as the disgraced Natale had at Charaka, Wingate received news that Aosta had surren-dered to Cunningham at Amba Alagi. He seized the opportunity to

---

*Ras Kassa was spotted watching these events while seated on a shooting stick, "like an English country gentleman watching a pheasant drive," according to Nott.

send Maraventano a letter with a brave Ethiopian who was paid one hundred Maria Theresas to cross the lines with it in a cleft stick and promised another hundred if he brought a reply. In it Wingate, who signed himself as commander of British and Ethiopian forces, played the Atrocity Card, explaining that he had been ordered to withdraw all British personnel and they would be at the mercy of Ras Kassa's Patriots:

> I linger here for perhaps 24 hours only in the hope that you will decide not to sacrifice needlessly the lives of so many brave men. . . . If you refuse this last offer, control passes out of my hand.

For a while the skirmishing continued, and then the next day Maraventano sent his reply, which declared that surrender was out of the question until his last bullet had been expended. "Danger, deprivation and fatigue we Italian soldiers will bear for the honour and grandeur of our motherland." Furthermore, he could not surrender without the permission of his superior. "I will send your letter to him by wireless telegraphy."

Meanwhile, Maraventano asked for bandages and medicines to treat the wounded Rowe, explaining that he no longer had these things. A radio intercept of his signal to General Nasi's HQ in Gondar revealed that medicine was not all he was short of. After three days of fighting he had used up most of his ammunition and food and his soldiers were exhausted.

Wingate responded by sending Rowe their last full bottle of whiskey, their only intact packet of cigarettes, and their only unused British army shell dressing. He wanted Maraventano to believe the British were so lavishly equipped that their quartermasters could afford to include comfort boxes in their mule trains. The truth was that Wingate not only had fewer men but less food and ammunition than the Italians. Undaunted, Wingate continued to bluff, flatter, and appeal to a common humanity. In a second letter, he told his adversary: "[Y]ou may well be described as having reached the point where surrender not only implies no disgrace but is the duty of a commander who has the welfare of his troops at heart."

Maraventano surrendered on 23 May 1941. In accordance with the terms of surrender and the whole nineteenth-century flavor of the campaign, a guard of honor—some of them Sudanese camel minders—

presented arms to him and his staff as they filed past. Wingate left a memorable description of the scene:

> Across a level plain sloping towards a hidden valley the Italian com-
> mander and his staff of thirty officers advanced on horseback. Be-
> hind them came eight hundred fascisti, and then phalanx after
> phalanx of Colonial troops (who did not want to surrender) with
> their 250 Italian officers, guns, mortars, machine guns and three mil-
> lion rounds of small arms ammunition. [Even if only half true, so
> much for the last bullet!] Altogether 14,000* men marched in order
> of battle, while to receive them stood 36 Sudanese. These formed
> five lanes through which the enemy poured, laying down his arms in
> heaps, reformed in units, and passed on over the edge of the valley
> where they expected to find the army that had beaten them. Instead
> they found myself with Ras Kassa and a few Patriots; but their arms
> already lay piled under guard of our Brens.

On the long march to Addis Ababa all the Italian officers and some of the men were allowed to keep their small arms and ten rounds of am-munition for their own protection. Among the stretcher cases carried by relays of four *ascari* was Rowe, who survived the journey only to die in hospital in Addis. Wingate would later put this down to a generally weakened condition brought about by their abysmal rations. The pris-oners occupied eighteen miles of narrow track and were escorted by about a dozen British officers and NCOs, sixty Sudanese soldiers, and a milling crowd of Patriots and hangers-on. According to Wingate all the latter exercised "their Christian forbearance and not a prisoner failed to reach the main road." How, one wonders, would he ever have noticed? But certainly there was no massacre.

Wingate brought up the end of the column, riding beside Major Nott, whom he kept amused by reciting chunks of Shakespeare. Gen-eral Wetherall forgave Wingate for disobeying orders and was gener-ous with his praise, describing, as well he might, the pursuit and capture of Maraventano as a brilliant and unparalleled action "against an enemy greatly superior in numbers."

After six months of hard and often dangerous campaigning it was the kind of moment most professional soldiers only dream about.

*Other eyewitnesses put the total at twelve thousand.

Years later Sir Wilfred Thesiger would tell the authors, "Wingate deserved a knighthood for what he did in Ethiopia."

But Wingate was not even allowed to take his place at the victory banquet that the emperor hosted for Sandford, Nott, Thesiger, and other members of the British team. Instead he got a summons to General Cunningham's HQ at Harar near the coast, where arrangements were made to put him on the next available flight to Cairo. "Everybody in force HQ distrusted him," recalled Captain Peter Molloy, a staff officer. "He had brought the Emperor in. They wanted him out as soon as possible . . . they were afraid he would meddle in politics."

It seemed that Cunningham, who would shortly be transferred to Egypt's Western Desert, and humiliation at the hands of Rommel, had heard all about Wingate's behavior in Palestine and was not going to tolerate any of that sort of hanky-panky on his patch. Around his headquarters there was no appreciation of what Wingate had achieved. Men who would never march all night on an empty stomach to fight at dawn, popinjays who thought hardship was not changing their shirt for three days, expressed their distaste for "a bearded, scruffy, unimpressive figure." Once again his differentness grated. It was as if the clock had been turned back twenty years and he was again at Woolwich. Wingate was not even allowed to return to Addis Ababa to say his good-byes to the emperor or collect Akavia, who still had his revolver. Which, as it turned out, was no bad thing.

Chapter 14

BACK IN CAIRO, Wingate walked into Middle East general headquarters a colonel—and walked out again an hour or two later a major. The reward for his key role in driving the Italians from Abyssinia, Britain's first enduring land victory of the war, was to be reduced to his substantive rank—"for political reasons," as he put it.

It was the first of a series of slights, real and imagined, other-inflicted and self-induced, which combined with a savage bout of ill health to reduce the victor of the Gojjam to the lowest point of his existence.

He might reasonably have expected his exploits in Ethiopia to have earned him if not acclaim at the very least confirmation in his temporary rank. But his prickly personality and his partisanship in Palestine had earned him the intense dislike of many at GHQ. As for Wavell, the erstwhile sponsor to whom Wingate might have appealed, he was on his way out, having earned Churchill's blame for the latest British setbacks in the Middle East.

For while Wingate had been busy routing an Italian army and restoring an emperor to his throne, the war had elsewhere in the region been going disastrously, reducing the Abyssinian campaign to a mere sideshow. The Axis had overrun Greece, Yugoslavia, and Crete, and in the Western Desert, Operation Battleaxe—a much-heralded British attempt to relieve the siege of Tobruk—had been easily contained by Rommel's Afrika Korps. The entire eastern Mediterranean was now at risk.

The hardships of the Abyssinian campaign had taken their toll of Wingate's physical resources. Worse, he was beginning to suffer the delayed effects of malaria. Worse still, no one at GHQ had any time for him or any suggestion as to where and how his talents might next be employed, even though a number of irregular units of the kind for which Wingate was eminently suited were either operating or in the process of formation.

One of these, known as the Special Interrogation Group, was employing at least one of Wingate's former Special Night Squadsmen, the German speaker Israel Carmi, behind enemy lines in Libya. Two other former squadsmen, Moshe Dayan and Dan Ram, were fighting with a mixed British, Australian, and Free French force against the pro-Axis Vichy French in Lebanon. But the man who had tutored them was left to seethe with frustration and resentment in a Cairo hotel, his hope shattered that victory in Ethiopia might revive his chances for command of a Jewish army.

Personal disappointment apart, Wingate was now beset by the conviction that the British were reneging on their promises to restore Abyssinia to full independence and intending to make it a protectorate under the Crown. There is absolutely no evidence that this was the case. Such a proposal was never discussed by Churchill's war cabinet, and Wavell's assurances to Haile Selassie were quite specific. "They [the British] reaffirm that they themselves have no territorial ambitions in Abyssinia. . . . Temporary measures of military guidance and control . . . will be brought to an end as soon as the situation permits."

But Wingate persisted in believing that his personal pledges to the emperor were to be dishonored. Haile Selassie himself more realistically focused his suspicions on the military authorities on the spot rather than on Whitehall. Sending Wingate four gold rings as a small token of his appreciation, he wrote: "It is distressing that the British [occupation] authorities are adopting a policy that is quite different to that of their government and the British public."

Wingate had taken the cause of Ethiopian independence to heart in much the same way—though with perhaps not quite the intensity—as he had the Zionist cause and was as quick to spring to the defense of the Abyssinians as he was of the Jews. "The Ethiopians were civilised and living in accordance with the laws of Moses when we were savages without a history," he upbraided a prominent Englishman who had published uncomplimentary comments about Haile Selassie's subjects. Wingate pointed to their "enlightened treatment of women" in contrast to the norms of Africa and the Middle East, and went on:

There is today more humanity and generosity of spirit among the Ethiopians than among us. I can supply you with details of Italian outrages against the Ethiopians which the Ethiopians rewarded with self restraint and humanity when they were in a position to exact revenge.

Wingate's spirits were raised a little when Tony Simonds arrived in Cairo from Abyssinia in mid-June. But Simonds, emaciated and suffering from jaundice, also met with indifference, if not hostility. On reporting to GHQ he found that for the six months he had been behind enemy lines in Abyssinia, "I had been credited no pay, no allowances, and I had been struck off the Army List." When he complained to the military secretary, he was told, "Awfully sorry. Thought you were dead." Subsequently Simonds was singled out as the only officer under Wingate's command in Abyssinia to be refused the decoration, the DSO, for which Wingate had recommended him—a fact that, to the end of his long life, Simonds attributed to his having been too close to "my dear old Orde." By contrast, Boustead and Thesiger, also recommended by Wingate for DSOs but neither of them on friendly terms with him, did receive their medals.

Then there was the case of Akavia, Wingate's particular favorite. As a civilian, and so not eligible to receive a military award, he had been recommended by Wingate for a civilian honor, the MBE.* This also was refused. Wingate himself could hardly be passed over and was awarded a bar to the DSO he had won in Palestine.

Another of Wingate's recommendations to be rejected by GHQ was his request for hardship allowances to be paid to the British NCOs who had served with Gideon Force. His claim was ruled inadmissible on the grounds that such allowances were available only to members of units "in the field," whereas his men had operated *behind* enemy lines. Such mean-spirited behavior only reinforced Wingate's conviction that the headquarters brass were out to get him.

With grounds like these for bitterness, suspicion, and resentment,

---

*Wingate's citation of Akavia said he was "frequently under fire in the course of his normal duties and [performed] the duties of an officer in charge of troops" showing "exceptional gifts and exceptional devotion to duty." When Akavia became an officer in a Palestinian unit of the British army he wore the bronze oak leaf of one who had been Mentioned in Despatches.

Wingate composed a lengthy but needlessly provocative "Appreciation of the Ethiopian Campaign." It was a document that Wavell said later "would almost have justified my placing him under arrest for insubordination." Although direct, cogent, and replete with shrewd observations and recommendations about the future conduct of irregular operations, the document also contained some of Wingate's most unfair judgments and least temperate language.

He described the British NCOs seconded to Gideon Force (those same NCOs for whom he had been trying to obtain hardship money!) as "the scum of an army," some of his officers as "mediocre or inferior," and some of his signalers as "lazy, ill-trained and sometimes cowardly." On the politics of the situation he declared his suspicions that Britain was planning to cheat the Abyssinians out of their independence:

> Cynicism in this war will defeat us but it is very prevalent in our councils. . . . [The] Ethiopians now begin to think . . . that we deliberately deceived them for gain. That so long as it was advantageous to us, we preached liberty to the captives. . . . If Ethiopia, always suspicious of White imperialism, thinks this today the world will find cause to think it tomorrow and we shall lose at one blow the support of millions. . . . Righteousness exalteth a nation.

To bolster his contention that the senior British commanders in East Africa were sympathetic toward fascism, Wingate went so far as to suggest that, prior to Italy's entry into the war, General Erskine had been undisguisedly pro-Italian and had accepted a rifle of honor from the Nazi propaganda chief, Joseph Goebbels. And as a parting shot, though without naming them directly, he described as "the mark of a military ape" the decision of Generals Cunningham* and Platt to disband Gideon Force before the campaign was quite over "and while the need for it still exists."

There is no question but that Wingate had been unjustly treated by Cunningham and, to a lesser extent, by Platt, but to call them "military apes" in a document intended for circulation at the highest level was provocation of a kind that even mentors like Wavell were not prepared to tolerate. Equally rash was the "scum of the army" remark, even

---

*Cunningham went on to become Britain's last colonial governor of Palestine, departing on the founding of the state of Israel in May 1948.

though Wingate's "appreciation" made it plain that there were honorable exceptions. Boustead's Sudanese battalion was singled out for special praise: "By the end of the campaign, the appearance of an Imma [turban] on a mountainside was worth a hundred men." Nor did he forget the excellence of some of the officers in the Second Ethiopian Battalion, such as Luyt, who was commissioned in the field for the way he served his Lewis gun at the Charaka River battle.

The admiration was often mutual. Tutton had long since shrugged off his reservations about Wingate. "I would seriously like to know if, when this campaign closes, there is any chance of my going along with you on any future adventurous enterprise,"* he wrote from a military hospital where he was recovering from dysentery. "I enjoyed our Gojjam campaign immensely. . . . It was a treat to serve under a commander of such boldness."

Even Boustead, though he certainly did not love Wingate, had also learned to respect his qualities. After their victory in the Gojjam he wrote Wingate a note, urging him on to bigger and better things: "The need for officers with your own strategic grasp and experience in the Middle East in the centre of things is patent to anyone who cares for the future. . . . So come out of these mountain fastnesses where all of importance is over . . . and go to where your services and experience and other qualities will be of greatest value. . . . Do not delay in what is now a minor theatre here, or you will be too late and the hurricane will already have swept over the real Middle East before you reach it."

The "scum" Wingate referred to were the officers and NCOs from the operational centers, the majority from the First Cavalry Division, which was in the process of being mechanized. At least half the centers never saw action, either because by the time they had finished training the Gojjam campaign was over or because they were held back around Burye to stiffen the emperor's household troops. The few who did see combat were mostly very good, especially the Australians of Number One Operational Centre, who all became fervent admirers of Wingate. Another center from an ordinary county infantry regiment, the Beds. and Herts., did very well with Thesiger, manning the Hotchkiss machine gun that helped seal the fate of Maraventano's column.

---

*This was not to be. Tutton was mortally wounded on 11 November 1941 as the campaign came to an end with the storming of the Italians' last mountain redoubt.

Despite these performances, Wingate's impressions seem to have been colored by the one mutinous center who very nearly surrendered to the Italians when they were serving with Simonds in Beghemder Force. This center had joined Simonds toward the end of March and was made up of an officer and four sergeants from a southern counties infantry regiment. The officer was a rather sheltered, religious young man who had been a schoolteacher in civilian life. The sergeants were all regulars, old sweats who, according to Simonds, thought that "training blacks" in Ethiopia was preferable to getting caught up in the bigger war in Libya. At least one of them had lost his stripes for some drunken misdemeanor and then had them restored before he was seconded to Gideon Force by a commanding officer who wanted to get rid of him. Within a short time all four sergeants had caught a venereal disease from women in the villages where they were operating. In his unpublished memoirs, Simonds mentioned that the sergeants moaned constantly about their rations:

> Our diet at this time, from February onwards, was semi-cooked meat, roasted barley, watt [a gray form of unleavened bread], rather bitter wild onions, rancid butter and stale, curdled milk. We had long beards and no soap at all.

Despite such hardships Simonds had no problems with his other operational center, composed of Territorial Army men from Northern Ireland who were genuine volunteers and good soldiers. Simonds recommended one of them, Sergeant Billy King, for a posthumous Victoria Cross after he deliberately blew himself up when he was discovered by Italians preparing to demolish a bridge. King died in an Italian field hospital a couple of days later, and the Italians sent Simonds a note saying he had been buried with the honors of war—"he was a very brave man." Wingate endorsed Simonds's recommendation for a VC, but King did not even get a Mention in Despatches.

The quality of the operational centers was obviously something that Wingate and Simonds raked over in Cairo, sick in body and sick at heart over the nonrecognition of their efforts and all the slights and obstructions to which they had been subject. Simonds's nerves were brittle as Melba toast. On his first day at GHQ he punched the staff officer responsible for calling him back to a job that no longer existed. And at his hotel one night he confronted a group of boisterous young cavalry officers with a revolver in one hand and a primed Italian grenade in the other for keeping him awake.

When Wingate's unfortunate "appreciation" reached headquarters, Wavell would recall, "my staff were, to put it mildly, pained at the tone. I sent for Wingate and had out with him as man to man the grievances he had voiced. Some were misunderstandings, a few were real and could be remedied, some more were imaginary. . . . He bore evidence of the great strain to which he had been subjected."

He did indeed. Although neither he nor anyone else could be aware of it at the time, malarial parasites were beginning to invade Wingate's brain as he typed his report. But although he was feeling wretched he would not go to an army doctor for fear of being put on an official sick list and perhaps shunted permanently aside by his detractors at GHQ. Instead, he went to a civilian doctor who prescribed Atabrine, a powerful antimalarial drug with depressive side effects.

Determined to regain his health without recourse to the Royal Army Medical Corps, Wingate began recklessly to overdose on Atabrine, which brought his temperature down but did not get to the root of his sickness. Matters came to a head on 4 July when, having run out of Atabrine, he staggered out of the hotel with a temperature of 104 and tried to find the doctor to obtain a fresh prescription. In his confused state of mind and, as he recorded later, beginning to entertain the thought of suicide "to make people pause and think," he lost his way in the steam heat of the Cairo back streets.

Holding on to walls for support he returned to the hotel and went up to his room. On the way there he passed a floor waiter and mumbled his thanks for the services the man had rendered him. By this time, convinced that the God in whom he believed so fervently had turned his back on him, Wingate had made up his befuddled mind to take his own life. Had he been in possession of a pistol and ammunition it would have been a simple enough matter. But, thanks to Cunningham's determination to get him out of Ethiopia in a hurry he had never had the chance to recover the service revolver he had lent to Akavia. And although he had acquired a small Italian automatic pistol, which he intended to give to Lorna, he had no ammunition for it. Akavia had packed the pistol in Wingate's suitcase and—following the concealment routine he had learned in Haganah training—packed the magazine separately in the bedroll that Wingate had left behind in Addis Ababa.

This sequence of happenstance undoubtedly saved Wingate's life. In the absence of a firearm he tried to kill himself with a hunting knife that he had been given by an American correspondent in Abyssinia. Standing in front of his bathroom mirror, he plunged the knife into the right side of his neck. Involuntarily, he had tensed his neck muscles and failed to penetrate the carotid artery, which carries blood to the brain. Bleeding profusely nonetheless, he staggered to his bedroom door to lock it before making a second attempt. Returning to the bathroom, he stabbed at the jugular vein on the left side of his neck. Again his neck muscles tensed involuntarily, and he missed the jugular. By now, he had lost so much blood that he fell heavily to the floor.

In the next-door bedroom Colonel Cudbert Thornhill had heard Wingate lock his door and, a few moments later, heard the thud as he fell to the floor. Realizing something was amiss, Thornhill tried to force his way in and, failing, dashed to the reception desk to get a passkey. He and the hotel manager got to Wingate just in time. An ambulance was summoned and the wounded man was rushed to a military hospital. There he was given an emergency transfusion of type O blood and operated on to repair the terrible wounds to his neck and throat.

In his delirium, Wingate cried out that he was dead and in hell. Church of England and Church of Scotland chaplains failed to calm him. Ironically, it was a priest of the Roman Catholic church—which regarded suicide as a mortal sin and of which the dissenting Wingate deeply disapproved—who persuaded him that God would forgive him. Finally, he fell asleep.

The next morning, the two doctors who had attended Wingate— Surgeon Captain F. P. Ellis, RN, and Colonel G. A. H. Buttle, RAMC—puzzled over the whys and wherefores of the case. A malaria specialist suggested an examination of blood drawn from Wingate's head. Remarkably, what this examination disclosed did not surface for almost four decades, when the *British Medical Journal* published an obituary of Buttle written by Ellis. "It [the blood slide] was swarming with malarial parasites," he wrote. "Wingate had cerebral malaria, not Atabrine poisoning as others have suggested."

On instructions from GHQ, neither officer had discussed Wingate's case with their contemporaries. Nor had they mentioned cerebral malaria in their official report or told either Wingate or his family that the malaria parasites had entered his brain.

———

Abraham Akavia arrived in Cairo from Addis, via Khartoum, the day after Wingate's suicide attempt. When he went to GHQ to report his arrival he was told what had happened and was "staggered" by the news. Yet when he went to the Fifteenth General Military Hospital to see Wingate—his commander's first nonmedical visitor—he studiously avoided any reference to what had happened. "He never told me what he'd done and I didn't enquire," Akavia told the authors. "We talked about everything else."

It must have been a slightly surreal encounter—Wingate drawn and haggard, and conspicuously bandaged about the throat, while his young acolyte pretended not to notice. Close though they were, a closeness tried and tempered in the heat of battle, their relationship was always one of superior to subordinate and, as Akavia put it at the age of eighty, "I never tried to cross the line—invariably I addressed him as 'sir'—and although I felt terribly sorry to see him in this state I never asked him how or why." He added: "My admiration for him was not changed or reduced in any way. And I was glad to feel that my Haganah training might have been instrumental in saving his life. You see, if I hadn't separated his pistol and its ammunition—putting the ammunition clip in his bedroll, which he left behind in Addis, and the gun in his suitcase—he would surely have used it on himself."

After visiting Wingate, Akavia saw Enzio Sereni,* a Palestinian Jew of Italian birth who was in Cairo editing a newspaper for Italian prisoners of war, and told him what had befallen Wingate. Sereni immediately passed the news on to Moshe Shertok at the Jewish Agency office in Cairo, and the following day the three of them went to visit the pa-

———

*Later in the war, Sereni, then aged thirty-nine, was parachuted into Nazi-occupied Italy as an agent for Britain's MI9, whose Cairo chief was Tony Simonds. Owing to a navigational error Sereni fell into German hands and was executed in Dachau concentration camp in 1944.

tient. Again, nothing was said about the reason for Wingate's condition until, first asking Sereni and Akavia to leave the room, Wingate made an emotional "confession" to Shertok, saying that the Zionist leadership, whom he hoped to serve in the future, were entitled to know the truth. Shertok assured him that their confidence in him would be in no way diminished, and Ben-Gurion, who visited a day or two later, gave Wingate the same assurance.

A visit from Hugh Boustead was a good deal less happy. It started amicably enough, but when Wingate mentioned his "appreciation" of the Abyssinian campaign and allowed Boustead to read a copy things turned nasty. When Boustead reached the passage containing Wingate's intemperate comments on the quality of his British officers and NCOs, he threw the papers to the ground and stormed out, telling Wingate that the next time he tried to do away with himself he should use a gun and make a thorough job of it.

Although he had made a clean breast of things to the Zionist leadership, Wingate had not yet told his wife the truth. Nor had anyone else, officially or otherwise. Ben-Gurion wrote to Lorna that "he has had some trouble with malaria . . . but when I saw him [he] seemed completely recovered and in good health." As for Wingate's neck wounds, Lorna had been told by a "secret source of information" that he had "had a fainting fit, fallen and cut himself," requiring several blood transfusions. She apparently swallowed this unlikely tale, though she did allow that "fainting fits don't sound at all like him."

By now Wingate was recovering rapidly in both body and spirit. He had overcome completely the paralyzing fear that God had forsaken him and had taken his rescue and recovery as a sign that he remained destined for some great purpose. To his mother—without telling her what had really happened—he wrote that "I feel better spiritually and bodily than I have done for years." Had he but realized it, the bungled suicide attempt may have saved his life: if he had not been hospitalized for his neck wounds he might well have succumbed to untreated cerebral malaria, which even under treatment often proves fatal.

The hospital's senior psychological consultant, Dr. G. W. B. James, who examined him on 22 July, only eighteen days after the suicide attempt, concluded that Wingate was no longer suicidal, had completely recovered his mind, and should soon be sent home for a lengthy con-valescence. And before long, exercising his remarkable knack for mak-ing valuable contacts among the movers and shakers, Wingate had struck up a friendship with an influential fellow patient, Mrs. Mary Newall, commandant of No. 11 Convoy, a motorized all-woman mili-tary ambulance unit. She was known in Cairo as "Pistol-Packing Mary" from her habit of wearing a huge service revolver in a holster at her waist. Stylish and crisply beautiful in her expensively tailored uni-forms, she was a celebrity in the enclosed British society of wartime Cairo, which she would later scandalize by conducting a very public affair with the British minister of state, Sir Walter Monckton. When she met Wingate she was in a private ward next to his, recovering from a duodenal ulcer, and, unaffected by the spiteful gossip of those who rejoiced in Wingate's downfall, she assured him that instances of sui-cide occurred in the best families, including her own.

She listened to him by the hour as he spoke on his pet subject, Zion-ism, and good-naturedly submitted to interminable readings from the Old Testament. One evening, after he had read most of the Book of Job to her, he exclaimed, "Isn't that magnificent!" to which she replied, "I really couldn't say; I've been asleep for the past half hour."

Two of Mary Newall's "gels" in the ambulance service were plan-ning a leave in Palestine, and at their commandant's request Wingate wrote them a brief guide to the country, which ran to three typed, sin-gle-spaced pages and was headed "How to See Palestine." It was a characteristic Wingate document:

> The usual organisation for depriving the traveller of comfort and
> means flourishes in Palestine as in Egypt. Any attempt to see sacred
> places, etc., after the usual manner delivers you straight into the
> hands of these sharks. The sequel is that you form part of a dusty,
> hot, uninterested crocodile, trailing after some semi-literate and ra-
> pacious Arab guide.

A characteristic Wingate document of rather more significance, his "appreciation" of the Abyssinian campaign, was passed on by Mary Newall to the most influential of all her acquaintances, Oliver Lyttleton (later Lord Chandos), Churchill's cabinet-ranking, newly appointed minister of state in Egypt and her lover Monckton's predecessor. Lyt-tleton invited Wingate to dinner at his temporary home near the Great

Pyramids and was impressed and intrigued by his guest's vivid and passionate discourse on Abyssinia, Palestine, the potential value of a Jewish fighting force, and the possibilities offered by future guerrilla-type operations. Lyttleton's impressions undoubtedly filtered back to Downing Street to be stored in the capacious memory of Churchill, who already had his own recollections of the spellbinding young officer he had met at a prewar dinner party.

On 10 August Wingate wrote to Haile Selassie, thanking him for the gift of four gold rings, delivered by Akavia, and explaining that, having been ill in hospital, "Your Majesty's rememberance of me was the more welcome." The letter suggests a professional soldier who, like his hero Cromwell, found no glory in battle, only "cruel necessity":

> There is little satisfaction to be found in the prosecution of war at the best of times, and it is only when such activities serve the cause of justice and humanity that we can feel pride in recollecting the share we bore in them. . . . I shall always be a devoted friend of Your Majesty and your people and shall confidently hope to see you established as an equal among equals in the better world order which will, please God, follow the present disastrous war.

One day in early September 1941, Akavia called in at the hospital to see Wingate and found an empty bed and a note saying: "Off at 12 hours' notice. Keep fit until I return, whatever happens. Many thanks for all your care and loyalty. If I could I would reward them." Signing off, he added in Hebrew the biblical exhortation "Be of good courage and strong."

Wingate was on his way home, on the hospital ship *Llandovery Castle,* via South Africa, the lengthy route taken by nonurgent traffic to avoid intensive enemy submarine activity in the enclosed waters of the Mediterranean. At Durban Wingate and other convalescent passengers were transferred to a nearby transit camp, and Wingate delighted Dick Luyt's parents by meeting them and telling them of their son's exploits. After three weeks in Cape Town he embarked on the troopship *Empress of Australia,* bound for Glasgow.

On this leg of the journey he took under his wing a young officer who, like him, had suffered severe mental stress and to whom he showed great kindness. This man left a heartfelt though unsigned testimonial to the moral support Wingate gave him:

> I saw him each day and came to know him as a real Christian. Frequently he would join me in my morning walk on deck and we had many interesting talks together, most of which were obviously designed to take my thoughts from myself and relieve me of my anxieties. . . . The doctors undoubtedly found treatment of my case difficult, and but for my most fortunate meeting with Major Wingate I am certain my recovery would have been considerably retarded. . . . His kindly actions, patient forebearance and thought for me during a voyage which, in my state of health was bound to be trying, apart from the hazards of war, will ever be remembered by me with gratitude.

This was surely a kinder, gentler Wingate, his sharp edges abraded by his own experience of breakdown, and a Wingate whom the senior medical officer on board had no hesitation in describing as fit for anything. "I have had the opportunity of close personal observation of this officer for the past ten weeks," he wrote, "and have formed the opinion that he is a man of unusual ability and high mental calibre."

> The latter part of the period of observation has been one of considerable strain due to war conditions at sea, when some nervous symptoms would not have been abnormal. But during this phase he shewed complete calm and was mentally alert. . . . The patient is now an officer of full mental and physical vigour and determined to get back to the firing line as quickly as possible. . . . His return to combatant duty in the field [is] most desirable from the national viewpoint.

Chapter 15

T H E *Empress of Australia* berthed in Glasgow on a cold, gray day in mid-November 1941, and Wingate, granted three months' convalescence leave, hurried down to London to be reunited with Lorna in their Mayfair flat. There, he confessed to her the truth of what had happened. "Don't you know?" he said. "I tried to kill myself."

Lorna had already begun to suspect that she had never been told the whole story, and Orde's admission, although a shock, was not entirely a surprise. Her main concern was to expunge any lingering feelings of guilt that Orde might harbor. Taking his hand, she said that people who lived at the cutting edge of great events were inevitably subject to highs and lows of greater intensity than those experienced by lesser mortals.

She mentioned Robert Clive, the founder of Britain's Indian empire and one of Wingate's personal heroes, who had attempted suicide three times and, like Orde, had believed his deliverance to be a sign that he was destined for greatness. "I forgot about him," said Orde, forgetting also that Clive had succeeded on his third attempt.

A bout of tonsillitis kept Wingate inactive for a couple of weeks, but once recovered he set about getting himself reclassified fit for active service as quickly as possible. With the help of his old friend and family doctor Ben Zion Kounine, he obtained an appointment with King George VI's physician, Lord Horder (who had coincidentally treated Ethel Wingate for her heart condition). Horder was favorably impressed by Wingate's mental and physical condition and more so when Chaim Weizmann, who happened to be in London at the time, weighed in with a personal guarantee of Wingate's mental stability. Although he had no official position vis-à-vis the War Office, Horder was obviously a man of great influence. Accordingly, his written assurance that Wingate was mentally and physically fit for active duty was a major factor in his being classified "Category A" by a War Office medical board on 30 December.

While all this was going on Wingate had been busy renewing old contacts and making new ones. These included, of course, Cousin Rex, and Leo Amery, the secretary of state for India. Sir Reginald congratulated Orde "most heartily" on his exploits in Abyssinia, adding: "We are all proud of the lustre you have so honourably and gallantly added to the family name." Amery urged him to write a fuller version of his report on the Abyssinian operation, with its recommendations for future guerrilla-type operations, and undertook to circulate it unofficially at the highest levels. On reading the draft, Amery tactfully urged Wingate to tone it down "very considerably" here and there:

> The passage at the bottom of page 18 would suggest that you looked upon General Cunningham as a military ape, and would certainly create the impression that your normal attitude towards the high military command is one of contempt. This would certainly not encourage the authorities to entrust you with the kind of organising work that you want. After all, your main purpose is action. . . . A little of both the dove and the serpent are required.

Wingate for once had the good sense to compromise, and Amery sent a copy of the amended draft to Sir Alan Brooke (later Lord Alanbrooke), chief of the Imperial General Staff, for circulation among the top brass at the War Office. Meanwhile, Sir Reginald sent copies to Sir Hastings (later Lord) Ismay, Churchill's military adviser, and Brigadier Sim, aide-de-camp to the king. In an accompanying note to Sim, Sir Reginald wrote: "His future seems uncertain—perhaps you can be of help in getting him employed in some capacity in which his exceptional experience could be utilised." To Ismay, he wrote: "I am sure it will interest you—not only as an achievement of value but largely as an important contribution to the method of warfare he adopted and which might well be adapted, with modifications, to other theatres of operations."

Orde was also making his mark with the media. An unidentified contributor to the influential *New Statesman and Nation* (probably Michael Foot) told how, on meeting Wingate the previous week, "for two hours I listened to a tale of epic quality."

If ever good propaganda was given to us by the gods, this story was supreme propaganda; the tale, for example, of how 14,000 Italian troops were bluffed into surrendering to less than 2,000 Patriots made one's blood tingle. But what is the Ministry of Information doing? Or the BBC? Here is a story that ought to go round the world. . . . Why this epic should be reserved for a few dinner tables I cannot imagine. Nor do I understand why the methods which worked so superbly in Abyssinia have not relevance of vital importance to other theatres of war.

The Americans, whose press had shown more interest in the Abyssinian campaign than the British, wanted Wingate to write a book. Thomas Costain of Doubleday and Doran, publishers in the United States of Lawrence's *Seven Pillars of Wisdom,* wrote, "There seems to us to be a parallel between what you have done and the part that Lawrence played in Arabia and it seems reasonable that sooner or later you will think of putting this story down on paper. If or when the time comes that you can do this we would like to have the opportunity of considering it for publication. . . ." Wingate replied with uncharacteristic restraint, withholding his poor opinion of his distant relative's military and political achievements but regretting that he lacked "Lawrence's literary gift."

As early as 20 November, only a day after his return to London, Wingate and Lorna were dining at the Dorchester with Chaim and Vera Weizmann and Blanche Dugdale and her husband, Edgar. "Orde by our desire held the floor all night," Baffy recorded in her diary. "His description of the Abyssinian campaign, his handling of the natives etc. quite brilliant. He is obviously a guerrilla leader of genius. But he is so pro-Abyssinian to be almost anti-British. I suppose it is part of his power to almost identify with the bands he leads."

Renewing his acquaintance with Weizmann must have been a pleasure tinged with a certain mutual awkwardness, given the harsh words Wingate had addressed to the Zionist leader, before departing for Ethiopia, for his failure to press hard enough for the creation of a Jewish fighting force. Whatever may or may not have been said on the subject that night, Wingate went out of his way to make his feelings clear in a subsequent letter:

As you know, we have differed—at times vehemently—as to the right policy to pursue from time to time. I have at times said and thought hard things of you, and I want you to know now that I have come to see that our differences were of temperament only and not of heart, and that I have come to realise the measure of your greatness, both in spirit and in work, and my own unworthiness to criticise as I have sometimes done. . . . I have grown to see the difficulties and also to comprehend the nobility of your patience and longsuffering. This is the greatness of the Jews.

It is doubtful that Wingate even bothered to mention to Weizmann a curious suggestion that had been made to him by Cousin Rex that perhaps the way out of the Palestine impasse would be to offer the Jews "a National Home in the reorganised Abyssinia":

> You know better than I do how much traditional connection there is between the two countries and having regard to the fact that recent events have shown that you have joint sympathies with the future of the two countries, you might perhaps be instrumental in sounding Haile Selassie and if he is agreeable the suggestion might come from him (through you) to H[is] M[ajesty's] G[overnment] and through the latter to the American Zionists with whom Weizmann has close relations.

The suggestion shows how unaware the doughty old Arabist was, not just of the strength of Zionist feelings for "the Land of Israel" but of Orde's determination that Abyssinia's hard-won independence should in no way be encroached upon. To have taken up his kinsman's notions—formulated in the course of "some interesting private correspondence with someone who holds an important position in H.M.G."—would have been to betray the two causes to which he was most passionately attached. And, as Baffy Dugdale had observed, he remained deeply suspicious that the British military and political leadership were planning to renege on their pledges of full independence to Haile Selassie.

These suspicions led him once more to interfere—dangerously, so far as his career prospects were concerned—in matters of high policy beyond the remit of a serving soldier. He had been introduced to a hyperactive bluestocking named Sylvia Pankhurst, daughter of the famed suffragette leader, who was editor of a fine-focused publication called *New Times and Ethiopia News,* which was dedicated to furthering the Abyssinian cause. In January 1942, this small-circulation but influential sheet published a series of articles that suggested a British conspiracy to keep Abyssinia under colonial rule. They bore Miss Pankhurst's byline but had Wingate's fingerprints all over them, giving fresh ammunition to those in military circles who deplored his political dabbling.

Although Wingate was not aware of it, Amery's and Sir Reginald's intercessions on his behalf were by now beginning to bear fruit. Learning that Wingate had been judged fit for active service, Wavell—now commander in chief in India—was considering sending for him to take charge of guerrilla operations in Burma, under threat of being overrun by the formidable Japanese imperial forces. Wingate did not yet know of this possibility and would not have been delighted if he had: his sights remained fixed on the Middle East and specifically on leading a Jewish fighting force in guerrilla operations against the Axis armies in the Western Desert.

Meanwhile, he had been refining his ideas about what we would nowadays call "special forces" and had come to the conclusion that ordinary soldiers, not necessarily elite troops, could be trained up to the required standards of morale and physical toughness. He had also refined the notion of what he called for the first time "long-range penetration," a concept that, if not uniquely his, was to influence strategic thinking throughout the rest of the war and up to the present day. He embodied these and other concepts in a lengthy—and in parts shamelessly self-promoting—memorandum that at Amery's urging he wrote in January 1942.

But all, it seemed, to no avail. On 7 February he received orders to report for regimental service with a Royal Artillery field battery at Wimborne, in Dorset. Wingate was devastated, convinced that his enemies in the War Office had finally "fixed" him. By sheerest coincidence, Wavell had sent a signal that very day from New Delhi, requesting Wingate's presence in Rangoon. But by an all-too-common type of military snafu, the message was sent not to the War Office but to the headquarters of East Africa Command.

Desperate to avoid what he considered relegation to limbo in Dorset, Wingate appealed urgently for help to another of Churchill's civilian advisers, Professor Harold Laski, who dashed off a note to the Great Man suggesting that the general staff were discriminating against Wingate on political grounds. Churchill sent back a reply through Ismay saying that in fact Wavell wanted Wingate in place quickly and "arrangements are therefore being made to send Wingate out by the fastest route at the first opportunity."

His posting to Wimborne was rescinded and Wingate readied himself to leave for the Far East. In tidying up his personal affairs he had cause to write to his mother-in-law concerning Lorna's health. "As you know," he wrote, "as the wife of a serving officer she is not liable for conscription but is liable to be directed to industrial work."

> I can say quite definitely that Lorna's health could not stand either normal conditions in any of the services or those in factories. She herself does not like to admit this but there is no doubt as to its truth. Any prolonged physical labour makes her rapidly and seriously ill—even six hours a day would prove too much. She is talented and able in any field where ideas, enthusiasm and successful personal contacts are the requirements for success. She is bad at looking after herself and easily victimised.

This is a curious letter. There is no evidence to suppose that Lorna suffered chronic ill health or that she was the kind of woman who could be "easily victimised." On the contrary, those who knew her all spoke of her forceful personality and her ability to out-argue even Orde himself. On the face of it, he seems to have been strangely overprotective. One might have expected Wingate to want his wife to play an active role of some kind in the war whose aims he so passionately believed in, yet here he was urging Ivy to shield Lorna by taking her on as an assistant in her worthy but scarcely vital Red Cross work of raising funds to send parcels to Allied prisoners of war.

One might have expected that Lorna, with her strong anti-Fascist and philo-semitic sentiments, would also have wished to play a more active role, however humble. She was intelligent, well educated, well connected, and had a flat in London where she could have been at the center of things. Legions of vacuous debutantes found work at the War Office, the Admiralty, in military intelligence and suchlike. Yet Lorna chose to shut herself away in Aberdeen, under the thumb of her domineering mother. It is a mystery that the authors have been unable to unravel.

———

When by 17 February 1942 Orde had received no precise information about the nature of his duties in the Far East, his chronic suspicions of the high command began to surface again. Their silence was "unusual and disquieting," he thought. When word of his disquiet reached Brooke, Wingate was summoned to the War Office at the unusual hour of 7:00 P.M. on 19 February, where he was ushered in to see General Sir Archibald Nye, the deputy CIGS. According to a chronology kept by Wingate (in which he referred to himself in the third person) Nye was "very affable" and explained that Wavell had still not stated exactly what job he had in mind for Wingate. "Therefore Wingate must go out as an unattached major without appointment of any kind and Wavell would fit him in when he got there. Was Wingate satisfied with this?"

He was not. There seemed little point in sending an officer who was an expert on the Middle East to the Far East, he told Nye. He went on to deliver "a brief resumé of his theses on modern war" and it became clear to him that Nye had never heard of him in connection with the Ethiopian campaign. Wingate pressed on with a personal overview of grand strategy, urging that a western front should be opened against the Axis by way of "a central thrust through [North] Africa." Nye nodded in apparent agreement, wrote Wingate, "but evidently did not wish a frank discussion. He remarked that he thought that the Far East was the place where 'things were going to happen.' The interview then came to an end with polite expressions on both sides."

Mulling over this inconclusive encounter, Wingate gave full rein to his suspicions. It was, of course, possible that he would be given a staff appointment on arrival in the Far East, but "what is much more likely is that Wingate as a supernumerary Major will be thrown into the first so-called irregular job that offers without rank or power to do anything." As for Nye, he must have had some ulterior motive in spending so much time on a relatively junior officer. It was "much as if a Principal Secretary of State were to interview a junior clerk for a quarter of an hour in order to tell him exactly nothing."

Wingate believed Nye's real purpose, in view of Churchill's interest, was "not to learn anything, nor yet to tell him anything; just to see him, with the view, one is justified in assuming, of saying that he has been seen." He concluded bitterly, "When the permanent officials go their own way regardless of the leaders of the nation, that nation is on the down grade."

Wingate flew out to the Far East on 27 February, still skeptical despite the implications of his priority passage by air and despite word from Ismay, through Cousin Rex, that his was to be "an important mission," and still resentful that he had not been allowed to fulfill his dream of leading a Jewish force in a flank attack from the south against the Axis armies in Libya. Rarely can a professional soldier have kept an appointment with destiny with such reluctance.

Book Four

BURMA

We have chosen to bear the burden and the heat of the day.
—ORDE WINGATE

Tonight you're going to find your souls.
—COLONEL PHILIP COCHRAN

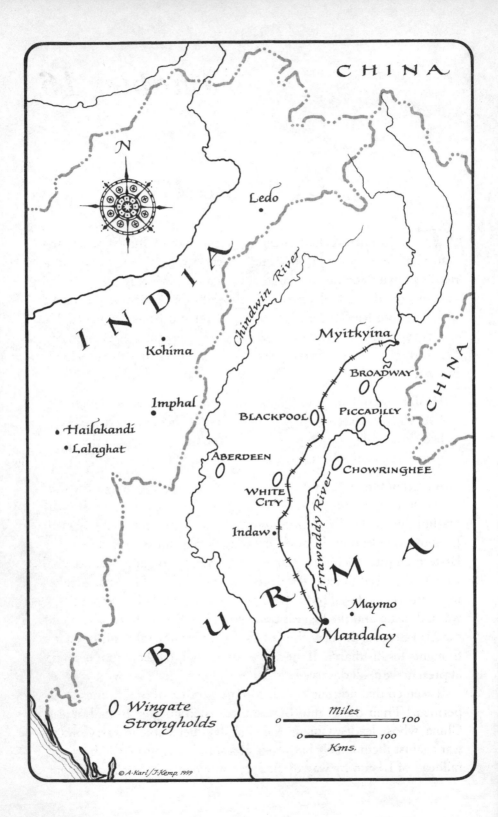

CHINA

N

INDIA

Ledo

Chindwin River

Myitkyina

BROADWAY

Kohima

BLACKPOOL   PICCADILLY

Imphal

CHINA

• Hailakandi
• Lalaghat

ABERDEEN

CHOWRINGHEE

WHITE
CITY

Irrawaddy River

Indaw •

B U R M A

Maymo •

Mandalay

O *Wingate*
Strongholds

Miles
0 —————— 100

0 —————— 100
Kms.

© A. Karl / J. Kemp. 1999

Chapter 16

THE JAPANESE had already overrun half of Burma when Iris
Appleton, a young secretary at British military and administrative headquarters, evacuated to the hill station of Maymyo after the fall
of Rangoon, dashed off a note to her parents to tell them of the arrival
of her school friend Lorna Paterson's husband from England. "He
seems very able and convincing and keen," she wrote. "His after dinner conversation is always very interesting though a bit tense and high-
brow at times."

> He did very well in Abyssinia. I hope he has a success out here but
> I am afraid he has a very hard nut to crack. The news here is very
> bad. Practically no air support and the Burmese are unfriendly
> towards us. In the occupied areas they are actually helping the Japs.

A hard nut indeed. Since the Japanese had entered the war the previous December with their sneak attack on the American fleet at Pearl
Harbor they had inflicted one humiliation after another on the British.
In about one hundred days they had overrun most of Britain's Far
Eastern empire, including Hong Kong, Singapore, and Malaya, and
were now poised to clear the British out of the rest of Burma, advancing to the very gates of India. Churchill called the fall of Singapore "the
worst disaster and the biggest capitulation" in British history. General
Sir Alan Brooke, the new chief of the Imperial General Staff, saved his
thoughts for his diary: "If the army cannot fight better than it is doing
at present we shall deserve to lose our Empire."

It seemed that nothing could stop the advance of the Japanese "supermen." Their thrust into Burma threatened not just India but also
China, whose leader, Chiang Kai-shek, had been able to carry on the
war against them largely by means of a supply line from the Burmese
railhead of Lashio by way of the legendary, seven-hundred-mile-long

Burma Road to his base at Kunming in Yunnan Province. When the American general Vinegar Joe Stilwell,* with Chinese troops under his command, failed to hold Lashio against the advancing Japanese, the only way to continue supplying Chiang was by air, a hazardous journey over "the Hump," the mountain range separating northern Burma from the Chinese plateau.

Burma's defense was largely left to a conglomeration of half-trained Indian troops—the best having been sent to the Middle East—and locally raised levies, bolstered by a British armored brigade that had seen action in the Western Desert against Rommel and all under the command of Lieutenant General (later Field Marshal Viscount) Sir Harold Alexander. The Indian troops and Burmese civilians were of sometimes doubtful loyalty, the Indians being urged by Japanese propaganda to desert and join the so-called Indian National Army for the liberation of their homeland from the British. The Burmese were subject to the blandishments of a homegrown national liberation movement led by Aung San, father of the present day Burmese opposition leader and Nobel laureate Aung San Suu Kyi.**

After the fall of Rangoon on 8 March 1942 Alexander's less than formidable army began to fall back to the Indian border in what would turn out to be the longest fighting retreat in British imperial history—nine hundred miles at the cost of almost fourteen thousand British, Indian, Burmese, and Gurkha lives. With them went long straggling lines of civilian refugees: the Eurasian families of the Scots teak wallahs (the Burmese women were famed for their beauty and intelligence) and Indian families desperate to get out before the country crumbled into anarchy. (Permitted by the British to settle, they had never been liked by the Burmese.) Where they could the British applied a scorched earth policy. At Yenangyaung black clouds hung over the blazing wells of the Far East's biggest oil fields.

*So called for his misanthropic demeanor and his Anglophobia, which disguised a clever and cultivated soldier whose courage and endurance belied his sixty years. Someone who knew the general well once suggested that if Saint Francis of Assisi had been forced to do Stilwell's job as head of the U.S. military mission to the devious and capricious Chiang, he might have been known as Vinegar Frank.

**Disillusioned with the Japanese, Aung San eventually changed sides and joined forces with the British. A statue in Rangoon shows him in British army officer's uniform. A statue in Prome shows him in Japanese uniform mounted on a charger. He was assassinated in 1947, on the eve of Burmese independence.

Amid the ruins the Burmese watched the departure of their colonial masters with mixed feelings. The ethnic minorities, especially the Karen, whose conversion to Christianity was mainly the work of American Baptist missionaries, had long been favorites of the British and dreaded the prospect of being left to the mercy of the Burman and Shan Buddhist majority.

Under the direction of its Japanese advisers, Aung San's Burmese Independence Army took the field, harassing British stragglers, providing guides and intelligence, and generally ensuring that Japanese troops advanced through a friendly populace just as the Patriots had for Wingate's Gideon Force in Ethiopia. For in Burma and the rest of its Southeast Asian possessions the British found themselves playing the same role as the Italians in East Africa: militarily inept colonizers, jumpy and often routed by numerically inferior forces while a formerly subject people pursued and tormented them.

Maymyo, where Wingate so impressed Iris Appleton with his after-dinner conversation, was a hill station thirty miles east of Mandalay, Burma's second city. For years the British had used it as their summer capital when, down in the Irrawaddy delta, Rangoon became too sticky and malarial for comfort. Wavell, as overall commander of British forces in the Far East, had sent Wingate to Maymyo with a vague brief to see what could be done about mounting some sort of guerrilla operation behind Japanese lines. By the time he got there it was obvious to Wingate that all Burma would soon fall and little could be done at present. "All concerned, military and civilian should disabuse their minds of the fallacy that there are going to be any guerrilla operations in Burma except those that can be carried out under the aegis and in the neighbourhood of regular columns," he advised Wavell.

> Guerrillas are born and not made. Essentially, a guerrilla is a man who prefers death on his own terms to life on the enemy's. Such were ... the Ethiopian guerrillas who continued to fight for five years after the Italian occupation; they were steadily being exterminated when we intervened.

In the same memo Wingate reveals a philosophy at odds with what has become a "special forces cult" of the kind that spawns Special Air Service groupies (not the SAS itself—a very professional force) and produces Hollywood fantasies of the Rambo type—or, more germane to Wingate's day, the wartime movie in which Errol Flynn liberated Burma virtually singlehandedly.

> The idea that toughness is a military quality much to be desired for the defeat of the enemy seems commonly held by the general public. The more savage and brutal the human being the better the soldier seems to be the argument. Those who have seen actual fighting are aware that the soldier must behave with the strictest rectitude, not only to his own side but also towards the enemy. The qualities that are of value in war are intelligence and courage. Savagery in fighting is a drawback . . . and the tendency to loot and rapine can do nothing but disservice to the side they serve.

What Wingate prized was endurance, a quality he had in abundance and encouraged in others. "The inexperienced soldier," he would write, "is apt to think that where he suffered there is something wrong instead of realising that suffering is a normal and necessary part of operations." Wavell was thinking very much on the same lines. Shortly before the fall of Singapore he had written to General Sir John Kennedy, planning chief at the War Office, deploring the lack of fighting spirit and general softness of Britain's increasingly conscript army:

> Until we have again soldiers capable of marching twenty or thirty miles a day for a number of days running and missing their full rations every second or third day, and his first idea is to push forward and get to grips with the enemy on any and every occasion, and whatever the difficulties and odds, we shall not recover our morale and reputation.

But Wavell was in distant Delhi, and Wingate could find no kindred spirits in Maymyo. Then one day he visited the headquarters of an organization called the Bush Warfare School, where he met a stocky Royal Engineers major named Michael Calvert. It was to be the start of a formidable partnership. Like Wingate, Calvert, the son of a district commissioner, had been born in India. He was a regular soldier who, unlike the man who was to become the greatest influence in his life, had flourished at Woolwich. He excelled at sports, particularly boxing and swimming, long-distance running and pistol shooting, but was not quite good enough a horseman and épée fencer to make the British pentathlon team for the 1936 Olympics.

His fighting career began in earnest in the spring of 1940 when he was one of the Anglo-French force sent to Norway in a futile attempt to stop the German invasion. As a demolition expert he was in the rear-guard, blowing up bridges and tunnels with the only available explosive devices—naval depth charges. While under air attack he tried, and only just failed, to bring down a German fighter by exploding a depth charge under it as it pulled out of a dive.

It was in the summer of 1941, some five months before Pearl Harbor, that he was posted to Burma as chief instructor at the Bush Warfare School, a rare example of the British actually preparing in advance for war against the Japanese. Its title was a deliberate misnomer. It had nothing to do with teaching bush or jungle warfare. It was part of a secret British military aid package* to Chiang Kai-shek intended to tie down as many Japanese troops as possible in China in the hope, forlorn as it turned out, that the Imperial Japanese Army would be too busy to get up to mischief elsewhere. Its task was to train Australian and British officers and NCOs to assist Chinese guerrillas in rather the same way that Wingate had organized the operational centers in Ethiopia. Indeed, at least two old Ethiopian hands had found employment there—Lord Bentinck of the Coldstreamers and Lieutenant Colonel Courtney Brocklehurst, the former Kenyan game warden Wingate had ordered Simonds to shoot on sight for his plan to suborn the emperor's authority by raising the Galla against the Amhara.

Wavell had returned Wingate to the rank of lieutenant colonel, shortly to be full colonel, though his substantive rank was still major, and had given him a rather loose brief to be a kind of supremo of all operations behind Japanese lines in Burma. Under this umbrella the hundred or so men at the Bush Warfare School, also known as Mission 204, came under his command, though by the time Wingate got there they were beginning to disperse.

When he met Wingate, Calvert had just returned from leading what he would later call the "showboat raid." Calvert had put seventy of his

*American aid was rather more effective and upfront. Major General Claire L. Chennault, a First World War flier who had retired from the U.S. Army Air Forces in 1937, recruited the famous Flying Tigers—a barnstorming bunch of well-paid American pilots, mostly ex-service, officially known as the American Volunteer Group, who became the cutting edge of Chiang Kai-shek's air force and later did their best to support the hard-pressed RAF in Burma.

men on an old paddle steamer skippered by a buccaneering Briton who knew the Irrawaddy's treacherous mudbanks and had taken it downstream as far as the town of Henzada, about seventy-five miles north of Japanese-occupied Rangoon. On the way they had gone ashore to wreck locomotives, bridges, boats, oil wells—anything that could conceivably be of use to the Japanese. Surprised at Henzada, they had almost accidentally led their pursuers into a brutal ambush laid by the covering party they had left on the bank.

Calvert returned to the Bush Warfare School HQ in Maymyo feeling tired and disgruntled. It seemed that some officers and colonial officials were still unable to digest the extent of the British defeat. Expecting congratulations, perhaps even a decoration for the "showboat raid," he had been reprimanded for endangering the lives of civilians employed by the Irrawaddy Flotilla Company and vandalizing the property of Burmah Oil. His mood was not improved by the sight of a large Wolseley-pattern sun helmet on his desk, behind which sat an unknown lieutenant colonel. "Who are you?" demanded Calvert, and the interloper told him his name.

He had never heard of Wingate, never been around when Brocklehurst had been laying down the poison against him. "Excuse me," Calvert said. "But that's my desk."

"I'm sorry," said Wingate, and allowed Calvert his chair. For the first time Calvert began to suspect that there was something unusual here:

> He showed no resentment of this somewhat disrespectful treatment by a major. He began talking quietly, asking questions about the showboat raid. And to my surprise they were the right sort of questions. . . . [H]ere was a man I could work for and follow. Clearly he knew all that I knew about unconventional warfare and a lot more. . . . Suddenly I no longer felt tired. For even at that first meeting something of the driving inspiration inside Orde Wingate transferred itself to me.

But this was not entirely the Wingate who had led Gideon Force, not yet anyway. This was more like the Wingate of his first year in Palestine, feeling his way, learning things, and in speech, if not always on paper, almost diffident at times. Calvert became his dragoman, and showed him around. One of the first things he did was take him down to Prome where Lieutenant General William Slim, who had served under Platt in Ethiopia, was trying to hold a line with his Anglo-Indian-Burmese formations. Wingate insisted that they take a stenographer from headquarters and, on the way down, dictated notes on the countryside. Calvert realized that he had never seen it properly before. When they got down to Slim they found that the situation was deteriorating fast. He was practically without air cover. Japanese fighters were superior to anything the RAF and the American Flying Tigers had available in Burma at that time, and they were overwhelmed. It was beginning to look as if Mandalay, Maymyo, and the rest of northern Burma would fall and the British would have to retreat west of the Chindwin to the jungle-covered hills of the Indian border.

Slim said he agreed with the idea of guerrilla operations in principle but did not have any troops to spare. It was suggested that Calvert might pull together an ad hoc force, using the Bush Warfare School instructors as a stiffener, from all the spare rear-echelon troops around Maymyo he could round up. These could be used as a rearguard screen to blow bridges or ambush the more pushy Japanese reconnaissance patrols.

When they got back to Maymyo Wingate and Calvert discovered that Chiang Kai-shek was visiting from his base in Chungking for a conference with General Alexander. Wingate flew back with the Chinese leader to learn something about Chinese guerrilla operations. Also on board was the American-educated Madame Chiang. Their C-47 was intercepted by Japanese fighters, and the American pilot had to take violent evasive action before he eventually found some cloud and lost them. Wingate, like many men before him, was utterly captivated by Madame Chiang, whose stunning good looks would shortly be celebrated on the cover of *Time* magazine.* He informed Calvert that she had retained her composure throughout and when she was air sick did so in a decorous manner into a paper cup. If his own equilibrium was any the worse for the experience he does not appear to have found it worth mentioning.

Shortly after his return from Chungking Wingate parted company with Calvert, who was press-ganging clerks and signalers and the recently mended into what would briefly be known as "Calvert's Com-

---

*She was still alive at this writing, aged over one hundred and living on Long Island in the United States.

mandos." In the best, or perhaps the worst, postwar Hollywood traditions he also recruited from the army's local detention barracks, though this was to prove a mixed blessing.

But Wingate felt that Burma was not yet ripe for guerrilla warfare in the classical sense. What was beginning to take shape in his fertile mind was something more akin to the cavalry raids of the American Civil War whereby regular troops penetrated enemy territory to wreak havoc behind his lines. When he came to explain it Wingate did so with a certain surgical relish:

> In the back areas are [the enemy's] unprotected kidneys, his midriff, his throat and other vulnerable points . . . the more vital and tender points of the enemy's anatomy. . . . [T]he enemy would have to withdraw troops from the front in order to protect them.

Before he left Burma Wingate borrowed a car and spent several days touring the few mostly unpaved roads between the Irrawaddy and Chindwin rivers accompanied by Captain George Dunlop, a close friend of Calvert's from the Bush Warfare School. On 17 May 1942, Wingate flew back to New Delhi, flying over the straggling columns of British troops and refugees as, racked by malaria and dysentery, they began their long walk to India through some of the cruelest hill country in the world. His parting words to Dunlop were, "There is only one seat. You shall make your own way to India and report to me there."

Not everybody was retreating. Calvert and what was officially designated the Bush Warfare Battalion had been told to hold the Gokteik viaduct—at ten thousand feet one of the highest in the world—about thirty miles east of Maymyo. When finally obliged to withdraw, he asked several times to be allowed to blow up the viaduct but to his puzzlement was always refused permission.

About a month later Calvert and a couple of his men, half-starved—Calvert had lost a third of his body weight—appeared at the headquarters of the Seventeenth Indian Division at Kalewa on the west bank of the Chindwin, unarmed and disguised as Indian peasant women in grubby saris. Calvert had survived a series of hair-raising encounters with the Japanese, including a nude wrestling match with a Japanese officer encountered while they were both bathing in a river. This ended with the athletic Calvert keeping his opponent's head under water until at last he floated away faceup, "like a ghastly yellow Ophelia."*

The authorities in India were overwhelmed by the refugees from the Great Retreat, civil and military. Calvert, after a nightmare rail journey crammed in a cattle truck with hardly any food and water, discovered his friend George Dunlop at a hospital of Crimean War squalor in the cantonment town of Ranchi northwest of Calcutta. The hospital had no nurses and the dead lay next to the living. Yet all around them, apparently oblivious to the suffering of this defeated army, the pukka sahibs were continuing to visit the clubs (some of which really did contain notices declaring that British Other Ranks—enlisted men—Indians, and dogs were barred), give dinner parties, and play tennis. Calvert went to complain to General Slim, who introduced him to a British nursing matron. Together they went knocking on the doors of clubs and bungalows and shamed their occupants into getting down to the hospitals to lend a hand.

The British called their latest defeat a "voluntary withdrawal." Stilwell, who had walked out of Burma to India with his staff and a field ambulance, including some nurses, and skirmished with the Japanese on the way, was not going to let the Limeys get away with that. "No commander in history ever made a voluntary withdrawal," he declared. "There's no such thing as a glorious retreat. All retreats are as ignominious as hell. I claim we got a hell of a licking and we ought to find out what went wrong and take it back."

In Delhi, Wavell had set up something called the Joint Planning Staff, which was supposed to be doing just that. On its staff was a monocled young Scots aristocrat, a major in the Black Watch, named Bernard Fergusson who wrote poetry and contributed nicely turned pieces to literary magazines. A Highlander and a romantic Tory whose hero was the Jacobite soldier-poet the earl of Montrose, Fergusson was nevertheless very much the professional soldier. He had seen action against Rommel's Afrika Korps during the siege of Tobruk and been

---

*Calvert was bathing apart from about a dozen men he had left with him at the time and guessed that his opponent was doing the same thing and did not want to raise the alarm in case the British were much stronger than his patrol and wiped them out. After Calvert killed him this is exactly what they did. Readers interested in a full account of Calvert's amazing adventures at this time should consult his autobiography, *Fighting Mad,* and David Rooney's biography *Mad Mike.*

an ADC to Wavell. He had known Wingate in Palestine, where he too had been engaged in intelligence duties. Now he was seeing a lot more of him:

> Only in one direction did there seem any prospect of action in the near future. It lay in the person of a broad-shouldered, uncouth, almost simian officer who used to drift gloomily into the office for two or three days at a time, audibly dream dreams, and drift out again. . . . We used to look on this visitor as one of those to be bowed out, as soon as it was possible to put a term to his ramblings; but as we became aware that he took no notice of us anyway, but that without our patronage he had the ear of the highest, we paid more attention to his schemes. . . . Briefly, his point was that the enemy was most vulnerable far behind his lines. . . . Here a small force could wreak havoc. . . . If it should be surprised, it could disintegrate into smaller prearranged parties to baffle pursuit, and meet again at a rendezvous fifteen to twenty miles further on its route. Supply should be by air, communication by wireless: these two weapons had not yet been properly exploited.

Under the propeller fans in Delhi, forbidden their normal peacetime flight to the hill station of Simla to escape the summer heat, the staff officers had begun to refer to Wingate as "Tarzan." But he had already won the first round. He tracked down Calvert and Dunlop, both still suffering from the exertions of the campaign, summoned them to Delhi, and informed them that his plan to form a long-range penetration unit and take it back into Burma had been approved. Training was to start immediately. Both agreed to join him as soon as they were well. Dunlop returned to hospital, this time in Delhi, and Calvert convalesced with his sister Eileen in Bangalore.

It was not until August 1942 that Calvert felt fit enough to return to duty, and by then Wingate had moved about 250 miles southeast of Delhi to the district of Sagar in Central Provinces. Here the land is quite like parts of northern Burma with scrub and thick undergrowth and a lot of small rivers that become raging torrents in the monsoon.

Calvert found him in a tented camp near the town of Pathari. Wingate had a brigadier's crown and three pips on his epaulettes and was in command of something called Seventy-seventh Indian Brigade, a title designed to confuse Japanese agents. For there were no Indians in Seventy-seventh Brigade unless you counted a newly raised battalion of Gurkha teenagers (most had lied about their age) from the independent kingdom of Nepal who did not consider themselves to be Indian any more than their British officers regarded them as mercenaries.

There was a battalion of Burma Rifles, who were all from the Karen, Kachin, or Chin minorities and had provided part of the rearguard during the retreat. Most of their officers were British reservists, some of them Eurasians, who had worked with the teak or mining companies and had a great rapport with their men. The Burrifs, as they were known within Seventy-seventh Brigade, were indirectly responsible for giving the formation the name by which they would eventually become known throughout the English-speaking world: the Chindits. This was a corruption of the Burmese *Chinthé,* the name of a mythical griffinlike creature, half lion, half dragon, whose stone effigies are to be found guarding their temples.

Also part of "Wingate's Circus," which is what his British troops were beginning to call themselves, were Royal Air Force officers and sergeants. The sergeants were Morse-key wireless telegraphers, but most of the officers were pilots. Both tended to be a bit bewildered by their new penguin role, which was to coordinate by radio with air transport headquarters for the parachuting of supplies—at the time a revolutionary concept. They also had to learn how to handle the mules that would carry their heavy radio equipment.

Then there was a unit called 142d Commando Company, about a hundred strong. These were the remnants of the training cadre from Calvert's Bush Warfare School, mixed in with a few reinforcements from Britain and the Middle East and volunteers from various British formations in India. Their main task was demolition, which explained the high number of Royal Engineers among them. Most of them were regular soldiers with "Palestine" among their campaign ribbons and the kind of off-duty habits Wingate deplored. Even their sergeant major, James Blain of the Argyll and Sutherland Highlanders, an intelligent man in his late thirties, had known his share of trouble with the military police. But at least they looked like soldiers, capable of frightening the enemy as well as everybody else.

But the British army's main contribution to Wingate's expedition was a unit that was, on the face of it, far less impressive. The Thirteenth Battalion King's (Liverpool) Regiment was old for frontline infantry. Many of the eight hundred or so rank and file were married men with an average age of thirty-three. Some were considerably older. "Not in their wildest dreams could they have considered themselves a picked force," wrote Major George Bromhead,* who was Wingate's brigade major.

It was a wartime battalion originally raised for coastal defense in Britain and, apart from a sprinkling of regular NCOs and reservists transferred from other regiments, most of the men had been conscripted from various concrete jungles in Liverpool, Glasgow, and Manchester. There were also a few Londoners in keeping with government policy not to make units too regional.** Other exceptions included some deserters from the Irish Free State army and, most exotic of all, a platoon commander named Willy Borge Erik Petersen, a Free Dane with the spirit of a Viking berserker.

Once the invasion scare was over the King's had been shipped out to India for internal security duties, which was considered a more appropriate role for them than active service in Africa or training for the invasion of Nazi-occupied Europe. Their new home was the old cantonment town of Secunderabad, where they seemed set for a safe and comfortable war, where even the men had bearers to clean and polish their kit and where there was a constant round of team sports, particularly soccer, and also cheap brothels. For the officers there was a chance to imitate the pukka sahibs from the Indian army with morning rides and even polo for those who could afford a decent string of ponies, tennis, mess nights, and clubs that staged dances. The sergeants and senior NCOs were catered for in friendly if slightly less pukka establishments where the dances were attended by good-looking young Eurasian women whose fathers worked on the railways.

Occasionally the Congress party might stir up the odd riot that needed to be put down or there would be a battalion exercise where they pretended to take on Japanese paratroopers. Then they were given, a little apologetically, to Wingate, who for once did not grumble,

---

*A descendent of the Gonville Bromhead who won a Victoria Cross keeping an impi at bay at Rorke's Drift, the part played by Michael Caine in the film *Zulu*.

**The previous war had shown that it was bad for civilian morale when disaster struck and entire communities were plunged into mourning.

for he knew that after the losses in Malaya and Burma there were no decent infantry to spare. Instead he decided to make the best of them and these mainly reluctant soldiers, so many on the nursery slopes of middle age, found themselves subjected to some of the toughest training ever devised for any regiment in the British army.

Chapter 17

SECOND LIEUTENANT PHILIP STIBBÉ was one of half a dozen young officers from the Royal Sussex Regiment seconded to the Thirteenth King's to bring them up to strength. They arrived bearing the normal accoutrements of young officers taking up their first posting in India: golf clubs, polo sticks, and tennis racquets. Stibbé was twenty and the grandson of a Dutch immigrant to Britain who had made his fortune selling knitting machines. He had recently been studying English literature at Merton College, Oxford, where his tutor was Edmund Blunden, the First World War poet. As soon as they met their new commanding officer the new arrivals realized that they would not be getting much use out of their sports equipment. But they were impressed:

> [I]t was his face which was so striking, particularly the deep set eyes. . . . He was inclined to stoop rather as he walked and with his head and jaw thrust forward and his eyes half closed, as though he was concentrating on some problem.

Wingate concluded his address by hoping the new arrivals would "all enjoy yourselves," an example of his sardonic sense of humor known to his close friends but rarely on public display. Even Calvert found the training tough. They marched until they dropped and then fought mock battles. They were taught to avoid ambush by eschewing well-used trails for the arduous business of hacking their way through thick jungle. Those who cheated when they thought nobody was looking sometimes found slabs of gun cotton exploding much too close for comfort. Nor could the exhausted always rely on a helping hand from their mates. "Fit men left behind to look after stragglers—absolutely forbidden," Wingate noted in the field notebook he carried everywhere—a very durable item with its waxed canvas waterproof cover.

Stibbé and the other young subaltern soon found themselves asking the question people had been asking about Wingate for some time now: was he a genius or a madman? In Patharia the subalterns mostly settled for the former:

> A constant stream of orders, pamphlets, information, encourage-ment and invective showered down on us from Brigade HQ. . . . Saluting was to be cut down to a minimum. Everything was to be done at the double. Everyone must eat at least one raw onion per day. Only shorts should be worn when it was raining. Swearing must stop. When marching in mass formation through the jungle thorn bushes were to be ignored and only thick plantations of bam-boo were to be looked upon as obstacles. [This order was subse-quently modified.] . . . No officer was to go sick, and a man must either be sick or fit; if he was sick he was to do nothing; if he was fit he was to do everything.

Their rations, mostly cheese and dates and a hard biscuit called *shakapura* that could be ground into a kind of porridge, were scarcely adequate, and they learned to forage for extra. With so much water around fish was an obvious item, but soon their diet began to sound as if it might have been inspired by the witches' brew in *Macbeth,* the menu including toads, frogs, snakes, lizards, and scraps of pigeons blown apart by .303 rifle rounds.

For some of the "old married men" in the King's it was all too much. They began to sicken. Before long their sick parades were probably the biggest the British army had seen since the Crimean cholera, with as many as 70 percent of the battalion, including officers, reporting sick. There were enough genuine cases for the malingerers to get them-selves taken seriously. A corporal and a sergeant died of dysentery the same day. There was a lot of malaria. Over a hundred of them were suf-fering from the tropical ulcers known as jungle sores, and they had not even left India yet.

Those staff wallahs who had poured scorn on "Tarzan" secretly re-joiced. Apart from anything else, the sick list provided useful ammuni-tion for those who argued that Wingate must follow British army tradition and use only volunteers for the kind of enterprise he was con-sidering. Failing that he should employ Indian soldiers who did not need to acclimatize. Wingate refused to accept this.

If the British soldier is allowed to get the notion that he cannot take hardships that men of other nations can, he better reconcile himself to being a member of a third rate nation. . . . I personally am quite satisfied the British soldier has a better body and a better mind than average humanity. He can not only equal but beat . . . the Japanese.

But the new Tommy Atkins, mostly citizen-soldier conscripts, had to learn things that were no longer taught in the soft democracies. He had to learn to take risks and hardships in his stride, to eat unfamiliar food, and to shrug off minor illnesses without running to a doctor. "Once you can teach him that," wrote Wingate, "he will win speedy and striking victories over the enemy."

This must have rung a bell with Wavell, who like many other senior officers felt that the bulldog breed had gone soft and must be hardened if the war was to be won and the empire saved. It also appeared to display the solid notions of national, not to say racial, superiority that were common to most Britons at the time. Wingate did not really share these views. Five years before he had made this quite plain in Palestine when he suggested that the average kibbutznik might one day make a better soldier than the average Tommy. What he did subscribe to, within reason, was the old maxim that there were no bad soldiers, only bad officers. Most fit young men could be transformed into competent soldiers providing they were were given the right training and, above all, leadership.

If he had any doubts about the raw material he was currently trying to work with he kept them to himself. Only in his field notebook does he give a clue to his real feelings about the King's. Below some figures on the large daily sick parades he wrote, "Hopeless." Alongside it is a small, tight, rather angry-looking doodle.

Charles Aves was one of the more unusual privates in the King's in that he was unmarried, under twenty-five, over six foot, and one of the few southerners—a Cockney born one hundred yards from Tower Bridge. Even by King's standards his soldiering at Secunderabad had been particularly cushy because he played the piano and piano accordion in the battalion's dance band, which the officers looked after because they liked it at their mess nights. Despite this background he was able to cope with the all-night marches and the bad food. Then the monsoon started:

That was absolute hell. We were never dry, night and day. There were mud holes five feet deep people would fall into. . . . [W]e get lost at night . . . could not find our way into our bivouac areas. It was during this period that we had our first casualties. A stream became a raging torrent. A number of men drowned.

The river Sunar had brimmed its banks as it did during most monsoons. One officer woke in his tent to discover he had been sleeping in six inches of water, which was steadily rising. The Gurkhas salvaged their rifles and took to the trees. It was a rare Gurkha who could swim, nor could at least half of the British Other Ranks even if they had lived near the sea or rivers.* This was a perfectly normal state of affairs for working-class Britons brought up in the 1920s and 1930s and educated up to the age of fourteen in poorly funded state schools with no swimming programs. Just as it was perfectly normal for men in their late twenties to have full sets of false teeth, which often made the consumption of hard biscuits and nuts a risky proposition.

Wingate did his best to try and do something about improving the swimming situation. Nonswimmers were to be "taken in hand at once" and taught to swim a minimum of fifty yards any style:

> Only first class swimmers will be able to cross even a small river in the monsoon season but the fact that a man can swim even a short distance engenders confidence and enables him to cross a wide stretch of deep water provided he is given the necessary buoyancy to keep his head above water.

Some officers took these instructions more seriously than others. But with the best will in the world there was hardly enough time to make up for deprived childhoods. There is no record of any of the officers not being able to swim, though standards obviously varied from the almost Olympic-class Calvert to exponents of the dog paddle. Wingate himself was quite a strong swimmer, though Calvert had plenty of opportunity to observe that his leader did not have his own athlete's build. "He had a weak body, in fact, but he hardened it as he

---

*The only British army corps that encouraged swimming was the Royal Engineers, the army's bridge builders, where sappers were given a small pay increase if they passed a swimming test.

hardened his will power and his sympathies, since he felt he had a mission and had to prepare himself for it."

Most of the officers were considerably taller than Wingate's five foot six, whereas the majority of the Gurkhas were under this. So were a good number of the British Other Ranks, especially the Glaswegians and Liverpudlians, where generations of poverty and bad diet among the urban poor had led to rickets and other stunting complaints somewhat at odds with the ferocity the same men could display in a pub brawl.

Sergeant Arthur Willshaw, a regular Royal Air Force wireless operator, was serving in RAF headquarters in Colombo when a notice went up asking for operators with a knowledge of ground to air communications to volunteer for an unspecified "special mission." Having been accepted Willshaw was told to report to no less than Air Vice Marshal Sir John D'Albiac, the RAF's commander-in-chief, at his headquarters in Delhi, who asked him what his teeth were like. Could he live on hard biscuits for a few weeks?

For those who had not been brought up to use a toothbrush there was not much to be done about bad teeth except to make sure that all the men with dentures had spare plates and impressions registered with the Royal Army Medical Corps so that spare sets could be parachuted to them. Wingate was sufficiently perturbed by the dental problem and interested rather before his time in the search for a balanced diet to give it his personal attention:

> I learn that there is a proposal to increase the nut diet. I am opposed to this on two grounds. Firstly the vast majority of British troops have bad teeth or false teeth and neither type can masticate nuts in the very thorough and complete way that is required if they are to be digested. Secondly, although we may start a campaign on almonds we are almost certain to end it on monkey nuts, which are thoroughly indigestible even when roasted.

Without doubt, dental care separated the two Englands as noticeably as height and the ability to swim and conjugate Latin verbs. The only officer with significant tooth loss was a kilt-wearing Scots commando captain named Geoffrey Lockett, who had had most of his front teeth removed, which made him look even fiercer when, like most of the others, he imitated Wingate by growing a beard.

Stibbé and the other new arrivals in Patharia were there as a result of a purge Wingate had instituted among senior and junior officers of the King's, including the battalion's commanding officer, who had brought them to India from the coastal defenses of Essex.

Over two hundred Other Ranks, about a quarter of their original strength, were also sifted out of the King's—some of them men who would never, however much they tried, be physically or mentally fit enough for the ordeal ahead, and some determined not to be. These were replaced by drafts from infantry reinforcement centers and British units throughout India.

Wingate ordered platoon commanders to examine any man who wished to report sick and in effect to become platoon physicians, taking temperatures, dishing out aspirin, and, not for the fainthearted, even inspecting latrines for visible evidence of dysentery. Wingate became fond of quoting Gordon of Khartoum on the subject of medical care: "A man is either a fool or his own physician by thirty." It was also pointed out that once they were inside Burma any man who, for whatever reason, sick or wounded, was unable to walk would not be going to hospital. He would be left in a village, if he was lucky, or more likely on the side of the trail. In either case he would be at the mercy of the Japanese—a quality the Japanese were not famous for. It began to work. Sick parades went down. Soon they were under 2 percent.

Aves was the son of a regular soldier wounded in the First World War and had no desire to follow his father's example. He was a conscript and quite happy to include himself among those who had adopted as their motto "Peace at Any Fucking Price." But he too began to fall under Wingate's spell:

> He realigned our perception of what was possible for ordinary people like ourselves. . . . He told us that we were going to be in for a very hard time training . . . and we were going to show the Japanese that the British could do as well and better. We were just amazed. We were in awe of him. . . . Those of us who did not malinger and drop out we called Pukka Kings . . . those who did malinger and drop out we called Jossers.* But we were proud to be PK's.

---

*Liverpool dialect word for the perpetrators of what Wingate would almost certainly have referred to as the Sin of Onan.

So were the PKs' officers now that the fainthearts, the comfort loving, and the more conservative military minds among them had been weeded out. The same could not always be said for some of the British officers of the Gurkhas, who often confronted Wingate with a languid insolence that bordered on insubordination. According to Calvert, they were encouraged in this "by certain senior officers in Delhi and the depots" who resented this upstart trying to teach the Indian army new tricks on its own turf.

Wingate never would get on with the officers of the Indian army, who were by no means all "Curry Colonels" but included some very professional soldiers who were genuinely devoted to their men, especially in the Gurkha regiments. Nor did Wingate help matters when he observed that this army was "the best organised system for outdoor relief in the world." Nor did he display the usual reverence for the courage of the Gurkhas under his command. The battalion allotted to him was such a young and untried unit of the rapidly expanding Indian army—it would shortly have a ration strength of over a million men—that he did right to suspect its inexperience. After almost four years of war there was a terrible shortage of suitable British officers, and yet a reluctance to promote Gurkhas to the commissioned ranks still prevailed. Within the Gurkha battalion in Wingate's brigade only one of its officers was capable of communicating with the men in their own language—Gurkhali.

To make matters worse, in the eyes of the mainly teenaged Gurkha soldiers, Wingate humiliated their officers by making them run everywhere. The only time a Gurkha wanted to see one of his officers running was when he led them in a charge. But it was one of Wingate's fads that British officers were too careful of their dignity and this wasted precious time. Wasting time was the worst sin of all, and Wingate was liable to turn up anywhere at any time, as Philip Stibbé soon learned when he took his platoon to a certain spot in the jungle where an instructor was to give a demonstration:

[W]hen we arrived the officer was not there so I told the men to sit down and have a smoke while I went to look for him. I returned with the officer two minutes later to find my platoon fallen in, with a fuming Brigadier pacing up and down in front of them. What was the meaning of this? Why was my platoon sitting here doing nothing? I explained the circumstances. Then why hadn't I given them something to do while they were waiting? Let them practise taking bearings with a compass, or climbing trees or doing anything as long as they were not wasting time. This must not happen again. It didn't!

It had probably not helped that Stibbé's platoon were not only idle but smoking. Wingate had given up smoking and now held advanced views on the nicotine habit:

I am very much against the inclusion of any cigarettes in the ration. Apart from the very real objection to the continuous coughing and expectorating they cause, they do, in fact, give rise to to the very evils they are supposed to alleviate. They are supposed to soothe the nerves, and one cigarette undoubtedly has this effect, but the habit of smoking promotes irritability and makes its victim unable to do without it. Since, in campaigns of this nature, men cannot depend on a constant supply of cigarettes they are ill advised to pursue the habit. From my own experience the habit can be abandoned and not missed a month afterwards. . . . Doctors' recommendations on this subject are biased as they are all inveterate smokers.

Wingate suggested that the space saved by cutting out cigarettes could be occupied by "a sardine tin, a pot of paste, cheese, Marmite* etcetera."

Alcohol could be a different matter. Some people believed that Wingate did not drink and put it down to his religious upbringing. The truth was that Wingate tended to be a feast or fast man, breaking days or weeks of abstinence with the occasional quiet bender—as in Addis Ababa after the restoration of Haile Selassie. Calvert recalls several pleasant evenings when Wingate would sit with his officers over a bottle of whisky or the dark navy rum, often issued to British soldiers in action, sometimes encouraging discussion and the challenging of his ideas or listening to some Wingatian discourse on subjects quite removed from their enterprise. (The disappearance of a snake under some floor matting became the occasion for a fresh look at Adam and Eve and the symbolism of the serpent.) As far as Calvert was concerned this sort of thing did not happen often enough: "But [Wingate]

---

*A blackish-brown yeast extract with the look and consistency of axle grease but extremely popular in Britain.

knew that he liked to party and so, on the whole, steeled himself against such frivolities."

For most of his time at Patharia Wingate's daily tipple was fresh buffalo's milk supplied by four animals kept at brigade headquarters and milked by the veterinary officer. Wingate's passion for buffalo milk became such that when the beasts got sick and nothing would seem to rouse them from a terminal lassitude, he turned to a shaman from a local Stone Age tribe whose ancestors had survived the Dravidian conquest. Watched by a curious audience this sage heated an iron in an open fire then touched the unfortunate buffalo in their nether parts to achieve an instantaneous cure.

There had been a time when some of the officers present would have liked to have seen the Miracle of the Buffalo performed on the more persistent malingerers, but those days were gone. Slowly, almost imperceptibly at first, Wingate was welding his unlikely and disparate material into something that was beginning to take on the appearance at least of a fighting formation. "We had toughened up considerably," recalled RAF radioman Arthur Willshaw. "Flabby flesh had disappeared, chests had filled out, muscles developed where only outlines existed before and we began to glory in a new feeling of self reliance that was so important in the coming task."

Wingate continued to be full of surprises. He had devised a theory whereby if troops were surprised in an ambush or were ambushing themselves and found they had bitten off more than they could chew, they would disperse and then rendezvous at a prearranged spot—usually forward from their present position and along the line of a ridge or a stream so they could walk up and down it to find the meeting place. In order to instruct platoon commanders such as Stibbé in tactics such as these, Wingate was a firm believer in what, in the alphabet soup of military life, were known as TEWTS—tactical exercises without troops. For this purpose he had had a massive sand tray constructed under the shelter of a palm thatch roof where he could explain his ideas by using matchsticks for soldiers. Stibbé recounts how, on one occasion, a group of officers was waiting here for Wingate to appear when

[s]uddenly, Wingate burst from the bushes behind them, dancing like a Dervish, firing his revolver just over their heads and shouting,

"Hands up the lot of you, hands up. You are all quite helpless, not one of you is armed." After that no-one was ever seen without his revolver.

Wingate began to hold jungle church parades and, as a result, Private Aves of the Pukka Kings began to see more of him. Aves's accordion had somehow survived the monsoon and he found himself providing the accompaniment for the hymn singing, often standing next to Wingate as he conducted the first part of the service. Afterward Wingate would sometimes linger and chat with the men and ask them how they were getting on with the training. One day Aves, who always found Wingate to be kind and considerate, told him that the main problem was that they did not get enough food and they were always hungry. Wingate appeared to listen sympathetically and told him that they would shortly be going off the three-day paratroopers' rations they had been living on for the last couple of months and back to general rations—the canned bully beef, vegetables, and plum duff that was the traditional fare of British troops. But once they were in Burma items like these would be luxuries and dependent on how much the RAF could carry on supply drops.

The emergency rations Wingate's men were living on were designed for brief operations by commandos and paratroopers. They were intended to keep men going for two or three days until the situation had changed and they could be properly fed. Perhaps because men at the very sharp end of combat, with the adrenaline flowing freely, are not much bothered by hunger until after the event, they were little more than a snack. Each consisted of twelve ounces of the famous Shakapura biscuits, of which Wingate was an ardent fan, mainly because they kept the bowels open;* two ounces of cheese; nine ounces of compressed almonds and raisins; one ounce of acid drops or chocolates; three quarters of an ounce of tea; one ounce of milk powder; four ounces of sugar; half an ounce of salt. Despite Wingate's strictures there were also twenty cigarettes and a box of matches.

It was intended that this ration would be supplemented by food bought from Burmese villages, for which a considerable amount of sil-

---

*"The roughage in it," he would write, "is a great element in passing healthy action of the bowel. Personally, I have never passed better looking stools."

ver rupees were issued. Game was also supposed to be another source of food, and for this some of the officers were given shotguns, which they carried in saddle boots on the chargers most of them had been given to ride up and down the long columns of mules and men and generally act as couriers.

On both counts this was hopelessly unrealistic. The Burmese countryside was far from teeming with game for the pot, and shooting it was neither easy nor safe—you might give your position away. The same applied to acquiring food from civilians. It could not always be assumed that they were friendly—far from it. In August 1942 Burma had become the first member of Japan's Greater East Asian Co-Prosperity Sphere to be granted "independence" by Tokyo. A national army, more like a militia, had been set up, and while rural areas were not as politicized as the towns it was generally true that Burmese and Shan villages had at best a neutral attitude toward the onetime colonial masters who had been so easily humiliated at the hands of other Asians.

According to George Bromhead, Wingate's brigade major, it was thought the men of Seventy-seventh Brigade would need about four thousand calories a day, of which three thousand would be provided by the ration and the rest by foraging. The daily four thousand calories was rarely achieved. Even if it had been it was not enough. An assessment of Wingate's first Burma expedition published in 1998 by Major General Julian Thompson,* a soldier with considerable experience of both jungle fighting and long marches, declared it "insufficient for men marching long distances." But this was something "Wingate's Circus" would have to learn the hard way.

Meanwhile, Wingate—with the help of his alarm clock—taught the Gurkhas how to cook rice. Gurkha officers insisted that their men required a halt of two and a half hours to prepare their main meal. This was mainly because the rice was slowly cooked in large pots, which took a long time to boil. Wingate did not speak Gurkhali, though he had picked up a few words, so he mimed a demonstration of his fast-food technique, which delighted the Gurkha soldiers. It was a simple solution but nobody seemed to have thought of it. Instead of cooking

---

*Chapter six of *War Behind Enemy Lines,* published by Sidgwick and Jackson and the Imperial War Museum. General Thompson fought as a young officer against Chinese Communist guerrillas in Malaya and later in Borneo during Britain's "confrontation" with Indonesia there.

their rice by platoons or companies in huge cauldrons, the Gurkhas would break up into smaller groups and boil it in smaller pots. Calvert watched him do it:

> He put his alarm clock down, started a fire with dry sticks from his pack, waited until he had really got it going then measured some rice from a spare sock—we always carried rice in socks—into a mess tin full of water. Everybody sat around and waited for about twenty minutes while he hummed to himself—Jewish or Arabic songs by the sound of it. By then the water had boiled away. He took a spoon to the rice, stirred it, blew on it and tasted a bit. After his first spoon full this great contented smile spread across his face and the Gurkhas were converted. We never heard anything more about two-and-a-half hour meal breaks after that.

Gradually Wingate assembled his senior team. His greatest coup was to poach the monocled Fergusson, who joined him despite the advice of everybody on the Joint Planning Staff to have nothing to do with "Tarzan." But Fergusson badly wanted some experience of fighting the Japanese before he rejoined his battalion of the Black Watch, who were engaged on internal security duties and unlikely to see action for several months. He took with him Corporal Peter Dorans, a Highland crofter who had been his batman—"servant" in the parlance of his regiment—since he joined the Black Watch in 1931. Even after they left Delhi Fergusson was warned to turn back while he still could. On the platform of the local station where they changed trains for the last part of his journey he met a major who asked him if he was Fergusson:

> When I acknowledged it, he said: "Well my advice to you is to turn round and go straight back to Delhi. Wingate is crackers and I'm off." I rightly guessed that I was witnessing the results of the process know as "cutting out dead wood" and was not therefore tempted to return to the dusty halls of the Joint Planning Staff.

One of the things Wingate had done was turn the normal battalion system upside down. Instead of platoons (usually between thirty and forty men) and companies (usually about one hundred), his brigade was divided into columns. There were eventually seven columns in all, three of them mainly British and four mainly Gurkha. Each column numbered about four hundred men, of which the nucleus was an infantry company. Added to this were various specialist platoons and smaller detachments. There was a reconnaissance platoon from the Burma Rifles who all carried civilian clothes in their packs to enable spies to be sent into villages to see if the enemy were at hand; there was a support platoon whose mules carried two three-inch mortars and their bombs plus Vickers machine guns—the kind of belt-fed machine gun on a tripod beloved by Hollywood and one of the best weapons the British infantry had, though it weighed ninety pounds. There was also a demolition platoon, sometimes called the commando platoon, whose mules carried so much explosive nobody wanted to get near them.

In addition there was a transport platoon almost invariably commanded by one of a batch of young British officers who had been sent to reinforce the Gurkha battalion. The muleteers were both British and Gurkha, normally one man for two mules, and both races became inordinately fond of their charges. Wingate, the equestrian, always insisted that mules and horses were well looked after—he once refused dinner in the Burma Rifles officers' mess because he noticed some badly tended mules nearby. But he had a shrewd idea what would happen to most of them and fought a losing battle trying to persuade his troops not to treat the mules as pets.

Then there were the "specialists." Since the whole enterprise depended on Wingate's novel and untested idea of resupplying his columns by air drops, probably the most important of these were the signalers. The two-man RAF teams were equipped with a very large and, by the standards of the day, powerful radio called a 1082/83, which broke down into three mule loads and, according to Fergusson, looked something like a barrel organ. These transmitters could reach an RAF HQ in Assam and request air drops of food and ammunition. Mules also carried the batteries and, if they were really unlucky, charging engines. In addition there were Royal Signals operators who kept the columns in touch with one another or with Wingate's headquarters group, which was attached to one of the columns. All communications were tapped out in coded Morse using the codes known as "one time pad" because they were changed daily.

The brigade was well served with medical personnel. Each column had a doctor and a couple of orderlies. There was plenty of morphine available and, quite apart from the medics' own store, every man carried morphine tablets and one morphine ampule—enough to give a fatal dose. From quite early on in the training it was made plain that only the fit and the walking wounded had any chance of getting out.

Fergusson did some poaching of his own. He persuaded an Australian captain named Duncan Menzies, a Rhodes scholar who had joined the Black Watch from Oxford and served with Fergusson in Tobruk, to join him as his adjutant. Menzies was the nephew of the Australian politician Robert Menzies, who had recently been prime minister and would shortly be again.

As far as his officers were concerned, Fergusson was well pleased with his team. He took a great delight in his unblooded, amateur subalterns and seems to have particularly enjoyed talking books—their favorite was Hardy—with Philip Stibbé. Stibbé and the other platoon commanders were mostly about ten years younger than Fergusson, straight down from university and politically somewhat to the left of the Old Etonian laird. This sometimes made for lively postprandial debate around their campfires, though they soon discovered they could go too far. When one of these newly appointed holders of the king's commission ventured doubts about the relevance in 1942 of fealty to a monarch he was, literally, banished to outer darkness for the evening. Less predictable perhaps was Fergusson's attitude when Lieutenant John Kerr offered to set up training sessions in the new science of unarmed combat. Fergusson was horrified by this attempt to introduce "low-life gangster fighting" including "biting, gouging and unpleasantly directed kicking" into his command. It was, he said, "barbaric," and he forbade it. "We've only ever fought decently in the British Army and I don't see why we should change now," he said.

Conscious of the number of river crossings they were about to undertake Fergusson was keener on what he called "bathing parades." He used the few strong swimmers he discovered among his British soldiers, particularly a former fisherman from Lowestoft known as "Sailor" Thomson, to teach the others and estimated that they taught a dozen men to swim who could not manage a stroke before. Alas, it was not enough.

By the end of 1942, training was almost over. There were two last grueling exercises involving the entire brigade, and the final weedings-out took place, of officers as well as men. The last exercise was not a great success. According to Wingate there were "an undue number of faint hearted stragglers." Quite suddenly his confidence, the one thing he always had in abundance, began to go.

He had never doubted that he was about to deal with a much tougher enemy than he had in Ethiopia. Now he wondered whether his troops were ready for it, indeed would ever be ready for it. He confided his fears to the avuncular General Gerard Wilcox, who as head of Central Command had overseen the provision of training facilities and been generally more supportive than some of his contemporaries in Delhi would have advised him.

To what extent this was a martial version of "first night nerves" or the onset of "my particular curse" as he called it is hard to say. General Wilcox seems to have easily vanquished these fears. Wavell had done the same a few weeks earlier after another exercise had made Wingate ponder the wisdom of the entire enterprise. Even in great captains, the temptation to quit before adding one's name to the list of great military blunders might seem almost irresistible at times. But this was Wingate, the man whose self-confidence bordered on the messianic—the man who told Calvert, after his most fervent disciple had passed on some of the nasty things they were saying about "Tarzan" at GHQ Delhi, "It is because I am what I am, objectionable though it may seem to my critics, that I win battles."

By Christmas 1942 the old certainties had returned and Wingate's brigade had settled in the cantonment town of Jhansi for the festivities, with officers and men as confident of his firm leadership as the Night Squads and Gideon Force had been. "Their faith in Wingate was implicit," observed Fergusson. "My serjeant-major,* Cairns, from Stranraer, used to get quite lyrical whenever he spoke of him; and the men were much the same."

For many of them it would be their last Christmas. Fergusson discovered he had several sweet-singing Welshmen in Five Column and organized a choir, which rehearsed for a carol service in one of those mock Norman churches with rifle rests in the pews to be found in garrison towns throughout British India. The officers organized mule derbies and mounted paper chases. The Pukka Kings drank and the

*The archaic spelling of "sergeant" was preferred by both Fergusson and his regiment, the Black Watch.

more adventurous whored, egged on by the old sweats who knew their
way around from their days of "proper soldierin' " in peacetime India.
More innocent pleasures were provided by Private Aves and his piano
accordion with what was left of the battalion dance band, some of
whom, when it came to jungle training, had turned out to be Jossers.
The Forces' favorites on Radio India, essentially an extension of the
BBC, were headed by Bing Crosby's new hit, "White Christmas."

On New Year's Eve Fergusson held a Hogmanay party for the officers of his column and invited guests—Scotland was well represented
in Fergusson's unit, where the Australian Menzies seemed to prefer to
flaunt his Caledonian rather than his Antipodean roots. Yet the
brigade had a very Australian look about them because, to their great
delight and at Wingate's insistence, they had all been issued with rak-
ish Digger hats with the left brim clipped up to the side of the crown.
The only person who did not wear one was Wingate, who stuck to his
solar topee.

While Wingate's men caroused, British and Indian soldiers had
started an offensive against the Japanese in Burma along the Arakan
coast on the Bay of Bengal, trying to push south toward Rangoon.
After some initial successes the offensive began to bog down and reinforcements were sent in. Elsewhere the war was going well for the Allies, but the British had yet to achieve any notable success against the
Sons of Nippon.

In various stages at the beginning of January Wingate's brigade
went by train to Assam. When they got to Imphal, Wingate had his
men bivouacked seven miles north of the township—"In order that the
troops might not be softened by the cinema." There was to be no last
picture show for Seventy-seventh Brigade. To keep their spirits up
they got an extra rum issue.

It rains on the high Imphal plain long before the monsoon starts in
neighboring Burma, which is lower down. In the early hours, a cold,
creeping mist often settles over these highlands, and the men shivered
in the banana-leaf and bamboo *bashas* they were now so good at building for themselves. These dwellings much impressed visiting staff officers, who expected this sort of thing from the Gurkhas and Burma
Rifles but were unaccustomed to British troops being so self-sufficient.

They were there for twelve days, not quite sure what the delay was
about. Nor were most of the officers any the wiser, though at some time

almost all of them were required to visit the Imphal golf club where Wingate had set up his headquarters and completely covered the floor of one room with a one-inch map. To receive a briefing there was rather like entering a mosque, for Wingate required that everybody remove footwear and enter his map room in stockinged feet. Dominic Neil and Peter Wormwell, two young British officers recently posted to the Gurkhas and transferred to the brigade as animal transport officers, were not the only ones to notice that Wingate had large holes in his socks.

Then Wavell flew in from Delhi and people began to understand why they were hanging about Imphal instead of heading into Burma and getting stuck into the Japs: the operation was about to be canceled. This was only partly true. Wavell was considering canceling, and for very good reasons. It had originally been intended that Wingate's operation would coincide with an offensive on three fronts—Stilwell's Chinese coming into Burma from the north; the plunge into the south from the Arakan, nearest to Wingate; and an advance by an Indian army corps under General Geoffrey Scoones from Imphal down to the Chindwin. Now the push into the Arakan had come to a halt, and it had been decided to postpone the other two for logistical reasons. Wavell was concerned that the Japanese would now be able to concentrate all their forces against Wingate and roll up his intrusion at their leisure. Wingate argued furiously that to cancel the operation now would be disastrous. The anticlimax would be unbearable for his soldiers. He would never be able to train them up to the same peak of efficiency again. Furthermore, if they did not go now they would never find out whether long-range penetration worked. It was probably what Wavell wanted to hear. He gave his consent, and at a farewell parade at their shanty camp rather startled the brigade by saluting *them*, quite the reverse of the normal etiquette with visiting generals, and saying, "Gentlemen, God bless you." Lieutenant Neil, one of the young officers attached to the Gurkhas who had not been able to take his eyes off the holes in Wingate's socks during the briefing at the golf club, thought that what Wavell meant to say was "God help you." But Neil would become one of those rare creatures, a young officer who served under Wingate and did not come under his spell.

Before he left Imphal Wingate gave an interview to a journalist named Alaric Jacob who worked for *The Daily Express,* one of a number he gave to selected reporters who were sworn to secrecy, aware that the lives of these men would be at peril if a word appeared before their return. Wingate told Jacob that if the operation succeeded it would save thousand of lives and went on:

> Most of my Chindits are not in their first youth, but married men between 28 and 35. . . . If ordinary family men from Liverpool and Manchester can be trained for specialised jungle war behind the enemy's lines, then any fit man in the British Army can be trained to do the same and we show ourselves to the world as fighting men second to none, which I believe we are.

This is the first recorded use of the word *Chindit*. Wingate, having coined it, was the first man to use it and the reporter Jacob the first to write it down. But at the time, if Seventy-seventh Brigade called themselves anything, it remained "Wingate's Circus." The ringmaster was not at all pleased with the code name the staff wallahs in Delhi had come up with for his show. They had dubbed it Operation Longcloth, a name that Wingate found utterly meaningless and rather absurd.

Chapter 18

THE CHINDWIN RIVER, the great tributary of the Irrawaddy, runs from north to south a few miles from Burma's western border with India. On average it is about half a mile wide, though frequently it runs narrower. By the beginning of 1943 the British held its west bank and the Japanese were on the east. Neither had enough troops to man the entire length of the river, and the commanders on both sides had to console themselves with Frederick the Great's advice on these matters: "He who defends everything defends nothing."

Instead they garrisoned obvious crossing points and patrolled in between. From time to time they also sent reconnaissance patrols across the river to explore each other's territory, though this tended to be done more by the British than the Japanese, who, at that point, were busy consolidating their extraordinary gains.

Wingate's initial objective was to get three thousand men and a thousand animals across the river without being detected then march them over the jungle-covered slopes of the Zibyutaungdan range to the north-south railway along which the Japanese were sending supplies to their troops fighting the Chinese in the north. They intended to render this line of communications useless for the next several months at least by blowing up bridges and culverts and breaking sections of track. Since the Chinese offensive from the north had been canceled, it was recognized from the beginning that, in military terms, this would not have much more than nuisance value. But it might get the Japanese to use troops to patrol the line who could be more profitably employed elsewhere. And from a propaganda point of view it would demonstrate to the northern Burmese villages that the British were not entirely a spent force and that membership in Japan's Greater East Asian Co-Prosperity Sphere was no more a protection from the ravages of war than finding themselves within the British Empire.

After he had dealt with the railway line, Wingate would decide whether to continue his penetration of the Japanese rear areas by making another river crossing, this time of the Irrawaddy, and going even farther east. All would depend on how effectively the RAF could resupply him. Out of their meager resources in what was still very much the Cinderella theater of Britain's war effort the RAF had earmarked six American-built aircraft for the job. Three of them were the new C-47 transports (the British called them Dakotas or DC-3s) and three Lockheed Hudson bombers, the military version of the airliner.

By 16 February 1943 Wingate's brigade had crossed the Chindwin, mostly with the aid of ropes, inflatable dinghies, and makeshift rafts with the mules swimming reluctantly alongside them. Immediately before the crossing officers were supposed to distribute Wingate's typewritten order of the day to the men, though some did not get a chance to look at it until after the crossing. It was a piece of pulpit oratory, meant to be heard rather than read and quite unlike the sort of thing field commanders were expected to deliver. Certainly, few regular officers would have considered it suitable fare for the British Tommy, with his reputation as a cynic and a Philistine to maintain. "Government of the world" and other Utopian phrases were not normally considered the stuff to give the troops; "United Nations" referred to the anti-Axis allies, not the world body we mean today. And although Wingate undoubtedly believed that the British Empire could be a force for good, it does not receive a single mention:

> To-day we stand on the threshold of battle. The time for preparation is over, and we are moving on the enemy to prove ourselves and our methods. At this moment we stand besides the soldiers of the United Nations in the front line trenches throughout the world. It is always a minority that occupies the front line. It is a still smaller minority that accepts with a good heart tasks like this that we have chosen to carry out. We need not, therefore, as we go forward into the conflict, suspect ourselves of selfish or interested motives. We have all had the opportunity of withdrawing and we are here because we have chosen to be here; that is, we have chosen to bear the burden and the heat of the day. Men who make this choice are above the average in courage. We therefore have no fear for the staunchness and guts of our comrades.

The motive which has led each and all of us to devote ourselves to what lies ahead cannot conceivably have been a bad motive. Comfort and security are not sacrificed voluntarily for the sake of others by ill-disposed people. Our motive, therefore, may be taken to be the desire to serve our day and generation in the way that seems nearest to our hand. The battle is not always to the strong or the race to the swift. Victory in war cannot be counted, but what can be counted is that we shall go forward determined to do what we can to bring this war to an end which we believe best for our friends and comrades in arms, without boastfulness or forgetting our duty, resolved to do right so far as we can see the right.

Our aim is to make possible a Government of the world in which all men can live at peace and with equal opportunity of service.

Finally, knowing the vanity of man's effort and the confusion of his purpose, let us pray that God may accept our service and direct our endeavours, so that when we shall have done all we shall see the fruit of our labours and be satisfied.

O. C. Wingate. Commander 77th Indian Infantry Brigade.

In Calvert's Number Three Column, Lieutenant Geoffrey Lockett passed a copy to Sergeant Major Blain, the tough Highland regular from the Argylls who was his senior NCO in the commando detachment. To his astonishment Blain read it and burst into tears.

Wingate had devised a complex deception plan, a cardsharp's performance of trickery and illusion, to keep the Japanese guessing as to his true intentions. He started by cutting his pack into two unequal groups. Number Two Group, which included his own headquarters party of about 250 and five of the columns, was the larger of the two, numbering about 2,200 men. The crossing would start with the Burma Rifle headquarters company under Lieutenant Colonel Lionel Wheeler, about 150 in all, getting over the river by boat and raft at a village called Tonhe. There would be no further movement at Tonhe for twenty-four hours. Meanwhile, the 800-strong Number One Group would begin to cross at Auktaung, another riverside hamlet about thirty-five miles south of Tonhe. To make sure that the Japanese were properly duped, the RAF parachuted a highly visible daylight supply drop onto the east bank. There was more.

Major John Jefferies, the commander of the demolition experts in

142d Independent Commando Company, was to stage yet another feint. Dressed as a general, complete with the scarlet collar tabs, Jefferies and his "staff," most of whom also wearing badges of rank to which they were not entitled, ventured south along the riverbank from Auktaung until they came to the village of Ta Nga, where the headman was known to be pro-Japanese.

Jefferies, tall and prematurely bald, threw himself enthusiastically into the role of General Blimp, the kind of officer who never saw the point of being discreet in front of the natives. First the general and his staff requisitioned the headman's house, graciously informing him that they would not be needing it for long and he and his family could remain if they wished. Then an enormous amount of food was ordered, haggled over, and paid for to feed the troops that were supposedly following him. Maps were ostentatiously spread out, orders dictated, place-names repeated and spelt out again by the stenographer. And all the while frantically saluting brigade majors and other staff officers rushed in and out of the headman's residence, stamping their hobnailed boots on his teak floors and thrusting written dispatches into the general's hand. Some months later Jefferies revealed the contents of these dispatches to Charles Rolo, a journalist who would later be employed by the British Information Service in New York:

> One officer solemnly handed Jefferies a message which read: "You have been invited to dine with Lady Snodgrass. 8 P.M., February 25. Black tie. The old harpie has been told you are coming." Another brought in a chit which announced he had drawn the favourite in the Irish sweepstake. A third mysteriously produced an ancient cable from Jefferies' bank informing him that his account was slightly overdrawn. The latter caused the "General's" face to twitch so violently that the watchful Burmese must have imagined momentous doings were afoot.

Then the general bid the headman a curt farewell, placed himself in the lead of his party, and marched out of the village in a southerly direction until he was sure he was not being followed. At that point they turned east and caught up with the main body of Number One Group.

Meanwhile, Wingate was getting the main party—2,200 men with 850 animals, including a couple of lumber elephants—across the river without being detected. The crossing was far from smooth despite months of training and moonlight bright enough to read a newspaper by. At times it seemed to live up to the Pukka Kings' insistence that they were "Wingate's Circus": naked men struggling with reluctant mules, which would go halfway over and then swim back the way they had come; lines of men shivering in the cold and sitting on their sixty-pound backpacks waiting to cross. Soon the columns were hours behind schedule and, as the dawn came up, Lockett thought it looked more like Blackpool beach than a tactical river crossing into enemy territory.

At one point Wingate came galloping across the sandy riverbank and called out to Lockett, who was naked in the river and struggling with the mules. "This is a perfect example of how a river should not be crossed." But their luck held. By the following evening the five columns of Number Two Group were all across and moving deep into Japanese-held territory in the long single files they called snakes.

Where they could, they avoided established tracks, with the lead men hacking their way through the undergrowth with Gurkha kukris.* Sometimes the columns moved together, sometimes separately. Rarely did they move fast enough to please Wingate.

One reason Wingate was in such a hurry was that an RAF supply drop, including letters from home, had been seen to fall into Japanese hands. It may seem odd to pamper troops who had been trained to give up most creature comforts with mail, especially when they had not been in the field very long. But from the beginning Wingate seems to have been determined not to miss a trick in keeping up morale.** Unfortunately, in this instance the mailman had, as Wingate put it, made the Japanese "a present of our order of battle."

---

*The *arme blanche* of the Nepalese highlands, a curved, broad-bladed, and heavy fighting knife more like a machete and rarely used for horticultural purposes by Gurkha soldiers.

**The RAF entered into the spirit of things and the parachute rations were sometimes supplemented with drops of bread, bully beef, chocolate specially made for them at Firpos, a famous Calcutta restaurant, and carefully packed bottles of rum. (Only 1 broke out of almost 170.) Magazines, newspapers, and books were dropped. Lockett had arranged to be resupplied with his favorite snuff but lost it to some Gurkhas who had never tasted such vile curry powder. When Fergusson lost his monocle, he was dropped a new one.

It was only a matter of time before Japanese military intelligence translated the letters, listed the ranks of the officers involved, and deduced the numerical strength of these raiders from their knowledge of the usual ratio of British officers to men. Wingate estimated, correctly as it turned out, that it would take the Japanese analysts about three days to do this. Yet for days the columns marched without encountering the enemy, and Wingate began to detect signs of slackness: march discipline was bad, and columns laid a paper trail through the jungle of cigarette cartons and other packings.

Philip Stibbé from Fergusson's Number Five Column was one of a number of young officers called to Wingate's headquarters to be lectured on column discipline. Quite apart from the litter problem, man and beast were making far too much noise, they were informed. Whinnying mules and horses were audible for miles and should be given a sharp tap on their nostrils every time they gave voice. "After a while the whinnying in our column almost ceased," reported Stibbé, "though whether this was the result of disciplinary action or whether the animals were too tired to whinny we could never tell. Billy, my horse, never learned his lesson and used to look at me reproachfully every time I beat him on the nose. He whinnied cheerfully to the end."

In the northern group all but Calvert's Number Three Column traveled along a secret mountain track, virtually a game trail, discovered by a British forestry officer trying to avoid the Japanese while leading a party out of Burma the year before. Once they were through they began to spread out toward their particular objectives, though they were often no more than two or three miles apart and easily concentrated against a single target.

Although the lost mail had given away the size of his force Wingate was confident that the Japanese remained utterly bewildered and had no idea what their objectives were. At one point Wingate even flouted all his own rules for caution and, in broad daylight, marched three of his columns down a motorable dirt road obviously used by enemy transport. The main risk was being spotted from the air. Otherwise, he made sure he blew the bridges behind him as he went and had what he called "a blocking party" ahead.

He continued to fine-tune his command, monitoring the performance of individual officers. The commander of Four Column could not tolerate the high-pitched hum from the battery charger necessary to keep their radios going, and as a result his column was frequently out of contact. Wingate transferred him to his headquarters as a supernumerary officer and he was replaced by George Bromhead, his brigade major—a brigadier's chief executive. Bromhead's position was filled by Captain Gilmour "Gim" Anderson, a sandy-haired solicitor from Glasgow. Anderson had originally commanded Six Column, mostly men from the King's, which had been broken up to reinforce the other columns following a final weeding out after the last, exhausting exercise at Jhansi.

Wingate now began to play undreamed-of remote-control games with his doggedly mobile foot columns, sending some to attack and some to distract and generally using tactics the Japanese had never encountered before, not even against Chinese guerrillas. By the beginning of March, some two weeks after they had set out from the Assam border, Fergusson and Five Column were closing on the Bon Chaung railway gorge with orders to destroy its bridges and block the line by dynamiting a section of the nearby cliff. Calvert and Three Column, having already amazed Wingate by calling him from as far east as the Wuntho Mountains, were approaching the country railway station of Nankan. Meanwhile, to keep the enemy's eye off the railway line, Wingate had dispatched two other columns to make diversionary attacks on rural garrisons at the market towns of Pinbon and Pinlebu. At the same time, Number One Group—having fulfilled its deception task—was also approaching the railway from a different direction.

Then came two major setbacks. Number Four Column under Bromhead was ambushed at a stream and split up—a mishap that Wingate would later blame on a disgraceful exhibition of "panic" by the mainly teenaged Gurkhas whom British and Burmese comrades had tried in vain to rally. The column took casualties and after collecting together the largest group of survivors Bromhead found his radio had been destroyed in the battle. Running low on food and ammunition, and unable to call for a supply drop, he decided to turn back for India with his half of the column while the other survivors marched north almost a thousand miles to the Chinese border. Afterward Wingate declared that Bromhead had displayed "judgment and courage throughout."

He was less forgiving about the second reverse. Colonel Hugh Alexander, heading with Number Two Column toward a rail junction

*Briefing the emperor: Wingate with Haile Selassie during Gideon
Force's campaign to return the monarch to his throne.*

*The Palestine connection: Wingate with Abraham Akavia,
the young Jew he sent for to be his man Friday in Abyssinia.*

*Victory parade: Wingate on horseback leads his men into Addis Ababa,
while Akavia and Sergeant Dick Luyt march immediately behind him
at the head of the Abyssinian Patriots.*

Column commander: Capt. Tony Simonds, bearded and disheveled,
led the backup column to Wingate's Gideon Force.

After Quadrant: Wingate in his London flat before the second Chindit campaign. Note his general's peaked cap and Wolseley helmet artfully arranged on the bookshelf.

"Flip Corkin" and The Man: After an unpromising first meeting,
Wingate and Col. Phil Cochran became firm friends and fast comrades.

Council of war: Wingate with Derek Tulloch, his chief staff officer
and oldest friend, in the run-up to Operation Thursday.

Finally I am feeling very much at the moment IM ESHHOKHEYTH YERUSHALAIM TISHKAH YAMINI & do you too pray that our lot takes us there together to the place & the work we love. Love to Ivy & your father. Tell my mother I am well & happy & hope not wholly useless or harmful.

Orde

Finally I am feeling very much at the moment
IM ESHKHOKHEYCH YERUSHALAIM TISH-
KAH YAMINI and do you too pray that our lot
takes us there together to the place and the
work we love.

Love to Ivy and your father. Tell my mother
I am well and happy and hope not wholly useless
or harmful.

מכתב אל לורנה

*If I forget thee: Amid frenzied preparations for Operation Thursday,
Wingate reveals that Jerusalem and Zion are very much on his mind.*

Churchill's stars: Mountbatten and Wingate at a training exercise
before the launching of the second Chindit campaign.

High anxiety: Wingate and his senior officers ponder the acute dilemma caused
when aerial photographs show a key landing site blocked by logs.

AFTERMATH

The son he never saw: Lorna Wingate with Orde Jonathan,
the child she bore three months after her husband's death.

he intended to sabotage, made the tactical error of marching directly down a branch line in daylight until he got to within three miles of his objective. He camped his mainly Gurkha column a couple of hundred yards off the track and waited for nightfall before sallying forth—only to walk slap into an ambush. In the ensuing battle this column, like Bromhead's, was split into two and failed to regroup. Half of the column headed east and eventually linked up with George Dunlop's Number One Column. The other half, under Major Arthur Emmett, an Indian army regular and fluent Gurkhali speaker, headed back toward India. Like Bromhead, Emmett was low on food and ammunition and without a working radio. But where Bromhead drew Wingate's praise, Emmett was to be denounced by his commanding officer as "unfit to command men." It seems a harsh judgment, and perhaps Wingate was ill-disposed toward Emmett as one of those rather superior Indian army officers who felt a cut above a Gunner from the Shop.

That other alumnus of Woolwich, Michael Calvert, began to redress the balance. On 6 March he celebrated his thirtieth birthday by blowing up two large railway bridges in the Nankan area, one of which had a three-hundred-foot span. He also cut the line in seventy other places and inflicted heavy losses on the Japanese:

> As expected, we ran into some resistance but I had placed ambush and covering parties and booby traps all around us and the Japs had an unpleasant day. We did not lose a single man though many a Jap did not live to see another dawn. At one stage a group of the enemy really got the jitters and decided to chance their all in a charge. They came at us yelling their heads off but for some reason we shall never know they chose a spot which meant crossing open country with no cover. Every one of them died.

Calvert had a couple of strokes of luck in this encounter—one of them almost the ballistic equivalent of winning the lottery. When the Japanese brought up several truckloads of reinforcements he used his two three-inch mortars on them. Against very long odds, he succeeded in dropping a mortar bomb directly into the back of one of the trucks. The second lucky stroke was the timely arrival of two platoons of Pukka Kings under the Free Dane Erik Petersen who had somehow become separated from their proper place with Seven Column. They were a tired and hungry bunch but flung themselves into the fray. Wingate was particularly impressed by the Dane's conduct and recommended him for a Military Cross:

> [H]is actions in these operations proved, if any proof was needed, that leadership is everything. . . . Some officers . . . would have gone back to the Chindwin. . . . Others would have blundered into the enemy. Petersen marched for the railway, outstripping everyone and arrived in Nankan railway station in the middle of a fight between the Japanese and 3 Column.

Calvert's casualties were nil. They lingered around Nankan long enough to booby trap the station with some of their mortar bombs before retiring to a prearranged rendezvous and making tea. The British and Gurkha soldiers in Wingate's brigade were all great believers in the restorative powers of hot, sweet tea—or *char* as it was called, from the Urdu *chai*—and there was something about the communal business of starting a fire and waiting for the water to boil that was a fillip to morale in itself. But woe betide the man who forgot, or could not be bothered, to split the bamboo generally used as kindling. Unsplit, it tended to explode and fly out of the fire with a report like a rifle shot, threatening to give their position away. There were also more immediate dangers: one of Fergusson's men lost an eye to a flying splinter. Flame and smoke were not a problem. The former could not be seen, not even in teak forest, which is the most open of jungle terrain, for more than one hundred yards. Smoke was not visible at night, and in daylight there was always a certain amount of smoke rising above the jungle canopy from the remoter villages.

Yet from quite early on Wingate urged column commanders not to delay their departure in the morning by "brewing up" immediately but to take advantage of the cool hours to get moving. This was extremely unpopular at first until it became apparent that a break in the march for a midmorning breakfast (rations permitting) gave you something to look forward to. "He [Wingate] proved plumb right as he nearly always was," observed Fergusson.

Fergusson's Five Column attacked the railway on the same day as Calvert but farther to the north, as did George Dunlop's One Column to the south. Both destroyed bridges, and Fergusson's commando platoon brought thousands of tons of rock onto the line from an overhanging cliff face. But Fergusson had taken casualties.

Lieutenant John Kerr, the officer who wanted to teach unarmed combat, lay wounded with four of his men, and four more had been killed by a Japanese machine gunner hidden close to where they had successfully ambushed a truckload of enemy soldiers. When he arrived, Fergusson counted sixteen Japanese on the ground. As he was squatting down beside Kerr, hit in a calf muscle and unable to stand, there was a shot immediately behind him. Fergusson turned to see the faithful Dorans with a smoking rifle in his hands, a "dead Jap" writhing on the ground, and still pointing in his direction one of the emperor's curiously long Arisaka rifles.* Fergusson now had to decide what to do with his wounded:

> The problem we had all so long dreaded had at last arisen. There were five of them unfit to move . . . the truck had got away and there was no knowing when the Japs would come back on us. We hoisted three of them on to mules, and bore them down to the village a hundred yards away; and there we left them with their packs and earthen jugs of water, in the shade under one of the houses. One of them said, "Thank God, no more walking for a bit"; one, Corporal Dale, said, "See and make a good job of that bridge"; and John Kerr said, "Don't you worry about us, sir, we'll be all right."

Before he left them Fergusson tried to do one more thing for his casualties. He found the headman of a nearby village who "agreed to accept responsibility for them." But even if he had been particularly pro-British, which would have been rare for a Burman in the spring of 1943, the chances of hiding wounded British soldiers without being caught and facing Japanese reprisals were slim. Fergusson must have realized that the headman would notify the Japanese as soon as he decently could, which is what he did.** Kerr was the only one of these five British soldiers to survive captivity in Rangoon jail despite beatings and torture. Shortly afterward, Calvert was put in a similar dilemma when five of his Gurkhas and one Burma Rifleman were

---

*Japanese gunsmiths had made the Arisaka long to try and achieve high velocity, but with bayonet fixed it was almost as tall as many Japanese soldiers and easily the longest rifle regularly used in World War II—a curious distinction for a nation that was to become so skilled at miniaturization.

**At least he did not have them publicly flogged as did a Shan headman who discovered two sick or wounded British soldiers abandoned in his village. A year later a Gurkha hacked this man to death with a kukri when he tried to escape.

wounded. Calvert having acquired some knowledge of the Japanese military psychology left his wounded with a note (in English) addressed to the local commander of the Imperial Japanese Army pointing out that, like him, these men had been fighting for king and country. "I leave them confidently in your charge, knowing that with your well known traditions of Bushido you will look after them as if they were your own."

Calvert, of course, knew no such thing, but it seemed worth a try. These new Knights of Bushido rarely honored the samurai code—though some of Wingate's men who survived captivity would report the occasional lapse into chivalry. Wingate always stressed that anybody who could not walk would have to be left behind:

> It is plain logic that a Column marching through an enemy country, hundreds of miles from help, must abandon any one who for any reason cannot move at the pace which tactical and strategical considerations impose.*

But Wingate knew that abandoning the wounded, however justified, was demoralizing for all concerned, and with his usual thoroughness he tried to make provision for the situation. Commanders were instructed to gather the gravely wounded at the end of the column then drop them off at selected villages together with some silver rupees and what medicines could be spared. He also had prepared printed proclamations in Burmese and English to be handed to the headman of the village. Fergusson appears to have given one to the headman with whom he left Kerr and the others. It contained a warning:

> The names of these men and the name of your village and your own name I have told to the British Government by wireless. They will send soldiers to enquire after them. You must be able to give a good account of them when the soldiers arrive.

The problem of the sick and wounded was one of the great weaknesses of the long-range penetration concept and Wingate knew it.

---

*Conveniently for a raiding party who could not be burdened with their own wounded, let alone prisoners, the determination of most Japanese soldiers to die rather than be captured spared Wingate the moral dilemma of what to do about prisoners.

Leaving the wounded was a disgrace, a denial of the comradeship that bound them together. One soldier poet with Wingate tried to imagine the feelings of the men they had left behind:

> Have you ever seen a column march away,
> And you left lying, too damned sick to care?
> Have you ever watched the night crawl into day
> With red-rimmed eyes that are too tired to stare?*

The attacks against the railway turned out to be the high-water mark of Operation Longcloth. The line had been cut in over seventy places. Had Chiang Kai-shek allowed Stilwell to launch an offensive the Japanese Eighteenth Chrysanthemum Division would have atrophied at the head of its severed main supply route and probably lost the battle. Alas, this was not the case. But the Japanese were deeply embarrassed by the mettle and initiative displayed by these British, no longer the plodding enemy of yesterday.

Wingate now had to make the most important decision of the campaign, perhaps of his career. After these successes, should he play safe and get back across the Chindwin before being cut off by the Japanese, who were beginning to deploy the best part of three divisions against him? Should he go north into the lands of the Kachin hill tribes as a springboard for guerrilla operations? Or should he continue to surprise the enemy with the unexpected, continue in an easterly direction, and cross the Irrawaddy?

Wingate had his mind made up for him. First he discovered that the best part of six hundred of his men were already over the river. These were the remnant of Number One Group. Following the debacle with Emmett's Number Two Column Alexander had been off the air for some time and Wingate had begun to fear the worst when one of Alexander's signalers tapped out the triumphant message that they had got across. Shortly afterward Wingate received signals from Calvert and Fergusson asking for permission to cross. Both believed that the Japanese were not in a position to oppose them providing they

---

*These lines are the start to a short poem by K. N. Batley entitled "Chindit" and published in Britain by Michael Joseph and Penguin in an anthology of servicemen's poetry from the Second World War compiled by the Salamander Oasis Trust. Little is known about Batley's service in Burma; it is possible he was in Fergusson's column.

could do it at once. Wingate felt he had to follow them and that he needed the experience of another major river crossing:

> Had I not crossed the Irrawaddy, I should have learned nothing real about crossing wide and swift streams, nor about opposed crossings. Further, although it is easy to be wise after the event, I had at this time every reason to believe that we would find conditions far easier on the East bank.

At first everything went splendidly. Dozens of boats were available and were soon plying a busy trade ferrying the brigade across the river while Fergusson placed his Vickers machine guns on high ground to cover them. It was obvious that the Japanese knew they were in the vicinity because one of their aircraft had been over dropping propaganda leaflets printed in English, Urdu, and Burmese calling on the "Pitiable Anglo-Indian Soldiery" to surrender. As dusk fell and the covering parties withdrew, the Japanese arrived. Fortunately for Five Column they did so with uncharacteristic caution, firing bursts of automatic fire from the outskirts of the town as if testing for reaction. Since they could not see any targets Fergusson and his rearguard remained true to Wingate's maxims of "When in doubt don't fire"* and "The answer to noise is silence."

Even so, the majority of the boatmen ran off, and those who remained did so only at gunpoint. Fergusson escaped on the last overcrowded boat, wading into the water to push it off. Weighed down by his heavy pack, he was dragged onto its stern where, since any further movement was liable to capsize the shallow craft, he was obliged to travel in a kneeling position with his bottom facing the enemy, who were still firing blindly into the night.**

Fergusson got his column across without incurring casualties. But when Calvert was ready to take his men over a few miles south of

---

*Students of tactics might be interested to know that this is exactly the opposite of what the Australians, who were highly rated as jungle fighters, generally did in New Guinea—or the Americans in Vietnam for that matter. But it is easy to imagine that in night fighting silence is much more unnerving for the enemy than blazing uselessly away in the wrong direction, however comforting this may seem. It just takes more discipline.

**Fergusson would later describe himself as "the first British officer ever to have crossed the Irrawaddy on all fours."

Tigyaing two days later the Japanese were much more alert. He found himself with a running fight on his hands in which he used his mortars and, being Calvert, personally led a counterattack. At one point most of his column was actually marooned on an island in the middle of the river with very few boats at their disposal. But just when things were looking really sticky a flotilla of Burmese trading craft glided up under sail. Calvert, who rarely missed an opportunity, pirated the lot and extricated his column, though half his mules and some equipment had to be abandoned. In all he lost twelve men, of whom five were wounded. These were the men he left behind with a note appealing to traditional notions of Japanese chivalry. The next day the Japanese air force made a rare appearance* and six bombers raided Calvert's abandoned bivouac on the west bank of the river.

"This shows the enemy's land attack had been driven off," noted Wingate, who crossed six days after Calvert with over one thousand men and almost as many mules at Hweibo, to the north of Tigyaing where Fergusson had crossed. The Irrawaddy can be a mile or more in width at times, but at Hweibo it was about a thousand yards. Since it was a fairly obvious crossing point Wingate had been expecting to have to deal with a Japanese patrol here, but the patrol had moved away the previous day. With the help of dozens of Burmese country boats with their crews and a few inflatable aircrew dinghies plus some canvas and wooden "reconnaissance boats" he was able to get the brigade headquarters group and the headquarters company of the Burma Rifles battalion over that night. The two columns, which were mostly made up of Pukka Kings, were all over by dawn. As the sun came up RAF Hurricanes called in from Imphal patrolled over the river in case any Japanese boats appeared. Wingate grumbled that, despite all their training, his men had made little progress in either boat handling or swimming. "The great majority could either not swim at all or were capable only of floundering a few yards," he noted. But on the whole he was proud of them:

> There was not another brigade in India that was capable of swimming a thousand mules over the Irrawaddy in a night, especially at

*The year before, the Japanese air force had dominated the skies over Burma and everywhere else in Southeast Asia, but by now several squadrons had been transferred to the Pacific to try to stop the Americans.

the end of such privations and long marches. The enemy himself could not have done it and he did not think we could or would.

Wingate's immediate plan was to dispatch the columns commanded by his two brightest stars, Calvert and Fergusson, to destroy the same Gokteik viaduct Calvert had sat on for ten days during the previous year's retreat, begging for permission to destroy it.* Calvert, promoted to acting lieutenant colonel, was to be in overall command, but Gokteik was over a hundred miles away to the southeast. Fergusson looked at his map and his heart sank. "The mountains between us and our goal were stinkers, nothing less."

Physical exhaustion was now setting in among all Wingate's troops. They had marched for too long—well over a month—on too little food. Some of the men no longer appeared hard and lean, but sick and gaunt. Bill Aird, Fergusson's Glaswegian doctor, urged a couple of weeks' rest on proper rations before anything else was asked of them. Instead Wingate came on the air to tell them that a supply drop they were all looking forward to had been postponed for a couple of days. Fergusson consulted his Bible and referred Wingate to Psalm 22, verse 17: "I can count all my bones: they stare and gloat over me." Back came word according to the Gospel of St. John: "Consider that it is expedient that one man should die for the people." Fergusson was not amused.

Wingate was beginning to understand that he may have gone a river too far. The largest part of the brigade—the columns of Calvert and Fergusson and Number One Group with Lieutenant Colonel Alexander and George Dunlop—were now corralled between two rivers: the Irrawaddy and the Shweli, which ran more or less parallel to it for mile after mile. To complete this effect of being almost surrounded by water, on his way southeast to attack the Gokteik viaduct Calvert would be obliged to cross the Nam Mit, a tributary of the Shweli. Meanwhile, as the monsoon approached it was getting hotter, sources of drinking water away from the Japanese patrols along the riverbanks

---

*General Alexander later explained to Calvert that he had been hoping he would disobey orders and blow the bridge up but for "political reasons" he had not been able to tell him to do it. Perhaps he felt that such an obvious indication that the British were scuttling out of northern Burma would undermine Chinese resolve to continue to fight.

were becoming increasingly hard to find, and now some of the columns were thirsty as well as hungry. Nonetheless, casualties had so far been light, and morale remained high. As the Japanese began to close they found some of Wingate's men a very prickly proposition.

First of all Fergusson's column was instrumental in getting a Japanese battalion very badly mauled by directing an RAF air strike onto it as they moved into a small village. Then on the Nam Mit River Calvert staged a murderous ambush of one of the large Japanese patrols that was attempting to fence them in, carefully picking the spot where he would least like to be ambushed himself:

> We let fly with everything we had and a lot of those Japs could never
> have known what hit them. It was one of the most one-sided actions
> I have ever fought in. We simply shot them to pieces. About a hun-
> dred of the enemy were killed. We lost one man, a Gurkha NCO.

Wingate was still toying with the idea of moving farther east into Kachin territory, but he knew that first he needed a big supply drop to feed his hungry men. He chose to have it on paddy fields near the village of Baw. Wingate knew it was possible that the village was garrisoned and brought to the problem the kind of tactics he had used with the Night Squads in Palestine. He decided to invest it. All tracks to it were to be blocked during the hours of darkness, but they would not reveal their presence until dawn, when Baw was to be entered with "preponderating force." Once the village had been secured the supply drop would take place.

But Wingate's plan was spoiled by "one officer failing to realise the importance of getting into position before it was light, while another blundered into Baw itself with his small road block party which was not strong enough to avail itself of the surprise its appearance caused."

What Wingate called "a dog fight of the usual type" now developed. The British, mostly Pukka Kings from Seven and Eight Columns under Major Walter Scott, in civilian life a junior local government official in Liverpool, cleared part of the village. In the course of this Erik Petersen, the Free Dane, received a bad head wound. Wingate took a look at him and was saddened to see there appeared to be little hope of getting him out of Burma alive.

Despite the fighting at the drop zone Wingate felt they were too short of rations to cancel the delivery. Also two badly needed extra signalers for brigade headquarters, a department always notoriously over-worked by Wingate, were dropping in with the supplies. Neither of these men, British volunteers from the Royal Corps of Signals, had ever parachuted before, and they landed in no-man's-land, were shot at by the Japanese, but managed to get to Wingate. Thereafter their luck ran out, for neither of them would survive the campaign.

The RAF had dropped about one-and-a-half-days' rations before they began to suspect that they might be feeding the Japanese—there was no direct ground-to-air radio link—and flew away. Eventually, both sides started to disengage, and the firing began to die down.

Perhaps it was his admiration for the grievously hurt Petersen, wounded in a skirmish that need never have unfolded the way it did had his orders been obeyed, that made Wingate boil over. All his anger and frustration for the failure to really hurt the Japanese at Baw as well as collect a major supply drop were directed at the young man who had lost them the crucial advantage of surprise. Without recourse to a court-martial or any other military flummery Wingate reduced the cul-prit to the ranks and transferred him to Fergusson's Five Column.*

The kilted commando officer Geoffrey Lockett claims that Wavell gave Wingate "special disciplinary powers" for the duration of Opera-tion Longcloth. If this is true, nothing was ever written down. Never-theless, although flogging was abolished in the British army in 1881, at least two men, one British and the other a Gurkha, were given a mild form of lashing for falling asleep on sentry duty.

The British soldier was from Philip Stibbé's platoon in Fergusson's Five Column. Stibbé was making his rounds before turning in himself when he discovered that one of his sentries was missing. Eventually he found the man curled up under his blanket. Stibbé felt it was too seri-ous a matter to handle himself and next day produced him before Fer-gusson, who gave the man the choice of walking back to the Chindwin on his own or being flogged by the column sergeant major. The youth-ful Stibbé, so recently down from Oxford and sometimes regarded by Fergusson as a bit of a dangerous radical, was in complete agreement:

> The punishment decided upon was in my opinion, the only possi-ble one under the circumstances and certainly it was none too harsh when one remembered that the man had, by his neglect of duty,

*Fergusson put the disgraced lieutenant in his column headquarters, and at the end of the campaign his rank was reinstated.

jeopardised the lives of all his comrades. I am glad to say that he bore his punishment well and subsequently bore no ill will.

Dominic Neill, the animal transport officer in Scott's Eight Column, had an almost identical experience and reaction with one of his Gurkha muleteers, who fell asleep on sentry duty. Neill decided to handle the matter himself:

> The only punishment I could give him was to flog him. So I told one of my senior naiks,* Naik Budemin, to tie him to a tree, take his shirt off, and to beat him with one of the mule's lead ropes. But I told him he must not under any circumstances break the boy's skin otherwise it would have been impossible for him to carry his pack. He was beaten so as to shame him . . . no harm was done except to his morale and everything was forgotten. He forgave us and we forgave him.

After the fight at Baw, Wingate received a radio message from the headquarters of Fourth Corps in Imphal saying that the RAF thought it would be difficult to continue to supply him if he went much farther east and instructing him to "consider a withdrawal." At about the same time he also received word from Calvert and Fergusson saying that lack of water and the almost daily increase in the temperature was "reducing their fighting efficiency." Eight days after he had crossed the Irrawaddy Wingate decided it was time to call it a day and take his brigade back to India.

About two thousand men were involved; the survivors of Columns Two and Four, having retired early after their various misfortunes, were already there. Of the five columns that had crossed the Irrawaddy, Wingate gathered the three British ones to him—Seven under Ken Gilkes, Eight under Walter Scott, and Five under Bernard Fergusson, plus the Karen and Kachin of the Burma Rifles headquarters company. Also with Wingate were John Jefferies's commandos, who had at last parted with Number One Group, the original decoy party for the crossing of the Chidwin. In all they totaled about twelve hundred men.

Still operating separately from Wingate were five hundred or so mainly Gurkha soldiers of George Dunlop's Number One Column

*Corporals.

and Number One Group's headquarters party under Colonel Alexander. They had penetrated farther than any of the others and were now camped west of Mong Mit, a small town not quite a hundred miles from China's Yunnan province.

Wingate now decided it would be a good idea if they took up their decoy role again and continued to move eastward in order to throw the Japanese off the scent while everybody else moved in a westerly direction. If Wingate's plan was "to mystify the Japanese of our intentions," Dunlop sometimes thought Wingate was doing his best to mystify him and Alexander. Brigade headquarters had not kept in very close touch, and even when a message had been deciphered a Bible often had to be consulted before its contents became clear. "Remember Lot's wife," Wingate urged them. "Return not whence thou came. Seek thy salvation in the mountains lest ye be consumed." It did not seem all that appropriate. Mong Mit was not exactly Sodom. Wearily, Dunlop gave his orders and they moved out.

Calvert was also away from the main group. Following his successful ambush along the Nam Mit he was once again heading toward the Gokteik viaduct, Calvert's very own white whale. When Wingate told him to forget about the viaduct and withdraw, he ordered him to find his own way back to India because he was so much farther south than anybody else. Calvert consoled himself with the thought that at least this time he was not leaving Burma as part of a defeated army. He told Geoffrey Lockett that on the way out he intended to blow up the railway line again. After Calvert had been turned back, Wingate had the RAF drop a large number of rations along the route Three Column would have taken to deceive the enemy into believing that his main thrust still lay in that direction.

On 26 March 1943 Wingate held a conference of all his other commanders on a *chaung* (a dried-up riverbed) called the Hehtin. They were hidden in thick jungle with pickets guarding all likely approaches. For officers and men it was the chance to meet up with old friends from other columns last seen when they assembled for Wavell's inspection at Imphal. There had been a supply drop including such luxuries as bully beef, beans, and rum. Some of the officers received special deliveries of whisky. Fergusson describes the atmosphere as being "like a Bardic festival."

By now the news was out that they were going back. Fergusson thought that this was a bad thing because the men would be less inclined to take the kind of risks that might get them out of trouble in a tight spot. It would have been better, he thought, had the officers been able to keep it to themselves. He found Wingate "a bit depressed" that his raid was coming to an end and also very much aware that recrossing the Irrawaddy might be the undoing of them. Fergusson too was under no illusions that with the enemy waiting for them along the banks of the Irrawaddy and the Shweli there was a distinct possibility that "we were already in the bag."

Just in case he didn't make it he got hold of Gim Anderson, the brigade major, and gave him his list of officers and men he was recommending for various decorations. Among them was a Military Cross for his Australian adjutant Duncan Menzies. He also made Anderson promise that if he survived and Fergusson did not he would seek out General Wavell* and tell him that in his opinion Wingate's methods worked. "I made him repeat several times over the arguments which, even should the expedition finish in disaster, seemed to me irrefutable proof that such enterprises were worthwhile."

---

*The bright and literary Fergusson had got on exceptionally well with Wavell during his spell as an aide-de-camp.

Chapter 19

*A*LL COMMANDERS dread a river crossing that might be opposed. To confront one twice in a matter of days was almost unthinkable. For the return journey Wingate had decided that he must do what the enemy would least expect him to do and go back the way he had come.

His columns would cross the Irrawaddy en masse close to the town of Inywa just below its confluence with the Shweli, where Wingate had brought brigade headquarters over after Fergusson and Calvert had gone across. Because swimming a large number of mules across the river would be such a time-consuming business and make the columns so vulnerable only those animals needed to carry radios and support weapons would be retained. The rest would be slaughtered.

Wingate set off for his second crossing of the Irrawaddy at one in the morning on 27 March 1943. The Burma Rifles, who were charged with brushing out their tracks, brought up the rear. Just before them was Fergusson's Five Column, which, because of its place in the line of march, was not able to get going until 3:00 A.M. Most them had spent the late afternoon and early evening trying to get some sleep, with varying degrees of success. Fergusson had been distracted by social calls from other columns and a taste of some of the whisky the RAF had dropped.

They went at a punishing pace, and as they went they murdered their mules and sometimes their horses, which they found a heartbreaking business; their animals had become part of the team and almost all had acquired names. Until now only with reluctance had the badly spavined been shot, and few of the men, however hungry, enjoyed the meat. Now Wingate sent word back that even revolvers were too noisy and they must do the killing silently. Fergusson did his best:

Now we tried the ghastly experiment of cutting their throats; but the first operation sickened us all so much I said we should try it no more. We had already disposed of sixteen animals since leaving the bivouac.*

Some columns just refused to do it and let the animals go instead, in the hope that local villagers would pick them up. This would have made Wingate furious had he known, for a string of abandoned animals was a sure indication to the Japanese that their tormentors were lightening their loads for the dash home.

Dominic Neill, one of the late-arrival Gurkha subalterns, had his "beloved horse" following him for miles until it took the hint and wandered away into a field of sugarcane. "I looked at my Syce and he was weeping too."

Five Column marched until the late afternoon, when they bivouacked and made the inevitable tea. Fergusson went forward and discovered Wingate eating rice and raisins in a cheerful mood. Fergusson returned to his column and about ten minutes later some shots rang out. From this moment Operation Longcloth began to unravel into its last desperate phase.

The shots were an exchange of fire between the tail-end Burma Rifles headquarters group and a Japanese patrol who had spotted one of their number defecating a few yards away from the main line of march. "Carelessness," grumbled Wingate, who rarely found reason to criticize his Burrifs. He sent Fergusson a message to set up an ambush in order to deter Japanese pursuit.

Fergusson thought something more than an ambush was called for, feeling it was likely that the Japanese would go around the tail of the column and attack its flanks. He spent the next few hours luring the enemy away from the main party, leaving a trail of footprints and litter along the sandy floor of the *chaung*. Shortly after dusk he staged the grande finale of his deception: a false bivouac with fires piled so high they could be seen for miles and some of the mules, gregarious creatures, tied to trees several yards apart from one another in the hope that they would bray to keep their spirits up. Mule saddles and some full-looking sacks were left around, most of them booby-trapped with grenades. Then, after brewing up some tea on the fires and a very light

*At least one mule got back to India. Flight Lieutenant Robert Thompson (later squadron leader) refused to be parted from his Argentine radio mule Yankee and believed the animal helped the morale of his party.

supper—for Five Column was already short of rations—they crept away and huddled in an unwarmed bivouac about six hundred yards off.

Fergusson allowed his column to sleep for a while and then, by no means satisfied that he had done enough to distract the Japanese from Wingate's party, went with a raiding party to a village where they believed they might find some Japanese. As they approached, Fergusson took out a grenade and strolled into the village accompanied by a couple of Burma Rifles and followed by the platoons of Stibbé and Lieutenant Jim Harman. Almost the first thing Fergusson saw was four men sitting around an open fire. He thought this was a good opportunity to use some of the few words of Burmese he had picked up and, with the grenade in his right hand, walked over and asked the name of the village. When the men looked up Fergusson saw complete terror on their faces:

> They were Japs. Resisting a curious instinct which was prompting me to apologise for interrupting them, I pulled the pin out of my grenade which had suddenly become sticky with sweat, and lobbed it—oh so neatly—into the fire and ran. It was a four-second grenade and went off almost at once. I looked round when I heard it go, and they were all sprawling on the ground.

Now followed a confused and deadly night fight with dozens of grenades thrown by both sides. Fergusson called in vain for Bren guns to be brought up, but these were not available because of what he later described as "the cowardice of three British soldiers" in charge of the mules that were carrying them.* Both sides continued to suffer casualties. Within a very short space of time at least three of Fergusson's men were dead, including his admin officer, Captain Alex MacDonald. Among the wounded were Stibbé and Harman. Stibbé had been shot through the body by a bullet that entered just below his left collarbone and made a ragged exit wound near his left shoulder blade. Even so, when his pack was removed so that a field dressing could be applied,

---

*Fergusson mentioned "the disgraceful business of the Bren guns at a crucial moment" in his classified report to Wingate, a copy of which is to be found in the Wingate Papers at the Imperial War Museum. But he censored it out of *Beyond the Chindwin,* the first of his war memoirs, which was published in 1945 when there were no cowards in the British army.

Stibbé removed the last of his bully beef and biscuits and stuffed them down the front of his blood-soaked shirt.

Fergusson had been wounded in the hip by grenade fragments but could still walk, albeit a little stiffly. One of the heroes of the hour turned out to be his batman, Dorans, who hid in a ditch while the Japanese were counterattacking then bowled some grenades among their feet, finishing off the survivors with his rifle.* Fergusson estimated Dorans had personally accounted for at least eight of the enemy, but he was not very satisfied with his own performance, convinced that a much weaker force of Japanese "did not receive the punishment they deserved for keeping such a lax lookout."

With a desultory exchange of shots still going on, Fergusson got his bugler to blow the signal to disperse, and the column broke up and went its separate ways. Stibbé, who had lost a lot of blood and was in some pain, was mounted on a pony by his dispersal party despite his protests that he must be left. Eventually he simply slipped out of the saddle and refused to go on. Rifleman Maung Tun of the Burma Rifles insisted on staying with him. Stibbé had always been popular with the Karen, and Tun would not abandon him.

Meanwhile Wingate, marching north toward Inywa, had not only lost contact with Fergusson's column but, more importantly, with Wheeler's Burma Rifles, who had been behind them brushing out their tracks whenever Wingate could not avoid crossing a motorable road. Wingate had been relying on Wheeler's Karen soldiers to procure craft for the crossing and on their skills as boatmen to get them across the half-mile stretch with its strong currents.

By the time they reached the east bank of the Irrawaddy at 3:00 A.M. on 29 March, Wingate and his men had marched through fifty miles of thick jungle in forty-eight hours. He was hoping that their reward for this epic feat of endurance would be the surprise they needed to cross the river unopposed. With luck Wheeler and his Burrifs might turn up at any moment. Meanwhile, delay was out of the question. Certainly, there could be no waiting around for it to get light. If possible, he

---

*Dorans was awarded the Distinguished Conduct Medal for this—at the time the British Other Ranks' equivalent of the Distinguished Service Order and second only to the Victoria Cross. Not until after the Gulf War of 1991 did the British army abolish the distinction between officers and men when it came to awards for gallantry.

wanted to establish a bridgehead on the opposite bank during the remaining hours of darkness.

He dispatched the two Burmese officers from his headquarters staff to rouse the local villagers, wave some silver rupees at them, and get boats. By dawn they had collected about twenty of the long, narrow wooden craft known as country boats, but they only had paddles for half of them. Wingate reproached himself for not having caused "hundreds of woven bamboo paddles to be prepared and carried" (surely only Wingate would have imagined his exhausted men would have had time to do this).

As the sun came up over the Irrawaddy, ten bright yellow RAF inflatable dinghies of the type issued to bomber crews were already in the water being towed across by country boats. The leading craft were carrying a couple of platoons of Pukka Kings from Seven Column. Private Aves, the piano accordionist, was in the third boat:

> As we approached the other side so the Japs opened up with mortars, machine guns and rifles. One of the boats behind me was hit by a mortar and I suppose everybody was blown up or drowned. . . . [W]hen I got ashore we sort of crawled up the bank and there I found one of the officers eating a piece of cheese. He didn't seem very concerned.

Looking at the scene from the east bank, Wingate was very concerned. His brigade signals sergeant was dying from a throat wound, and Eight Column commander Major Scott had just survived a bullet through his map case. It was his worst nightmare—an opposed crossing with the situation deteriorating by the minute:

> The native oarsmen all scurried for safety. Nothing could induce them to function. . . . [W]e were left with a small number of country boats with perhaps a dozen oarsmen who knew enough to avoid capsizing them and who could do the round journey in perhaps an hour-and-a-half.

Wingate calculated that at that rate, with a payload of twenty-five men to a boat, it would take about two and a half days to get the thousand or so men he had with him across, longer if he was joined by the missing Burma Rifles and Fergusson's column. The mortar and machine-gun fire had stopped—there were no longer any targets for them since all the boats had fled to one bank or the other. Sniping continued, but the presence of the bridgehead party on the west bank deterred the Japanese from pressing home their attack. Wingate guessed that for the moment he was probably opposed by a small number, though it was obvious that they would be reinforced in a matter of hours:

> Caught strung out on the banks we could easily be pinned down while [the Japanese commander] brought up the superior forces at his disposal. Finally looking around I saw most of the men asleep and exhausted. I therefore decided to abandon the crossing.

He had decided much more than that. Wingate had concluded that he would have to break up his brigade in order to save it. This was the most controversial decision he ever made in the field and not popular with all the men under his command. According to the young Gurkha lieutenant Dominic Neill, Wingate, looking more than ever like some Victorian throwback with his Wolseley helmet and enormous beard, shouted, "Disperse, disperse, get back to India."

> I thought the man had gone stark staring mad. . . . He had taken us so far but he wasn't going to take us back. Here we were a force of 700 strong [in fact stronger] with a platoon already across the river and he wasn't prepared to cross. I realise we would have taken casualties crossing, but far fewer than we eventually did in small groups and getting piecemeal to India.

Neill had joined the brigade late in its training. Officers who had been with Seventy-seventh Brigade since its inception, Wingate noted, greeted his decision with "complete cheerfulness." They were totally conversant with the notion of dispersal,* splitting up when they felt it was time to disappear to meet up again at a prearranged spot. Just as a fighter pilot knows he might one day have to use his parachute, it had always been in the cards that in order to survive the brigade might have to come home a platoon at a time.

There was not always safety in numbers. Trying to force a crossing of the Irrawaddy might delay them to the point where the enemy

---

*Wingate claimed that the dispersal tactic was originally practiced by the thirteenth-century Scots warrior King Robert the Bruce while fighting the English.

would have time to assemble a hammer on one bank and an anvil on the other. The trick now was to be as slippery as possible and not to offer the enemy a large and slow-moving target.

Fifty minutes after the firing started Wingate had a "short and sad meeting" with the commanders of Seven and Eight columns, put himself at the head of his headquarters party, and led them back the way they had come until "I found what I regarded as a secure enough bivouac." Very soon the only people in the camp who were not sound asleep were the sentries, trying to keep awake on hot and highly sugared tea boiled over bamboo fires, and the signalers calling Imphal to arrange their last supply drop before they set off.

Wingate's brigade headquarters was about 220 strong and he divided it into five dispersal units, each with maps and compasses. All the thousand or so men who had gathered with Wingate on the east bank of the Irrawaddy now began to go their separate ways, and not always in the same direction. About 150 of Seven Column under its commander Ken Gilkes headed north toward China. Among them was the wounded Dane Erik Petersen, held on a horse by some of his loyal Pukka Kings, who refused to be parted from him.

Fergusson's column had already dispersed after the night fight at Hintha. Some were with Gilkes's party. One hundred and twenty had remained with Fergusson, who never regained contact with Wingate. The Burma Rifles headquarters group who had failed to meet up with Wingate at Inywa were going to try to cross the Irrawaddy intact, which Wingate thought a good idea, "owing to their many talents, good spirit and knowledge of the country."

Farther to the east Alexander and Ford with their Gurkhas of Number One Group had decided that they had remembered Lot's wife for quite long enough. After successfully ambushing some of their pursuers they turned back to the west, still traveling as a formation.

Calvert, still a long way to the south of Wingate, was also reluctant to dismantle his column, which had done so well and whose repeated successes, from bridge blowing to ambushes, had made it Wingate's favorite. But he knew that some of his Gurkhas were too exhausted to fight so the column was divided into ten groups of forty. Typically, Calvert chose to have a lot of the lame ducks in his group, though he also made sure he had Geoffrey Lockett and some of his commandos with him. Before they set out the leaders met to toast the king with the remains of their rum ration, and Calvert delivered one last piece of advice: "Tiredness makes cowards of us all," he warned them. "If you are really up against it, sit down and make a cup of tea, and the problem will usually get solved."

Wingate too was meeting uncertainty by putting the kettle on. For an entire week his party continued to linger a couple of miles east of the river in what appeared to be a safe bivouac. Here they were dining on mule meat and the remains of their last parachute drop, sleeping long hours. But if idle physically, their minds were being stimulated by a virtuoso display of debate between Wingate and the affable Irishman and master of deception Major John Jefferies, who later gave an account of these conversations to the journalist Charles Rolo*:

> In those seven days he talked like a man possessed, rather as if he was striving to set in order the sum total of his beliefs. . . . Wingate talked of books, painting and the future of mankind. He lectured them on the paintings of the eighteenth century. He argued heatedly with Jefferies that the symphony and not—as Jefferies held—the piano concerto was the highest form of art. There were great possibilities for the cinema, he said, but they had never been fully exploited, except perhaps by Walt Disney. . . . He analysed the art of detective fiction, quoted Leonardo da Vinci. . . . He talked a great deal about the good in various religions. He dissected the characters in the comic strips. His favourites were "Jane"** of the *Daily Mirror* and J. Wellington Wimpy whose lack of courage, Wingate argued, was more human than Popeye's impossible feats of bravery.

Certainly, Wingate would not be the first great captain to surface into a tranquil interlude from his particular hell, take a deep breath, and feel the need to talk about the finer things of life. But few, with the business at hand unfinished, would have gone about recharging their intellectual batteries with such deliberation.

---

*Rolo, who was born in Alexandria, Egypt, of British parents and educated, like Wingate, at Charterhouse School, was employed during World War II by the British Information Services, Churchill's propaganda arm, and in 1944 published the first book on Wingate.

**The daily adventures—considered quite racy at the time and a great favorite with the troops—of a young woman who found it difficult to keep her clothes on.

In their last supply drop the RAF had delivered Jefferies, as part of its "personal service," a recently published biography of George Bernard Shaw, which Wingate managed to read first. "Most English writers are sterile," he flattered the Wexford man. Their library also boasted a copy of Plato's *Dialogues* that Wingate had brought along, Mark Twain's *The Innocents Abroad,* and Palgrave's verse anthology *The Golden Treasury,* the property of Gim Anderson, Wingate's adjutant, from which Wingate's favorite reading to them aloud was all thirty-one verses of Thomas Gray's "Elegy Written in a Country Churchyard." It is its ninth verse that ends "The paths of glory lead but to the grave."

Much of Wingate's talk was the kind of conversation he might have had in Lorna's company. Some of it was about what they were fighting for in the first place and what they should do to see that they would never have to do so again. There was of course Zionism and utopian talk of a world federation and the need for peace enforcers to deal harshly with nations that stepped out of line. Good soldiers would be needed here of course.

Yet at the same time Wingate demonstrated a contempt for the feebleness of contemporary Western man, his guts and initiative eroded like poor J. Wellington Wimpy. "European civilization," Wingate told them, "prevents men from thinking and acting for themselves." There was the usual talk of "military apes." The Burmese officer Aung Thin asked him why on earth he had ever chosen a military career. So Wingate explained about family tradition, and a boyhood spent playing soldiers, and the inevitability of it all, combing his beard as he spoke.

The cool early morning hours were spent preparing for the trek ahead. All the heavy equipment—mortars, Vickers machine guns, and even the Bren light machine guns, which weighed almost twice as much as a rifle—were dismantled and buried in separate pieces. The radio, their umbilical cord to the supply drops that had nourished them, would be the last to go. The rifles, Tommy guns, and revolvers they would take with them were stripped and cleaned and lightly oiled. Magazines were reloaded and every round of ammunition was polished, every grenade had its priming checked. Determined to be ready this time, Wingate ordered dozens of bamboo paddles to be made with instructions given on how best to cut the wood so as not to attract the attention of any passing Japanese patrol. The chopping must be irregular: one loud thwack, half a dozen shorter hacks, and then a pause.

The sad slaughter of the remaining mules and horses went on with all the carcasses butchered and eaten—cooking fires being allowed for an hour during the evening and early morning. Wingate demonstrated the way he wanted the animals dispatched silently with a knife. Perhaps it was something he had picked up from the vets at the army riding school at Weedon all those years before, useful campaigning tips when cut off in enemy territory. Once the mule was bound and pushed to the ground, one entirely naked soldier would sit on its head while Wingate felt along the stretched neck for its carotid artery.

The geyser of blood that ensued would completely cover the naked man, who left the scene afterward to bathe in a nearby *chaung*, looking as if he had prepared himself for some obscene and pagan ceremony. One Indian muleteer, who had prayed with his animals all night the morning before they were to be killed, wept for three days. For Wingate the equestrian it could not have been any easier. One day he called Jefferies to his side with urgent gestures that he should be quiet as he did so. Jefferies feared the worst, only to find his leader gazing utterly entranced at a butterfly.

Why did Wingate delay his departure for seven days? Some of his critics have alleged that he was unfairly allowing the other dispersal parties to draw the heat away from him. There is probably a much simpler and kinder explanation: he was tired. Calvert had noted that Wingate did not have a particularly strong physique. What he had was the willpower to endure when others would have given up. He had just passed his fortieth birthday and had marched as hard and fast as men half his age. By any standards, the last forced march to Inywa had been a killer. At the end of it, he had confided to Anderson, his brigade major, that he had reached his limits. Wingate knew that if he did not rest and allow himself a chance to recuperate he would never make it back. It was as simple as that.

Gorged on mule meat—grilled tongue and kidneys was a favorite— they broke camp and set out for the Irrawaddy on 7 April. It took them two days of dodging Japanese patrols before Wingate and most of his group slipped across at the spot where Calvert had crossed almost a month before. Seven of the British headquarters staff were missing—

among them Squadron Leader Charles Longmore, the senior RAF man, and Lieutenant Lionel Rose, who commanded the Gurkhas in the headquarters defense platoon, a young man Wingate had grown fond of, not least because he was Jewish.

Knowing that the British were about, the Japanese were trying to keep a tight control on all small-boat traffic on the river. Nevertheless, Aung Thin had persuaded a village headman to hire them a boat that had permission to be on the water, because it was transferring a corpse for burial downstream. Five trips were made without incident, but on the sixth the boatman became alarmed that a Japanese patrol had arrived on the east bank. This caused a delay, and Rose and the others never caught Wingate up.

Wingate reached the Chindwin on 29 April 1943—twenty-two days after leaving his camp east of the Irrawaddy—with thirty-two of the forty-two men he started out with.* In addition to the seven who went missing during the Irrawaddy crossing, three more were lost on the way to the Chindwin. One was a British lance corporal whose legs were infected with deep and septic jungle sores, which made it increasingly difficult for him to walk. One day the man stepped out of line, and though Wingate called a halt and went to look for him he was never seen again. Lost or noble self-sacrifice? This was 1943, when heroic explanations were preferred.

There was nothing ambiguous about the next casualty. Wingate had to make the agonizing decision to abandon one of his headquarters officers, Lieutenant Ken Spurlock, whom he had worked with every day since crossing the Chindwin. Spurlock went down with dysentery and was too sick to march.

To varying degrees they were all sick by now. Malaria had been kept at bay by Atabrine tablets. Wingate also had a theory that marching and physical exertion generally were very good for keeping malaria away, an exclusive theory and still ahead of medical science. Apart from malaria, most people were suffering from bad stomachs. This ranged from mild diarrhea to full-blown dysentery.

Wingate's party had sighted the Chindwin on 23 April—St.

*In his printed report of the expedition Wingate says his dispersal party numbered forty-three. He then goes on to give a breakdown of exactly who they were, but there is no way they add up to any more than forty-two.

George's Day. A Burmese guide led them up a fifteen-hundred-foot escarpment. From the top a blue haze only partly obscured the glorious sight of the Chindwin River Valley. Wingate, looking more than ever like some Old Testament prophet with his bamboo staff and his matted beard, knew what was expected of him. "There in that blue mist lies the Jordan," he told them. "And beyond is our Promised Land."

It took them five days to get there, for one eight-mile stretch wading waist deep in water along a fast-running *chaung*, barking their spindly shins on submerged rocks. For days they had known nothing but hunger and thirst, pain and the torment of mosquitos and lice, which deprived exhausted men of sleep.

Wingate, with his extraordinary feel for terrain, led the way, rifle slung over shoulder, machete in his right hand, scouting ahead, testing how noisy a stretch over fallen teak leaves would be (like walking over broken crockery was the answer). And all the time he chivvied them along, telling them to close up, not to bother about their diarrhea, just to keep marching. And they had to remember that they were still soldiers: mosquito repellent was only to be used to keep the bolt actions of their Lee-Enfields working—they had long since run out of gun oil.

Daydreaming was regarded as almost as dangerous as a jammed rifle. Jefferies was inclined to act as if they were home and dry with talk of the champagne he was going to drink in Calcutta and the mince pies—most of them were craving for sugar—he was going to consume at Firpos restaurant. Wingate told him that he would do better to concentrate on getting out of Burma alive. "We're still a long way from Firpos and crossing the Chindwin is going to be the toughest hurdle of all."

And so it proved. There were no boats and the usual swimming problem. Even some who could swim wondered whether they would have the strength to cross. Wingate decided he and five others would attempt to swim across and arrange boats for the rest of the party, who would remain in hiding under the command of Major Anderson until a pickup had been arranged. A recognition signal, a flashed Morse letter, was agreed to.

Wingate's way to the river was impeded by a huge stand of fifteen-foot-high, razor-sharp elephant grass, which left their hands and forearms bloody from cuts and the remains of their shirts in rags. They started at 5:30 A.M. and after four hours had got through about five hundred yards. It was almost as noisy as the teak leaves.

Wingate called a halt, followed a buffalo track down to a swamp, and extracted enough moisture from its ooze to boil a little rice over the kindling they always carried with them, dispersing the smoke with their hats. Revived by this breakfast they went back to their task.

According to the map the grass ended a few hundred yards short of the river, and Wingate decided they would have to lie up until dusk before risking a dash down to the water's edge. Then Wingate, in the lead, prised apart a few blades and discovered that the map was wrong: the river was almost at their feet and at most two hundred yards wide.* It was three in the afternoon and Wingate said there would be no waiting for dusk: they would go now.

They emptied their packs and attached them to lengths of bamboo for buoyancy. Some put their boots inside. At the top of his Wingate attached his inverted Wolseley helmet. Those with rifles rested them across their packs. The RAF signaler Sergeant Arthur Willshaw had kept his air-force-issue Mae West life jacket throughout the expedition, using it as a pillow. Now he could put it to its proper use. It was filthy, but as he entered the Chindwin he was horribly conscious that the water would soon restore it to its pristine orange and make a wonderful target for a Japanese patrol.

They got across without being spotted and made their way to a nearby hut whose owner served them the delicious and reviving juice of green coconuts. Wingate shook each man solemnly by the hand. Then they were led to the nearest British troops, a Gurkha battalion about five miles away, where they feasted on the staple diet of the British army in the field: hot sweet tea with condensed milk, bully beef stew, and rum.

While the others slept, Wingate took the Gurkhas back to the place along the riverbank where he had arranged to exchange signals with Anderson. All night he waited. No signal came. Next day two swimmers from Anderson's party got across. Four had set out, one turned back, and the other drowned. They brought word of another pickup point Anderson wanted to try that night. The Japanese were closing in

---

*Sykes says up to five hundred yards wide, but we base our figure on Flight Sergeant Willshaw's account published in 1997 in Philip D. Chinnery's *March or Die,* which contains by far the best account of the dispersal.

on his party and he had been unable to go to the spot they had originally agreed on.*

The Gurkhas picked up Anderson's party that night, beating off
with mortar and Bren gunfire a last-minute attempt by the Japanese to
intervene as they crossed by country boat. Wingate, Jefferies, and the
others were waiting to greet them, rifles in hand. The idea of leaving it
to the Gurkhas while they went back to Imphal and soft beds does not
seem to have occurred to them.

In all, thirty-seven of the original forty-two in Wingate's dispersal
party got back to India in 1943—thirty-three with him plus four of the
seven who had become separated during the Irrawaddy crossing.
Much to everyone's amazement Lieutenant Spurlock was picked up
by the Japanese and survived captivity in Rangoon, as did Squadron
Leader Longmore and Lieutenant Rose.

Wingate's was the fourth group to return. First home, on 15 April,
was Calvert's dispersal party. Not only had he not lost a single man, but
he succeeded in blowing up the railway again a couple of hundred
yards from a Japanese post, an incident in which Calvert lit a match
under Lockett's kilt when he needed to check a detonator in the dark.

Despite the worst fears of some of his officers, Fergusson's hip
wound healed up. He arrived in Assam on 25 April though his party
were in poor shape and he thought that with their Ben Gunn beards,
bamboo staves, and spindly shanks they looked "more like a collection
of Damascus beggars than a fighting force."

He had been obliged to abandon over forty of his men, almost all
nonswimmers, on a sandbank in the Shweli River when they had refused to budge after others had been swept away and drowned. Dominic Menzies, the Australian who had made a secret pact with
Dorans to return for Fergusson if they had to leave him, was not so
lucky. Colonel Wheeler's Burma Rifles discovered him and another
British soldier tied to trees in a village where they had just driven out

---

*After this depressing night, which fueled fears that none of Wingate's party had
survived to alert the British lines to their presence, Captain Motilal Katju had volunteered to try to find some boats and had gone off with one of the Burma Riflemen.
They came to a village where the Burrif made some inquiries and was warned that
there were Japanese in the vicinity. Katju insisted on going in. Shortly afterward the
Burrif, who was hiding outside, heard a burst of gunfire. He waited but the brave
Katju, a journalist in civilian life who had joined Wingate's brigade at the last moment without any special training, did not return.

the Japanese. Both had been shot or bayoneted, possibly both, and had their beards shaven off—Japan's peasant soldiers were fascinated by the amount of body hair these barbarians could produce.

Kerr and Stibbé, the two wounded subalterns Fergusson had left behind, both survived captivity and the ill treatment and starvation that were the lot of most Allied servicemen who fell into the hands of the Japanese. Maung Tun, the Karen rifleman who volunteered to stay with Stibbé, did not survive. Seventeen sick and wounded with Scott's Eight Column were luckier. On 28 April, the day before Wingate swam the Chindwin, Scott, who still had a radio, had called for an air drop. When he got to the dropping zone he realized that an aircraft could easily land there—it was one of the biggest clearings in northern Burma—and since there were no ground-to-air communications he marked out a message: "PLANE LAND HERE."

After some reconnaissance, the RAF chanced it, taking along with them William Vandivert, an American photographer for *Life* magazine. As the gaunt and hollow-eyed British soldiers came aboard the Dakota, one man holding up the Japanese rifle bullet that had passed straight through him, Vandivert started taking a series of pictures that would eventually go around the world. This was the war's first airborne medical evacuation from behind enemy lines. In a year it would become commonplace in Burma, but in April 1943 nobody had ever seen anything like it.

Private Aves returned with a lieutenant and nine others, having fired his only shots in anger at what might have been a mixed patrol of Burmese National Army and Japanese. Tired and hungry, when they were jumped, most of the men with him, including two officers, had bolted. When Wingate visited him in hospital, where Aves had spent forty-eight hours delirious with malaria, the private told him of his disgust at the way he had been abandoned. "We won't wash our dirty linen in public, will we," urged Wingate. And Private Aves held his silence for half a century.

The last of Wingate's men to get back across the Chindwin were Lieutenant Dominic Neill, one other British officer, and eight Gurkhas who arrived by boat on 6 June 1943. Neill thought their part in the campaign, through no fault of their own, had been a fiasco. "I killed a lot of lice. Not many Japs. . . . In my view only Number Three Column under Mike Calvert had achieved anything." But when he opened *The*

Times of India Neill was astonished to find that he belonged to something called the Chindits and had participated in a military triumph.

Almost all the surviving Chindits found themselves at Nineteenth Military Clearing Station, which was under Matron Agnes MacGeary, a no-nonsense Scotswoman who had been decorated for the bravery she displayed at Dunkirk. MacGeary found she had to start getting tough with some of them. Men who had kept themselves going on visions of a soft bed and clean sheets started dying as soon as they slipped in between them. The antidote was to get them up and clothed, give them some errands to make them walk, and then gradually reintroduce them to bed and sleep. The matron soon realized that Wingate was as sick as some of his men. Since he wanted somewhere quiet to write his report she made two rooms available for him in the hospital, which he would leave from time to time to patrol the wards in search of the latest arrivals. By the end of April it was obvious that losses were high. Out of the 3,000, perhaps slightly more, who had gone into Burma, a total of 2,182 returned.* Only six hundred of the survivors would be fit for future active service.

If Wingate's exploits in Ethiopia two years before had received too little recognition, his first expedition in Burma perhaps received more than it merited by military calculation, or even by his own reckoning. "Abyssinia was one of the most thrilling campaigns you can imagine," he told a friend. "Far more so than my long walk in Burma."

But the British badly needed a success in Southeast Asia. There had just been another failure—the offensive in the Arakan along Burma's west coast on the Bay of Bengal had come to naught. Now, even before the last of Wingate's men had straggled in, Britain's propaganda machine began trumpeting their achievements.

In Delhi and Calcutta, where most of the reporters covering the Burma front were gathered, it was well known among the press that there had been some kind of large-scale raid behind Japanese lines.

*The Thirteenth King's were the worst hit, losing almost half the battalion. Of the 721 who went in only 384 returned to India in 1943. Seventy-one more survived captivity.

Some correspondents, among them Stewart Emeny of London's *News Chronicle,* had even been allowed to go as far as the Chindwin to see them off. There had also been a series of interviews such as the one Wingate granted Alaric Jacob of the *Express* at Imphal in which he mentioned the word *Chindit* for the first time. All this had been done on the understanding that nobody would attempt to publish anything until the time was right, and everybody concerned obeyed the rules. Scoops that might somehow assist the enemy were not considered an acceptable form of journalism in 1943.

The big moment came on 20 May when army public relations unveiled Wingate at a press conference in Delhi. It was standing room only, and the next day British and American front pages were covered with accounts of what the Reuters News Agency dubbed "The British Ghost Army," while the London *Daily Mail* hailed Wingate as "Clive of Burma." In the *News Chronicle* Emeny was at last able to publish the pen-portrait of Wingate he had compiled on the march to the Chindwin back in February. It depicted the kind of military eccentric the British always love:

> You may hear him chanting to himself in Arabic, which he speaks fluently, in his tent in the morning. Then for hours he will be silent and meditative. . . . He has very definite ideas on diet and frequently flabbergasts his visitors by pulling out a handful of raw onions and inviting his guests to join him. His conversation ranges through philosophy, literature, art, music, politics and economics to international affairs.

Nor were the Germans spared this propaganda blitz. On 21 May a BBC German-language broadcast from London told how the British had run rings around the Japanese while subsisting on a diet of python steaks, vulture cutlets, banana leaves, bamboo shoots, jungle pig, and roast elephant. This last embroidery was apparently preferred to the unpalatable business of the mules' final contribution to the Allied war effort.

On the same day, Alaric Jacob's piece from the Delhi press conference appeared in the *Express* in which he used the word *Chindit.* There was resistance to the term at first, especially from the Chindits themselves. "It makes me feel I should have a fur coat and live up a tree," said one. But gradually, in the way of these things, it caught on. Wingate's detractors at GHQ Delhi mut have hated all this adulation, but their objections, if voiced, were easily overridden by the immense propaganda rewards to be derived from showing the world that ordinary British Tommies could beat Japan's "jungle supermen," especially after the defeat of British conventional forces in the Arakan. Wingate's exploits would reassure the skeptical Americans that the British really were pulling their weight against Japan and also give a much needed fillip to domestic morale, depressed by a seemingly endless succession of Japanese victories over British arms. As well, it would help strengthen the British hold on India, where public opinion was increasingly beginning to dwell on the possibility and implications of an outright Japanese victory.

As anyone who was alive at the time will recall, the Home Front was electrified. "Everyone was thrilled to the core," Wingate's old hunting friend Derek Tulloch would write. "Officers who had been content to sit on their bottoms placidly at home felt a stirring of conscience and a desire for active service."

Lorna cabled her husband:

SWEETHEART WHOLE COUNTRY TALKING OF YOUR SUCCESS. GLADDEN-
ING HEARTS WITH PERFECT CONFIDENCE GO FORWARD WITH HUMILITY
AND COURAGE. YOURS ALWAYS.

She had been inundated with messages of congratulation from all levels, ranging from Buckingham Palace and British governmental luminaries such as Leo Amery to the wives of serving soldiers. The Zionist leadership was especially delighted that The Friend should have won such acclaim, and a young Jewish refugee from Nazi Germany, just about to enter the British forces, felt moved to tell Lorna that he would be "more than proud" to serve under Wingate in a Jewish army.

This time there was interest from the book trade on the British side of the Atlantic. The publisher Hamish Hamilton predicted that all his rivals would be writing to Orde in the hope of signing him up. "If, remembering our conversation when he was bedridden in London last year, he should feel like entrusting his story to my firm, I should be proud and happy." Perhaps the most sage comment came from Wingate's redoubtable mother. She, of course, thanked God for his deliverance, but her next point was worthy of a Clausewitz: "To me, dear son, all ignoramus as I am, the outstanding contribution of your exploit to military science and knowledge is that you made your lines of communication vertical and not horizontal."

Publicity and Wingate were usually a happenstance affair. Unlike the pearl-handled Patton or the cap-badged Montgomery, off the battlefield, he lacked the instincts of a natural showman. There was nothing contrived. He was wearing his beard and Wolseley helmet long before they first appeared on a front page. Now he was about to become famous, a warrior icon, and it did not displease him. But he did not seek it out.

Reporters did not quite know what to make of Wingate. He tended to treat them with the same sort of capriciousness he treated everybody else. Emeny's amusing companion around the campfire was not what the Australian communist Wilfred Burchett, then working for the *Daily Express,* discovered when he visited Wingate in a hotel room in Delhi:

> I found him sitting naked on his bed, eyes buried deep in a book. He hardly glanced up as I entered and rather gruffly asked what I wanted. . . . He wasn't interested in me or my requirements, but seemed most excited about the book he was reading. Then Bernard Fergusson came in and the two of them started an animated discussion about this book, which turned out to be a critical commentary on Emily Brontë and her work.

At this time Wingate was doing some writing himself. On 17 June he finished composing his report on Operation Longcloth, which, with its sixteen appendices, numbered over sixty pages. By his standards the language is mild, nothing like the intemperate stuff that almost got him court-martialed after the Ethiopian campaign.*

It is possible that Wingate thought that the acclaim and recognition he was receiving required a little reciprocal humility. Certainly, it is a very modest document, infuriatingly so for the biographer. He devotes one line to his own escape from Burma: "[M]y own story is merely one of many similar ones."

But there was enough in it to excite Churchill, to whom Leo Amery sent a copy, as the memo the prime minister dictated to Pug Ismay, his military secretary, reveals:

---

*Lieutenant General Geoffrey Scoones, corps commander on the Chindwin front, had urged Wingate not to put anything in it GHQ Delhi would not like to show the Americans.

I consider Wingate should command the army against the Japanese in Burma. He is a man of genius and audacity and has rightly been discerned by all eyes as a figure quite above the ordinary level. . . . There is no doubt that in the welter of inefficiency and lassitude which have characterized our operations on the India front, this man, his force, and achievements, stand out, and no mere question of seniority must obstruct the advance of real personalities to their proper station in war.

Wingate, Churchill added, should return to Britain for discussions as soon as possible. He left on 30 July 1943, having had no time to acquire a more suitable uniform than his tropical outfit run up by an Indian tailor. Churchill merely wanted "to have a look at him" before he left for a summit meeting with President Roosevelt in Quebec City, but, in the event, things were to turn out rather differently.

Chapter 20

A BRAHAM AKAVIA, Wingate's one-time translator and faithful Sancho Panza throughout the Abyssinian campaign, was an officer wearing British uniform when Wingate arrived in Cairo, en route for London. The British had not fully relented on their refusal to permit the creation of a Jewish fighting force of the kind Wingate had advocated so energetically, but they had, under pressure from Rommel's Afrika Korps, raised a number of volunteer infantry companies for rear-echelon duties in Palestine and Egypt,* and Akavia was a lieutenant in these so-called Palestine Buffs.

His two-hundred-strong company was based on the outskirts of Suez, guarding an oil refinery, when on 1 August 1943 it received a formal visit from Moshe Shertok of the Jewish Agency. As the company lined up for his inspection, Shertok murmured to Akavia in Hebrew: "Hayedid is in Cairo, but just for a few hours." Akavia turned immediately to his company commander, a British major, and asked: "May I fall out, sir?" The major showed surprise but assented. Akavia walked out onto the main road beside the camp and flagged down an army lorry heading west toward Cairo.

Once in the capital he made straight for Shepheard's,** the five-star hotel on the Nile corniche where senior officers in transit customarily stayed. At the reception desk he was told that Brigadier Wingate was out but expected back shortly. Akavia took a seat on the hotel veranda and waited, from time to time checking at reception to make sure Wingate had not come in by the rear entrance.

---

*Subsequently a Palestine Jewish brigade group was deployed for service with the Eighth Army in Italy.

**Shepheard's was burned to the ground during anti-British riots in January 1952; a new hotel of the same name now stands on the site.

Returning to the veranda from one such excursion, he literally bumped into his former commander. "*Shalom,* Avtam," said Wingate. "Hello, sir," replied Akavia. "*Shalom,* Avtam," Wingate repeated with heavy empasis, and Akavia realized that he was insisting on the Hebrew greeting. "*Shalom,*" replied Akavia, and the ice was broken.

Wingate was still wearing jungle green, by no means inappropriate for the searing heat of Cairo in August, and Akavia noticed that he carried a blue canvas bag, chained to his wrist. "Let me hold that for you, sir," Akavia offered. "No," replied Wingate. "This contains my plans for a new campaign against the Japanese. There are too many people who'd be glad to see me court-martialed if they got lost."

For the next two or three hours, until it was time for Wingate to catch his top-priority flight to Britain, he and Akavia talked but he never, as Akavia would recall, uttered a word about his recent exploits. "He did not mention Burma or say why he had been called to London, and I felt it was not my place to enquire," explained Akavia. "His talk was all about Palestine, Zionism, the people we had both known, and the prospects for a Jewish state. Before we parted I asked him if he could find me a job on his staff and he promised to let me know what the chances were after he returned to the Far East."

On arrival in England, Wingate was met by a representative of the chief of the Imperial General Staff, Field Marshal Sir Alan Brooke, and was driven straight to the War Office to meet him. Wingate assured the CIGS that what he had achieved with a comparatively small force against the Japanese in Burma could be repeated on a far larger scale, given sufficient manpower and resources. "He required, however, for these forces the cream of everything," Brooke recalled later, "the best men, the best NCOs, the best officers, the best equipment and a larger airlift." Brooke said he was about to leave for Canada with Churchill to confer with the American chiefs of staff, but promised Wingate that when he returned he would go into the whole matter with him and see that he got what he wanted. He had no inkling that Wingate would be a last-minute participant in the same conference—the Quadrant summit between Churchill and Roosevelt and their respective military chiefs in Quebec City.

Wingate had just enough time to put in a phone call to Lorna, at her parents' country home in Aberdeenshire, to tell her he was back in Britain before leaving for his next appointment. This was at 10 Downing Street, where Churchill intended to see him before leaving in the greatest secrecy that same night for Quebec. Churchill was about to sit down to dinner with his brother Jack and daughter Mary, his wife having decided to dine alone in her room, when he was told that Wingate had arrived. Churchill immediately sent word for him to join them, and Wingate presented himself still in his jungle green.

Mary Churchill, a lieutenant in an anti-aircraft unit of the women's Auxiliary Territorial Service, was to accompany her father to Quebec as an extra ADC, a forgivable and minor act of favoritism by a doting father. She sized Wingate up over predinner drinks as "a tiger of a man." When they sat down to eat, as the prime minister would recall, Wingate "plunged into his theme of how the Japanese could be mastered in jungle warfare by long range penetration groups landed by air behind the enemy lines." Churchill was enthralled:

> I felt myself in the presence of a man of the highest quality [and] decided at once to take him with me on the voyage. I told him our train would leave at ten. It was then nearly nine. . . . He was, of course, quite ready to go, but expressed regret that he would not be able to see his wife.

Lorna was already on her way south aboard the night express from Aberdeen. Churchill immediately issued instructions to his private office to have her taken off the train at Edinburgh, put into a hotel for the night, and transferred early the next morning to the special train that was taking him and his entourage, including Wingate, to join the liner *Queen Mary* on the Clyde for the five-day voyage to Canada. For security reasons, Lorna was to be offered no explanation for the interruption of her journey, and she passed an anxious night until she was reunited with Orde the next morning on the platform of Edinburgh's Waverley Station.

There was a greater surprise yet to come. As the train rattled on toward the Clyde and Orde introduced Lorna to the prime minister in his carriage, Churchill, in avuncular mood and visibly pleased with his small logistical feat in bringing the couple together, said to Lorna, "Well, my dear, you must be glad to be seeing your husband." She replied, "Yes sir, of course, but I wish we had more time together."

Whereupon Churchill replied, "And so you shall. You must come with us to Quebec."

For Orde and Lorna, this totally unexpected turn of events must have seemed heaven-sent. The few surviving letters from their eighteen months of separation reflect a deep longing for each other. "You know that I love you as no other being on earth and that life is quite incomplete without you," he had written to her from New Delhi while preparing for the first Chindit operation. They were living through "a dreadful age for humanity," he said, but he had faith in the future: "For you and I there is the hope that somewhere somehow we may meet again to live a life of peace and delight in living."

He was clearly too busy to fall prey to depression: "I have on the whole been comfortably free from my particular curse and hope to remain so." And always, and despite the intense challenge of his Burma assignment, Palestine and the Jews remained on his mind. En route to India by flying boat, he had flown "over the mountains of Israel to land on Gennesaret [the Sea of Galilee]. . . . How lovely it would be if you and I were there now, working to defend *Haaretz* [the land]. Let it happen, please God."*

On his return to base from what he modestly called "certain adventures," Orde assured Lorna that he was "very well, beloved—happy and greatly benefitted by the last few months' experiences."

I have a deep sense of the faithfulness of God and meaning of my life and while I may still go astray, as so often in the past, I may hope to receive again the heavenly vision and thrust on through the jungle to the eternal city. . . . I love you as no one else I know or have ever

---

*In this letter Wingate describes a visit to the palace of the Great Mogul in Delhi—"[M]uch of the glory and colour are gone, but enough remains to carry you back to those days of poetry and cruelty, beauty and vain endeavour, art and childishness." He discusses the character of "the unfortunate Nietzsche," whose biography he has been reading—"too German, too humourless, too hysterical. . . . Besides, neither he nor anyone else knows what he was trying to say." And, having just been to Chungking with Chiang Kai-shek, he sketches the character of the "charming" Chinese people—"Their dominant characteristic is cheerfulness. Under conditions which reduce Europeans to a gloomy despair smiles of pure joy break constantly over the Chinese face."

known: there is a peculiar bond between us that has stood the test of rage and violence on my part and you know that I am always yours.

And to underline his obsession with the Jewish cause: "I am feeling very much at the moment IM ESHKOKHEYTH YERUSHALAIM TISHKAH YAMINI [If I forget thee, O Jerusalem, let my right hand lose her cunning] and do you too pray that our lot takes us there together to the place and the work we love."

Another recurring theme was his concern for Lorna's health: "I often think of my time in the cold weather without coal or heating [it was December]. You must take to wearing clothes for warmth or pneumonia is a certainty." And in July: "Sweetheart, I hear you are in the clutches of the doctors. As far as you can, avoid them; a most dangerous profession. Above all, avoid operations by the nose, throat and ear fraternity. . . . I do wish, my own, we were likely to meet soon. I am entirely unenthusiastic for a bloodstained career and only want to be with you for the rest of time." Lorna had assured him in May that "I bloom and flourish, but only to 50 percent of my capacity, as half my entrails are strung out across the seas." Now she cabled: "Disregard health rumours. Am anaemic but well. No operations specialist. Preserve yourself. I will follow suit. Your well-being basis of my own."

<hr />

It was an all-star cast that boarded the eighty-thousand-ton *Queen Mary* on the morning of 5 August as, clad in wartime gray, she spread her thousand-foot length at anchor in midstream at Gourock, in the Clyde. Churchill's retinue of advisers, service chiefs, secretaries, and senior ministers numbered 250, including Foreign Secretary Anthony Eden, and among the service chiefs were Lord Louis Mountbatten (later Earl Mountbatten of Burma), the king's cousin and head of Combined Operations, who had been earmarked by Churchill—with American approval—to become supreme commander of Allied forces in Southeast Asia; Brooke, the CIGS; and Sir Charles (later Lord) Portal, the chief of Air Staff. As well as Wingate, the *Queen Mary* carried another outstanding hero of the moment—Group Captain Guy Gibson, VC, leader of the Dam Busters, the RAF Bomber Command force that had won fame by breaching the Germans' vital Ruhr Valley dams.

Here was a striking contrast in personal styles: Gibson, the quintessential RAF "type," affecting the nonchalant, almost flippant manner that hid the steely resolve he had shown under fire,* and Wingate, the intense, taut military intellectual, ruthless in action, brilliant in exposition, but virtually incapable of small talk.

The giant Cunarder, with her assemblage of the best and brightest of wartime Britain, would have been the juiciest possible target for Hitler's marauding U-boats. "You are my war machine," Churchill had told Eden before setting sail, in explanation of his veto on their flying to Quebec, "Brookie, Portal, you and Dickie [Mountbatten]. I simply couldn't replace you." Security was correspondingly tight. Churchill was traveling under the cover name of "Colonel Warden," and the ship had been plastered with notices in Dutch, apparently to give the impression to dockyard workers that the exiled Queen Wilhelmina of the occupied Netherlands was the VIP for whom the liner was being prepared. The *QM*, modified to hold as many as an entire division of soldiers in her troop-carrying role, was to be escorted across the Atlantic by a cruiser and an anti-submarine screen of destroyers, although with a top speed of thirty knots she could easily outrun any U-boat yet built.

The Wingates were the objects of considerable gossip and attention, if only because of the dramatic—not to say romantic—circumstances of their reunion and last-minute inclusion in Churchill's party. Many of the women passengers, concerned that Lorna was traveling without a suitable wardrobe, hastened to offer her articles of clothing. (Orde had exchanged his jungle kit for naval battledress, the only uniform available in his size.) But the clouds of sympathy soon evaporated. Lorna was determined not to be cast as the gallant little wartime wife, keeping the home fires burning for her warrior husband. She ignored the gush, eschewed small talk, and insisted on delivering her views on such subjects as Palestine and Zionism and the sociology of everyday life in wartime Scotland.

She was young, she was beautiful, and her voice was strikingly melodious, but her manner seemed to those expecting only a little girlish chit-chat to be schoolmarmish and even ominously left wing. Eyes

---

*Gibson was shot down and killed by a German night fighter while leading a Mosquito light bomber raid over occupied Holland in September 1944. His last words, radioed to his squadron after they had dropped their bombs on target, were, "Nice work, chaps. Now beat it home."

began to glaze over at the dinner table, and Guy Gibson, who was the same age as Lorna—twenty-six—was heard to describe her as "a sententious prig," to which Portal was heard to agree. This was a period when a young woman was supposed to be decorative if possible, but in any case to know her place and not to "hold forth" on serious matters. Orde, as a man of forty and a triple DSO (his second bar had been gazetted while he was on his way home from India), was of course above any such criticism.

The *Queen Mary*, on that voyage, was no ship of fools—far from it; her passengers, from Churchill down, represented the cream of a great if fading empire, on a mission of the utmost importance and gravity. The five days of the crossing were spent, for the most part, in intensive preparation for the coming conference. But the company's collective "off-duty" style at dinner or over cocktails could be characterized as "World War II insouciant." To keep up morale, if for no other reason, the British affected a lighthearted approach to the grim business of war, and gravitas was not appreciated, still less the Manichean worldview of the Wingates.

On the third day out Churchill sent for Wingate, wanting to have a more detailed discussion of his memorandum on future operations in Burma. The premier questioned him closely, point by point, and ended up satisfied that his initial enthusiasm for Wingate's plan had not been misplaced. More than purely military considerations were involved here, however: relations between the two great allies were somewhat strained over a variety of issues—not least the timing and starting point for an invasion of Europe—and Churchill was anxious to show the Americans that he shared their resolve to put maximum pressure on the Japanese in the Far East.

In a note to the Chiefs of Staff Committee he said that before meeting the Americans they must agree upon "positive proposals for attacking the enemy and proving our zeal in this theatre of war, which by its failures and sluggishness is in a measure under reasonable reproach." In this connection, Wingate and the dashing and personable Mountbatten were to be his star turns at Quebec.

Thick fog enveloped the *Queen Mary* as she approached the Grand Banks, off Newfoundland. Despite an equally dense blanket of security, the citizens of Halifax, Nova Scotia, were sufficiently well informed to turn out in their flag-waving thousands to greet Churchill and his entourage. From Halifax, the summit party went by train to Quebec City, where Churchill was to stay at the Canadian governor-general's summer residence while the rest of his party were accommodated in the massive Château Frontenac, a fairytale castle of a hotel with steep, verdigrised roofs and rows of dormer windows, set on a dramatic promontory high above the St. Lawrence River.

The winking lights of the lower town were a delight to the British visitors after four years of blackout, as was the abundance of food and drink after four years of rationing.* For Orde and Lorna it must all have seemed like some kind of dream, but there was serious business to be done and they had little chance to be alone together.

The British party reached Quebec three days before the Americans were due and spent the time in more intensive committee work, at which Wingate proved unexpectedly adept. He presented his revised plans for the second Chindit campaign to the British staff chiefs and the Joint Planning Staff on 10 August—"a first class talk," said Brooke—and they approved his demands for manpower and matériel with only slight modifications. Churchill was delighted with the performance of his protégé and went out of his way to mention him by name in a message to the king: "Brigadier Wingate made a deep impression on all during the voyage, and I look forward to a new turn being given to the campaign in Upper Burma."

On 14 August Wingate's plan was approved by the American top brass at a meeting of the combined chiefs of staff. And on the eighteenth Wingate was wheeled in to sell his ideas to Roosevelt himself, in the presence of Churchill and Mountbatten. Wingate was crisp, concise, brilliantly persuasive. Said Churchill: "You have expounded a large and very complex subject with exemplary lucidity." "Such is always my practice, sir," replied Wingate, without a trace of false modesty. The plan called for a long-range penetration force of 26,500 men, to be divided into three groups, each of eight columns. These would be inserted deep behind Japanese lines to soften up the enemy before a three-pronged frontal main assault by the British in the west, the Chi-

---

*Mary Churchill was struck by how white the bread was, compared with the gray of the wartime British variety.

nese in the east, and Stilwell's Sino-American force in the north, the overall objective being "the conquest of Burma north of the 23rd parallel." But although Churchill, Roosevelt, the American service chiefs, and the British service chiefs all liked the plan—indeed, it was the one unequivocal point of agreement in an otherwise tense and disputatious conference—British military headquarters in New Delhi did not.

They had been told by cable from Quebec City of its gist and of the combined chiefs' approval and asked for their comments by 20 August. But the commander in chief in India, Field Marshal Claude Auchinleck, while paying lip service to Wingate's zeal and leadership, did not see him as a corps commander. Further, he had been persuaded by his staff that Wingate's wish list would place an intolerable demand on their limited resources of manpower and equipment. As well, they argued that the Chindits' role, as a guerrilla force, was not to engage the enemy in pitched battle but to harass them while avoiding direct contact wherever possible. "Therefore," Auchinleck cabled, "in my opinion the proposal is unsound and uneconomical as it would break up divisions which will certainly be required for prosecution of the main campaign in 1944/45."

When this cable arrived in Quebec, Churchill exploded and Wingate mounted a counterattack in the form of an eight-page memorandum in which he did not hesitate to disparage the performance of the command so far:

> Everywhere except in one instance [i.e., the Chindits] the troops given the task of fighting the enemy have been worsted and made fools of. It is not too bold to say that this is due to faulty methods. . . . The statement that the object of LRPGs is not to fight but to evade the enemy is the reverse of the fact. . . . Troops of these columns must have seen many more Japanese during the Chindit operation than normal infantry have seen of this enemy in years. . . . The longer this war in Assam lasts, the less ready to advance the formations seem to become. . . . As long as a year ago we were speaking with confidence of our intention to make these advances not in 43–44 but in 42–43! The longer the war goes on the further this prospect of an advance recedes.

This was entirely in line with Churchill's own feelings that the high command in New Delhi had been dragging its feet far too long. And in any case, there could be no question now of going back in any way on the agreement just reached with the Americans. Wingate won the contest hands down, including his insistence on being allowed to establish his own headquarters. His ascendancy was further underlined when on 25 August the conference formally established the Southeast Asia Command (SEAC) under Mountbatten, who believed in him 100 percent. There were those at Quebec and elsewhere who were not certain that Mountbatten had the experience to hold down the job of supremo, but as Anthony Eden's private secretary Oliver Harvey put it, Wingate was "a good second." And "Mountbatten-Wingate is at least a refreshing contrast to Wavell-Auchinleck."

In political terms, Quadrant was the high point of Wingate's career. It was unprecedented for an officer of his comparatively junior rank to find himself in a position of such influence over strategic decision-making at so high a level. But before he had time to savor his triumph, personal tragedy intervened to cast him down when he learned belatedly that his mother had died suddenly on 8 August of angina, the heart condition that had plagued her for years. Thinking him still to be in India, his sister Rachel had cabled him there on the ninth, while Sybil had followed up with a letter: "It was quite sudden in that she had been better for some time past, right up to yesterday. In fact, she was downstairs playing the piano on Saturday evening."

Neither letter nor cable, of course, reached Wingate, and a few days later the family heard rumors that he was in England. They tried and failed to get confirmation of this—Lorna, too, being out of contact—so Sybil Wingate telephoned Leo Amery at the India Office. Amery knew but felt unable to tell her where her brother was, offering instead to see that the news reached him. It did so, just as he was about to leave Quebec for Washington with Mountbatten on further business connected with the forthcoming Burma operation.

As in childhood, so throughout his adult life Wingate had been especially close to his mother, whose lively intelligence remained with her to the end despite chronic sickness and the intellectual limitations imposed by her cast-iron fundamentalist beliefs. In her final letter to him, just over a month before her death, she seemed to sense that he was planning to repeat his success in long-range penetration. "Stick to your praying, darling," she admonished and went on:

> I was much struck a week ago by the fact that David never took God's guidance for granted, nor made his plans first and expected

God to endorse them afterwards. I was reading 2 Sam. 5.19–25 and saw that David did not take it for granted that if God had guided one form of attack one time that he wanted David to follow that same method the second time.

Even more remarkable was the fact that her death should coincide—quite possibly to the very day—with the conception of her first grandchild. After a hitherto childless marriage of eight years, Lorna became pregnant while in Quebec or on the way there. Blind coincidence or God's will? Ethel Wingate would surely have believed the latter.

Chapter 21

T HE FIRST MEETING between Wingate and Lieutenant Colonel Philip Cochran, the breezy, shoot-'em-up American who was to command the Chindits' unique aerial task force, was a less than unqualified success—and an almost perfect paradigm of the occasionally uneasy Anglo-American alliance as it stood in the late summer of 1943.

In the aftermath of the Quadrant Conference, Cochran had been sent to London by the U.S. Army Air Forces chief of staff, General H. H. "Hap" Arnold, to confer with Wingate about the aerial assistance the Americans had promised for the next Chindit operation. But his first encounter with Wingate left Cochran with the feeling that there was little common ground between them. Cochran, the son of a well-to-do Irish-American couple from Erie, Pennsylvania, had a problem with English accents at the best of times, and to his ear Wingate's plummy tones were "exaggerated" and "obfuscating." To make matters worse, Cochran would recall, Wingate "mixed everything up with scholarship and the history of war" so that "I didn't know what he was talking about." There is no record of what kind of impression Cochran made on Wingate, but it seems safe to assume that the incomprehension was mutual.

Cochran enjoyed a certain wry celebrity within the U.S. Army Air Forces as the model for Flip Corkin, the hero of the hugely popular syndicated comic strip "Terry and the Pirates," whose inventor, the cartoonist Milton Caniff, had been his high school classmate. As a fighter pilot, Cochran had more solid grounds for the respect of his contemporaries and superiors in the shape of the Distinguished Flying Cross with two clusters, the Croix de Guerre, and a Silver Star, earned against the Germans in North Africa, where he was credited with four enemy kills.

Cochran was one of the two battle-hardened combat flyers Arnold had sent as potential commanders of the top-secret unit, initially code-named "Project Nine," that was to be the Chindits' private air force. The second candidate was Cochran's old friend, flat-mate, and fellow regular officer, John Alison—also a lieutenant colonel—who had shot down six Japanese warplanes while serving in China with Claire Chennault's legendary Flying Tigers. He too was much decorated, holding the Distinguished Service Cross, the Distinguished Flying Cross, the Purple Heart, the Silver Star, and the Legion of Merit. Cochran was the more extroverted of the two, an ex–high school football star with a taste for nightclubbing and a way with "the chicks"; Alison was retiring, steady, and diplomatic, and in those days teetotal, in keeping with his Southern Bible Belt upbringing. In their different fashions both had strong leadership and organizational skills; both were now training rookie pilots in the United States; both were eager to return to action. As Alison recalls it,* Project Nine was conceived by Hap Arnold—ostensibly at least—as little more than a casualty evacuation unit, operating with unarmed light aircraft and not at all the kind of work that a gung-ho fighter pilot might be expected to relish. Privately, Arnold had much greater ambitions for the project, but initially he kept them to himself.

> He called us into his office in the Pentagon and said, "One of you boys have got to do it. Which one is it going to be?" I had been assigned to command a fighter group in Britain and told him straight out that I wasn't interested. Phil said, "General, he doesn't mean that." I said, "General, I do mean it." Then, seeing that neither of us wanted the job, Arnold told us his full plan.

> What the general had in mind was nothing less than a miniature air force—dedicated entirely to the Chindit operation and therefore beyond interservice rivalry and immune to the pull of competing priorities—equipped not just with air ambulances but with transport aircraft of all types, plus fighter planes for air cover and close support. "I'll give you anything you want," said Arnold. "The best aircraft, the best pilots, the best ground crews. Now, which one of you wants the job?" Alison and Cochran conferred quickly together. Now they were really interested.

---

*Cochran died of a heart attack in August 1979, while riding with the hunt club in Saratoga, New York.

We said, "Can we both go?" and Arnold said, "Okay." Then he said, "Alison, you're the senior so you're in command." I said, "No, Phil outranks me by a couple of months," so he said, "Okay, you'll be co-commanders." That arrangement didn't work so well in practice, if only because of the confusion it caused in the Pentagon, so after a while I said to Phil, "You command, I'll be deputy." And that's how it was.

One of Cochran's first assignments was his trip from Washington to London to confer with Mountbatten and Wingate. After an amiable lunch with Lord Louis and his wife, Edwina, Cochran made his way to Combined Operations headquarters in Richmond Terrace, next to Scotland Yard, where Wingate had been allocated a temporary office before returning to India. Cochran found him at work in an untidy cubbyhole on the top floor and was hardly more impressed by the accommodation than he was by its occupant. Their unpromising first meeting was succeeded by a second the next day, which went a good deal better. This time Wingate was able to get across to the American what he meant by "long-range penetration," and as they spoke Cochran "suddenly realised that, with his radio direction, Wingate used his guerrilla columns in the same way that fighter-control headquarters directs planes out on a mission":

> I saw it as an adaptation of air to jungle, an application of air-war tactics to a walking war in the trees and the weeds. Wingate had hit upon the idea independently. . . . In his own tough element he was thinking along the same radio lines that an airman would about tactics among the clouds. I realised that there was something very deep about him. . . . He was a thinker and a philosopher. . . . When I left him I was beginning to assimilate some of the flame about this guy Wingate.

On his return to Washington, Cochran, with Alison, plunged into a hectic round of procurement. They soon found Arnold to be as good as his word: they could have whatever they wanted, provided they pushed hard enough. Within a month Project Nine, soon to be renamed Number One Air Commando, had acquired 100 L-1 Vigilant and L-5 Sentinel light planes for ambulance and resupply duties; 12 single-engined UC-64 Norseman cargo planes, each capable of carrying a two-thousand-pound payload; 30 single-engined P-51 Mustang fighters, equipped with the new rocket launchers; 13 twin-engined DC-3 Dakota transports*; 150 CG-4 Waco cargo- and troop-carrying gliders, with 50 more in the pipeline; and 6 new-fangled helicopters, the first to be deployed anywhere in the world. Subsequently, they would add 15 B-25 Mitchell light bombers to this formidable little air force.

Quite beyond the enormous morale-boosting effect casualty-evacuation capability would have on Wingate's men, this unexpected American munificence would add an entirely new dimension to his long-range penetration concept—especially so in the provision of gliders, which would make it possible to insert his Chindits deep into the enemy's vitals within hours ("I don't want those guys to walk," Arnold had said) while ensuring that they had more than the light weaponry to which they would otherwise have been restricted. Now, using the Waco gliders as cargo carriers, they could deploy heavy mortars, jeeps, and light artillery.

On the last day of August 1943, Wingate's old friend and fox-hunting companion Derek Tulloch, now a lieutenant colonel commanding a light anti-aircraft regiment in Britain, was enjoying the first day of a fortnight's leave at his home in Lancashire. After a morning spent shooting partridge in the pouring rain, he returned for lunch to find a telegram that read: "Am in London and require your help. Come up immediately. Orde Wingate." Tulloch, thrilled that this old friend, now a national celebrity, had not forgotten him, changed, packed an overnight bag, and caught the next train south with his wife, Mary.

The following morning the Tullochs joined Wingate and Lorna at their flat in Mayfair. "Wingate looked extremely well, was full of self-confidence and obviously keyed up with well-repressed excitement over the future." He told Tulloch what had transpired at Quebec, gave him a copy of his report on the first Chindit operation, and said that—with War Office approval, of course—he needed Tulloch's help in recruiting a nucleus of suitable staff officers to take out to India with him.

---

*More commonly designated by the Americans as the C-47 Skytrain.

Tulloch himself would be second in command of one of Wingate's long-range penetration brigades.

Time was of the essence. They had little more than a week before Wingate, now about to be promoted from brigadier to major general, was due to leave for India. But preparations for the invasion of France were siphoning off the cream of the army, and with only a couple of days in hand Tulloch had to report that he had been unable to fill the most important post—brigadier general, staff. Of the two best available candidates, one had declined on grounds of ill health while the other had been severely wounded in Italy even as the telegram offering him the appointment was on its way. To Tulloch's surprise Wingate said he had hoped for such an outcome; he wanted Tulloch himself to be his chief of staff. The self-effacing Tulloch accepted with trepidation, flattered by the offer but fearing he might not be up to the job.*

While in London, Tulloch had another task—to evaluate some of the new weaponry that was being developed for use by special forces and commando groups. At Special Operations Executive headquarters he ordered a number of silenced pistols, for dealing with enemy sentries, and a new version of the Sten gun, which was reputed to be fully efficient even after being immersed in water or sand for long periods. He also ordered a number of portable "Lifebuoy" flamethrowers and some lightweight American M1 carbines, more suitable for jungle warfare than the elderly British Lee-Enfield.

One night shortly before leaving England Wingate and Tulloch took their wives to dinner at the In and Out Club in Piccadilly. Walking back to the Wingates' flat afterward, Wingate told Mary Tulloch how deeply he had been affected by having been forced to leave the sick and wounded behind during the first Chindit operation. He was confident that thanks to the American ambulance planes this would not happen next time. Wingate also found time for a brief reunion with Chaim and Vera Weizmann and to have lunch with his sister Sybil, by now a senior civil servant with the Ministry of War Production. She would "remember vividly the emphasis in his voice as he walked down the Charing Cross Road . . . saying to me (in what context I do not recall), 'You must have faith, you must have faith in God.' " The context

---

*"How nice Wingate could be," Tulloch observed parenthetically in his memoir, "and invariably was, when dealing with me, though very naturally he lost his temper on occasion, and usually I deserved it!"

almost certainly was that while he was still a fervent believer, Sybil, an equally fervent Socialist, no longer was.

On 11 September, Wingate and Tulloch and four other officers, the nucleus of his staff, left London by train for the RAF base at Lyneham in Wiltshire, where they were to emplane for India. Before boarding, Wingate and Tulloch had time to take a stroll around the deserted grounds of Marlborough College—closed for the holidays—and up to a hill on the surrounding downs. "It was a glorious autumn evening," Tulloch would recall, "and Wiltshire was looking very lovely. It was fitting that Wingate's last sight of England should have been that of the county where he had spent so much of his life and of which he was so fond."

Tulloch's impressions of their flight to India are somewhat less elegiac. They traveled in a Liberator bomber, and since their first stop was at neutral Lisbon they were wearing civilian clothes.

> We were a somewhat comical-looking party in our mufti, and the comedy was given a fillip when Wingate opened his suitcase to take out some papers and his Major-General's hat fell out, was caught in the slipstream of the aircraft, and bowled merrily down the runway with a Portuguese policeman in pursuit.

In letters to his wife, Tulloch reported with amused tolerance on Wingate's less than rigorous personal habits. From Lisbon, he wrote: "We both share a room and O, not having made any provision for such things(!) also shares my razor and soap, etc. . . . We have a private bathroom and the water is hot. There is a footbath in there which O uses for a somewhat different purpose [than] for what it was intended—by mistake at first, but he is continuing happily. He has been chanting outlandish songs, so I think he is enjoying himself." From Cairo he wrote: "Orde and I share a room here. He has not cleaned his teeth since we started! and shows little inclination to start. . . . It was jolly lucky I brought those travellers' cheques as they won't change English currency. I have been able to finance Orde."

One incident en route that was to have near-fatal consequences occurred during a fueling stop at Castel Benito in North Africa. It was hot and dry and they were all thirsty, but the airfield bar was closed and there was no one about to tend to them. Wingate, displaying an astonishing lack of elementary caution, seized a vase full of flowers and drank the water. "I have never been able to fathom how he came to break one of his own strongest rules in this way," observed Tulloch later.

In Cairo, where they stayed two nights before flying on to India, Wingate displayed once more his utter lack of inhibition about nudity. "He stood on the verandah at Shepheards under the neon lights for at least half an hour with nothing on," reported Tulloch, "quite unperturbed when I pointed out how visible he was." Before leaving Cairo by Sunderland flying boat, Wingate had an unexpected and necessarily brief reunion with his younger brother Nigel, an anti-aircraft artillery officer on sick leave from Tunisia.*

On arrival in Delhi, Wingate and his party got a chilly reception. They had only five months to raise, organize, equip, and train six long-range penetration brigades and get them into action before the onset of the 1944 monsoon. But Mountbatten had not yet arrived to take over as supremo and Auchinleck, who was soon to be moved sideways, had made no secret of his objections to the whole project. His staff—the "Curry Colonels" as they were contemputously called by those in the field, who viewed them as motivated mainly by sloth and selfish ambition—were virtually unanimous in believing that the decisions reached at Quebec were political rather than strategic and that there was no real intention to carry them through. Beyond that, Wingate was widely viewed as a scruffy upstart who must be put in his place. He, in turn, made absolutely no attempt to make himself agreeable, or even diplomatically polite, to those he considered "military apes."

Consequently, the first planning conference on Chindit Two turned out to be, in Tulloch's phrase, "an ugly fiasco." Invited to outline his plans and requirements, Wingate was met by the proverbial wall of cotton wool. As Tulloch put it, "One after another officer gave reasons why they could not help the project." And when one senior officer complained that "this is the first I've ever heard about all this," Wingate rose to his feet and snapped, "Why should you have been told before? I'm telling you now."

It was obvious, he said, that none of the Quadrant decisions had been carried out and that there was no intention to carry them out. Under those circumstances there was no point in continuing the discussion, but he wanted the meeting to know that unless there was a

*Later that year Nigel received crippling wounds in action in Italy.

change of heart he would be forced to make use of his direct channel of communication with the prime minister and tell him what kind of a reception he had received. With that he left the conference room, taking Tulloch with him.

> He turned to me with a wry grin and said, "Derek, do you think I was too bloody?" To this I replied, "No—we were getting absolutely nowhere. It was the only thing to do." By this action Wingate had virtually declared war on the entire staff of GHQ India.

And war it was. At Quebec Wingate had been promised his own office, his own car, his own aircraft. He got none of them, not even a secretary. From Central Command headquarters at Agra, a week after that disastrous first meeting, Tulloch wrote to his wife, "So far we have had no staff at all. We had one room between the lot of us at Delhi and eventually co-opted the services of a Wren,* who came and acted as a stenographer for Orde, but I have had no one. Consequently everything is down in my notebook or on scrap paper."

While Tulloch battled with his organizational problems, Wingate continued the fight for his project in Delhi, at a series of often rancorous top-level staff conferences, and made whirlwind visits to the Bangalore headquarters of Seventieth British Division, which, in the teeth of general staff opposition, was to be broken up in favor of his long-range penetration force, and to Assam, where he met Major General Eugene Stratemeyer, the American commander of Allied air operations in Burma. With Mountbatten not expected from London until the first week in October, Wingate encountered continued foot-dragging on his return to Delhi. "God, there are some loathsome people in this city," fumed Tulloch. "There are rows of people who are dead and have been dead for years but are still walking about and drawing good money." Even in the midst of such major controversies, Wingate's Zionist obsession kept showing itself. In a memorandum to the chief of staff he recommended that the Chindits should in future be known officially as Gideon Force—a suggestion that was turned down**

---

*A member of the Women's Royal Naval Service (WRNS).
**Possibly for reasons of security. Japanese intelligence might have spotted the Abyssinian connection and concluded that a major Wingate-led operation was in the offing.

in favor of Special Force. On greeting Bernard Fergusson, who was to command one of the Chindit brigades, and spotting the Palestine Medal ribbon on his chest, he growled that it was "a badge of disgrace." And in a letter to Akavia, regretting that he could not find a suitable job for him in India, Wingate added in Hebrew script the words "If I forget thee, O Jerusalem . . ."

Two days before Mountbatten's arrival Wingate fell victim to a mysterious illness, which left him weak and feverish. Disregarding medical advice that he should go to hospital, he dragged himself to the airport to meet the new supreme commander. He had pointedly not been invited to join the official reception committee but was determined to tell Mountbatten about the difficulties he was encountering before giving in to his malady, whatever it might be.

The next day Wingate was admitted to hospital. The doctors failed at first to diagnose what was wrong with him, thinking, as Tulloch noted, "that it might be dysentery or malaria, or malaria and dysentery combined, or it might be enteric." Wingate characteristically railed at the doctors. Pale and haggard, but combative as ever, he told Tulloch: "They are treating me for all kinds of diseases. I would have done better to stay at Maiden's Hotel." After eight days the army doctors came to the belated conclusion that he was suffering from typhoid—doubtless the result of his ill-advised drink from the vase of tainted water at Castel Benito.

On 15 October, Tulloch recorded: "News is bad. Orde is vile—typhoid, and is at the peak tonight." Five days later he confessed himself "worried stiff" about Wingate's condition and the treatment he was getting. "I loathe the nurses at the hospital," Tulloch said in a letter to his wife, "they seem quite inhuman and uninterested." He added the curious information that he had been "combing Delhi for champagne for [Wingate].*

---

*It may seem strange that the desperately ill Wingate should feel the need for so frivolous a drink, but despite his asceticism he was not entirely immune to the delights of the palate. Akavia recalls that during the Abyssinian campaign they would imbibe freely from cases of Spumante, captured from the Italians. And in a letter to a friend in England while convalescing from his typhoid attack Wingate looked forward to "a tremendous blow-out" once "this tiresome war" was over: "I dream of oysters, smoked salmon, caviar, lobsters, etc., assisted on its way by champaign [sic] and hocks."

Determined to secure better care for his friend and commander, Tulloch sent an urgent message to Mountbatten, who was in Chungking to confer with the Chinese leadership, urging that the redoubtable Matron MacGeary be brought to Delhi from Imphal. Mountbatten agreed immediately and at his behest an RAF Dakota was diverted to bring her to the capital posthaste, traveling all night in the copilot's seat. With some justification Tulloch exulted. "The way I got her will be a classic in good organisation for ever! I achieved the impossible in 14 hours. Needless to say, I had an open sesame behind me."

There can be little doubt that Matron MacGeary's prompt arrival was instrumental in saving Wingate's life. He immediately "settled down and ceased to worry about his condition," said Tulloch. "He had complete faith in her and obeyed her instructions implicitly." A hospital visit from Cochran and Alison, with their buoyant optimism and enthusiasm for the coming campaign—plus the news that the bulk of their gliders, fighters, transports, bombers, and ambulance planes had arrived by sea from the United States—did much to raise Wingate's spirits.

Back in Scotland, Lorna was by now three and a half months pregnant. She had not been having an easy time of it, and the shock of receiving Tulloch's cable, telling of Orde's grave illness, almost caused her to miscarry. "She lost a stone in about ten days," said her mother, "and the sickness which was already bad became much worse." Lorna was admitted to a nursing home, where she remained until the news that Matron MacGeary was on hand and Orde was recovering caused her own state of health to pick up. From her mother's house in Aberdeen, she wrote to her "dearest twin" to urge him not to rush back to work:

> You may as well make up your mind to get better properly for the sake of the job, if not for the sake of the Jews, yourself, me, and the rest of the world. Your stubbornness, indeed senselessness, in the matter of reasonable care has nothing fine about it. It simply causes endless trouble and destroys your efficiency.

Lorna's ongoing preoccupation with the Jews and Zionism, despite her concerns for Orde's health and her own difficult pregnancy, is made clear in a number of her letters during this period. In one, she mentions that Chaim Weizmann was "upset by the anti-semitism in England" and about a trial in Palestine that was "an absolute put-up job by the police in an effort to incriminate the [Jewish] Agency and smash the Histadrut." In another, she comments concernedly on an article in *The Times* about Britain's postwar Middle East policy, which involved "arranging an Arab federation including Palestine." And so forth.

Likewise, Orde, while convalescing as the Wavells' houseguest at Viceregal Lodge, discussed the Middle East with his host: "Talked to Wavell of Eretz Yisrael. He said danger was to A[rabs] from J[ews]. I differed, giving much chapter and verse from my own experience." But for once Wingate did not allow a fundamental divergence of view to sour a relationship. Wavell was "a likeable man," he told Lorna, "—most kind to me."

But naturally enough, much of their correspondence focused on the expected child. She told him that his sisters and aunts were "very thrilled about the baby":

> We are all collecting its trousseau, quite a business in these days. If it is a boy, do you have any ideas about names? Orde for one, I think. And supposing it is a girl? You must give the matter your earnest attention. . . . Darling boy, I miss you so much and I love you more than I can say. It won't matter if you are very great and famous or just a major growing cabbages, I shall always think you are just the best thing that ever happened to me. . . . I needn't tell you how proud I am of your exploits and much more of your goodness and courage and patience. Beloved, don't be cast down by the jealousy and faithlessness of some people. They destroy themselves if only one can wait long enough!

Accompanied at Viceregal Lodge by the ever-vigilant Matron MacGeary, Wingate was making rapid progress back to health. A cable from Churchill—one of three from the prime minister, who had been receiving daily bulletins on Wingate's condition—urged him to make sure he was quite better before returning to duty: "On no account hurry. Take your time." To which Wingate replied, "Will go as slow as I can but hope to be at work in week or two." And to Mountbatten: "I know my own body and assure you that I am fitter for work at this moment than I have frequently been in the past in the midst of campaigns." In the event, Wingate was back on duty after three weeks' convalescence, instead of the three months recommended by the doctors, assuming formal command of Special Force on 1 December.

For her part, Lorna had received "some extraordinarily charming and sympathetic letters" from Churchill's wife, Clementine. And by mid-November she was assuring her husband that she was now feeling much better herself and was "hardly sick at all. . . . There is no outward or visible sign of the inward Wingate, but after poking me about yesterday the doctor said the little creature was certainly there."

From Faridkot House, where he completed his convalescence as houseguest of the Mountbattens, Wingate wrote to Lorna in a mood of uncharacteristic calm, even serenity:

> This present ambitious phase of our lives may well end in obscurity. If so, beloved, I look forward to life together as peasants. Our life together has been a joy to me in spite of failings and faults on my own side. And since I have found you I have had no dreams of a better companion or lover. . . . Finally, my own, I am peaceful and happy in mind and only miss you. God bless you and all our friends, especially the Jews who now are in great distress. I am sure they will yet reap in joy the harvest of so many tears.

"Peaceful and happy in mind"—this is hardly the fire-eating Wingate of old. Had illness mellowed him? Wingate apparently thought so. "I sometimes think my typhoid has deprived me of some of my mental force," he told Lorna,"—that although placid, fat and happy I have lost some of the mental acuteness and vigour that I enjoyed before the removal of my gut." That was certainly not the impression he gave to those around him as—still under the watchful eye of Matron MacGeary—he hustled to make up for lost time and get his greatly enlarged Chindit force ready for the coming operation. As Tulloch noted:

> Orde has been difficult of late. All his staff except [Lt. Col.] Neville Marks and myself are terrified of him, though they respect and like him. He has two distinct natures: Jekyll and Hyde. One is charming, kind, almost deprecating. The other is nothing short of tyrannical, overweening and despotic. His energy and forcefulness are quite incomparable.

Clearly, the strain of trying to mount an operation of such complexity in so short a time, combined with the aftereffects of his near-fatal illness, was taking its toll. Nevertheless, Wingate remained deeply concerned about the welfare of the men under his command, past and present, as one small incident may illustrate. Lorna had written to say that she had received an enquiry from the wife of one of Wingate's officers who had not returned from the first Chindit expedition. This was Lieutenant Lionel Rose of the Sherwood Foresters, the defense platoon commander at Wingate's brigade HQ, who had got as far as the Chindwin on the return journey, only to fall into Japanese hands. "Would you ask someone to get what details there are for this poor woman?" asked Lorna. Wingate wrote back describing Rose as "a splendid boy" who was "instrumental in saving my own life on one occasion."

> I felt very badly about his loss, which was perhaps partly my fault. He was missing from the time he was last seen, about May 1st, on the Chindwin. I fear the worst, though don't say so to Mrs. Rose. If she is in any want now or in the future we must help her. I feel I am responsible to Rose for that. . . . Rose behaved with the greatest courage and unselfishness. He was devoted to his Ghurkas and owes his present absence to that devotion—otherwise he would have come in my boat, as I asked him to do. I often lost my temper with him and even struck him, but he understood.

Six weeks later, Wingate received "the glad news that certain of my old brigade officers are prisoners of war in Burma" and immediately wrote to tell Lorna that "Rose is said to be one of them."* He added: "I do not think they are badly treated by all accounts. They get the Japanese rations which are poor for Englishmen but there does not seem to be any deliberate ill-treatment there at present."

Even amid the turmoil of training his Chindits for the coming campaign and conducting his battles with headquarters, Wingate found time for serious reading and for thinking about "the meaning of existence." His reading list brought him back to the gospels of Matthew and Mark and the Book of Isaiah and to Rousseau's *Confessions*. The first volume of the Rousseau was "good," he thought, but the second "mainly paranoia. . . . Tolstoy said this book was one of the great influences of his life. I can understand the first vol. being so—not the sec-

---

*It is unclear whether Rose survived captivity. Some prisoners were in such poor condition when liberated by the advancing British in April 1945 that they died shortly after.

ond." Wingate's ruminations on the subject of war, while on the threshold of his most testing campaign, are especially revealing. War, he supposed, was "a necessary evil—as is a surgical operation."

> The drugging of one human being by another, the hideous mutilation by the knife, are in themselves an evil but become good through the motive. Can one fight in war with good motives? If not, one ought not to fight. I believe one can. I do not believe in carrying on war with hatred for one's enemy. On the contrary, it is a police operation which has in view the welfare of the criminal as well as of the community protected.

And on faith: "Life would be easier for us if we had a dogma like the aunts. But while I acknowledge the goodness of Christ and the sweetness of his teaching and would feel honoured beyond expectation to be described as a Christian, yet I do not know the Christian dogma—Christ is God, blood redemption, operative only by expressing a belief in the resurrection and doctrine, new birth on this etc.—to be necessary. If it is, may God guide us to that knowledge."

Chapter 22

*A*LTHOUGH WINGATE was only partly aware of it, war strategies had changed significantly since the heady days of his triumph at Quebec. During his illness and convalescence, Quadrant had been followed by Sextant, at which sharp disagreements came to the surface among the Big Four allies—Churchill, Roosevelt, Stalin, and Chiang Kai-shek—and new priorities emerged.

The first phase of the Sextant Conference, held in Cairo, reaffirmed the objectives of Quadrant for the conquest of northern Burma by means of an offensive to be launched and consolidated before the onset of the monsoon in mid-May made operations impossible. The ultimate objective was the liberation of the entire country, through a seven-point airborne, overland, and amphibious operation, code-named Buccaneer, of which Wingate's long-range penetration group was an essential element. But Buccaneer came under threat when the conference moved on to Tehran and was joined by the Soviet leader.

Stalin, who as yet had no part in the war against Japan, insisted on the opening of an Anglo-American second front in Western Europe by mid-1944 to take pressure off the Red Army in the east. To a certain extent, Roosevelt shared Stalin's doubts about Churchill's commitment to a full-scale invasion of Hitler's "Festung Europa" and supported the Russian leader's argument. Under the circumstances, Churchill had no choice but to agree to a massive allotment of resources to an early invasion of France. This, in effect, relegated a major Burma offensive to third place. Buccaneer was canceled, and Chiang went into a sulk, convinced that his strategic interests mattered little to his Anglo-Saxon allies.

But shifting global priorities were only part of the political, strategic, tactical, and personal witches' brew in which Wingate's plans for the second Chindit expedition were left to simmer. He had to contend not only with the normal vagaries of wartime supply and planning,* with inter-Allied and interservice rivalry, and with the hostility of skeptical or ill-intentioned senior staff officers and the duplicity of superiors—including Mountbatten—whose priorities changed with those of their political masters; he also had to navigate the complexities of an unusually tangled command structure.

He was immediately answerable to Lieutenant General (later Field Marshal Viscount) Sir William Slim, the recently appointed Fourteenth Army commander, who in turn was responsible to General Sir George Giffard, commander of the Eleventh Army Group and head of all Allied land forces in Southeast Asia. Giffard answered directly to Mountbatten, whose chief of staff, Lieutenant General Sir Henry Pownall, had conceived an avid dislike of Wingate. Another player near the top of the command structure was the cantankerous American general Vinegar Joe Stilwell, who had an avid dislike of *all* Britons. He commanded a mixed Sino-American force based at Ledo in the far north of Assam and, although officially subordinate to Mountbatten, whom he despised, owed allegiance to Chiang and refused to consider himself answerable to Giffard.

The reordering of strategic priorities at Sextant and its full implications were not made clear to Wingate, or even to Mountbatten's more immediate subordinates, but it soon became evident to the Curry Colonels in New Delhi that something had happened to clip the high-flying Wingate's wings. Thus encouraged, they renewed their attempts to bring him down. And, without a full-scale offensive to back it up, a Chindit long-range penetration (LRP) operation could indeed look like a pointless waste of men and matériel. True, Mountbatten insisted that he had "absolutely no intention of allowing the operation in northern Burma to fade away," but this may have been no more than a sop to the Americans, who suspected that the British were more interested in recovering their Far East empire than keeping the Chinese in the war. Despite changing global strategies, therefore, Roosevelt continued to demand action on the Burma front to open up the overland supply route to China.

---

*During this period, apart from Buccaneer, Mountbatten's staff produced a proliferation of bizarrely code-named plans—Culverin, Bullfrog, Pigstick, Tarzan, Dracula, Toreador, and Axiom. All were either disapproved or abandoned.

Consequently, Mountbatten conceded that Wingate's long-range penetration "Operation Thursday" should go ahead. It was to be co-ordinated with an offensive by Stilwell, whose troops were supposed in theory to link up with Yoke Force, a Chinese army of fifteen divisions deployed across the Salween River on the Sino-Burmese border, and reopen the precipitous Burma Road from Lashio to Chiang's operational headquarters at Yunnan.

But Chiang, still sulking, was refusing to send Yoke Force across the Salween unless and until his allies had first cleared the Japanese out of northern Burma. And Stilwell was sulking, too. Though eager enough for action, he was less than keen on the idea of Wingate's Chindits "muscling in" on his operation and deeply resentful that the U.S. Army Air Forces should have assigned its Number One Air Commando—jocularly known as "Phil Cochran's Flying Circus" and less jocularly as Wingate's private air force—to the despised British. Other Allied commanders had also been casting envious eyes on the lavish air power resources put at Wingate's disposal, and to deter them Hap Arnold, at Cochran's urgent request, drafted a letter to "Dear Dickie" (Mountbatten), underlining that the Air Commando was in India specifically to support the Chindits and must continue in that role.

The British commanders in the field were as reluctant as Chiang to commit their main force, the Fourteenth Army, to a full-scale offensive. Despite Mountbatten's brave words, there could be no question of his ordering Slim to support a Chindit operation with a major drive across the Assamese frontier. Churchill's attention was focused elsewhere, and Wingate's critics—and even some of his Chindit officers—began to believe not only that his ascendancy was over but that the days of his Special Force were numbered. Indeed, in his frustration Wingate himself went so far as to suggest disbanding the Chindits, offering to return to regimental duty at his substantive rank of lieutenant colonel.

It may have been a bluff, for he no doubt calculated correctly that Mountbatten had to keep Special Force alive, if only to appear determined to honor the promises that had been made at Quebec. But it took Roosevelt's insistence and mounting evidence that the Japanese were preparing to launch a major offensive of their own, across the Burmese frontier into Assam, to save Operation Thursday from being discarded. In the event of a Japanese offensive, an LRP operation to disrupt supply lines and attack airfields and communication behind enemy lines seemed both desirable and viable, if risky, especially in the light of Wingate's formulation of a bold and brilliant new tactical concept.

This was his idea for the creation of a pattern of so-called strong-holds, fully fledged, semipermanent operational bases that were to be inserted by airlift deep inside enemy territory. These were to be no mere jungle outposts but brigade headquarters in every sense of the term, each with its field hospital and post office, officers' and NCOs' messes, and canteen for the enlisted men. More than that, each "demesne," as Wingate called it, was to have shops and cultivated fields. Nor did Wingate neglect the need for light entertainment: he had inherited a divisional dance band—and chose for its signature tune the current favorite "Praise the Lord and Pass the Ammuni-tion"—which he intended should visit the strongholds once they were securely established.* This was shrewd psychology; a flying visit from a dance band would be more than mere entertainment—it would serve as a powerful morale booster, suggesting the normality of a base two hundred miles beyond the front line.

The very name for these beyond-the-lines HQs was inspired by a passage in the Old Testament—"Turn you to the stronghold, ye pris-oners of hope" (Zechariah 9:12). Their feasibility was the product of Wingate's belief that the boldest methods were the safest, combined with American optimism and technical know-how. It was expressed by Wingate in these sonorous terms:

> The Stronghold is a *machan*** overlooking a kid, tied up to en-tice the Japanese tiger.
> The Stronghold is an asylum for Long Range Penetration Group wounded.
> The Stronghold is a magazine of stores.
> The Stronghold is a defended air-strip.
> The Stronghold is an administration centre for loyal inhabitants.

---

*The bandmaster, Colonel John Lancaster, told one of the authors in a 1997 in-terview, "If Wingate had not died we would have been flown into one of his strong-holds—probably White City—to entertain the lads. It would have been the only concert ever given behind enemy lines during World War II. It would have been a great thumbing of the nose at the Japs. I could have dined out on it for years."

**A raised observation platform.

The Stronghold is an orbit around which columns of the Brigade circulate. It is suitably placed with reference to the main objective of the Brigade.

The Stronghold is a base for light planes operating with columns on the main objective.

In a training memorandum. Wingate explained his idea in more detail: "The ideal situation for a Stronghold is the centre of a circle of 30 miles radius of closely wooded and very broken country, only passable to pack transport owing to great natural obstacles, and capable only of slow improvement. This centre should ideally consist of a level upland with a cleared strip for Dakotas, a separate supply-dropping area, taxiways to the Stronghold, a neighbouring friendly village or two, and an inexhaustible and uncontaminated water supply within the Stronghold." He demonstrated how such an area might be organized in accompanying sketches and concluded: "The motto of the Stronghold is 'No Surrender!' "

Fergusson, a by no means uncritical admirer of Wingate, was deeply impressed by "the clarity in which [the concept] now blazed from his triumphant paper."

The conception was masterly and daring; the very word "Stronghold" was typical of his taste for the challenging word; his sense of drama, his unashamed and flaunting use of archaic phrases invested what might have been a drab life with a sense of history. . . . The quotation from Zechariah . . . flared across the top of the first page and blazoned itself on my mind; its comforting rhythm and heavy beat fitted my step along many miles of jungle path.

The American know-how that underpinned the strongholds came from Cochran and Alison. They had convinced the initially skeptical Wingate that their gliders, towed two at a time, could fly troops and bulldozers into any suitable jungle clearing. Once the combat engineers accompanying the initial landing party had created a landing strip, Dakota transport planes would put down a full brigade of troops with all the weapons and equipment needed to establish a secure base for offensive operations within thirty-six hours. What was more, undamaged gliders could be reused, thanks to an ingenious device, involving a line stretched across two poles and a contraption like a giant fishing reel inside a DC-3, with which they could be snatched off the ground and towed back to base.

It was all startlingly novel, disconcertingly daring. The Germans had pioneered the use of troop-carrying gliders, notably in their invasion of Crete in 1941, where they took horrendous casualties but won the battle. The Allies had been playing catch-up ever since and made their first large-scale use of gliders in the Sicily landings in June 1943. But no one had ever contemplated using them in jungle terrain, and the notion would be anathema to the naysayers at GHQ Delhi with their "it can't be done" mentality. To an innovative mind like Wingate's it was music. He needed only one successful demonstration to convince him that this was the way to go.

That materialized at a realistic fly-in exercise at a jungle clearing in Gwalior, central India, not far from Wingate's Special Force training headquarters. He looked on as first a pair of pathfinder gliders, one of them copiloted by Cochran, made a successful landing, to be followed half an hour later by the main force, a battalion of the Black Watch. The airborne Scottish infantrymen fanned out to defend the perimeter from an "attacking" force of West Africans, while successive waves of gliders brought in heavy equipment, supplies, and ammunition, plus mules for ground transportation. When the fly-in had been successfully accomplished and the perimeter secured, poles were set up and the DC-3s returned to snatch the gliders from the muddy clearing. The jubilant Wingate insisted on flying out in a glider snatch, first instructing his aide-de-camp to "tell the RAF that I have not only seen it, I've done it!" And in an exultant message to Mountbatten, Wingate declared, "Cochran's gliding was a complete success and can revolutionize the whole campaign."

That daytime exercise was followed by an equally successful night fly-in and pickup that was witnessed by, among others, the supreme commander—"Louie the Lord," as the Americans called him—who was so impressed that he offered Wingate ("The Man" to the Americans) promotion to the rank of lieutenant general. Wingate demurred, saying he would accept after he had proved his ideas in action.

Before he could put the stronghold to the ultimate test, Wingate had to win over the somewhat cautious Slim and also persuade the Royal Air Force to second the pilots and wireless operators he wanted with his units on the ground to handle the vital task of coordinating forward air operations. That was an absolutely revolutionary notion at the time, and initially the RAF top brass were totally against releasing aircrews for such a purpose. Eventually, Wingate won this and other such arguments, but only at the cost of making new enemies because of the sometimes undiplomatic and frequently downright rude way in which he fought his corner. As Tulloch would put it:

> Conservatism in the armed forces has always striven to stifle "non-conformity" and there were many senior officers of both services in India in 1943 who honestly thought that Wingate's plan of putting a force of corps strength behind the enemy's lines and maintaining it solely by air was suicidal and impossible to achieve. . . . [Wingate's] direct approach and scornful rejection of what he considered to be out-of-date and effete gained him no friends.

On the credit side of this situation, some of the best and brightest young officers in India volunteered to join Wingate—"not misfits or wastrels," as Tulloch would say, "but genuine enthusiasts who willingly gave up their temporary rank in order to join the Force." The downside was that a good proportion of those volunteers were weeded out by the rigors of Wingate's training regime and were returned to their units embittered against him.

By mid-January 1944, Wingate moved the headquarters of Special Force—now, for security reasons, officially named the Third Indian Division—to the Imphal Valley in Assam, near the Indo-Burmese frontier. Three of his six brigades came with him: Calvert's Seventy-seventh, Fergusson's Sixteenth, and the 111th, commanded by an ex-Glurkha officer, Brigadier William (Joe) Lentaigne. Another three brigades completed their training in central India, and an American formation commanded by Brigadier General Frank Merrill, which had been training with the Chindits, was hived off to join Stilwell at Ledo. They were to achieve fame—and heavy casualties—as Merrill's Marauders.

Wingate's relations with Stilwell remained fraught. In an obvious reference to him, Wingate told his wife: "I like the Americans here very much and rely much on them—all but one, who normally resides far away." Yet the Limey-loathing Stilwell may have nursed a grudging respect for Wingate. The worst he could find to say of him was that he was "an exhibitionist"—practically a compliment by comparison with

what he had to say of Mountbatten ("a fatuous ass") and British soldiery in general ("pig-fuckers").

As part of Operation Thursday, Fergusson's brigade was to move to
Ledo by rail, their mission being to march down into Burma on Stilwell's right before setting up a stronghold with aerial support and seizing an important Japanese airfield at Indaw. Calvert's and Lentaigne's
brigades were to fly in from an airfield in the vicinity of Wingate's
headquarters to establish strongholds in the central sector, within operational distance of Fergusson's. From there they would fan out to attack Japanese supply lines and installations and block road and rail
communications. Air support would be provided by the RAF as well
as Cochran's "Flying Circus."

Wingate had determined that he would need extra battalions of infantry to garrison his strongholds, so freeing the intensively trained
Chindits to foray as "floater" units beyond the perimeter. He thought
he had obtained Slim's unconditional agreement to provide these. But
on 25 January, during a tour of inspection, he learned that Slim had
changed his mind. In view of the threatening Japanese offensive, the
Fourteenth Army commander was not prepared to deplete his reserves, and Wingate was told he would have to garrison the strongholds out of his own specialized manpower resources. In fury, he wrote
to Mountbatten offering once more to resign and return to regimental
duty. Without the garrison battalions, he said, Special Force might as
well be disbanded and Operation Thursday cancelled:

> Not because it is inadvisable; on the contrary, if it were backed by
> the military command it would have a great chance of success; not
> because the Air think it is impossible; they're playing; but simply
> and solely because the commanding British generals are not at heart
> for it. That is to say, they are opposed to making the minimum con-
> tribution necessary to its success. Not only has this already preju-
> diced the success of the operation but who can tell its deadly effect
> in the future when at the height of some crisis I shall wish to count
> on loyal support? It is a change of heart that is required and I cannot
> change their hearts. I believe that the cancellation of the operation
> will be disgraceful to our arms, but to court probable disaster might
> be still more disgraceful.

Pownall, Mountbatten's chief of staff, already thought Wingate was
"quite a bit mad," and on reading this latest tirade became alarmed at

the possible consequences. Wingate had "succeeded in selling himself to the PM . . . and Winston has sold him to Roosevelt, also to Mountbatten who at present thinks him the cat's whiskers" and if Wingate should appeal directly to Churchill the prime minister might even sack Slim and give Wingate command of the Fourteenth Army—an appointment he had considered before appointing Slim in the first place. This would be "a most dangerous affair," Pownall felt. "Wingate may (or may not) be all right as a specialist, but he simply hasn't the knowledge or the balance to be in high command."

Pownall's dislike of Wingate knew no bounds, his diary notes—not intended for publication—reflecting perfectly the hostility felt by so many senior officers of conventional mind-set. "I think that at last Mountbatten is beginning to see through him," he observed hopefully after a subsequent testy exchange between Wingate and the supreme commander. "I shouldn't be at all surprised if within the next three months it is proved that Wingate is bogus; at any rate he is a thoroughly nasty bit of work."

In the event, the dispute over the garrison battalions was smoothed over by Giffard, who prevailed on Slim to order a Gurkha battalion to join Calvert's brigade for training in stronghold garrison duties and to provide twenty-five-pounder artillery and anti-aircraft guns for stronghold protection. Although Wingate accepted the offer with reluctance it did nothing for his volcanic temper. Even the loyal Tulloch felt the lash of his tongue from time to time. "My relations with Orde are 90% delightful and 10% bloody awful," he informed his wife.

On one occasion Wingate became so angry over botched transport arrangements that he kicked his transport officer, Lieutenant Colonel Francis Piggott, out of a taxiing Dakota. "God, how I laughed when I heard," said Tulloch. "It was very naughty of Orde, though, and he had the grace to apologise. . . . Orde's story was 'a slight push after the plane had stopped.' Francis' story was 'kicked out violently when the plane had only just touched down!' India is full of disembodied spirits who started with us and faded out. I fear poor Francis is going to join them."

———————

When Wingate moved to his operational headquarters Number One Air Commando followed, establishing two airfields in the Imphal Valley about one hundred miles from the border. One, at Hailakandi, was for fighters and bombers; the other, at Lalaghat a dozen miles away, was for gliders and their towing transports. The light ambulance and communications aircraft could use either. Number One Air Commando now numbered 87 officers and 436 enlisted men, with a total of 348 aircraft. It was soon to be joined by a combat engineering company, equipped with air-transportable tractors, bulldozers, and graders.

At Hailakandi and Lalaghat, the American air and ground crews set to work stripped to the waist to improve the two fields, employing native labor with elephants to help them lengthen and widen the landing strips to six thousand feet by three hundred, and building bamboo huts, or *bashas,* for accommodation and administration. It was sweaty work, and Cochran's men had little regard for spit and polish; many of them grew beards, and when USAAF Brigadier General William Old, the head of Troop Carrier Command, made an inspection visit he was not pleased by their slovenly appearance. They looked more like hoboes than soldiers, he complained, and Cochran, on being told to make his men smarten up, posted an order that must stand as a classic of its kind:

> Look, Sports, the beards and attempts at beards are not appreciated by visitors. Since we can't explain to all strangers that the fuzz is a gag, we must avoid their reporting that we are unshaven (regulations say shave) by appearing like Saturday night in Jersey. Work comes before shaving. You can never be criticized for being unkempt if you are so damn busy you can't take time to doll up. But be clean while you can. Ain't it awful?

From the two improved airstrips the Americans trained intensively, practicing glider landings with Wingate's troops. Inevitably, these exercises were not without mishap as the pilots of gliders and towing planes alike learned to master unfamiliar techniques. In one night exercise involving a double tow, the lead glider got into the propeller wash of the towing plane and went out of control. Both gliders made an emergency release. One landed safely but the other crashed, killing four Britons and three Americans. This experience did not deter the Chindits. The following day Captain Bill Taylor, leader of the glider pilots, received a message from them, saying, "Please be assured that we will go with your boys, any place, any time, any where." The last six words became the official motto of Number One Air Commando.

One of the many problems to be overcome was the transportation of the mules Wingate had requisitioned as jungle pack animals. Some went aboard willingly enough; others had to be dragged and prodded. And once aboard and airborne, how could one be sure they would not panic and kick holes in the flimsy walls of the gliders? The gliders' floors were reinforced, the mules' legs were hobbled, their heads were tied down to keep their ears out of the control cables, and their movement was restricted in slinglike contraptions. Muleteers were ordered to shoot the animals if they became unmanageable and endangered the aircraft, but in the event this was never necessary; they were invariably unexpectedly passive.

During February, while awaiting the green light for Operation Thursday, the Air Commando flew regular combat missions. Daily sorties were made by Mustangs and Mitchell bombers, not only to hit ground installations and for general reconnaissance, but to photograph likely landing sites for the eventual Chindit fly-in. The city of Mandalay was a major target, and returning from a raid there one day in February a squadron of Air Commando Mustangs spotted a large concentration of Japanese bombers on the ground at Shwebo. Ignoring the Japanese fighter cover over the airfield, the Mustangs attacked the grounded bombers with cannon fire, destroying many of them for the loss of one of their own. A dozen Mitchell bombers from Hailakandi followed up, arriving over Shwebo just before sundown, escorted by a squadron of RAF Hurricane fighters. Flying in at under one thousand feet, they caught the Japanese by surprise with fragmentation bombs.

An RAF reconnaissance flight the next day counted more than a hundred destroyed Japanese bombers and Zero fighters. "This raid must have broken the back of the Japanese air force in Burma," said Alison in a postwar memoir.

As well as attacking trains, ammunition dumps, river barges, and highway traffic, the American fighter pilots devised a daring method of disrupting Japanese telephone and telegraph communications. Flying low, trailing a cable with a hook on the end, they would snag telegraph wires, cutting them and occasionally uprooting their poles. One Mustang actually returned to base dragging a telegraph pole behind it. The light ambulance planes were active, too, flying into the scene of fighting along the Arakan coast where a British division was heavily engaged and flying out a total of seven hundred casualties.

And Cochran's gliders were busy on more than just training flights.

Two of them were towed to the support of Fergusson's brigade as it marched south on Stilwell's right flank, landing on a sandbar in the Chindwin with folding boats, outboard engines, and gasoline for a river crossing before being snatched off again. The Air Commando also flew Wingate in by light aircraft for a conference with Fergusson while the latter's brigade was on the march.* The bonds of confidence and comradeship between Wingate's men and Cochran's were growing to the extent that, as Mountbatten would say after the war, "I do not suppose there has been a finer example of inter-service, inter-allied cooperation."

By mid-February Wingate had decided on the location of six potential landing sites straddling the strategic railway line linking Mandalay with important Japanese air bases at Indaw and Myitkyina. These sites were code-named Piccadilly, Broadway, Blackpool, White City, Aberdeen, and Chowringhee. The initial fly-in, by Calvert's Seventy-seventh Brigade on the night of 5 March, would be to Broadway, Piccadilly, and Chowringhee. Lentaigne's men would fly in to various sites during the next six days while Fergusson, whose men had been on the march for over a month, would set up his headquarters at Aberdeen before attacking the Indaw air base.

To avoid arousing Japanese suspicions, Wingate banned all reconnaissance flights in the vicinity of Piccadilly, Broadway, and Chowringhee for a week before D-day—an order that, fortunately for all concerned, Cochran ignored. A few hours before the gliders were due to be towed off from Lalaghat, he ordered one of his Mitchells to hive off from a routine bombing mission and photograph the landing sites. A scant fifteen minutes before the first glider was due to leave, Lieutenant Charles Russhon, head of the Air Commando's photographic unit, made a hurried landing in a light plane from Hailakandi, where the B-25s were based. He ran to where Wingate, Tulloch, and Cochran stood in a huddle with some of SEAC's most senior officers,** including the visiting generals Slim and Stratemeyer and the RAF's Air Mar-

---

*"If ye be willing and obedient ye shall possess the land," Wingate had messaged Fergusson, adding: "Keep me personally informed by signal of any important difficulties and remember if you are in a jam I am the person most likely to help you out. Seek therefore for opportunities to see me by suggesting places where I can visit you by Light Plane."

**Mountbatten was not present, due to a painful eye infection.

shal Sir John Baldwin. In his hand Russhon carried still-wet blowup prints of the three landing sites.

Eighty gliders were deployed in pairs along the tarmac, their three-hundred-foot nylon towlines stretched out ahead of them. Under their wings sat Calvert's men, quietly waiting the order to embark. Breathlessly, Russhon handed Cochran his prints. Broadway and Chowringhee were clear; Piccadilly was covered with teak logs—a death trap for any gliders that might land there.

Wingate's first shocked reaction, according to Tulloch, who stood next to him, was to demand to know who had disobeyed his instructions not to fly over the landing sites. Cochran took full responsibility and Wingate apologized for his outburst. Then began an anxious debate about the implications of the reconnaissance photographs.

Wingate initially suspected that his plans had been betrayed by loose talk in Chungking. It was well known that Chiang Kai-shek's headquarters was a hotbed of Japanese spies. And since one of the main objectives of the operation was to show Stilwell's Chinese that they were not alone by severing the main supply line of Japan's elite Eighteenth Division, they had been kept informed of Anglo-American plans. But if a spy had got hold of the blueprint for Operation Thursday, why was only Piccadilly blocked? Had the Japanese left the other sites open as a trap and dug themselves in there, waiting to ambush the Chindits when they landed?

Or was there a less sinister explanation? After all, Piccadilly had been discovered by Wingate's expedition the year before, when Scott's Eight Column had persuaded the RAF to land there and pick up the sick and wounded. It was one of the largest clearings in northern Burma, easily the most obvious of potential landing zones. Furthermore, pictures of it had appeared in the June 1943 issue of *Life* magazine, when it ran the photojournalist William Vandivert's photographs of Scott's casualties flying out. It was possible that the enemy had located and strewn Piccadilly with logs simply as a routine precaution against airborne landings. It was also possible that Burmese peasant foresters had left the logs there to dry before floating them down the Irrawaddy just as they did in peacetime. It could mean whatever you wanted it to mean, and Wingate soon found some grounds for optimism: "[T]he blocking of Piccadilly by the enemy did not necessarily imply any knowledge of the plan, and the fact that none of the other three had been blocked (so far as we were aware) entitled me to hope that this interference by the enemy at Piccadilly was merely a routine measure. . . . It can be imagined, however, how ominous at the time the discovery appeared."

For whatever reason, Piccadilly was clearly unusable, and at literally the last moment Wingate was having to contemplate the possibility of postponing or even abandoning Operation Thursday altogether. He consulted Cochran and, most crucially, Calvert, who would land with his battalion in the first wave. If the Japanese were waiting in ambush he and his men would be flying to virtually certain death. Nevertheless, both Calvert and Cochran urged Wingate that the fly-in should go ahead, only cutting out Piccadilly. Calvert had just one stipulation— that his entire force should be put down on Broadway instead of being split between Broadway and Chowringhee, on the opposite side of the Irrawaddy, so that if the landing was opposed his brigade would not be divided by the river.

At Wingate's urging, Slim, who as army commander would take ul- timate responsibility if the landings ended in disaster, endorsed the de- cision to go ahead,* and Cochran rounded up the Dakota and glider pilots whose destination had now been changed. Leaping onto the bonnet of a jeep he began his rebriefing by calling out: "Say, fellers, we've got a better place to go to." At 6:10 P.M.—only seventy minutes behind schedule and despite the radical change in flight plans—the first glider became airborne, bound for Broadway.

At his final briefing, even the laconic Cochran had been moved to the kind of language he normally avoided: "Nothing you've ever done, nothing you're ever going to do, counts now—only the next few hours. Tonight you're going to find your souls."

---

*For Slim's much later, contrary, version of events, see the Epilogue.

Chapter 23

OHN ALISON was flying one of the Pathfinder teams of eight gliders that had taken off shortly after 6:00 P.M. just as the light was beginning to fade. Their job was to secure the strip and mark out the landing zone for the first wave, which would include the American airfield engineers whose task it was to make a runway capable of taking DC-3 Dakotas.

Ideally, the Waco gliders were supposed to have two-man crews—a pilot and copilot—but Number One Air Commando did not have the manpower for that sort of luxury. Since arriving in India, accidents and sickness had taken their toll, and they hardly had one glider pilot per aircraft. As a career officer, Alison, though by temperament and training a fighter pilot, had flown just about every kind of aircraft the United States Army Air Forces had to offer. Gliders were a different matter. He had flown one for the first time the previous day when he got one of the Dakotas to tow him up and did a couple of circuits above Lalaghat.

Lieutenant Colonel Walter Scott—the same Scott who had discovered Piccadilly the year before—and the other twelve men sitting in the dark on the floor behind him did not know that, and Alison thought it better not to tell them. They had quite enough to worry about. For most of them the very idea of being airborne was a disturbing novelty. Talking quietly to Scott was another American, the writer and broadcaster James Warner Bellah,* who had flown with Britain's Royal Fly-

---

*Bellah is probably best remembered for the screenplay he wrote for the enormously successful western *She Wore a Yellow Ribbon*. A much better known Hollywood face among Number One Air Commandos was Jackie "The Kid" Coogan, the child actor, who was a glider pilot. At the time he was probably more famous for his recent divorce from the forces' pinup Betty Grable and he knew it. "Congratulations," he would say on being introduced. "You have just shaken the hand that holds the prick that . . ." This did not make him universally popular.

ing Corps during World War I. Now he had managed to get a job with Armed Forces Radio. He was carrying a pistol and a carbine and had confided to Alison that it was his ambition to earn the Combat Infantryman's Medal. Alison too was armed to the teeth, and besides his issue .45 automatic had equipped himself with a carbine, a bag of grenades, and his personal .22 Colt, because he always knew he could hit something with it. He had studied the aerial reconnaissance photographs of the Broadway site and had decided that if the Japanese were waiting for them it would be in a spear of jungle that jutted into the clearing like a finger. Meanwhile, his main concern was getting there.

With two gliders attached to each Dakota tow it had taken them forty-five minutes of circling Lalaghat field to gain sufficient altitude to clear the Chin Mountains. Now that they were in more or less level flight Alison could make out in the hazy moonlight the silhouette of the C-47 tug plane ahead of him and the other glider on his left-hand side, which contained Calvert and some of the headquarters staff of Seventy-seventh Brigade. The only problem he had with this unpowered flight was the tow cable, the start of which he could see stretching out before him and rather ragged looking because it was festooned with the field telephone wire that was their link with the tugs. Every so often they would sail too close to the tow and get too much slack in it, which could lead to breaks if it straightened out again too suddenly. The trick was to move slowly out to the side and allow it to become taut again slowly. Seated in the copilot's seat alongside Alison was the third American on the glider, a young air force surgeon named James Tulloch. The British also had a doctor aboard one of the gliders. Even if the Japanese were not waiting for them, landing gliders in rough country in the dark was hardly likely to be painless. The aircraft rose and fell like a boat in a gentle swell. For most of the Chindits this was only the second or third time they had ever been airborne—there had not been enough time to do any more than a couple of training circuits with them. Alison noticed that his passengers were mostly silent.

Across a very small expanse of sky, in the tug's other glider, Calvert too saw that most of his companions were slumped against their heavy packs, asleep. Below him he glimpsed the thin silver ribbon of the

Chindwin and he reflected that this was the fourth time he had crossed that river: twice swimming and the third time by boat with the Japs in pursuit. They went over the Zibyutaungdan Range and then shortly afterward crossed the railway line where almost exactly a year ago he had celebrated his thirtieth birthday by blowing up bridges. It was his birthday again tomorrow. He wondered what it would bring. He watched Donald Seese, his pilot. Seese was chewing gum, slowly working his lower mandible as if he didn't have a care in the world. Cochran had asked Calvert who he wanted as a pilot, and he had chosen Seese because he had noticed him in their earlier trials and thought him one of those taciturn, Scandinavian-looking Americans who never lost their heads. They bumped and they swayed and Calvert's stomach went into his mouth while the wind whistled alarmingly around them. For a moment he was envious of Fergusson, walking in. All he wanted to do was get out of this flimsy contraption and get his feet back on the ground.

Wingate walked into the control tent at Lalaghat to find all his distinguished British and American visitors—Slim, Air Marshal Sir John Baldwin, and the American Army Air Forces generals Old and Stratemeyer—squatting on a roll of tentage. They were being served sweet tea by Tulloch's batman, who, as if to put an Anglo-American stamp on the occasion, was wearing a red baseball cap given to him by one of Cochran's Air Commandos. All the VIPs were staring at Tulloch, who was seated behind a table on which there were three telephones. One of them was connected to Cochran's headquarters at Hailakandi twenty miles away, which was in radio contact with the Dakota tugs. So far the news had been mixed.

According to Tulloch's figures sixty gliders had now been dispatched and most of them appeared to be on course. But three gliders had crash-landed shortly after takeoff—probably because they were badly loaded. Others had broken their tow ropes and disappeared into the night. In the most dramatic incident, Gurkhas in two gliders that had come down near Slim's headquarters at Imphal had assumed they were in Burma and initiated a brisk exchange of fire with the guards.

The first gliders were due to touch down at Broadway at about 10:00 P.M. Once they were down Tulloch had arranged two code words with

Calvert and Scott to indicate the state of affairs at Broadway. PORK SAUSAGE would mean that so far all was well at Broadway; SOYA LINK, the detested wartime sausage substitute in food-rationed Britain, would indicate that there was trouble at Broadway and no further gliders should land. Slim, poker-faced, and the others were staring intently at Tulloch and his telephone. It made him feel uncomfortable. The only sign Wingate gave that he might be feeling the strain was that he was constantly stroking his beard. When he had a chance Tulloch whispered to Wingate that he would appreciate it if Slim and the others moved out of his line of vision as it was putting him off. Wingate gave him an understanding smile. The next time Tulloch looked up the VIPs had gone. Shortly afterward the first gliders were released over Broadway, and initial radio reports from the tugs said there was no sign of any red distress flares or any other indication that anything was going wrong.

Under an almost full moon, Bill Taylor, the leader of Cochran's glider pilots, took the first glider down onto the dark shadow the planners had so confidently called Broadway and made a good landing. The second glider smashed its undercarriage and there was considerable noise, but no one was hurt. Alison managed to put his own glider down intact. Then Seese with Calvert's party on board came onto the field from a different direction. Taylor held his breath as he stood at the edge of the field and watched it heading remorselessly for his own aircraft, which was more or less empty apart from a few stores. But at the last moment Seese pulled back the stick and jumped the stationary aircraft like a steeplechaser.

Inside Calvert had been conscious of "a big bump and we took off, nose in the air." He noticed his pilot was still chewing gum. Then:

> A crash, a stanchion hit me in the small of the back and we were down. Sgt. McDermott who was next to me shouted that his hand was jammed between the stanchions. I gave the order to deplane while my air force officer Sqn. Ldr. Bobbie Thompson and I tried to lever the sergeant's hand free. We broke a rifle in doing so and wasted valuable time. His hand was crushed.

Outside, Colonel Scott and his men were taking the first steps to secure the landing zone. Alison accompanied them together with the apprentice infantryman and radio correspondent Bellah.* The first thing they did was to advance in an extended line toward the finger of jungle jutting into the clearing that Alison had noted from the aerial reconnaissance photograph as being the most likely spot to conceal an ambush party. There was a single shot and they all hit the ground, panting and cocking weapons, pressing their cheeks to the grass. After a while, people started whispering that some fool had been firing at shadows, but nobody moved. Then Scott told everybody to stay as they were, got to his feet, and silhouetted by the moonlight, walked briskly toward the dark and menacing strip of jungle. Alison was impressed. He held his breath. Nothing happened. Scott's men rose and joined him at the edge of the strip and then walked through it. The Japanese were noted for their bravery, not their fire discipline, which was usually much worse than the British. Either they were dealing with some very cool customers indeed or there were no Japanese at Broadway.

This proved to be the case, but their troubles were only just beginning. In theory, they should have been able to manhandle the Pathfinder gliders to the side of the clearing to make way for the first wave, which in turn would be pushed aside. In most cases this was not possible because the gliders had lost their undercarriages. Some had been snapped off in a channel made by teak logs being dragged across the clearing by work elephants during the logging season and others had crumpled against logs hidden in the long grass. It turned out that the greater number of logs spotted at the aborted Piccadilly landing zone were just as innocent and not Japanese anti-landing devices.

To make matters worse, the glider carrying the airfield's lighting beacons had been seen to miss the Broadway clearing altogether and crash near some tall trees in thick jungle. They were hoping that survivors would shortly come straggling in and lead them back to where their aircraft and the missing equipment lay, but so far no one had appeared.** They did have some petroleum flares, and Calvert helped Alison to try to line them up in such a way that the new arrivals would miss the glid-

---

*Strangely, Bellah was not the only war correspondent to be allowed a seat with the Pathfinders. William Vandivert, whose pictures of Scott's haggard wounded being evacuated from behind Japanese lines during Longcloth had made him something of an honorary Chindit, was also there.

**It would eventually take sixteen hours to find the wreck. All on board were dead.

ers that had collapsed onto their bellies and were now stubbornly static. But it was difficult in the dark to line the flares up properly, and they were running out of time. The inevitable happened. The next wave began to arrive with all the finesse of a delivery of coal, smashing into one another and becoming hazards for the gliders behind them.

Wrecks soon littered the clearing. The noise was terrible. Gliders were built like drums, all stretched canvas and light wood. When they collided they made an enormous booming sound often to be followed by the screams and groans of maimed and dying men. Alison and Calvert led rescue parties from glider to glider. But extricating the injured was often an impossible job in the dark. They would be struggling to untangle them when again they would hear the distinctive whistling sound that heralded the approach of another glider, catch a glimpse of its shadow, and have to run for their lives. Alison fell down so many times his new carbine was covered with mud and he was exhausted. And all the time they had the feeling that the Japanese could turn up any moment, just when they were at their most vulnerable. Among the latest stunned arrivals was Alison's signals team; their radio was slightly damaged and they were trying to repair it.

Almost all the first wave were down now, and Calvert was convinced that they had to call at least a temporary halt. At last Alison's signalers got their radio working, and Calvert sent his brief message. Afterward, he advised Alison, as they curled up alongside each other on the ground, to get some sleep. "Things always look better in the morning," he told him.

But the best Calvert was hoping for was that the dawn would reveal that they could make enough space to land some light planes and evacuate the injured, who at the last count amounted to almost thirty. So far two bodies had been recovered. There was, he thought, a very good chance he would shortly be walking back to India again. And Calvert was determined that none of their wounded would be left behind. Not this time.

It was 2:30 A.M. when Tulloch received the code words he had been dreading all evening: SOYA LINK. Trouble at Broadway. What kind of trouble he didn't know. Returning pilots had reported that the landing lights were now clearly visible. Were the Japs attacking? Air Marshal

Baldwin set about arranging an RAF fighter sweep of the area at first light. Meanwhile, all Dakotas currently bound for Broadway were to return to base. Tulloch went in search of his boss.

After his earlier setbacks—Piccadilly blocked and then the gliders lost en route—Wingate seemed to regard the SOYA LINK message as the last straw. He told Tulloch it looked like it was all over; they had failed. On the face of it, Tulloch could easily have agreed with him, but he knew that was not what Wingate wanted to hear:

> He should not worry too much, I argued; we had plenty of troops on the ground, and perhaps I was to blame for giving Calvert two code words instead of five or six. Wingate very rarely swore but on this occasion he called me "a bloody optimist."

Afterward, Tulloch walked Wingate to his *basha*—for they slept in slightly grander versions of the bamboo and palm thatch huts the Chindits made for themselves in the jungle—and told him to get a good night's sleep and to expect better news in the morning. Tulloch was not a particularly brilliant man, and some military historians, among them at least one successful field commander, have suggested over the half century or so that has elapsed since that fateful evening in March 1943 that he was sometimes hopelessly out of his depth. But Wingate knew what he was doing when he appointed his old and loyal friend as his chief of staff. Nor was Tulloch's confidence unfounded. At about 6:30 A.M. the duty radio operator began to pick up over his headphones a faint Morse message from Broadway, which began with the letter P. By the time it was finished he had written on his message pad PORK SAUSAGE. All was now well at the landing zone.

Tulloch went over to Wingate's *basha*, found him deep in sleep, and woke him with the welcome words. It is fair to assume that Wingate had never been served a finer breakfast. "Ye Gods, it was a night," Tulloch wrote to his wife shortly afterward. "And then came that code word to top it all. . . . It was a night that I shall remember always."

When he got back to the control tent Tulloch discovered that there was another message from Broadway requesting light aircraft to evacuate casualties. As far as the Chindits were concerned this was the acid test for Cochran and his Air Commandos. Would the Americans do it? Would they really be prepared to fly unarmed aircraft 165 miles behind Japanese lines in broad daylight and put down on a rough strip where,

for all they knew, the situation could have changed dramatically between takeoff and landing? The Japanese air force in Burma was weak,
but it had recently been reinforced for their army's forthcoming offensive. A couple of Zeros would have a grouse shoot.

Major Andy Rebori, the commander of Cochran's light plane
squadron, led twelve of his little L-5 high-wing monoplanes at treetop
height and put them down on a crude but discernible runway. Even as
they landed the first casualties were loaded for what would turn out to
be a safe return to Assam. Waiting to greet Rebori were Alison and
Calvert, their tired and grimy faces wreathed in smiles. Calvert was
particularly thrilled by the arrival of these men who had risked their
lives to take out his wounded. "This was our first experience in the
field of those very gallant pilots. Later perhaps we took their gallantry
too much for granted."

Broadway was in business. In the four hours that had elapsed between SOYA LINK and PORK SAUSAGE there had occurred one of those pe-
culiarly American sagas of the "can do" spirit. It was a combination of
the right people being in the right place with the right equipment at the
right time, albeit rather late in the day. It had started shortly after
Calvert had told Alison that things might look better in the morning.

Just as he had been getting to sleep Alison had heard the sound of
another aircraft above Broadway. He had groaned and told his men to
douse the flare lights, something he thought he should have done earlier. But when he managed to get in touch with the Dakota on one of
the ground-to-air radios he had with him the crew told him that they
did not have enough fuel left to tow the single glider they were tugging
back to Assam. There was nothing for it but to light up the flares again
and let it land.

The glider came in and to his horror Alison watched it pass straight
between two trees that neatly sheared its wings off and made a sound
"like a hundred kettle drums going off" as it careered off into the jungle.
Alison and the others ran to see whether there was anybody left alive.

They discovered, shaken but unhurt, the luckiest people to land
that night. Flight Officer Gene Kelly and his copilot Sergeant Joseph
Desalvo had no passengers aboard their Waco. Instead, they were
bringing in a mini-bulldozer belonging to 900th Airborne Engineer
Aviation Company. As they crash-landed, the bulldozer broke free
from its lashings and hurtled forward toward the cockpit. The crew

should have been crushed to death, but they were saved by a wonderful stroke of luck. As it came forward the bulldozer tripped the wire that raised the cockpit and nose of the Waco for loading heavy freight. Up went the astonished Kelly and Desalvo and out underneath them went the bulldozer, which came to a halt against a tree, a little damaged but still in working order.

The commanding officer of the American engineers had died in one of the wrecked gliders. In charge was a Lieutenant Robert Brackett. Alison asked Brackett (who would be killed in Burma two months later) if he could use the bulldozer to make a landing strip from which the L-5s could evacuate the casualties. Brackett thought he could. What about something bigger, big enough to take C-47s? That would take a little longer. How long? Would this afternoon be okay? The first six Dakotas—the lead aircraft piloted by Brigadier General Bill Old himself—landed shortly before dusk. Another sixty-three Dakotas came in before midnight. "La Guardia has nothing on us. Can take over a hundred a night," a jubilant Bobbie Thompson, the senior RAF officer attached to Calvert's brigade, signaled Cochran.

Between 5 and 11 March 1943 Cochran's Air Commandos and the Royal Air Force between them flew a total of 579 Dakota sorties into Broadway, ferrying just over nine thousand personnel, almost fourteen hundred animals, several jeeps, and over 250 tons of weapons and stores including Bofors anti-aircraft guns and a complete four-gun battery of twenty-five-pounder field howitzers. The Japanese eventually got around to attacking Broadway about three weeks after Alison and Calvert first arrived there with the Pathfinder gliders. They were beaten off with heavy casualties. One of the reasons for their uncharacteristically slow response was that at least eight gliders had come down in wildly different places behind their lines. These scattered landings—one came down on a divisional headquarters and the Chindits escaped before the Japanese got over the shock—sowed considerable confusion about the Allies' true intentions.*

*Some of the occupants of these gliders were killed or captured. Perhaps half managed to evade the Japanese and either find their way to Broadway or get back to Assam. Among them was Lieutenant Colonel Peter Fleming, the author and Calvert's old friend, who crash-landed with part of Calvert's brigade headquarters company and got all but one of his party of fifteen home in a week. The casualty drowned while crossing the Chindwin.

On 13 March 1944 Wingate's order of the day was distributed to all Chindits and Air Commandos:

Our first task is fulfilled. We have inflicted a complete surprise on the enemy. All our Columns are inside the enemy's guts. The time has come to reap the fruit of the advantage we have gained. . . . Let us Thank God for the great success he has vouchsafed us and we must press forward with our sword in the enemy's ribs.

Chapter 24

HAVING PLACED HIS SWORD in the enemy's ribs, Wingate began to twist it. On 7 March he flew into Broadway traveling on one of the Dakotas that were flying a regular shuttle from Lalaghat. He carried with him a rifle and fifty rounds of ammunition, not the normal equipment of a major general but then not all that many major generals needed to fly 160 miles behind enemy lines to visit their forward troops. Besides, he had carried a rifle throughout the first Chindit expedition and, like the beard and the Wolseley helmet, it had become one of his props.

His visit to Broadway had to be brief. He had twelve thousand men under him now—seventeen British battalions, five Gurkha, and three West African, mostly from the Gold Coast (Ghana) and Nigeria. The days when he could lead from the front were over. John Alison showed him around the stronghold, pointed out the wrecked gliders from the night of the fly-in. It seemed much longer than a mere forty-eight hours ago. Broadway bustled with men and equipment. It looked like something that had been going on for a very long time. Then he put Wingate into an L-5 and flew him over to a satellite strip they called Chowringhee after Calcutta's busiest street.

An advance party from another Chindit brigade—Joe Lentaigne's 111th—had arrived here by glider to prepare a runway for Dakotas. Just as Wingate had done the previous year Lentaigne's brigade was going to cross the Irrawaddy and raid the Japanese communications there. Calvert's brigade was about to move south out of Broadway and establish a block across the rail and road communications to the Japanese Eighteenth Division, the heroes of Malaya, who were facing Stilwell's offensive in the north. Calvert had already picked his spot—a place called Mawlu where the railway and the road ran only a few yards apart and where it would be easy to cut both. Meanwhile, the three thousand men and four hundred animals that were Fergusson's Sixteenth Brigade—the only brigade not to arrive by air—was coming toward the end of the four-hundred-mile trek it had started on 5 February—exactly a month before Calvert flew into Broadway. Fergusson's task was to protect Stilwell's right flank by establishing a stronghold west of the Japanese air and road communications center at Indaw, which it was to attack.

Wingate spent the night at Broadway then flew back to Lalaghat the next day to find that Tulloch had some disturbing news for him. During his absence Slim had paid a visit and told him that intelligence sources and air reconnaissance had confirmed that a Japanese offensive was pending. There were indications* that Lieutenant General Renya Mutaguchi was intending to enter India with his Fifteenth Army and attempt to seize the towns of Imphal and Kohima, with their massive supply dumps. If this was the case, the commander of Fourteenth Army told Tulloch, he might have to take the Chindits' two reserve brigades, which Wingate had intended to rotate with the ones in place so that his troops on the ground were always reasonably fresh. It was Slim's intention to let Mutaguchi come across the Chindwin and then, with his superior numbers and greater air power, destroy the Japanese on ground of his own choice.

Before he departed Slim assured Tulloch that taking Wingate's reserve brigades away from him was something that would only happen as a last resort and he should not concern Wingate about something that might never happen. It is hard to believe that Slim really expected Tulloch not to tell Wingate—it was well known that Tulloch was a close friend. Knowing how Wingate was likely to react to any attempt to reduce his command, perhaps Slim thought that if he got his most volatile and best connected subordinate used to the idea Wingate might be more amenable.

This was never very likely, and when Tulloch told him Wingate was furious. It had been agreed with Mountbatten, he reminded Tulloch, that in the event of such a Japanese offensive he would retain command of these brigades in order to harass their lines of communication. He would, he said, fly to Imphal in the morning and confront Slim, and if

---

*Slim was privy to the ULTRA code-breaking secrets, which, in the Far East, the Allies called MAGIC.

he persisted with this nonsense he would resign. Up to the moment Wingate boarded the plane the next morning the crestfallen Tulloch was trying to persuade him not to do it, convinced that at the moment of his greatest triumph and after all they had gone through together Wingate was about to push his luck too far:

> The next few hours went very slowly indeed and I expected a signal advising me that Wingate's resignation had been accepted and naming his successor. But to my great relief there came a message that Wingate was on his way back to Lalaghat, and later, as he jumped down from the Dakota, I could see from his cheerful expression that all was well.

Slim had denied any intention of taking his brigades off him. If they did go into Burma earlier than intended because of a Japanese offensive then they would, of course, remain under Wingate's command. The square-jawed Slim is normally portrayed as the epitome of the bluff and honest soldier, but presumably he felt that a little duplicity was called for when dealing with a man with a direct line to the prime minister. For as it happens both these brigades—Fourteenth and Twenty-third—were indeed used to harass the rear of the attacking Japanese when Mutaguchi's offensive came, but neither came under the command of Special Force. In any event, Slim's man management worked, Wingate was calmed, and he returned to his headquarters. But soon he was involved in another of those paper battles with headquarters to which he was so prone—and this time without genuine grounds.

After considerable discussion as to whether publicity was advisable, and without consulting Wingate, Mountbatten's public relations staff had issued a brief handout to the press, declaring that "troops of the 14th Army" had taken part in a successful airborne operation but making no mention of Wingate, the Chindits, or First Air Commando. It was intended as the first installment of an unfolding story in which, once public interest had been whetted and security considerations superseded, full credit was to be given to the Chindits and their American comrades.

Unaware of this strategy, Wingate was concerned not just about the failure to mention the Chindits but also about the perceived slight to Cochran's men, to whom he owed so much. He had only just succeeded in mollifying Cochran over an incident in which the RAF had sent six of its Spitfires to operate out of the airstrip at Broadway before Cochran had put his own Mustangs in there. Cochran considered he had been bounced out of the airfield his own men had constructed and reacted accordingly. Assuming the unaccustomed role of peace-maker—perhaps because in the crush of work he had failed to consult Cochran in advance about the move—Wingate damped down the American's understandable ire.* Now, he feared, it would be ignited again by the headquarters' handout.

The same day, Wingate sent a furious telegram, in clear, to Mount-batten's head of publicity, Air Marshal Sir Philip Joubert: "Consider whole story grossly unfair and calculated to cause despondency amongst the troops now engaged in fighting the Japanese under the most arduous conditions. . . . The whole operation was planned solely by staff of Special Force with assistance of No. 1 Air Commando and [USAAF] Troops Carrier Command only. Your representation is a travesty of the truth. . . ." And so forth.

He followed up with a letter in similar vein to Mountbatten, who replied with a sharp rebuke for Wingate's "temperamental outburst." Explaining that he and Joubert were already planning how best to give the most effective publicity "both to your force and, as a matter of fact, personally to you," the supreme commander wrote, "Your astounding telegram to Joubert has made me realise how you have achieved such amazing success in getting yourself disliked by people who are only too ready to be on your side." In a rambling six-page reply that he drafted the next day, Wingate grumbled on, saying that he had only made "a very modest request that . . . the truth should be told or if the time is not ripe . . . that nothing should be said." Mercifully, he had second thoughts and never sent it.

Meanwhile, the Chindits themselves were involved in rather more pressing causes. Calvert had moved down to Mawlu to establish his block. But the Japanese were already there, and he immediately be-came embroiled in a small action—there were no more than two hun-

---

*As it happens the problem was soon resolved when, after a glorious opening act in which the Spitfires surprised some Japanese fighter-bombers raiding Broadway and inflicted heavy losses, they were all destroyed either on the ground or in the air. The last one to go was piloted by the squadron leader commanding this detachment who, in the spirit of the Few, took off alone against considerable odds.

dred or so on each side—that would become the high-water mark of Wingate's rejuvenation of the British infantry in Burma.

Calvert had taken with him some Gurkhas and his battalion of South Staffords. The Staffords were part of Wingate's inheritance from Seventieth Division. In theory they were a regular battalion—the same newly arrived unit that had done so badly in Tiberias in 1938 when the Arab raiders came in. Since then they had seen action in the Western Desert, notably at the siege of Tobruk, and a lot of its old sweats were dead or in German prison camps or had been rotated home.

Their replacements were often conscripts and their officers wartime volunteers with respectable peacetime jobs to go back to. Men, for instance, like the lanky mortar platoon officer Lieutenant George Cairns, a scholarship boy from a Fulham grammar school who had landed a job with Banque Belge in the City of London. Cairns was newly married and in his early thirties, a bit long in the tooth for an infantry subaltern. But he fitted in well with a regiment who knew their worth and were without pretension, where the accents to be heard in its officers' and sergeants' messes were often indistinguishable.

Now some of the Staffords, Cairns among them, had got themselves in trouble. They had moved onto the railway line itself and were trying to dig in when the Japanese opened fire with machine guns and mortars from some nearby low hills. They were without proper cover and beginning to take casualties. Calvert, who had taken to wearing a flat service cap with his newly acquired brigadier's red band around it, set off with his headquarters company to investigate, spoiling for a fight. "I was determined that we must win our first engagement."

He got to a ridge where he could observe the Japanese "milling about a pagoda on top of a little knoll." On another small hill but lower down were the Staffords—clouds of dust coming from the mortar bombs exploding around them. They were trying to retaliate with their Vickers machine guns and their own mortars. But the Staffords were in a hopeless position, overlooked and without much cover. It looked like the Japanese had seized the initiative and thwarted Calvert's plan to establish a rail- and roadblock before he could get started.

While the Gurkhas cleared the Japanese off another of the hills Calvert ran down to the Staffords accompanied by the RAF liaison officer Bobbie Thompson; Corporal Young, his Anglo-Chinese batman; and Paddy Dermody, who had once earned his living as a jockey. He arrived a little breathless to be greeted by cries of, "Thank God you've come, sir."

Calvert looked around him and saw a number of dead and wounded, noted the absence of cover, and realized that something had to be done quickly:

> I then told everybody that we were going to charge Pagoda Hill. There were reinforcements on our left flank (the Gurkhas) who were going to charge as well. So, standing up, I shouted out "charge" and ran down the hill with Bobbie [Thompson] and the two orderlies. Half of the South Staffords joined in. Then looking back I found a lot had not. So I told them to bloody well "Charge, what the hell do you think you're doing." So they charged. Machine-gunners, mortar teams, all officers—everybody who was on that hill.

Among them were Lieutenants Norman Durant, who was in charge of the Vickers guns, and his friend George Cairns. Calvert, who was carrying a rifle with a fixed bayonet, was originally in the lead, but as they ran down the hill the Staffords had been occupying, crossed the dirt road to Mawlu, and began to climb Pagoda Hill he was soon overtaken by Cairns and Durant, who recalled:

> I went up the hill like a two-year-old. . . . To this day I'm not quite certain what I expected to see—the place deserted or the Japs on the run I suppose, but what I actually saw was a Jap section climbing out of their trenches . . . and coming straight at me; the leading two with bayonets fixed and rather unfriendly expressions being about 20 yards to my right. I fired my revolver twice and nothing happened—I was later to find the hammer had worked loose.

Durant tossed a grenade and immediately threw himself down the side of the hill, catching a bullet in the leg as he did so. Then, despite his wound still able to get to his feet, he limped back up the hill, picked a Japanese rifle off the ground, and attempted to join the extraordinary melée taking place at the summit where bayonets and rifles butts, kukris and samurai swords were all being employed. One of the first things Durant saw was George Cairns and a Japanese soldier wrestling

on the ground. He watched Cairns break free, pick up a rifle and bayonet, and "stab the Jap again and again like a madman."

> It was only when I got near that I saw he himself had already been
> bayoneted twice through the side and that his left arm was hanging
> on by a few strips of muscle. How he found the strength to fight was
> a miracle. . . . There were a lot of our dead and Jap dead lying
> about. But the Japs still held the top of the hill and things were look-
> ing critical. We might have been pushed back if the Brigadier had
> not shouted, "Come on now, one more effort, you've got them on
> the run" . . . and before we knew what was happening the Japs were
> running.

The Battle of Pagoda Hill was over. The Staffords' casualties were
twenty-three killed and sixty-four wounded. Calvert said that the sav-
agery of the fighting was "not unlike that depicted in scenes from ancient battles." According to Calvert and other eyewitnesses, George
Cairns was not bayoneted but had his arm practically severed by a Japanese officer wielding a samurai sword, which Cairns picked up after
shooting the officer. A sergeant literally kicked in the head of a Japanese soldier who had feigned death and then shot an unsuspecting
lieutenant in the Staffords. In all, fourteen British officers participated
in the charge, of whom three were killed and four wounded. Cairns lingered for three days before he died of his terrible injuries. On Calvert's
recommendation he was awarded a posthumous Victoria Cross.

Many of his officers and men thought Calvert himself had earned a
VC for the valor and leadership he displayed that day. He was surely
the only brigadier in any of the World War Two armies to personally
lead a bayonet charge. His prompt action had saved the block, which
he now reinforced with the rest of his brigade. Soon it would have its
own airstrip, a battery of field guns, anti-aircraft guns, and bunkers
roofed with sleepers torn out of the railway. With almost daily supply
drops from the RAF and Cochran's Air Commandos there were soon
so many parachutes hanging off the surrounding vegetation that the pilots gave it the name White City.

The Japanese only ever made one attempt, rather halfhearted by
their standards, to attack the Broadway stronghold on the ground. But
for weeks they tried to break Calvert's grip on White City, this con-
striction in the throat of Eighteenth Division, which was increasingly

obliged to live off the land and husband its ammunition. Hundreds of
decomposing Japanese corpses lay around its perimeter—some of
them suicide squads who had blown themselves up trying to blast a
path through the barbed wire entanglements Calvert had put down.
Cochran's light-plane pilots coming in to pick up the wounded told
one another that you did not need a compass to get to White City: all
that was required was a decent nose. The determination of the American fliers to get the British wounded away from these horrors often
meant that their unarmed planes were grossly overloaded and could
hardly get into the air.

Meanwhile, the headquarters party of Fergusson's Sixteenth
Brigade had completed its epic four-hundred-mile march from Ledo
to reach its operational area and set up a stronghold, not far from one
of Wingate's most prized objectives, the twin Japanese airfields of
Indaw East and West. This stronghold was to be called Aberdeen,
after Lorna Wingate's home town. Fergusson and his men arrived utterly exhausted by their trek, which had taken them over some of the
most difficult and mountainous jungle terrain to be found anywhere in
Southeast Asia. "The march was the heaviest imaginable," Fergusson
would recall:

> No single stretch of level going existed between Tagap and Hkalak
> and few thereafter. The cold was intense, particularly at bivouacs
> over 5,000 feet. The seventy pounds which men were carrying were
> greatly increased in weight due to saturation with water. A dry
> bivouac was practically unknown. Leeches were innumerable, but
> less unpleasant than the Polaung fly, whose vicious bites hardened
> to a septic lump.

One of the RAF liaison officers who made the march with Fergusson's brigade was a Brooklyn-born, twenty-year-old flight lieutenant
named John Knowles. Inspired by Britain's lone stand against the
Nazis, he had gone north, before Pearl Harbor brought America into
the war, to join the Royal Canadian Air Force and had found himself
flying Hurricane fighters against the Japanese from an RAF base on the
Indo-Burmese border. When word came around seeking volunteers
for the Chindit operation Knowles traded the relative comfort of a
fighter pilot's existence for the gruelling footslog from Ledo to the Aberdeen stronghold. "We were completely beat by the time we got

there," he recalls. "I weighed one hundred twenty-six pounds and we were all walking skeletons."

> I had auditory hallucinations during the march, kept hearing an orchestra playing the same tune over and over and—would you believe it?—it was "I'll Walk Beside You." I mentioned this to the brigadier and he told me he'd been having visual hallucinations: he kept seeing Christmas trees, decked out in colored lights. As for the packs we carried, they were a good deal more than the official seventy pounds. After an air-supply drop it would take two men to lift your full pack onto your back. You'd get on to your knees so they'd put it on you and then you'd gradually stand upright. How did we do it? I guess you just don't know what you can do until you have to.

Two columns had been hived off from the brigade en route to attack a Japanese garrison at Lonkin, on Stilwell's right flank, and would not catch up with Fergusson for another ten days. Other elements were still footslogging down the trail, three or four days away. So Sixteenth Brigade was tired and significantly understrength when Wingate flew in by light plane on 20 March 1944 to confer with Fergusson.

The monocled Scots brigadier wanted desperately to give his men a few days' rest and consolidate his force. But Wingate insisted on an immediate assault on the airfields at Indaw, arguing that delay might give the Japanese the chance to bring in reinforcements to defend them. He told Fergusson he planned to fly Fourteenth Brigade into Aberdeen as soon as the airstrip was ready, and that these troops would attack Indaw from the west while Fergusson launched an assault from the northeast. His doubts overcome, Fergusson agreed to move on Indaw on 24 March, fully expecting to be backed up by Fourteenth Brigade. But it was not to be.

When on 21 March Wingate flew back to army headquarters at Comilla to meet Slim he found that changing circumstances required Fourteenth Brigade to be assigned a different task—to set up a new stronghold, about sixty miles southwest of Aberdeen, and disrupt the rear communications of the Japanese divisions that were attacking Imphal. But because of a communications snarl-up that has never been fully explained—but was probably a result of Wingate's decision to move his operational headquarters from Imphal to Sylhet—Fergusson was not informed of this change of plan. The consequences were calamitous for Fergusson: his unrested brigade's attack on Indaw was driven off with heavy casualties.

Still, it was, as Wellington said of Waterloo, a close-run thing. A column of the Royal Leicester Regiment, skillfully aided by close support from Cochran's fighter-bombers, came close to capturing the Indaw East airfield, only withdrawing when Fergusson—"damned angry" that his calls for support to Fourteenth Brigade had gone unanswered—ordered a general pullback on 29 March.

Some five days before Wingate had made another grand tour of his possessions. He had first visited Broadway, then flown on to Aberdeen, and finally dropped in on White City, where Calvert gave him a guided tour:

> Wingate had sensible suggestions for everyone, whether it was the siting of a machine gun, the lie of a three inch mortar, a point of hygiene to the doctor, the means by which the Protestant and Roman Catholic padres could keep up morale, the places for burying the dead, or the siting of the wireless aerials etcetera.

Calvert took him for a stroll along the railway and Wingate kicked the lines and said, "So, this is Eighteenth Division's rail communications." They had known each other for almost exactly two years now since they first met at the Bush Warfare School in Maymyo on the eve of the great retreat. During that time they had achieved so much, packed so much into it that it must have seemed much longer.

Wingate showed him the messages of congratulation he had received from Churchill and grumbled that now Mutaguchi's offensive had at last started there were threats to take Special Force's air support away from them. He confided that he had sent Churchill a message saying that if he was given another three Dakota squadrons he could take the whole of northern Burma. Before he took off, Wingate informed Calvert that he had been awarded a bar to his DSO. "Let it go to your heart and not your head," he told him.

"Yes, sir. Thank you, sir," said Calvert, and he watched Wingate climb back into the L-5 that had brought him from Broadway. He never saw him again.

From White City Wingate flew back to Imphal for a meeting with Air Commodore S. F. Vincent of the Royal Air Force to discuss problems arising out of his decision to transfer Chindit advance headquarters from Imphal to Sylhet. Wingate had ordered the shift to safeguard his HQ in the event of a further Japanese advance into the Kohima Plain, but the RAF were concerned that the move might impair communications between the Chindits and air headquarters at Comilla. In an hour-long discussion Wingate and Vincent sorted out their difficulties and both prepared to leave by nightfall—Vincent for Comilla and Wingate for Hailakandi, where he planned to discuss operational matters with Cochran and spend the night.

Before boarding the Air Commando B-25 Mitchell bomber that had brought him from Broadway and was waiting to take him to Hailakandi, Wingate did something that in retrospect might seem almost valedictory. For no obvious reason, he turned back to his office to have a few words with his personal clerk and stenographer, Sergeant Walter Foreman. Foreman had served Wingate well since the start of preparations for the second Chindit expedition. He had been the attentive scribe, taking down Wingate's torrent of thoughts and plans for action during his convalescence at Viceregal House and at the Mountbattens' residence and throughout the hectic period leading up to the Operation Thursday fly-in and beyond. During those difficult weeks and months Foreman had received many signs of Wingate's regard.* He had also on occasion felt the rough edge of Wingate's tongue, and now his commander turned back to make amends. As Tulloch would recall, he patted Foreman on the back, "telling him that he had worked wonderfully well for him and apologising for having cursed him at times."

It may have been with the benefit of hindsight that Tulloch came to see Wingate's desire to make amends to his clerk as "a strong premonition of disaster." Following his own recent narrow escape, when a kite hawk hit his plane shortly after takeoff, Tulloch and Wingate had made a pact never to fly together, feeling that "one of us was bound by the law of averages to take a bender." There was also the risk of being shot down by marauding enemy warplanes during an inspection trip behind the lines. In the previous ten days the Japanese had twice

---

*In an interview with his hometown newspaper, Foreman would recall that Wingate "took an intense interest in my personal welfare and of my four-year-old son at home." He told of the time how, when he was taking notes at an important conference, tea was brought in for the officers and Wingate insisted that a cup be brought for him, too. Foreman also recalled that Wingate's "sly sense of humour was terrific."

bombed the airstrip at Broadway, and although the flight from Imphal to Hailakandi was over friendly territory the possibility of enemy action was not entirely remote. It was for all these reasons that, as Tulloch would tell it, he "pressed [Wingate] no less than four times not to take this particular trip and he nearly weakened and called it off."

Whether or not Wingate did have a premonition of disaster, there is persuasive evidence that USAAF Lieutenant Brian Hodges, the B-25 pilot, had some misgivings about one of his aircraft's twin engines. While waiting at Broadway to take Wingate on to Imphal, Hodges had told Lieutenant Colonel Claud Rome, the British officer in command of the garrison there, that the engine was not developing its proper power and asked him to persuade Wingate to wait for a relief aircraft. The pilot was "obviously rather in awe of Wingate and pretty worried," Rome told Tulloch long after the event. But Wingate "was inclined to pooh-pooh the matter," and after he exchanged a few words with Hodges the plane prepared for takeoff. According to Rome's account, the B-25 "fairly staggered off the runway, using every inch of it, and climbed very slowly."

Given Rome's description of that takeoff, and of Hodges's remarks to him preceeding it, it seems curious that after landing at Imphal Hodges did not have the suspect engine checked. It may be that, Wingate being in no mood to brook delay, the young American was afraid of incurring the legendary displeasure of "The Man." As it was, Hodges was not an ideal choice for this particular mission and would not have flown it at all had he been luckier at cards. According to Howard Sparks, a Texan who was a nineteen-year-old navigator with the Air Commando, Hodges was one of a rota of B-25 aircrew whose duties included taking turns to fly Wingate about the frequently mist-shrouded jungle highlands his Chindits had just seized from the Japanese.

In the early hours of 24 March, Sparks, Hodges, and his own navigator, the recently arrived reinforcement Second Lieutenant Stephen Wanderer, were among seven B-25 crewmen playing "high-low, split the pot" poker by the light of a hurricane lamp at Hailakandi when their game was interrupted by a message from Wingate asking to be picked up from Imphal for the trip that would take him to Broadway, where he would transfer to a light plane to visit the Aberdeen stronghold and Calvert at White City. (Afterward, the light-plane shuttle would return him to Broadway, where he would pick up the B-25 again.)

For Sparks and his pilot, Wingate's latest demands were the first bad luck of the game. All night they had been blessed with good hands, and now they stood to win the eight hundred rupees left in the pot. But their names were first on the duty rota, and an immediate take-off was required. Hodges and Wanderer had not been so lucky and had just dropped out. So they volunteered to go instead, leaving Sparks and the others to reshuffle the pack. Shortly afterward, as their game was coming to an end, the poker players heard the B-25 take off, and Sparks and his pilot began to wonder whether they had done the right thing. Wanderer was new to navigating aircraft around the Chin Hills, and they recalled that Hodges always found flying after sunset a strain. "Nervous at night," was the way one of the card players described him.

Yet now, as night fell, it was Hodges who, despite his reservations about the engine, was preparing to take Wingate on the last leg of the trip from Imphal back to Hailakandi. If Wingate had been assigned his own aircraft and personal RAF pilot, as promised at Quebec, it might have been a different story. A British pilot, given time to develop a relationship of trust with the demanding Chindit leader, might have better understood his moods and been less reluctant to risk his anger. Despite Hodges's concerns, the B-25 was neither inspected nor serviced during its hour and a half on the ground at Imphal. But it was kept under guard according to routine, and there is no chance that it could have been tampered with. (This close to the front, the Allies were wary of Japanese attempts to get Indian nationalist saboteurs onto their airfields.)

The weather forecast was good, though with the possibility of localized storms, as Wingate boarded the plane with his ADC, Captain George Barrow, and took his usual place in the copilot's seat alongside Hodges. Barrow carried a briefcase laden with documents for Wingate's attention, among them Calvert's scribbled citation recommending Cairns for a Victoria Cross in recognition of his heroism at Pagoda Hill. Boarding with Wingate and the ADC were two British war correspondents, Stuart Emeny of the *News Chronicle* and Stanley Wills of the *Daily Herald,* both of whom had been with Wingate to visit Broadway earlier that day. Navigator Wanderer was crouched over his maps, and farther down the fuselage were three American sergeants—radio operator James Hickey, gunner Frank Sadoski, and engineer Vernon McIninch.

The B-25 took off at precisely 8:05 P.M. and headed west into a moonless night for Hailakandi. This time, unlike Rome at Broadway, nobody noticed anything unusual about the takeoff. Whatever it was that caused it to make a near-vertical plunge into a three-thousand-foot hillside twenty minutes later happened too quickly for Hodges or his radio operator to send out a distress signal. The official USAAF investigation that opened a week after the crash concluded that while no definite cause could be established it was probably the result of a spin caused by engine failure and that there was no evidence of sabotage or negligence. Major Rome was not among the witnesses at that enquiry, and he gave his recollections to Tulloch twenty-five years after the event. His recall may have been colored to a certain extent by time and hindsight, but it does reinforce the belief that engine failure caused the disaster.

"What a pity. Oh, what a pity," wrote Tulloch in his diary when news broke that Wingate's plane had crashed. "God, what enemies we have and now I shall have to fight them alone." Calvert, bravest of the brave, put his hand to his head and said, "Oh, who will look after us now?" Richard Rhodes James, a cipher officer in Lentaigne's 111th Brigade, had the same feeling of abandonment: "Our master was gone and we, his masterpiece, were now ownerless."

John Knowles felt a similar sense of abandonment: "We had tremendous faith in him. You just knew that as long as he was there everything was going to be fine and when we heard he'd been killed we thought 'Oh God, what's going to happen to us?' "

Deprived of Wingate's inspired—some would say manic—leadership, the Chindits were destined for early extinction as a military formation. The choice of Wingate's successor may have had as much to do with their demise as the shifting fortunes and priorities of the Burma campaign after the failure of the Japanese offensive against Imphal and Kohima.

Tulloch ruled himself out of the succession on the very valid grounds that he lacked the field experience for the job. Calvert and

Fergusson had both proved themselves thoroughly by virtue of their outstanding roles in both Chindit expeditions, and both believed wholeheartedly in the correctness of Wingate's military doctrines. But Joe Lentaigne was the most senior of the Special Force brigadiers and, partly on the strength of Tulloch's advice to Slim, he took over. It was a recommendation Tulloch would regret to his dying day.

Lentaigne, a brave but essentially conventional Gurkha officer, had never been wholly convinced by Wingate's theories of long-range penetration, and when Slim decided to hive off Twenty-third Brigade from Special Force and assign it to the defense of Kohima, Lentaigne raised no objection. It was the start of an inexorable process. In early April Slim put the Chindits under the operational command of the Limey-hating Stilwell and to Calvert's great disgust ordered him to abandon the White City stronghold, which he had founded with the bayonet charge at Pagoda Hill and held against all comers, diverting men and materials the Japanese would have preferred to use elsewhere. Slim later ordered Special Force troops out of Broadway and Aberdeen, while Fergusson's brigade, exhausted by its long march from Ledo and badly mauled in the battle for Indaw, was evacuated by air to India. A stronghold called Blackpool was hard pressed, and the survivors could not be extracted by air. Rather than allow them to fall into Japanese hands Chindit doctors and medics shot the most grievously wounded.

The smaller elements of Special Force—Lieutenant Colonel Jumbo Morris's battalion-strength Gurkha "Morrisforce," which was ambushing Japanese convoys and attacking supply dumps, and Lieutenant Colonel Fish Herring's "Dahforce" Kachin tribesmen, who were harrying the Japanese to the north of Morris—were seriously compromised by the new deployment of the brigades.

As his command crumbled under him, Lentaigne tried to invoke his predecessor's special relationship with Churchill to stop the rot. "Operation conceived by Wingate successfully completed, but lack of follow-up troops makes withdrawal inevitable," he said in a message to Mountbatten in which he requested that Churchill be informed of the situation. But the supreme commander had no intention of allowing Lentaigne a direct channel to the prime minister. The Chindits had lost their most powerful friend, and the process of dissolution continued.

In being moved to the north and put under Stilwell's command, the

Chindit brigades lost their role as a long-range penetration force and became, in effect, regular infantry formations, though without support from armor or artillery. After horrific casualties, Calvert's brigade took Mogaung—the first city in northern Burma to fall to the Allies. They fought well but their raison d'être had been removed. At the end of August 1944 they were withdrawn, exhausted, to India, and at the beginning of 1945 Special Force was formally disbanded. In doing so, Mountbatten paid an indirect tribute to the enduring value of many of Wingate's innovations—in particular his methods of aerial supply and coordination between ground troops and the air force—in the Burma campaign that was now moving toward a victorious conclusion. "There is no need for Chindits," said the supremo. "We are all Chindits now."

Epilogue

WINGATE INHABITS an unquiet and overcrowded grave. Although the discord and controversy that accompanied much of his life ceased after his death, as befits the demise of a national hero in time of war, old antipathies came to the surface a few years later and reverberate distantly to this day.

The disposition of Wingate's sparse mortal remains and those of his traveling companions has been hardly less troubled a matter. The first men on the scene of the B-25 crash, Air Commando light aircraft pilots Lloyd Samp and Bill Walters, nearly lost their lives getting there. The two sergeants were sent out together at first light on 26 March in an L-5 to make an aerial search while a British land party made its laborious way on foot. While circling the scene the carburetor of Samp and Walters's plane iced up, forcing Samp to make a crash landing into a bamboo thicket. Walters broke his leg in the crash and the pair of them had to be rescued by the overland party, which arrived some hours later. The searchers found a crater eight feet deep by twenty wide, with wreckage and unidentifiable body parts scattered over a hundred-yard radius. Wingate's pith helmet, scorched but recognizable, was one of the very few pieces of debris that could be positively identified. Such had been the force of the impact that the scattered body parts were inextricably intermixed. These were collected and hastily buried at the scene.

Three months later, the Chindits' chief chaplain, Lieutenant Colonel Christopher Perowne,* led another party overland to the crash site, where they found and buried several more bone fragments. They erected a cross on the spot with a bronze plaque bearing the

---

*Brother of Brigadier Lance Perowne, who went to school with Wingate and commanded the Chindits' 23rd brigade.

names of the dead, and Perowne, wearing his sacramental robes, conducted a brief service. "The cross is facing towards Burma and has the wonderful backdrop of the Naga Hills with its beautiful colours," Perowne informed Lorna, adding, "I think it would have pleased Orde to know that I was wearing robes for the service in the middle of the jungle." He was almost certainly mistaken there. The totally Nonconformist Wingate hated all manifestations of ecclesiastical pomp.

In April 1947, an Anglo-American search party made its way overland to the crash site to disinter the remains and bring them back for reburial in the British war cemetery at Imphal. But within months the American authorities were making representation to have the remains moved once again. Citing an Anglo-U.S. agreement, they argued that since the majority of those killed in the B-25 crash were Americans, and since the remains could not be separated and identified, they should find their final resting place in a U.S. war cemetery. At first they suggested Manila or Guam, but eventually it was decided that the Arlington National Cemetery, just across the Potomac from Washington, D.C., was the most appropriate place.

Arlington is hallowed ground to the Americans, but the British were not pleased. In both world wars it was Britain's policy to bury its dead where they fell. Without prior notification to the Wingate family, or the families of his ADC and the two British correspondents, the remains were reinterred in a single grave at Arlington on 10 November 1950, prompting a furious controversy in the British press and Parliament and a letter of protest to Winston Churchill from the family. "If an American general, say Patton, had been killed in a plane flown by a British crew, would the Americans ever have allowed his body to be transported to Britain and put into an RAF cemetery?" demanded Rachel Wingate. And in a letter to *The Times,* she wanted to know "why at no stage of these removals—which we learn have been in hand for over a year—did we ever hear from an official? The Imperial War Graves Commission . . . has been unable to offer any explanation for deliberately keeping the British relatives in the dark."

A gesture was made toward family grievances when the grave site was rededicated with a handsome upright headstone on 24 March 1974, the thirtieth anniversary of Wingate's death. A wreath was laid by the son he never saw, Orde Jonathan, by then a captain in the Royal Artillery. Every year since, the Israeli ambassador to Washington has also laid a wreath there, accompanied by Jewish-American war veterans, in fond memory of "The Friend."

This is only one sign of the Jewish state's regard. In Israel itself there is scarcely a town or city that does not have its Wingate Avenue or Wingate Square, and the country's principle sporting and athletics institute, near the Mediterranean city of Netanya, is named after him— if somewhat incongruously since, although fanatical about fitness, he had no time at all for team sports or ball games.

Half a century after its founding, the Jewish state for which Wingate longed so fervently may be divided and troubled—and, for all its accomplishments, not quite the "light unto the nations" that he and its founders had intended—but it is at least secure. The same cannot be said for Wingate's reputation in his own country.

As might be expected, the public eulogies immediately following his fatal crash were lavish enough, reaching their height when, on 22 August 1944, Churchill rose to his feet in the House of Commons to deliver a report on the progress of the fighting in Burma and to pay to the fallen Chindit commander a tribute that rings down the decades: "There was a man of genius, who might well have become also a man of destiny." Wingate's detractors no doubt muttered that he had ever been the Old Man's pet and that anyway Churchill had not proved himself an invariably good judge of men. But the private tributes, not intended for the building of morale or the consolation of the bereaved, were no less heartfelt.

Perhaps the most striking of these came from Mountbatten: "I cannot tell you how much I am going to miss Wingate," he said in a letter to his wife, Edwina. "Not only had we become close personal friends, but he was such a fire-eater and it was such a help to me having a man with a burning desire to fight. He was a pain in the neck to the generals over him, but I loved his wild enthusiasm and it will be very difficult for me to try and inculcate it from above."

Fergusson, coming out of the jungle after his unfortunate experience at Indaw, and in any case never an unalloyed admirer of Wingate, nevertheless described his commander in a 1945 memoir as "a military genius of a grandeur and stature seen not more than once or twice in a century":

No other officer I have heard of could have dreamed the dream, planned the plan, obtained, trained, inspired and led the force. There are men who shine at planning, or at training, or at leading; here was a man who excelled at all three, and whose vision at the council table matched his genius in the field.

One who spoke both admiringly and candidly about Wingate— "dark, fiery and eager [he] might have sat for the portrait of a leader of Spanish partisans in the Peninsular War"—was Wavell, who thought him a man of "remarkable power and genius":

> He was not, I think, easy to know. His forcible, challenging personality invoked antagonism—he often exasperated my staff by the vehement importunity with which his demands for priority of equipment and personnel were pressed; nor did his subordinates find him an easy man to serve.

But the eulogy that was to come from Slim was entirely without ambivalence. Slim's relations with his prickly subordinate had always been somewhat edgy, yet the Fourteenth Army commander took up the theme of "genius" with even more emphasis than Churchill or Wavell in an appreciation that was published while the Burma campaign still raged and victory was yet to be assured:

> Genius is a word that should not be easily used but I say without hesitation that Wingate had sparks of genius in him. . . . The number of men of our race in this war who are really irreplaceable can be counted on the fingers of one hand. Wingate is one of them. The force he built is his own; no one else could have produced it. He designed it, he raised it, he led it, inspired it and finally placed it where he meant to place it—in the enemy's vitals.

Throughout the early postwar period Wingate's reputation remained unquestioned in public. At a 1951 memorial service at Wingate's old school, Charterhouse, Pownall (of all people) read a tribute from Churchill—"here indeed is a name which deserves lasting honour"— while Mountbatten unveiled a commemorative plaque. By then styled Earl Mountbatten of Burma, and assured of a place in history as the last viceroy of India, the former supreme commander described Wingate as "a great fighter, a fearless leader of men, a brilliant originator." Boilerplate praise, perhaps, but lest anyone should imagine that Wingate was driven by personal ambition, Mountbatten went out of his way to recall how he had refused the offer of a promotion until Operation Thursday had been proved a success.

Five years later Wingate's many detractors in high military places began to find their voices. Their cue came in 1956 when Slim published his war memoirs and, to the shock and surprise of many, presented a considerably less than admiring picture of his celebrated subordinate. "Uncle Bill" Slim, by now a retired field marshal, a peer of the realm, and governor-general of Australia, was as widely admired by his former troops and the British public as a whole as Wingate had been, if for less theatrical qualities. His memoirs overall reflected an engaging tendency for self-deprecation. Here was no self-absorbed glory seeker or petty time server, so when he wrote that Operation Longcloth had been "an expensive failure" that had given "little tangible return for the losses it had suffered and the resources it had absorbed," people sat up.

In moving on to consider Operation Thursday, Slim depicted Wingate as "a man who so fanatically pursued his own purposes without regard to any other consideration or purposes." No longer a genius, Wingate was now "strangely naive when it came to the business of actually fighting the Japanese." But perhaps Slim's most damaging and, to Wingate's partisans, most unjust, inference was that Wingate panicked at that defining moment on the airstrip at Lalaghat on the night of the fly-in, when reconnaissance photographs arrived showing the landing site at Piccadilly blocked by teak logs. Up to then "Wingate, though obviously feeling the mounting strain, had been quiet and controlled," wrote Slim. He continued:

> Now, not unnaturally perhaps, he became very moved. His immediate reaction was to declare emphatically to me that the whole plan had been betrayed—probably by the Chinese—and that it would be dangerous to go on with it. . . . Wingate was now in a very emotional state, and to avoid discussion with him before an audience, I drew him on one side. I said I did not think the Chinese had betrayed him . . . but he reiterated that someone had betrayed the plan and that the fly-in should be cancelled. . . . With great feeling he said it would be "murder" [to proceed]. I told him I doubted if

these places [Broadway and Chowringhee] were ambushed. Had the Japanese known of the plan I was sure they would have either ambushed or obstructed all three landing grounds. Wingate was by now calmer and much more in control of himself. After thinking for a moment, he said there would be great risk. I agreed. He paused, then looked straight at me: "The responsibility is yours," he said.

This was an astonishing revision of the previously accepted version of events at the launch of Operation Thursday and one that, it must be emphasized, none of those present has ever endorsed. Few would happily go out of their way to give the lie publicly to so popular a figure as Bill Slim, but Air Marshal Baldwin for one has described his story as "decidedly inaccurate." And how, knowing what we do of Wingate's uncompromising personality, could it be otherwise? Whatever his faults, indecisiveness was never one of them, and it seems unbelievable that at the most crucial moment of his career Wingate would simply throw in his hand and, in so doing, deliver himself to the mercies of his detractors. For if the fly-in had been so much as delayed it would have meant cancellation; moon conditions would not be right again for some time, and the Chindits' eve-of-battle zeal could never be fully rekindled.

Of course, the final decision had to be Slim's; as Fourteenth Army commander he would "carry the can" if the fly-in should end in disaster. But as Tulloch and other eyewitnesses have made plain—and as a dramatic photograph of the scene confirms—Slim stood apart from the huddle as Wingate discussed the situation with those most directly involved. At what point, then, did Slim "draw him aside"? It was surely only after Calvert and Cochran had assured Wingate that they were ready to go ahead with the fly-in.

Colonel (later Major General) Alison, who took part in the airstrip discussions—and who, with Calvert, was the last survivor of the event at the time of this writing*—told the authors he had absolutely no recollection of Slim taking Wingate aside before the active participants had reached their decision. He was quite definite that Wingate was not at all "emotional." "It was all quite businesslike," Alison recalled, "and

---

*Alison, although eighty-four years old, was in remarkably good shape, still active in military-related business affairs and very much, as the Americans say, "on the ball."

the matter was really decided by Wingate." In an appreciation produced in the 1960s by the Chindits Old Comrades Association, Colonel (later Brigadier) Walter Scott, another one of the group who stood around discussing the implications of the fateful photograph, said Wingate gave an "unforgettable demonstration of cool, determined and inspired leadership" on that occasion. "If ever I saw greatness in a human being I saw it in General Wingate that night."

And when Slim eventually endorsed the decision of his subordinates, which he was surely bound to do, Tulloch, who was "watching him closely at this moment of crisis, gained the impression, which has always remained, that he had the utmost confidence both in Wingate and in the success of the operation."

Certainly, the photograph of those involved in those tense discussion seems to confirm that, contrary to Slim's account, Wingate remained perfectly calm. He stands, slightly apart from his fellow officers, hands on hips and head slightly bowed in an attitude that suggests thoughtfulness rather than agitation. If body language means anything, Wingate's—as caught in that decisive moment by the camera lens—surely refutes Slim as convincingly as do the recollections of the other players in that night's drama.

What could have induced Slim to issue such a damning new version of a pivotal event a decade later and such a critical account overall of Operation Thursday? He was a bluff, jovial figure, much loved by his men, a highly effective if cautious commander who would achieve well deserved fame and prominence and who, according to his authorized biographer, was "incapable of telling a lie." That is no doubt so, in the sense that a lie should be defined as a deliberate and calculated falsehood. But in his assessment of Wingate it does seem either that Slim's memory played him false or that he allowed himself to be prompted, perhaps subliminally, by prejudiced parties and by reawakened memories of past disagreements.

However that might be, one feels bound to ask: if Slim was displaying a characteristic forthright honesty when he accused Wingate of going to pieces at a moment of crisis, what on earth was he displaying when he described him in 1944 as "irreplaceable" and "a genius"? Yes, Slim would have felt circumscribed then by both the custom of *"de mortuis nil nisi bonum"* and the need to bolster wartime morale and, yes, he might feel that such considerations no longer applied ten years on. But speaking no ill of the dead surely does not mean going to the opposite extreme and lavishing superlatives on someone about whom you have serious doubts.

Wingate's siblings, understandably outraged by Slim's criticisms, suggested a possible reason for his change of heart. Sybil Wingate told Tulloch: "I suspect my brother Nigel is right in attributing it to Churchill's publication of the fact [in *The Second World War,* volume 5] that he had contemplated putting Orde over Slim's head. Wounded vanity is one of the strongest of mortal feelings."

Whatever his motive, by the time Slim wrote his memoirs all the old dislike of Wingate within the military establishment—for his rebellious scorn, his arrogance, his paranoid touchiness, his reckless rudeness, his flouting of convention, his personal scruffiness, his leftish ideas, and (dare one suggest it?) his strange obsession with Zionism and the Jews*—was coming to the surface. Perhaps Slim, a likable but essentially conventional man, was infected by a climate of opinion in which Palestine had been merely a series of skirmishes against a native rabble; Abyssinia was largely forgotten and was, anyway, a victory over an enemy whose fighting qualities were not highly rated; Operation Longcloth was a needlessly costly adventure without strategic significance; and Thursday was at best a costly and unproven operation that would never have been undertaken but for Wingate's unsoldierly machinations in high places.

This mind-set was manifested most damagingly in volume 3 of the official history of the Second World War in Asia, *The War Against Japan.* It was published in 1961, but researched and written during the 1950s, during which time Slim and other senior officers had been intensively consulted and in turn quite possibly influenced by its principal author, Major General S. Woodburn Kirby.

Certainly, in dealing with Wingate this volume falls far short of the cool, detached, and rigorously objective standards an official history should surely reflect. It contains a highly unusual six-page assessment of the Chindit commander—unusual insofar as, in all five volumes of *The War Against Japan,* no other commander receives a separate as-

---

*Some of Wingate's detractors liked to insist that he *was* a Jew. The American John Knowles recalls hearing staff officers in Calcutta referring to him as "that Jew-boy."

sessment, not even Mountbatten or Slim. This would be a remarkable testimony to Wingate's significance but for the fact that the assessment is almost entirely negative.

Kirby had been deputy chief of the general staff in New Delhi in 1943 and as such had many a bruising encounter with Wingate when the latter arrived from Quebec with demands for men, supplies, and equipment that Auchinleck and his staff felt should be allocated elsewhere. In one message to Mountbatten, complaining of GHQ's failure to meet his demands for weaponry and rations, Wingate rashly named Kirby as one of those who "should be sacked for iniquitous and unpatriotic conduct." Could it be that, armed with the authorship of the official history, Kirby took the opportunity to avenge such slights? Or was it in the spirit of objective scholarship that he portrayed his former adversary as a soldier of modest ability, uncooperative disposition, and overweening ambition who, by seducing Churchill, won promotion far beyond his abilities and by selfish use of Churchill's favor obtained an unfair amount of scarce war matériel, which he used to little strategic advantage?*

Disregarding all favorable comment about Wingate, Kirby described him as "petulant," "obsessed," and having "neither the knowledge, stability, nor balance to make a great commander." Wingate's Special Force, Kirby wrote, had done little to help Fourteenth Army defeat the Japanese at Imphal and Kohima—"They had indeed the reverse effect." Wingate's "fertile imagination would make an interesting psychological study," Kirby suggested, and he capped it all by concluding that "just as timing played a great part in his rise to prominence, so the moment of his death may have been equally propitious for him." In other words, Wingate was killed before he was found out.

The suggestion that Wingate's death was well timed seems especially offensive, particularly in an official history, and one rear-echelon general who uttered a similar opinion at an officers' club in Delhi in

---

*Wingate, in fact, only once ever used his access to Churchill to make a direct representation. It was an ultimate weapon to be wielded only as an implicit threat. Other British military historians down the decades have echoed the themes of Kirby and his team, although the American official military historians, Charles F. Romanus and Riley Sunderland, have been a good deal more complimentary. For a point-by-point rebuttal of Kirby, see Derek Tulloch's *Wingate in Peace and War,* Peter Mead's *Orde Wingate and the Historians,* and David Rooney's *Wingate and the Chindits.*

1944 was thrown fully clothed into a fountain by assailants who, though never caught and punished, were undoubtedly young Chindit officers. More senior Chindit officers felt the same way. An unidentified brigadier and six colonels sent Lorna, as "a small token in memory of our late general," a few lines of heartfelt if lumbering verse: "I cannot stomach the revolting orgy / Of jackals gloating over their escape / From tongue of genius, lashing them with fury / The crashing of a fist which made them quake."

How, though, to account for the strength of the official military animus against Wingate that persists to this day in staff college lectures and in occasional articles in the press and specialized publications? Calvert stumbled across a possible explanation in 1947 when, as a member of Field Marshal Viscount Montgomery's planning staff, he turned up an Army Council minute that he summarized as saying that Wingate was a divisive influence and "we don't want any more Wingates in the British Army. Therefore we must write down Wingate and the Chindits."

However that might be, and whatever the army establishment and many like-minded military historians may say, the dwindling band of Chindit veterans who served under him remember Wingate with fierce affection and undiminished loyalty, as anyone privileged enough to attend a Chindit reunion will discover. Years after the war, the dying utterance of his clerk Sergeant Foreman, repeated over and over again, was the name of his old commander.

But perhaps the most effective witnesses to Wingate's prowess at arms are the Japanese commanders who felt the edge of his "terrible swift sword" and who can hardly be accused of taking sides in an internal British military controversy. The official Japanese view, based on statements taken from more than thirty commanders in the Burma theater, states unequivocally that "the raiding force [Chindits] greatly affected Army operations and eventually led to the total abandonment of Northern Burma." And Lieutenant General Mutaguchi, the Fifteenth Army's commander, writing to one of Kirby's researchers shortly before his death in 1968, asserted that "General Wingate's airborne tactics put a great obstacle in the way of our Imphal plan and were an important reason for its failure." Recalling his reaction to the news of Wingate's death, Mutaguchi added: "I realised what a loss this was to the British Army and said a prayer for the soul of this man in whom I had found my match." None of this was reflected in Kirby's official history. Sir Robert (Bobbie) Thompson, who was an RAF liaison officer with both Chindit operations and won postwar fame as a principal architect of the successful campaign against the Malayan Chinese Communist uprising and an adviser on counterinsurgency to American presidents, has perhaps best characterized the significance of Operation Thursday by posing the following question: "What would have been the effect if two days after the D-day landings in Normandy in 1944 two German airborne divisions had landed in central southern England and blocked several of the main roads to the south coast ports? No analogy is exact, but that is roughly what Wingate did."

The public controversy over Wingate's place in military history, both as a field commander and as an innovator whose ideas have changed the face of war, rumbles on, erupting now and then with extraordinary vehemence on each side, though, it must be said, with some of the heaviest guns ranged against him. That the debate continues after more than half a century is in itself a backhanded tribute, ensuring that he is at least not forgotten.

Although it was almost certainly not meant kindly, Kirby's observation that the timing of Wingate's death "may have been propitious for him" is not entirely without substance. He died at the apogee of his military career, the initial success of Operation Thursday having seemed to validate his daring innovations. But let us play the admittedly sterile game of "what if?" for a moment and wonder how, had Wingate survived World War II, he would have responded to the dismal final events of the Palestine mandate, when the British were no longer merely unsympathetic to but engaged in open warfare against armed Zionists—the very situation Wingate had urged the Jewish Agency and Haganah to avoid at all costs before he left Palestine in 1938.

One can reasonably surmise that postwar revelations of the full horrors of the Nazi holocaust—and the stupidities, insensitivities, and contradictions of British policy as the Holocaust survivors straggled into the Holy Land—would have combined to make Wingate's attachment to the Zionist cause more fervent than ever. But how would he have reacted to the Zionist extremism that murdered Lord Moyne in Cairo and Count Bernadotte in Jerusalem, which blew up British headquarters at the King David Hotel killing 91 Britons, Arabs, and Jews, which hanged two British sergeants in an orange grove, and which perpetrated the massacre of 250 Arab civilians at Dir Yassin? These incidents were all the work of Revisionist Zionists with whom, during his years in Palestine, Wingate had no truck. His contacts and friendships had all been with the mainstream Zionist leadership, even if he felt at times that they were rather too moderate. But during the closing stages of the Zionist struggle, his friends and disciples of the Haganah gave at least tacit support to the gunmen of the far-right Irgun Zvai Leumi and Lehi, the Stern Gang. To what extent would that connection have strained Wingate's loyalties?

And finally what if, when the British finally pulled out, the Jewish Agency had offered him his longed-for chance to lead a Jewish army in Israel's War of Independence? The Jews were certainly in need of someone of Wingate's talents: their chief of staff, General Yaakov Dori, was bedridden, and his deputy, General Yigael Yadin, an archaeologist by training, was a man of extremely limited military experience. In the end, of course, it made little difference; the Israelis won the war without help from outside. But just imagine the consequences of a situation in which a Jewish army commanded by one British general had taken the field against Jordan's Arab Legion, commanded by another British general, John Glubb.*

In a very real sense, of course, Wingate's guiding spirit as a military leader was present throughout the early years of the Jewish state, informing the doctrines that won the War of Independence and led to the stunning victories of the 1956 Sinai campaign and the 1967 Six Day War. The period after the Six Day War when Israel, by now very much the upper dog, began to pursue the path of territorial expansion and the army Wingate inspired became an army of occupation, might conceivably have tested his uncritical constancy. But that is perhaps one "what if?" too far.

Although the two cannot, of course, be separated, Wingate the Man

---

*At least one distinguished ex-Chindit joined Glubb Pasha's forces as a contract officer—Geoffrey Lockett, beneath whose kilt Calvert had checked his fuses when he blew up the railway for the second time during the first Chindit expedition.

presents a figure at least as interesting as Wingate the Soldier. And it was perhaps the left-wing journalist and future Labour party leader Michael Foot who pinned down what it was about Wingate that makes him a man to remember. Describing him as "a great rebel, a great Puritan, a great man of God in the Old Testament sense, a great Englishman," Foot went on:

> For the glory of England all over the globe, the fact which has allied her name with that of Freedom and of Humanity, that tradition which has made her loved despite the crimes committed beneath her flag, are that men such as Wingate have left these shores and gone forth to make their own the cause of some unhappy people, suppliant in their agony and looking to England as their champion. Without this our Empire is infamy; without such men we are little better than bloated conquerors.

It is a cruel irony of history—and no derogation of the legitimacy of the Jewish state—that its creation and expansion should have left another "unhappy people, suppliant in their agony" homeless, despairing, and looking for a champion.

In ways not always predictable, those who were close to Orde Wingate were marked for life. Peggy Jelley remained unmarried because, as she said, "after Orde, all other men seemed uninteresting." Nevertheless, she told Judy Wingate a year before her solitary death in 1996 that "I have lived a contented and for the most part happy life."

Lorna remained a passionate partisan of Zionism for some years, but, refused the necessary passport endorsement, was unable to return to Palestine until the end of the British mandate. "The black books of MI5 contain many unfriendly references to me and my doings," she said in a letter to a friend in Palestine. "I think that as long as there is a British Raj in Palestine I shall be warned off the country."

She did manage to return in time for Israel's declaration of independence in May 1948, and despite her close relations with the most senior officials of the nascent Jewish state she chose to spend Independence Day in Haifa with Akavia and his wife. When Ben-Gurion's proclamation of Israel's statehood was relayed by radio she turned impulsively to kiss the person standing next to her. "It was the Sephardic chief rabbi of Haifa," recalls Akavia. "They were both quite embarrassed."

Lorna tried to get permission from the Israeli military authorities to fly over Yemin Orde, a Galilean kibbutz named after her husband that was under siege from Arab forces. Her idea was to drop Wingate's personal Bible to the defenders. Contrary to popular Israeli legend, she was refused permission to make the flight for reasons of her own safety. Instead, she handed the Bible to a group of women who, with their children, had been evacuated from the settlement. She inscribed it:

> 7/5/48. To the Defenders of Yemin Orde. Since Orde Wingate is with you in spirit, though he cannot lead you in the flesh, I send you the Bible he carried in all his campaigns and from which he drew the inspiration of his victories. May it be a covenant between you and him, in triumph or defeat, now and always.

That Bible is now preserved in a glass case at Ein Harod, in a museum named for Wingate's friend Chaim Sturmann.

As principal keeper of the flame, Lorna rigorously vetted would-be authorized biographers of her husband, rejecting all of them before deciding on Christopher Sykes. It was a choice she later felt cause to regret. She had apparently hoped that Sykes might perform the impossible feat of combining scholarly objectivity with an inability to discern fault in his subject. Even more forbidding was her attitude toward the cinema, a popular art form for which she felt considerable disdain. Numerous Hollywood producers vied for permission to make Wingate the Movie, but by insisting on veto rights over the selection of screenwriters, directors, and stars and censorship rights over the scripts, she eventually drove off even the most persistent. For journalists seeking an interview, she had even less tolerance, driving some of them off her property with a shotgun.

In April 1953, in the presence of Ben-Gurion and the Israeli chief of staff Moshe Dayan, Lorna formally opened Yemin Orde as a youth center, near Haifa. It was her final act as a champion of Zionism. In the following year, she broke with her past life and interests to become plain Mrs. John Smith, wife of a well-to-do Scottish landowner who had farmed during the war and never been a soldier. She became a convert to Roman Catholicism, bore her new husband two children, and also broke off all contact with her mother. Predeceased by her second husband, Lorna left Scotland to live on Guernsey, in the Channel Islands, where she spent a lot of money refurbishing a secluded granite farmhouse called Le Monnaie de Haut, infuriating local builders by importing English artisans to do much of the work. The once beautiful and articulate teenager who had swept Wingate off his feet became a hard-drinking recluse, rejecting the friendship offered by the numerous retired officers and their families on the island. "She kept herself to herself—I think you'll discover she had a problem with bottles," one of the authors was told. By 1990 Lorna had moved to a nursing home in England, where she died aged seventy-four.

Orde Jonathan Wingate, conceived on the Atlantic crossing in 1943, followed his father into the Royal Artillery. Like most British soldiers of his generation his only experience of active service was in Northern Ireland. He left the army in 1978 but continued to serve as a part-time soldier in the Territorial Army's Honourable Artillery Company, whose wartime mission would have appealed to his father—they train to hide in the enemy's rear with a radio and direct gunfire onto selected targets. He retired from the Territorials in 1994 with the rank of lieutenant colonel.

Tulloch went through agonies of uncertainty and apprehension after he illegally took possession of his friend and commander's official and private papers, anticipating correctly that the military establishment would attempt to do Wingate down. He took the papers back to England after the war at the considerable risk of court-martial, dismissal from the service, and loss of pension and remained "worried stiff" that he might be found out. Eventually, having retired from the army as a major general, he used the papers as the basis for a book— *Wingate in Peace and War*—in which he sought to rebut the criticisms leveled by Slim and the official historian, General Kirby, among others.

By no means a natural writer, Tulloch found authorship a stressful experience. Friends and family attribute his relatively early death, two years after publication, to the mental and emotional wear and tear he suffered in bringing his book to fruition.

Like Tulloch, the redoubtable Matron MacGeary also suffered because of her close association with Wingate. Like him, she was intolerant of the sloth of GHQ in dealing with deficiencies, and she alleged that the medical authorities started "a campaign of petty tyranny" against her when, in charge of the Special Force hospital at Imphal, she complained to Mountbatten. "I have fought hard against them," she told Lorna, "and twice this month I have been told that unless I mend my ways I will be sacked. Yesterday I sent in my resignation."

The postwar careers of Fergusson and Calvert, both regular army officers and Wingate's best pupils, are of such wild contrast that it is difficult to believe that fate can be so capricious. Fergusson, the smooth aristocrat and old Etonian, went on to reap all the rewards of an arduous and dangerous wartime career, fulfilling earlier literary ambitions with poetry and prose, including three very well received volumes of war memoirs, and achieving high office. He was knighted, became governor-general of New Zealand, and by the time of his death in 1980 had been made a life peer and taken the title Lord Ballantrae.

Calvert, perhaps the bravest and most tactically brilliant of all Wingate's senior officers and certainly the most devoted of his acolytes, ended the war commanding a unit of French and Belgian Special Air Service commandos in Germany. By the summer of 1945 he was one of Britain's most decorated soldiers, for apart from his two DSOs he held the American Silver Star, the French Legion d'honneur, and the Belgian Order of Leopold.

Peace required that he drop a couple of rungs from brigadier to lieutenant colonel, and staff college was followed by a boring spell in military government in Trieste. But in 1950 Field Marshal Slim, who had succeeded Montgomery as chief of staff, remembered Calvert's jungle fighting skills and sent him to Malaya to fight Communist guerrillas. Calvert devised new tactics and was allowed to raise his own unit called the Malayan Scouts, which recruited several former Chindits and became the foundation of the revived Special Air Service regiment.

The tactics Calvert pioneered undoubtedly contributed to eventual British victory, but the Malayan Scouts turned out to be a mixed blessing for both the army and Calvert. Many of the Scouts acquired a reputation for being drunk and undisciplined, and that included their commanding officer. Nonetheless, Calvert was still a name to conjure with, and the army were saved the embarrassment of replacing him when he was invalided back to Britain suffering from amoebic dysentery and malaria. He spent a long convalescence writing *Prisoners of Hope*, a much-praised account of his role in Wingate's second Chindit campaign. Then came disaster.

In July 1952 a court-martial in Germany convicted Calvert, who was then almost forty and had never married, of gross indecency with German youths aged between seventeen and eighteen and dismissed him from the army. Calvert had always vehemently denied the charges. In 1996 one of the German witnesses, now in his sixties, denied that any homosexual acts had ever taken place, with Calvert explaining that they had visited his flat in the hope of stealing sugar and cigarettes, rare commodities on the black market. The German told Calvert's biographer David Rooney* that the British military police had fabricated the evidence.

In 1952 homosexuality was a criminal offense in Britain. Whether Calvert was merely the victim of a "queer bashing" mentality among the military police or whether, as in his later years Calvert sometimes liked to think, the charges were part of some deeper conspiracy by the anti-Wingate faction in the army will probably never be known. Whatever the reason, it left Calvert a broken man, and the rest of his life became a protracted battle with alcoholism. He wrote some more books, but none were as successful as *Prisoners of Hope*, which has twice been reprinted, and by the time he reached retirement age the hero of Pagoda Hill was working as a gardener.

There was, however, something of a happy ending. A campaign to recognize Calvert's heroism gained momentum. In 1995, when Britain celebrated the fiftieth anniversary of the end of World War II, it was Calvert who was chosen to lead the Chindit contingent in a parade of veterans before the queen. Like many of the men who followed him, Brigadier Calvert, now always referred to by his wartime rank, made his salute from a wheelchair. He died in 1998, aged eighty-eight.

Wingate's devoted sisters all remained unmarried, all pursuing demanding careers. Sybil, the left-wing intellectual and senior civil servant, left behind an unpublished poem, found by one of the authors in a tin trunk in the garage of Wingate's widowed sister-in-law, Judith, in 1997. Sybil composed it on 20 April 1944, sitting by the window of her London flat, overlooking the Thames:

> Far beyond where, long river-miles eastward,
> The rippling water meets water, the sweet to the salt, and the river
> Nests its head on the breast of the sea,

Mad Mike by David Rooney was published by the British military publisher Leo Cooper in 1997.

Its tide holding the hulls of vessels, the violet, the black-begrimed
    boats,
Sun-steeped, spice-breathed, pass eastward, eastward,
Sun-seeking, and sight the deep, the gulf of the pathless forest,
The mountain, the cry, O my brother, the fire in the night.

Half begun, well done and ended,
Sealed with the fire of the achieving sun, washed
By waters that meet the waters in the womb of the sea;
Here was thy spring, thy straight run, where the streams part
From under my feet.

Acknowledgments and Sources

The principal primary sources for this biography are the private papers of Major General Orde Charles Wingate, formerly held by his son, Lieutenant Colonel Orde Jonathan Wingate (Ret.), and a random but extensive collection of letters, photographs, and other family memorabilia in the possession of Mrs. Judy Wingate, the widow of General Wingate's youngest brother, Granville.

Colonel Wingate put his father's papers up for sale at auction by Sotheby's in London in the summer of 1996, and, by agreement, these were split into two lots. One of these, relating to Wingate's early life, his Abyssinian campaign, and his two Chindit campaigns in Burma, was purchased by the Imperial War Museum in London. The other lot, concerning Wingate's activities in prewar Palestine, was purchased on behalf of the Collection of Steve Forbes, New York.

In the ensuing chapter notes, the papers now held by the Imperial War Museum are classified under the headings Early Life (WPEL/IWM), Abyssinia (WPA/IWM), and Chindit (WPC/IWM). Those held by the Steve Forbes Collection are designated Palestine (WPP/Forbes). Those held by Judy Wingate are designated Family (WPF).

Before the Palestine papers were allowed to leave the United Kingdom they were microfilmed by the British Library. The curators of the Steve Forbes Collection, waiving their right to a seven-year embargo, kindly gave the authors permission to examine the Palestine papers on microfilm and to quote from them.

At the time the authors consulted the IWM and Forbes acquisitions, during 1996 and 1997, neither collection had yet been comprehensively sorted and classified; consequently we have been unable to cite box and file numbers.

At the Imperial War Museum the authors consulted numerous other primary sources, all of which are cited in the chapter notes below. Other relevant documentary sources are in the Public Record Office (PRO) at Kew and in the papers of Major General Derek Tulloch and Ivy Hay of Seaton (formerly Paterson) at Manchester University's John Rylands Library.

These and other documentary primary sources were enhanced and enlivened by the oral recollections of a number of men and women in Britain, Israel, the United States, and Cyprus who knew Wingate and whose lives were altered as a result. These included (in alphabetical order) Avraham Akavia, John Alison, Zvi Brenner, Michael Calvert, Israel Carmi, Ruth Dayan, George Dunlop, Michael Foot, Chaim and Tchia Geyari, Patrick Graves, Rex King-Clark, John Knowles, John Lancaster, Robert Schieferstein, Tony Simonds, Lady (Mary) Soames, née Churchill, and Sir Wilfred Thesiger. We are deeply indebted to all of them.

The recollections of others, some deceased before we began our research, are contained in numerous autobiographies and memoirs, etc., cited below. Of special value were certain chapters, translated into English by Abraham Akavia, of his published Hebrew memoir *With Wingate in Ethiopia* and his campaign diary, which is to be found in the Public Record Office. Tony Simonds directed us to, and gave us permission to quote from, his unpublished memoir, "Pieces of War," copies of which he lodged in various places, including the Imperial War Museum, after his first draft was lost when his home was destroyed during the Turkish invasion of Cyprus in 1974. Also in the Imperial War Museum we found the fascinating journal kept by Michael Tutton during the Ethiopian campaign in which he was mortally wounded.

Throughout our research, the staff of Roderick Suddaby, chief keeper at the IWM's Department of Documents, produced every file and book we ever asked for. The authors are greatly indebted to them as they are to Merav Segal, curator of the Weizmann Archives in Israel, and to all who have given permission to quote from written works.

Quotations from the letters of Sir Reginald Wingate are reproduced with the kind permission of his granddaughter, Mrs. Josephine Street; quotations from the letters and diaries of General Derek Tulloch with the kind permission of his son, James Tulloch; and quotations from the published works of Brigadier Bernard Fergusson by kind permission of his son, the Hon. George Fergusson.

Finally, in recording our thanks to Judy Wingate for allowing us to delve into her tin trunk full of photographs, letters, documents, and other memorabilia, we should also note our gratitude for the information she was able to give us about Peggy Jelley, an important influence in Wingate's early life.

The following abbreviations are used throughout the Notes:

PJ   Peggy Jelley
RKC   Rex King-Clark
IP   Ivy Patterson
TS   A. C. (Tony) Simonds
DT   Derek Tulloch

CW   Chaim Weizmann
EW   Ethel Wingate
GW   George Wingate
JW   Judy Wingate
LW   Lorna Wingate
OW   Orde Wingate
RW   Reginald Wingate
SW   Sybil Wingate

Chapter 1

PAGE

7   "an unusually fine": GW to Mrs. Orde-Browne, 3 March 1903, WPEL/IWM.

7   "I never lost hope": ibid.

10   "Mummy is always thinking": GW to daughters, 28 April 1904, WPF.

11   "the most unhappy, the most lonely": SW manuscript, WPF.

11   "a temple of gloom": Nigel Wingate to Monica Wingate, 3 January 1934, WPF.

11   "we realise more": OW to GW, 26 September 1932, WPF.

12   "very considerable mental gifts": Sybil Wingate in *The Spectator*, 29 May 1959.

13   carried off to heaven: Hay, *There Was a Man of Genius*, p. 25.

13   "The dramatis personae": SW manuscript, WPF.

14   "the sort of boy": Jossleyn Hennessy in BBC broadcast, 20 April 1959.

14   "a little rat-like fellow": Adrian Daintrey, quoted in Sykes, *Orde Wingate*, p. 34.

14   "If you go": Phillip Radcliffe, quoted in Sykes, p. 35.

14   "no memory of him"—Holden, *The Charterhouse We Knew*, p. 12.

16   "one basic common belief": Colonel F. Wintle to DT, 2 February 1967, WPF.

17   "On the following day": Tulloch, *Wingate in Peace and War*, p. 16.

18   "Orde walked, very slowly": Tulloch essay, WPEL/IWM.

19   "His mind had suddenly awakened": Sybil Wingate, *The Spectator*, 29 May 1959.

Chapter 2

20   "on morning parades": Tulloch essay, WPEL/IWM.

21   "As the seasons went on": ibid.

21   "a day of pure happiness": OW to Claud Fothergill, undated, WPEL/IWM.

22   "Don't run through": Monica Wingate to OW, undated, WPEL/IWM.

23   "no use for girls": Tulloch essay, WPEL/IWM.

24   "I am proud": EW to OW, undated, WPEL/IWM.

24   "Is it a warning?": GW to OW, undated, WPEL/IWM.

24-25   "Before the first race": OW diary, 25 March 1925, WPF.

25   "Sunday. Went to church": ibid., 4 January 1925.

25   "that rude young man": Royle, *Orde Wingate,* p. 46.

27   "Personally, I do not profess": OW to Hartley Holmes, undated, WPEL/IWM.

27   "I have the strongest belief": OW to SW, 15 April 1934, WPF.

Chapter 3

31   "at the top of the tree": EW to OW, undated, WPEL/IWM.

31   "the best-behaved officials": OW to GW, 31 October 1927, WPEL/IWM.

33   "Expenses here are terrible": OW to GW, 20 November 1927, WPEL/IWM.

34   sporting a moustache: OW to GW, 25 February 1928, WPEL/IWM.

35   "I lived and moved": OW to PJ, undated, WPEL/IWM.

35   "I said to myself": ibid.

36   "I doubt very much": OW to GW, 13 June 1928, WPEL/IWM.

36   "such a state of nerves": OW to PJ, 12 April 1931, WPEL/IWM.

37   "God is good": ibid.

37   "I know how you feel": OW to PJ, undated, WPEL/IWM.

38   "I don't like the things you say": General Sir Terence Airey quoted in Sykes, *Orde Wingate,* p. 66.

39   "He only possessed": OW to PJ, undated, WPEL/IWM.

39   "It has two sides": OW to SW, 15 February 1936, WPF.

39   "Death is no respecter": OW to PJ, 12 April 1931, WPEL/IWM.

42   "this high and ghostly waste": Wingate, "The Search for Zerzura," *Geographical Journal,* 83, April 1934, pp. 281–308.

Chapter 4

44   the bright yellow shoes: Hay, *There Was a Man of Genius,* p. 19 et seq.

47   "It would have been": PJ in Tulloch, *Wingate in Peace and War,* p. 41.

48   "looking like death": Mary Jelley to DT, WPEL/IWM.
48   "I was in a daze": JW, author interview.
49   "Of course, it was hateful": PJ to JW, 5 April 1995.
50   "It was imperative": OW to IP, 1 October 1934, WPEL/IWM.
51   "Affairs are in such a state": OW to SW, 13 January 1935, WPF.
51   "masses of mimosa": Hay, *There Was a Man of Genius*, p. 35.
52   "Lorna heard the batman": Tulloch essay, WPEL/IWM.
53   "very pretty, very young": TS, author interview, Cyprus, August 1996.
53   "I am at a dangerous age": OW to GW, 14 April 1934, WPF.
53   "I hated the life": OW to EW, 12 August 1941, WPF.
54   "if you would like to see me": OW to RW, RW papers, Centre for Middle East Studies, Durham University.

Chapter 5

60   "the saviour of our people": Begin quoted in Bethell, *The Palestine Triangle*, p. 21.
60   "with little short of dismay": RW to Sir Mark Sykes, 28 November 1917, Sledmere papers, quoted in Sanders, *The High Walls of Jerusalem*, p. 619.
63   "famous for their hospitality": Peres, *Battling for Peace*, p. 21.
63   "Certainly, the Jews were white": Corporal (later Lieutenant Colonel) Ivor Thomas, unpublished ms., WPF.
63   "Everyone's against the Jews": TS interview, August 1996.
63   "small, pale nondescript": Hay, *There Was a Man of Genius*, p. 24.
64   "wicked persecution": GW to OW, undated, 1924, WPEL/IWM.
64   "We need only . . . arm": OW to RW, 12 January 1937, WPP/Forbes.
66   "two sides to the Palestine problem": Abraham Akavia, author interview, Haifa, 1997.
68   "a truly great man": OW to RW, 12 January 1937, WPP/Forbes.
68   "more noisy, more vociferous": TS interview, August 1996.
69   "I designed the furniture": LW to Monica Wingate, undated, WPF.
69   "I can speak": OW to EW, 24 April 1937, WPP/Forbes.
69   "1,000 millim Ivrit": OW to CW, Weizmann Archives.
69   "It always seems alive": OW to EW, 20 April 1937, WPF.
70   "She was very young": Ruth Dayan, author interview, Jerusalem, 30 October 1997.
70   "I knew at once": Thomas, unpublished ms., WPF.

PAGE

72   "In my position": OW to CW, 31 May 1937, WPP/Forbes.

72   "Lucky for us": Rose, *The Diaries of Blanche Dugdale*, p. 80.

72   "literally sick with indegestion": CW to IP, 13 July 1937, Weizmann Archives.

73   "The Kingdom of David": CW to IP, 7 July 1937, Weizmann Archives.

74   "He suddenly decided": Thomas, unpublished ms., WPF.

Chapter 6

75   concealed radio transmitter: Zvi Brenner, author interview, Kibbutz Afikim, August 1996.

76   a light-colored suit: Israel Carmi, author interview, Haifa, September 1997.

77   "He claims the government": Eshkol, *A Common Soldier*, p. 73.

78   "Zvi, you're in charge": Brenner interview, August 1996.

78   "The great advantage": OW to Ritchie, 7 April 1938, WPP/Forbes.

79   "a most reliable source": ibid.

79   "the tremendous din": ibid.

80   "There, standing in the foyer": King-Clark, *Free for a Blast*, p. 158.

81   "After all, he was": Eshkol, *A Common Soldier*, p. 110.

81   "I opened his suitcase": Ruth Dayan, author interview, Tel Aviv, October 1997.

82   [OW] was confronted by a young woman: Brenner interview, August 1996.

83   "doing something great": ibid.

84   "From the very first": Eshkol, *A Common Soldier*, p. 90.

85   "Before going on an action": Moshe Dayan, *Story of My Life* (London: Weidenfeld and Nicholson, 1976), p. 89.

85   "They are quite unable": OW to Ritchie, 7 April 1938, WPP/Forbes.

86   "His name at once caught": Wavell in Foreword to Rolo, *Wingate's Raiders*.

86   "Only one way"—OW to Ritchie, 7 April 1938, WPP/Forbes.

Chapter 7

88   "no very large battles": RKC, Palestine diary, IWM.

PAGE

89   "so much time with your enemies": Sykes, *Orde Wingate,* p. 144.
89   sideshow of a sideshow: Bond, *Oxford History of the British Army,*
        p. 265.
89   "Sending troops to Palestine": Bond, ed., *Chief of Staff.*
90   "chase them by night": Sykes, *Orde Wingate,* p. 149.
90   "Don't imitate the British Tommy": Eshkol, *A Common Soldier,* p.
        150.
90   shilling a day: Lieutenant Colonel M. R. L. Grove, IWM sound
        archives (004510/03).
91   "Saul was a bloody fool": Akavia interview, 1997.
91   "An odd gentleman" et seq.: RKC, Palestine diary, IWM.
92   "able to adjust to the terrain": Eshkol, *A Common Soldier,* p. 105.
92   "He was shouting 'Jews' and 'guns' ": ibid., p 106, and Brenner
        interview, August 1996.
93   "again Wingate led us": Eshkol, *A Common Soldier,* p. 106.
93   "beyond the wire": Brenner interview, August 1996.
94   "Wingate was walking along": Grove, sound archives, IWM.
94   "a species the infantry": RKC, author interview, 1997.
95   "Not chauffeurs": Brenner interview, August 1996.
95   felt uncomfortable, et seq.: Carmi interview, September 1997.
96   slapping or punching: Eshkol, *A Common Soldier,* p. 179, and
        Brenner interview, August 1996.
96   "He was our father": Brenner, author interview, August 1996.
97   liked Wingate's style: Cpl. Howbrook, IWM sound archives
        (004619/03).

Chapter 8

98   "moving ambushes" et seq.: OW to Ritchie, 17 July 1938,
        WPP/Forbes.
98   a tedious country walk: Grove, op. cit.
100   "without a hitch": ibid.
100   "a cock-up of the first water": RKC, author interview, Rhu, Scot-
        land, 1997.
101   "I was advancing": OW to Ritchie, 17 July 1938, WPP/Forbes.
102   "white as a sheet": RKC, Palestine diary, IWM.
102   "He looked very pale": Brenner interview, August 1996.
103   "gallantry of a very high order": *London Gazette,* September 1938.
103   "My leg goes on well": OW to RKC, 17 July 1938, WPP/Forbes.

PAGE

103   "We learned, however": ibid.

104   "Should the time ever come": ibid.

104   "I am quite well again": OW to EW, 2 August 1938, WPP/Forbes.

105   "God gave it to us": Akavia interview, 1997.

105   "we all made a great many mistakes": quoted in Sykes, *Orde Wingate*, pp. 167–68.

105   "It's not his legs": Humphrey Bredin quoted in RKC interview, 30 July 1997.

109   "a sort of circus comedian": John Hackett, IWM sound archives (004527/06).

110   "[T]hey appeared at dawn": Grove, op. cit.

111   it worked like a dream: Humphrey Bredin quoted in the *Jewish Observer and Middle East Review*, 17 October 1969.

111   "As we advanced": King-Clark, *Free for a Blast*, p. 198.

112   "A minute later": ibid.

112   "He was trying to reload": Howbrook, op. cit.

113   "the first soldiers": Akavia interview, 16 June 1997.

114   barred his audience from taking notes: ibid.

114   "He gave out a cry": Eshkol, *A Common Soldier*, p. 175.

115   "The problem of punishment": ibid., p. 176.

116   "Some of the things we did": Carmi interview, 18 June 1997.

116   Tiberias massacre details: Colonial Office annual report, 1938, and Ironside, quoted in Sykes, *Orde Wingate*, p. 179.

118   "And who are you?": Ironside, quoted in Sykes, *Orde Wingate*, p. 180.

Chapter 9

120   shrewd analysis with reckless advice: Dov Yosef to CW, 10 October 1938, Weizmann Archives.

120   OW testimony to Woodhead Commission: Brig. Leslie Wieler, quoted in Sykes, *Orde Wingate*, p. 166.

122   "ordered to shut my mouth": Rebecca Sieff, ibid., p. 192.

122   "apprehensive of the lines": W. C. Ritchie, report on OW, 13 July 1939, WPP/Forbes.

123   "fundamentally an individualist": Ritchie, report on OW, 18 November 1938, WPP/Forbes.

123   "In the interests of the Service": Lt. Gen. Robert Haining, report on OW, 27 December 1938, WPP/Forbes.

123   "scrupulously fair": OW to Ritchie, 30 December 1938, WPP/ Forbes.

124   "dressing up of Jews": OW to Brig. John Evetts, 31 March 1939, WPP/Forbes.

126   "OFFERED IMMEDIATE TRANSFER": OW to CW; 12 March 1939, Weizmann Archives.

127   "The time for self-restraint": David Hacohen, quoted in Sykes, *Orde Wingate*, p. 197.

127   "I am sent away": Brenner, author interview, Afikim, 30 September 1996.

127–28 "The time has come": Mosley, *Gideon Goes to War*, p. 58.

128   "If you ever resort": Sykes, *Orde Wingate*, p. 203.

Chapter 10

130   "We must foster" et seq.: OW, "Palestine in Imperial Strategy," WPP/Forbes.

133   "complete agreement": Gen. Edmund Ironside to OW, 8 June 1939, WPP/Forbes.

134   "Many exceptional qualities": Ritchie, Report on OW, 9 June 1939, WPP/Forbes.

134   "The tendency": Haining, Report on OW, 10 July 1939, WPP/ Forbes.

134   "The views he held": OW to Army Council, 27 June 1939, WPP/ Forbes.

135   "very valuable qualities": Ironside to Leslie Hore-Belisha, 3 November 1939, quoted in Sykes, *Orde Wingate*, p. 217.

136   "a kind of mystical belief": Michael Foot, author interview, London, 3 November 1997.

138   "beside themselves": Rose, ed., *The Diary of Blanche Dugdale*, entry for 1 November 1939.

138   "The idea": Ironside, quoted in Sykes, *Orde Wingate*, p. 217.

138   "more than a right": David Ben-Gurion, "A Jewish Army" (unidentified publication, 1940, cutting in Wiener Library, London).

139   "much upset by Vera": Rose, ed., *The Diary of Blanche Dugdale*, entry for 25 May 1940.

140   "It is not thus": OW chronology, WPEL/IWM.

141   "a much more virile": Leopold Amery, quoted in Sykes, *Orde Wingate*, p. 230.

PAGE

141   "A lucky day": Rose, ed., *The Diary of Blanche Dugdale,* entry for 13 September 1940.

142   "He lost his temper": ibid., 14 September 1940.

143   "tried my best": CW to LW, 23 January 1941, WPP/Forbes.

143   "I knew in what spirit": Weizmann, *Trial and Error* (London: Hamish Hamilton, 1949), p. 490.

143   "Our readiness to serve": CW to Winston Churchill, 10 September 1941, WPP/Forbes.

143   "You ought to go": quoted in Norman Rose, *Chaim Weizmann: A Biography,* p. 356.

Chapter 11

148   "The curse of this war": Sir Wilfred Thesiger, author interview, London, July 1997.

148   "more like a Baptist missionary" et seq.: F. O. Reginald Collis and Sgt. Frank Bavin-Smith, "Operation Wingate," *Aeroplane Monthly,* August-September 1993.

153   "a real fighting force": OW, "Appreciation of the Ethiopian Campaign," 18 June 1941, WPA/IWM.

154   "Don't bore me": Collis and Bavin-Smith, "Operation Wingate," *Aeroplane Monthly,* August-September 1993.

155   "wrist watches are no damned good": ibid.

155   "his ruthless energy": Maj. Gen. I. S. O. Playfair, *The Mediterranean and the Middle East,* vol. 1, *Early Successes Against Italy,* HMSO, p. 404.

156   "They would regret being conquered": Mosley, *Gideon Goes to War,* p. 75.

157   "an indispensable part of British war aims": OW, "Appreciation of the Ethiopian Campaign," WPA/IWM.

158   "My dear Wingate": Major George Green to OW, 14 December 1940, WPA/IWM.

158   "Fifty-two nations let you down": OW, "Appreciation of the Ethiopian Campaign," WPA/IWM.

160   "While it's not denied": ibid.

161   "you will shoot him": TS interview, September 1996.

161   "A clerkless officer": OW, "Appreciation of the Ethiopian Campaign," WPA/IWM.

162   "The time was an odd one": Sykes, *Orde Wingate,* p. 246.

163   "They didn't like Wingate": TS, unpublished memoir, IWM.

PAGE

164   "Here is a traitor": TS interview, September 1996.
165   "Everyone was milling around": Allen, *Guerrilla War in Abyssinia*,
        p. 47.
166   "I'm not happy": Thesiger, *The Life of My Choice*, p. 333.
166   "every weapon, every round": OW, "Appreciation of the
        Ethiopian Campaign," WPA/IWM.

Chapter 12

167   "without a single mistake:" Shirreff, *Bare Feet and Bandoliers*, p.
        73.
167   "the sound of the war drums": Thesiger, *The Life of My Choice*, p.
        329.
168   "Mosley, Matthews and Monckton": WPA/IWM.
168   "Are we going to have tanks": Akavia, unpublished English-
        language typescript, privately held.
169   "The lorry carrying the Emperor": *The Abyssinian Campaigns: The
        Official Story of the Conquest of East Africa*, HMSO, 1942, p. 62.
170   "gallantly padding along": Shirreff, *Bare Feet and Bandoliers*, p. 73.
170–71 "I hope when we meet my people": Mosley, *Gideon Goes to War*,
        p. 95.
172   "that average combination": Allen, *Guerrilla War in Abyssinia*, p.
        105.
172   "Wingate's tactics": ibid., p. 92.
173   "He lacked Wingate's vision": Thesiger interview, July 1997.
176   cracked the Italian army's high-grade cypher: *Oxford Companion
        to the Second World War*, p. 317.
178   "looks (and tastes) like earth": Akavia, unpublished typescript,
        privately held.
179   "It is my intention": OW Order of the Day, 18 February 1941,
        WPA/IWM.
181   "The comforts which we now lack": Akavia campaign diary, PRO,
        London.

Chapter 13

182   "a very different matter": Simonds, author interview, August 1996.
184   "a brooding and sinister influence": TS unpublished memoir, pri-
        vately held.
185   "I would divide my force": OW lecture notes, WPA/IWM.
186   "I marched from Engiabara": ibid.

PAGE

186   "Wingate and Boyle were . . . less reconcilable": Michael Tutton, unpublished diary, IWM.

187   "The milling camels": ibid.

187   "Wingate now borrowed my electric torch": Akavia, *With Wingate in Ethiopia,* unpublished English translation.

188   "The vivid imagination of the enemy": OW lecture notes, WPA/IWM.

190   "a wrong done in 1935": OW to Lt. Col. Hugh Boustead, 18 March 1941, WPA/IWM.

192   "I ran over with the Sudanese": Akavia, *With Wingate in Ethiopia.*

194   "[T]he 2nd Ethiopian Battalion": OW, "Appreciation of the Ethiopian Campaign," WPA/IWM.

195   "The Italians halted": Thesiger, *The Life of My Choice,* p. 335.

195   "shot him through from side to side": Tutton diary, IWM.

196   "A strong force appeared": Captain Allen Smith to OW, undated but probably 6 March 1941, WPA/IWM.

197   "A wounded Italian officer": Tutton diary, IWM.

199   "scrambling about on a great pile of burst tins": Thesiger, *The Life of My Choice,* p. 336, and interview, July 1997.

200   "like living torches": Thesiger interview, July 1997.

200   "He never uttered a complaint": Akavia, *With Wingate in Ethiopia.*

200   "it makes me feel a brute": Thesiger, *The Life of My Choice,* p. 336.

201   "enemy morale is obviously shaken": Akavia, *With Wingate in Ethiopia.*

202   "Wingate demanded fast movement": ibid.

203   "I came out here": Sandford to OW, 21 March 1941, WPA/IWM.

203   "The value of Patriot fighting": quoted in Akavia, *With Wingate in Ethiopia.*

204   "I was more than sorry": OW to Platt, 9 April 1941, WPAI/IWM.

204   "Fortunately . . . I didn't hit them": TS, unpublished memoir, privately held.

207   "I gave the handle . . . a vigorous crank": Edmund Stevens, *Life,* 15 September 1941.

207   "unexpectedly understanding": Thesiger, *The Life of My Choice,* p. 339.

208   "A doc! A doc!": TS, unpublished memoir, privately held.

208   "a moving Zionist speech": Akavia, *With Wingate in Ethiopia.*

208   "The best type of latrine": OW Order of the Day, 5 April 1941, WPA/IWM.

210   "ferocious looking savages": Tutton diary, IWM.

PAGE

210   "So I followed": Akavia, *With Wingate in Ethiopia*.

211   "I really appreciated his greatness": Thesiger, *The Life of My Choice*, p. 344.

212   "I intended, as far as possible": OW, "Appreciation of the Ethiopian Campaign," revised, WPA/IWM.

212   "Joining this massif": ibid.

213   "Their morale is bad": Thesiger, *The Life of My Choice*, p. 345.

213   "displayed great courage": Akavia, *With Wingate in Ethiopia*.

214   "I linger here": OW to Maraventano, 20 May 1941, WPA/IWM.

215   "Across a level plain": OW, "Appreciation of the Ethiopian Campaign," revised, WPA/IWM.

215   "Wingate deserved a knighthood": Thesiger interview, July 1997.

216   "Everybody . . . distrusted him": Shirreff, *Bare Feet and Bandoliers*, p. 213.

216   "bearded, scruffy, unimpressive": ibid.

Chapter 14

218   "[the British] reaffirm": Gen. Wavell to Haile Selassie, February 1941, WPA/IWM.

218   "It is distressing": Haile Selassie to OW, 26 June 1941, WPA/IWM.

218   "The Ethiopians were civilised": OW to Lord Noel Buxton, undated, WPA/IWM.

219   "no pay, no allowances": TS interview, September 1996.

220   "would almost have justified": Wavell in Preface to Rolo, *Wingate's Raiders*.

220   "the scum of an army": OW, "Appreciation of the Campaign in Ethiopia," WPA/IWM.

221   "I would seriously like": Tutton to OW, 27 May 1941, WPA/IWM.

221   "The need for officers": Boustead to OW, 31 May 1941, WPA/IWM.

223   "my staff were . . . pained": Wavell in Preface to Rolo, *Wingate's Raiders*.

223   The missing firearms: Akavia interview, 1997.

224   "It . . . was swarming": Dr. Frank Ellis, *British Medical Journal*, vol. 287, 9 July 1983.

226   "[he] seemed completely recovered": David Ben-Gurion to LW, 18 August 1941, WPA/IWM.

226   "I feel better": OW to EW, 12 August 1941, WPF.

227   "Isn't that magnificent!": Mary Newall, quoted in Sykes, *Orde Wingate,* p. 336.

227   "How to See Palestine": original donated by Dorothy Stewart, Wingate Institute, Israel.

228   "There is little satisfaction": OW to Haile Selassie, 10 August 1941, WPA/IWM.

228   "Off at 12 hours' notice": OW to Akavia, 3 September 1941, WPA/IPM.

229   "I saw him each day": anonymous undated document, WPA/IWM.

229   "I have had the opportunity": unsigned clinical notes, 13 November 1941, WPA/IWM.

Chapter 15

230   "Don't you know?": LW, quoted in Sykes, *Orde Wingate,* p. 340.

231   "We are all proud": RW to OW, 12 December 1941, WPA/IWM.

231   "The passage": Amery to OW, 30 December 1941, WPA/IWM.

231   "I am sure it will": RW to Sir Hastings Ismay, 17 January 1942, WPA/IWM.

231   "for two hours": *New Statesman,* 19 December 1941.

232   "There seems to us": Thomas Costain to OW, 16 September 1941, WPA/IWM.

232   "Orde by our desire": Rose, ed., *The Diaries of Blanche Dugdale,* entry for 20 November 1941.

232   "As you know": OW to CW, 7 February 1942, Weizmann Archive.

233   "You know better than I do": RW to OW, 20 June 1941, Centre for Middle East Studies, Durham University.

235   "arrangements are therefore being made": Ismay to Harold Laski, 13 February 1942, WPC/IWM.

235   "As you know": OW to IP, undated, WPC/IWM.

236   "unusual and disquieting" et seq.: OW diary entries, 17 February and 19 February 1942, WPC/IWM.

237   "an important mission": RW to OW, 20 February 1942, WPC/IWM.

Chapter 16

241   "He seems very able": Iris Appleton to parents, 30 March 1942, WPC/IWM.

PAGE

241   "If the army cannot fight better": *Oxford History of the British Army*, p. 278.

243   "should disabuse their minds": OW to Wavell, 6 April 1942, WPC/IWM.

244   "The idea that toughness": ibid.

244   "Until we have again soldiers": Kennedy, *The Business of War*, p. 51.

246   "He showed no resentment": Calvert, *Fighting Mad*, p. 66.

248   "In the back areas": OW to Wavell, 6 April 1942, WPC/IWM.

249   "a ghastly yellow Ophelia": Calvert, *Fighting Mad*, p. 93.

249   "No commander in history": Gen. Joseph Stilwell, quoted in *Oxford Companion to Second World War* (London, Oxford University Press, 1995), p. 1065.

250   "uncouth, almost simian": Fergusson, *Beyond the Chindwin*, pp. 20–21.

252   "Not in their wildest dreams": Maj. George Bromhead, quoted in Julian Thompson, *War Behind Enemy Lines*, p. 140.

Chapter 17

254   "[I]t was his face": Stibbé, *Return via Rangoon*, p. 25.

255   "A constant stream": ibid.

256   "If the British soldier": OW to Wavell, 14 December 1942, WPC/IWM.

257   "absolute hell": Charles Aves, IWM sound archives (15486/4).

257   "Only first class swimmers": OW, "Report on Operations of 77 Indian Infantry Brigade in Burma, Feb–June 1943" (henceforth "Report"), WPC/IWM.

257   "He had a weak body": Calvert, *Prisoners of Hope*, p. 86.

258   "a proposal to increase": OW, "Report," WPC/IWM.

259   "realigned our perception": Aves, sound archives, IWM.

260   "[W]hen we arrived": Stibbé, *Return via Rangoon*, p. 25.

261   "much against . . . cigarettes": OW, "Report," WPC/IWM.

262   "toughened up considerably": Arthur Willshaw, quoted in Philip Chinnery, *March or Die*, p. 29.

262   "burst from the bushes": Stibbé, *Return via Rangoon*, p. 34.

265   "put his alarm clock down": Calvert, author interview, July 1997.

265   "Wingate is crackers": Fergusson, *Beyond the Chindwin*, p. 24.

267   "low-life gangster fighting": ibid., p. 32.

268   "faith in Wingate was implicit": ibid., p. 48.

271   "Most of my Chindits": *Daily Express,* 21 May 1943.

Chapter 18

273   "on the threshold of battle": Order of Day, 16 February 1943, WPC/IWM.

274   Blain burst into tears: Lt. Geoffrey Lockett, quoted in Tulloch, *Wingate in Peace and War,* p. 77.

275   "handed Jefferies a message": Rolo, *Wingate' Raiders,* p. 61.

277   "the whinnying . . . ceased": Stibbé, *Return via Rangoon,* p. 51.

279   "ran into some resistance": Calvert, *Fighting Mad,* p. 121.

280   "[H]is actions . . . proved": OW, "Report," WPC/IWM.

281   "The problem we had . . . dreaded": Fergusson, *Beyond the Chindwin,* p. 96.

282   "It is plain logic": OW, "Report," WPC/IWM.

282   "The names of these men": ibid.

284   "Had I not crossed": ibid.

285   "not another brigade in India": ibid.

287   "We let fly with everything": Calvert, *Prisoners of Hope,* p. 126.

288   "The punishment decided": Stibbé, *Return via Rangoon,* p. 82.

289   "The only punishment": Dominic Neill, IWM sound archives (133299/8).

290   "Remember Lot's wife": Capt. George Dunlop, author interview, May 1998.

Chapter 19

292   "the ghastly experiment": Fergusson, *Beyond the Chindwin,* p. 145.

293   "my Syce . . . was weeping": Neill, op. cit.

294   "They were Japs": Fergusson, *Beyond the Chindwin,* p. 151.

296   "As we approached": Aves, op. cit.

297   "strung out on the banks": OW, "Report," WPC/IWM.

297   "stark staring mad": Neil, op. cit.

299   "In those seven days": Rolo, *Wingate's Raiders,* p. 131.

300   "European civilization": ibid., p. 132.

301   entranced at a butterfly: ibid., p. 131.

303   "There in that blue mist": ibid., p. 139.

305   "Damascus beggars": Fergusson, *Beyond the Chindwin,* p. 191.

PAGE

306   "our dirty linen": Aves, op. cit.

306   "I killed a lot of lice": Neill, op. cit.

307   "my long walk in Burma": OW to Constance Reynolds, 16 November 1943, WPC/IWM.

308   "You may hear him": *News Chronicle,* 21 May 1943.

309   "Everyone was thrilled": Tulloch essay, WPC/IWM.

309   "WHOLE COUNTRY TALKING": LW to OW, 4 June 1943, WPC/IWM.

309   "more than proud": G. Frey to LW, 23 May 1943, WPC/IWM.

309   "remembering our conversation": Hamish Hamilton to LW, 22 May 1943, WPC/IWM.

309   "To me, dear son": EW to OW, 25 May 1943, WPC/IWM.

310   "I found him sitting naked": quoted in Sykes, *Orde Wingate,* p. 436.

311   "Wingate should command": Churchill, *The Second World War,* vol. 5, p. 507.

311   "to have a look at him": ibid., p. 62.

Chapter 20

312   "Hayedid is in Cairo": Akavia interview, 1997.

313   "He required, however": Viscount Alanbrooke, quoted in Sir Arthur Bryant, *The Turn of the Tide: 1939–1943* (London: Collins, 1957).

314   "a tiger of a man": Mary, Lady Soames, author interview, 24 October 1997.

314   "plunged into his theme": Churchill, *The Second World War,* vol. 5, p. 62.

314   "Well, my dear": LW, in postwar conversation with Akavia, as told to authors.

315   "You know that I love you": OW to LW, 27 April 1942, WPC/IWM.

315   "very well, beloved": OW to LW, 4 May 1943, WPC/IWM.

316   "I often think": OW to LW, 21 December 1942, WPC/IWM.

316   "Sweetheart, I hear": OW to LW, 14 July 1943, WPC/IWM.

316   "I bloom and flourish": LW to OW, 19 May 1943, WPC/IWM.

316   "Disregard health rumours": LW to OW, 22 July 1943, WPC/IWM.

317   "You are my war machine": Anthony Eden, *The Reckoning,* p. 404.

318   "positive proposals for attacking the enemy": Churchill, *The Second World War*, vol. 5, p. 76.

319   "Wingate made a deep impression": ibid., p. 77.

319   "You have expounded": Col. Anthony Head, quoted in Sykes, *Orde Wingate*, p. 456.

320   "Everywhere except in one instance": OW memorandum, 22 August 1943, WPC/IWM.

321   "a good second": Oliver Harvey, *The War Diaries of Oliver Harvey*, p. 286.

321   "Stick to your praying": EW to OW, 25 May 1943, WPC/IWM.

Chapter 21

323   "mixed everything up": Lowell Thomas, *Back to Mandalay*, p. 19.

324   "He called us into his office": Lt. Col. John Alison in author interview, 26 November 1997.

325   Cochran "suddenly realised": Thomas, *Back to Mandalay*, p. 76.

326   "Am in London": Tulloch, *Wingate in Peace and War*, p. 57.

326   "Wingate looked extremely well": ibid., p. 126.

327   "How nice Wingate could be": ibid., p. 127–28.

327   "remember vividly": Sybil Wingate, *The Spectator*, 29 May 1959.

328   "a somewhat comical-looking party": Tulloch, *Wingate in Peace and War*, p. 130.

328   "We both share a room": DT to Mary Tulloch, 12 September 1943, WPC/IWM.

328   "Orde and I share": ibid., 14 September 1943.

328   "I have never been able": Tulloch, *Wingate in Peace and War*, p. 130.

330   "He turned to me": ibid., p. 136.

330   "So far . . . no staff": DT to Mary Tulloch, 26 September 1943, WPC/IWM.

330   "some loathsome people": ibid., 21 October 1943.

331   "News is bad": ibid., 15 October 1943.

331   "worried stiff": ibid., 20 October 1943.

331   "a tremendous blow-out": OW to unidentified friend, 16 November 1943, WPC/IWM.

332   "He had complete faith in her": Tulloch, *Wingate in Peace and War*, p. 139.

332   "She lost a stone": IP to OW, 18 November 1943, WPC/IWM.

332   "You may as well make up your mind": LW to OW, 7 November 1943, WPC/IWM.

333   "Talked to Wavell": OW to LW, 19 November 1943, WPC/IWM.

333   "On no account": Churchill to OW, 3 November 1943, WPC/IWM.

333   "as slow as I can": OW to Churchill, 5 November 1943, WPC/IWM.

333   "I know my own body": OW to Lord Mountbatten, 14 November 1943, WPC/IWM.

334   "hardly sick at all": LW to OW, 18 November 1943, WPC/IWM.

334   "This present ambitious phase": OW to LW, 3 December 1943, WPC/IWM.

334   "I sometimes think": OW to LW, undated but early January 1944, WPC/IWM.

334   "Orde has been difficult": DT to Mary Tulloch, 25 December 1943, WPC/IWM.

335   "a splendid boy": OW to LW, 22 December 1943, WPC/IWM.

335   "the glad news": OW to LW, 7 February 1944, WPC/IWM.

335   "the meaning of existence": ibid.

336   "a necessary evil": OW to LW, undated January or February 1944, WPC/IWM.

336   "Life would be easier": ibid.

Chapter 22

340   "The Stronghold is": OW memorandum, undated, WPC/IWM.

341   "The conception was masterly": Fergusson, *The Wild Green Earth*, p. 73.

342   "tell the RAF": Thomas, *Back to Mandalay*, p. 134.

342   "a complete success": OW to Mountbatten, 1 January 1944, PRO file HS/AL/2005.

343   "Conservatism in the armed forces": Tulloch, *Wingate in Peace and War*, pp. 147–48.

343   "I like the Americans here": OW to LW, 23 December 1943, WPC/IWM.

344   "Not because it is inadvisable": OW to Mountbatten, 26 January 1944, WPC/IWM.

344   "quite a bit mad": Pownall/Bond, *Diaries of Lt. Gen. Sir Henry Pownall* (London: Leo Cooper, 1974), entry for 17 October 1943.

345   "a most dangerous affair": ibid., entry for 28 January 1944.

345   "beginning to see through him": ibid., entry for 19 February 1944.

345   "My relations with Orde": DT to Mary Tulloch, 27 January 1944, WPC/IWM.
345   "God, how I laughed": ibid., 15 February 1944.
346   "Look, Sports": R. D. Van Wagner, *1st Air Commando Group*, p. 52.
346   "Please be assured": Chinnery, *Air Commando*, p. 7.
347   "This raid": Tulloch, *Wingate in Peace and War*, p. 276.
348   "I do not suppose": *The Carthusian*, June 1951.
350   "we've got a better place to go": Slim, *Defeat into Victory*, p. 263.
350   "Nothing you've ever done": Van Wagner, *1st Air Commando Group*, p. 64.

Chapter 23

352   Fly-in details: Alison, author interview, June 1998, and Calvert, *Prisoners of Hope*, pp. 23–27.
353   a red baseball cap: Tulloch, *Wingate in Peace and War*, p. 201.
355   Alison was impressed: Alison interviews, September 1997, June 1998.
357   "Ye Gods, it was a night": DT diary letter to Mary Tulloch, 6 March 1944, WPC/IWM.
358   "those very gallant pilots": Calvert, *Prisoners of Hope*, p. 32.
358   "a hundred kettle drums": Alison interview 1997.
359   a total of 579 Dakota sorties: Cabinet Papers HS/AL 2178, PRO London.

Chapter 24

363   "The next few hours": Tulloch, *Wingate in Peace and War*, p. 210.
364   "Consider whole story grossly unfair": OW to Air Marshal Joubert, 16 March 1944, WPC/IWM.
364   "Your astounding telegram": Mountbatten to OW, 17 March 1944, WPC/IWM.
364   "a very modest request": OW to Mountbatten, 18 March 1944, WPC/IWM.
366   "Thank God you've come": Calvert, *Prisoners of Hope*, p. 50.
366   "up the hill like a two year-old": Lt. Norman Durant memoir, IWM.
368   "the heaviest imaginable": Fergusson, *The Wild Green Earth*, p. 48.

370   "sensible suggestions for everyone": Calvert, *Prisoners of Hope*, p. 62.

371   "a strong premonition": DT to Mary Tulloch, 24 March 1944, WPC/IWM.

371   "an intense interest": *Portsmouth Evening News*, 1 July 1944.

372   "rather in awe of Wingate": Tulloch, *Wingate in Peace and War*, pp. 229–30.

374   "What a pity": DT to Mary Tulloch, 24 March 1944, WPC/IWM.

374   "who will look after us now?": Rooney, *Mad Mike*, p. 82.

374   "Our master was gone": Rhodes-James, *Chindit*, p. 206.

374   "We had tremendous": author interview, 1998.

375   "Operation conceived by Wingate": Brig. William Lentaigne to Mountbatten, 28 April 1944, WO 203/5221.

Epilogue

378   "facing towards Burma": Lt. Col. Christopher Perowne to LW, 15 July 1944, WPC/IWM.

378   "If . . . Patton had been killed": Rachel Wingate to Churchill, 12 November 1950, PRO.WO.32/12967.

378   "at no stage of these removals": Letter to the editor, *The Times*, 27 November 1950.

379   "I cannot tell you": Mountbatten to Edwina Mountbatten, 2 April 1944, quoted in Philip Ziegler, *Mountbatten*, p. 276.

379   "grandeur and stature": Fergusson, *Beyond the Chindwin*, p. 242.

380   "dark, fiery and eager": Wavell, *Central Asian Review*, June 1944.

380   "Genius is a word": Slim, SEAC pamphlet "The Chindits," October 1944.

381   "obviously feeling the mounting strain": Slim, *Defeat into Victory*, pp. 260–61.

383   "watching him closely": Tulloch, *Wingate in Peace and War*, p. 200.

383   "incapable of telling a lie": Lewin, *Slim the Standard Bearer*, p. 163.

384   "I suspect my brother . . . is right": SW to DT, 22 February 1964, Rylands.

385   "iniquitous and unpatriotic conduct": OW to Mountbatten, 1 January 1944, PRO file HS/AL/2005.

385   "Petulant . . . obsessed": Kirby, *The War Against Japan*, vol. 3, pp. 217–23 and 444.

PAGE

386   "a small token in memory": WPC/IWM.

386   "the raiding force": Monograph 134 in Japanese Defence Archives, quoted in Tulloch, *Wingate in Peace and War,* p. 264.

386   "a great obstacle": Lt. Gen. Mutaguchi to Lt. Col. J. E. B. Barker, ibid., p. 265.

387   "What would have been the effect": Sir Robert Thompson in Foreword to Mead, *Wingate and the Historians.*

389   "The black books of MI5": LW to David Hacohen, 20 September 1947, WPC/IWM.

391   "a campaign of petty tyranny": Agnes McGeary to LW, undated, WPC/IWM.

Bibliography

Allen, Louis. *Burma, The Longest War, 1941–5* (London: J. M. Dent, 1984).

Allen, W. E. D. *Guerrilla War in Abyssinia* (London: Penguin Books, 1943).

Bethell, Nicholas. *The Palestine Triangle* (London: Andre Deutsch, 1979).

Bidwell, Shelford. *The Chindit War* (London: Hodder and Stoughton, 1979).

Bond, Brian, ed. *Chief of Staff: The Diaries of Lt. Gen. Sir Henry Pownall,* vol. 2 (London: Leo Cooper, 1974).

Boustead, Hugh. *The Wind of Morning* (London: Chatto and Windus, 1971).

Burchett, Wilfred. *Wingate's Phantom Army* (London: Frederick Muller, 1947).

Calvert, Michael. *Fighting Mad,* rev. ed. (London: Airlife Publishing, 1996).

———. *Prisoners of Hope,* rev. ed. (London: Leo Cooper, 1971).

Chandler, David, ed. *The Oxford History of the British Army* (Oxford: Oxford University Press, 1996).

Chinnery, Philip D. *Air Commando* (New York: St. Martin's Press, 1997).

———. *March or Die* (London: Airlife Publishing, 1997).

Churchill, Winston. *The Second World War,* vol. 5 (London: Cassell, 1952).

Connell, John. *Wavell: Scholar and Soldier* (London: Collins, 1964).

Cooper, Artemis. *Cairo in the War* (London: Hamish Hamilton, 1989).

Dear, I. C. B., ed. *The Oxford History of the Second World War* (Oxford: Oxford University Press, 1995).

Eshkol, Yosef. *A Common Soldier: The Story of Zvi Brenner,* trans. by Shmuel Himmelstein (Tel Aviv: MOD Books, 1993).

Fergusson, Bernard. *Beyond the Chindwin* (London: Collins, 1945).

———. *The Trumpet in the Hall* (London: Collins, 1970).

———. *The Wild Green Earth* (London: Collins, 1946).

Foot, M. R. D. *SOE: The Special Operations Executive* (London: BBC Books, 1984).

Fromkin, David. *A Peace to End All Peace* (New York: Henry Holt, 1989).

Hay, Alice Ivy. *There Was a Man of Genius* (London: Neville Spearman, 1963).

Hawley, Dennis. *The Death of Wingate* (Braunton: Merlin Books, 1994).

Horne, Edward. *A Job Well Done: A History of the Palestine Police Force, 1920–1948* (London: Palestine Police Old Comrades Association, 1982).

Kennedy, John. *The Business of War* (London: Macmillan, 1957).

King-Clark, Rex. *Free for a Blast* (London: Grenville Publishing, 1988).

Kirby, Woodburn, ed. *The War Against Japan,* vol. 3 (London: HM Stationery Office, 1958).

Laffin, John. *British VCs of World War Two* (Gloucester, UK: Sutton Publishing, 1997).

Lewin, Ronald. *Slim the Standard Bearer* (London: Leo Cooper, 1976).

Mason, H. A., R. G. Bergeron, and J. A. Renfrow. *Operation Thursday* (Washington, D.C.: USAF History and Museums Program, 1994).

Masters, John. *The Road Past Mandalay* (New York: Harper & Row, 1961).

Mead, Peter. *Wingate and the Historians* (Braunton, UK: Merlin Books, 1987).

Mosely, Leonard. *Gideon Goes to War* (London: Arthur Barker, 1955).

Parkinson, Roger. *The Auk* (London: Granada Publishing, 1997).

Pearlman, Maurice. *Mufti of Jerusalem* (London: Gollancz, 1947).

Peres, Shimon. *Battling for Peace,* ed. by D. Landau (London: Weidenfeld and Nicolson, 1995).

Probert, Henry. *The Forgotten Air Force* (London: Brassey's, 1995).

Rhodes-James, Richard. *Chindit* (London: John Murray, 1980).

Rolo, Charles. *Wingate's Raiders* (London: Harrap, 1944).

Romanus, Charles F., and Riley Sunderland, eds. *United States Army in World War II: China-Burma-India Theater: Stilwell's Mission to China* (Washington, D.C.: Office of the Chief of Military History, 1953).

Rooney, David. *Burma Victory* (London: Arms and Armour Press, 1992).

———. *Mad Mike: A Life of Michael Calvert* (London: Leo Cooper, 1996).

———. *Wingate and the Chindits: Redressing the Balance* (London: Arms and Armour Press, 1994).

Rose, Norman, ed. *Baffy: The Diaries of Blanche Dugdale, 1936–47* (London: Valentine Mitchell, 1973).

———. *Chaim Weizmann: A Biography* (New York: Viking-Penguin, 1986).

Royle, Trevor. *Orde Wingate: Irregular Soldier* (London: Weidenfeld and Nicolson, 1995).

Sanders, Ronald. *The High Walls of Jerusalem* (New York: Holt, Rinehart and Winston, 1983).

Sharpe, Phil. *To Be a Chindit* (Lewes, Sussex: The Book Guild, 1995).

Shirreff, David. *Bare Feet and Bandoliers* (London, Radcliffe Press, 1995).

Slim, William. *Defeat into Victory* (London: Cassell, 1956).

Stibbé, Philip. *Return via Rangoon,* rev. ed. (Barnsley: Leo Cooper, 1995).

Sykes, Christopher. *Orde Wingate* (London: Collins, 1959).

Thesiger, Wilfred. *The Life of My Choice* (London: HarperCollins, 1987).

Thomas, Lowell. *Back to Mandalay* (New York: Greystone Press, 1951).

Thompson, Julian. *War Behind Enemy Lines* (London: IWM/Sidgwick and Jackson, 1998).

Thompson, Robert. *Make for the Hills* (Barnsley, UK: Leo Cooper, 1989).

Tuchman, Barbara. *Stilwell and the American Experience in China* (New York: Macmillan, 1970).

Tulloch, Derek. *Wingate in Peace and War* (London: MacDonald, 1972).

Van Wagner, R. D. *1st Air Commando Group,* USAF Air Command Military History Series 86-1, Washington, DC.

Whiting, Charles. *The Poor Bloody Infantry* (London: Stanley Paul, 1987).

Ziegler, Philip. *Mountbatten* (London: Collins, 1985).

Index

Grateful acknowledgment is made to the following for permission to reprint previously published and preexisting material:

AIRLIFE PUBLISHING LIMITED: Excerpts from *Fighting Mad* by Michael Calvert and *March or Die* by Philip D. Chinnery, both published by Airlife Publishing Limited, Shrewsbury, England. Reprinted by permission.

CONTROLLER OF HER MAJESTY'S STATIONERY OFFICE: Excerpts from *The War Against Japan, Volume II.* Crown copyright is reproduced with the permission of the Controller of Her Majesty's Stationery Office.

CURTIS BROWN LTD., LONDON: Excerpts from *Gideon Goes to War* by Leonard Mosley. Copyright the Estate of Leonard Mosley. Reprinted by permission of Curtis Brown Ltd., London, on behalf of the Estate of Leonard Mosley.

THE C. W. DANIEL COMPANY LTD.: Excerpts from *There Was a Man of Genius* by Alice Ivy Hay. Reprinted by permission of The C. W. Daniel Company Ltd., Essex, England.

JOHN DURANT: Excerpts from the papers of Lieutenant N. Durant (housed at the Imperial War Museum, London). Reprinted by permission of John Durant.

THE FORBES MAGAZINE COLLECTION: Excerpts from Orde Wingate archival material housed in the Collection of Steve Forbes, New York. Used by permission.

FRANK CASS & CO. LTD.: Excerpts from *Baffy: The Diaries of Blanche Dugdale.* Reprinted by permission of Frank Cass & Co., Ltd., Ilford, Essex, England.

IMPERIAL WAR MUSEUM: Excerpts from interview with Charles Alfred William Aves, Imperial War Museum Sound Archive, 15486/4, Code A; excerpts from interview with Dominic Fitzgerald Neill, Imperial War Museum Sound Archive, 13299/A, Code A; excerpts from interview with Sir Gawain Bell, Imperial War Museum Sound Archive, 10256/5, Code A; excerpts from John Winthrop Hackett, Imperial War Museum Sound Archive, 4527/6, Code B; excerpts from interview with M.R.L. Grove, Imperial War Museum Sound Archive, 004510/03, Code A; excerpts from interview with Fred Howbrook, Imperial War Museum Sound Archive, 004619/03, Code A. All excerpts reprinted by permission.

THE ISRAEL M.O.D. PUBLISHING HOUSE: Excerpts from *A Common Soldier* by Yosef Eshkol. Reprinted by permission of The Israel M.O.D. Publishing House, Tel Aviv.

LT. COL. R. KING-CLARK: Photographs, sketches, and letters relating to Palestine, India, and Burma; diary entries; excerpts from *Free for a Blast* (London, Grenville, 1988), a copy of which is housed at the Imperial War Museum. Reprinted by permission of Lt. Col. R. King-Clark.

LITTLE, BROWN AND COMPANY (UK): Excerpts from *Wingate in Peace and War* by Derek Tulloch. Reprinted by permission of Little, Brown and Company (UK).

VERONICA PAWLUK: Excerpts from a journal by Captain Michael Tutton housed at the Imperial War Museum, London. Used by permission of Veronica Pawluk.

PEN & SWORD BOOKS LIMITED: Excerpts from *Prisoners of Hope* by Michael Calvert, *Make for the Hills* by Robert Thompson, *Return via Rangoon* by Phillip Stibbe, and *Chief of Staff: The Diaries of Lt. Gen. Sir Henry Pownall* edited by Brian Bond. All material reprinted by permission of Pen & Sword Books Limited, South Yorkshire, England.

PETERS FRASER & DUNLOP: Excerpts from *Wingate* by Christopher Sykes. Reprinted by permission of Peters Fraser & Dunlop on behalf of the Estate of Christopher Sykes.

COL. ANTHONY SIMONDS: Excerpt from unpublished memoir entitled "Pieces of War" by Col. Anthony Simonds and housed at the Imperial War Museum. Reprinted by permission.

THE WEIZMANN ARCHIVES: Excerpts from various papers housed at The Weizmann Archives. Used by permission.

HD 8/12/66